ENGLISH WOMEN, RELIGION, ... PRODUCTION, 1500–

This excellent collection breaks new ground, admirably theorizing early modern women's agency in religious communities and intertextual prose genres.
—*Margaret P. Hannay, Siena College, USA*
and author of Mary Sidney, Lady Wroth

Contributing to the growing interest in early modern women and religion, this essay collection advances scholarship by introducing readers to recently recovered or little-studied texts and by offering new paradigms for the analysis of women's religious literary activities. Contributors underscore the fact that women had complex, multi-dimensional relationships to the religio-political order, engaging as activists for specific causes but also departing from confessional norms in creative ways and engaging in intra- as well as extra-confessional conflict. The volume thus includes essays that reflect on the complex dynamics of religious culture itself and that illuminate the importance of women's engagement with Catholicism throughout the period. The collection also highlights the vitality of neglected intertextual genres such as prayers, meditations, and translations, and it focuses attention on diverse forms of textual production such as literary writing, patronage, epistolary exchanges, public reading, and epitaphs. Collectively, *English Women, Religion, and Textual Production, 1500–1625* offers a comprehensive treatment of the historical, literary, and methodological issues preoccupying scholars of women and religious writing.

Women and Gender in the Early Modern World

Series Editors:
Allyson Poska, The University of Mary Washington, USA
Abby Zanger

The study of women and gender offers some of the most vital and innovative challenges to current scholarship on the early modern period. For more than a decade now, Women and Gender in the Early Modern World has served as a forum for presenting fresh ideas and original approaches to the field. Interdisciplinary and multidisciplinary in scope, this Ashgate book series strives to reach beyond geographical limitations to explore the experiences of early modern women and the nature of gender in Europe, the Americas, Asia, and Africa. We welcome proposals for both single-author volumes and edited collections which expand and develop this continually evolving field of study.

Titles in the series

Gender, Sexuality, and Material Objects in English Renaissance Verse
Pamela S. Hammons

Early Modern Women and Transnational Communities of Letters
Edited by Julie D. Campbell and Anne R. Larsen

Rape and the Rise of the Author
Amy Greenstadt

Biblical Women's Voices in Early Modern England
Michele Osherow

Women's Wealth and Women's Writing in Early Modern England
Elizabeth Mazzola

English Printing, Verse Translation, and the Battle of the Sexes, 1476–1557
Anne E.B. Coldiron

English Women, Religion, and Textual Production, 1500–1625

Edited by
MICHELINE WHITE
Carleton University, Canada

Routledge
Taylor & Francis Group
LONDON AND NEW YORK

First published 2011 by Ashgate Publishing

2 Park Square, Milton Park, Abingdon, Oxon OX14 4RN
711 Third Avenue, New York, NY 10017, USA

Routledge is an imprint of the Taylor & Francis Group, an informa business

First issued in paperback 2016

British Library Cataloguing in Publication Data
English women, religion, and textual production, 1500–1625. – (Women and gender in the early modern world)
1. Christian literature, English – Women authors – History and criticism. 2. English literature – Early modern, 1500–1700 – History and criticism. 3. Women and literature – England – History – 16th century. 4. Women and literature – England – History – 17th century. 5. Women and religion – England – History – 16th century. 6. Women and religion – England – History – 17th century. 7. Christian women – England – Intellectual life – 16th century. 8. Christian women – England – Intellectual life – 17th century.
I. Series II. White, Micheline.
820.9'3823082'09031–dc22

Library of Congress Cataloging-in-Publication Data
English women, religion, and textual production, 1500–1625 / edited by Micheline White.
p. cm. — (Women and gender in the early modern world)
Includes bibliographical references and index.
1. English literature—Early modern, 1500–1700—History and criticism. 2. English literature—Women authors—History and criticism. 3. Women and literature—England—History—16th century. 4. Women and literature—England—History—17th century. 5. Religion and literature—England—History—16th century. 6. Religion and literature—England—History—17th century. 7. Women and religion—England—History—16th century. 8. Women and religion—England—History—17th century. 9. Religion in literature. I. White, Micheline.
PR113.E54 2011
809'.89287—dc22

2010053822

ISBN 978-1-4094-0651-8 (hbk)
ISBN 978-1-138-26080-1 (pbk)

Contents

List of Figures

List of Contributors

Julie Crawford is Associate Professor of English and Comparative Literature at Columbia University.

Patricia Demers is Professor of English and Film Studies at the University of Alberta.

Susan M. Felch is Professor of English at Calvin College.

Jaime Goodrich is Assistant Professor of English at Wayne State University.

Brenda M. Hosington is Professeur honoraire in the Département de linguistique et traduction at the Université de Montréal and Associate Research Fellow in the Centre for the Study of the Renaissance at the University of Warwick.

Susannah Brietz Monta is the John Cardinal O'Hara, C.S.C. and Glynn Family Honors Associate Professor of English at the University of Notre Dame.

Janel Mueller is William Rainey Harper Distinguished Service Professor Emerita, Department of English and the College, University of Chicago.

Kate Narveson is Associate Professor of English at Luther College.

Patricia Phillippy is Professor of English at Kingston University, London.

Mary Trull is Associate Professor of English at St. Olaf College.

Micheline White is Associate Professor of English and Humanities at Carleton University, Ottawa.

Acknowledgements

It is my pleasure to thank the many people who made this project possible. First, I would like to thank the ten contributors, many of whom participated at a research seminar at the SAA in 2007 on Tudor and Stuart women's religious writing or at a session at the RSA in 2008 on women and religious conflict. I am grateful for their patience as they waited out a maternity leave and for their promptness in responding to my requests for revisions. It was a true pleasure to work with such a talented and energetic group of scholars. I would also like to thank Margaret Hannay and Kimberly Coles for their support and helpful suggestions.

I am also grateful for the support provided by Carleton University. Dean John Osborne (Faculty of Arts and Social Sciences), the Department of English, and the College of the Humanities offered generous assistance at various stages of this project. In particular, I would like to thank three students—Céline Pitre, Janice Pringle, and Sarah Trick—for their excellent help with proofreading and other editorial tasks. It was a pleasure for me to work with Erika Gaffney at Ashgate Press, and I thank the anonymous Ashgate readers for their suggestions.

Finally, I would like to thank my husband, Fraser Cole, and my parents, George and Julienne White, for their constant encouragement and support.

List of Abbreviations

EETS Early English Text Society

EME Early Modern Englishwoman: A Facsimile Library of Essential Works—Printed Writings, 1500–1640

NRSV New Revised Standard Version

ODNB *Oxford Dictionary of National Biography*, online ed., edited by Lawrence Goldman. Oxford: Oxford University Press.

TNA The National Archives (formerly The Public Record Office)

STC *A Short-Title Catalogue of Books Printed in England, Scotland, and Ireland and of English Books Printed Abroad, 1475–1640*. First compiled by A.W. Pollard & G.R. Redgrave. 2nd ed. revised and enlarged by W.A. Jackson and F.S. Ferguson, and completed by Katharine F. Pantzer. London: Bibliographical Society, 1976–1991.

Introduction: Women, Religious Communities, Prose Genres, and Textual Production

Micheline White

It is widely recognized that the religious works produced or circulated by Tudor and Jacobean women present a particular set of challenges for feminist literary criticism. On the one hand, the sheer number of these works demonstrates that religious topics and genres were central to women's intellectual lives and everyday experience. On the other hand, many of these works are composed in genres that are marginal to early modern literary criticism,[1] and the works do not, for the most part, explicitly engage with issues that have been of interest to feminists: that is, most of them do not openly criticize the patriarchal understanding of male–female relations or dwell at length on marriage, female education, female authorship, maternity, sexuality, or female ecclesiastical authority.[2] The primary goal of these texts is to promulgate Christian convictions and record religious experience. Thus while feminists have worked hard to recover and disseminate these lesser-known works to a broad readership, it has not always been easy to incorporate them into narratives about the development of feminist thought or the development of early modern literature.

The first critical studies to grapple with these issues were published in the mid-1980s and early 1990s: they offered groundbreaking analyses of female authors and patrons, and they focused sustained attention on male attitudes towards female education, silence, and authorship.[3] These studies also drew on a

[1] Such genres include prose translations of theological works, prayers, meditations, psalm versifications, hymns, dream visions, catechisms, and martyrologies.

[2] There are a few important exceptions: Anne Askew, Aemilia Lanyer, Lady Anne Southwell, and the authors of the "mother's legacies" explicitly deal with gender in their religious works. Not surprisingly, these texts have received extensive critical treatment; by contrast, most of the texts treated in this volume have not yet been studied carefully.

[3] See Betty Travitsky, ed., *The Paradise of Women: Writings by Englishwomen of the Renaissance* (Westport, CT: Greenwood Press, 1981); Margaret P. Hannay, ed., *Silent But for the Word: Tudor Women as Patrons, Translators, and Writers of Religious Works* (Kent, OH: Kent State University Press, 1985); Elaine V. Beilin, *Redeeming Eve: Women Writers of the English Renaissance* (Princeton: Princeton University Press, 1987); Tina Krontiris, *Oppositional Voices: Women as Writers and Translators of Literature in the English Renaissance* (London: Routledge, 1992); Barbara Kiefer Lewalski, *Writing Women in Jacobean England* (Cambridge, MA: Harvard University Press, 1993); Louise Schleiner,

series of assumptions about women and religion that often minimized the cultural significance of women's religious activities even as they sought to incorporate them into the field of early modern studies. Like many gynocritical studies from this period, they tended to focus on authors' apparent resistance to patriarchal attitudes, and like many new historical studies, they often treated the *religious* content of women's texts in secular terms. Moreover, they often assumed that religion was a safe form of discourse deemed suitable for women; that religious genres afforded women minimal forms of literary or political agency; and that women's texts were circulated by men to bolster their own religiopolitical interests. As a result, scholars viewed many female-authored religious works as marginal or depressingly acquiescent, and those that did not appear to resist gender norms were largely overlooked.

Over the course of the past twenty-five years, two intertwined strands of critical activity have transformed the field: first, scholars have recalibrated many of their theoretical assumptions about the cultural significance of religious discourse and about the categories and methodologies required to analyze women's religious texts. At the same time, scholars have recovered a large number of previously unknown works and have offered micro-historical analyses of their contributions to political, social, theological, and aesthetic movements.[4] In considering this significant critical reorientation, we might note that new interpretive paradigms emerged as scholars began acknowledging the central (rather than marginal) place of religious writing in Renaissance England; began reading women's religious texts as *religious* texts; and began positioning them in relation to a range of religio–cultural developments rather than solely in relation to early modern gender norms.[5] Debora Shuger and Kate Narveson, for example, emphasized that religion was "the cultural matrix for explorations of virtually every topic" during this period,[6] and argued that religious texts were best approached by a methodology

---

Tudor and Stuart Women Writers (Bloomington: Indiana University Press, 1994); and the early scholarship on Aemilia Lanyer.

4 So many new texts have been recovered that the field of study looks entirely different than it did twenty-five years ago. The effects of this process of historical recovery are unpredictable, though, and the long-term implications of these new texts will only become clear in the decades to come.

5 It is impossible to document all the scholarship that has contributed to this disciplinary shift. In addition to the critical editions cited in this collection, recent monographs include Jennifer Summit, *Lost Property: The Woman Writer and English Literary History, 1380–1589* (Chicago: University of Chicago Press, 2000); Erica Longfellow, *Women and Religious Writing in Early Modern England* (Cambridge: Cambridge University Press, 2004); Edith Snook, *Women, Reading, and the Cultural Politics of Early Modern England* (Aldershot: Ashgate, 2005); and Kimberly Anne Coles, *Religion, Reform, and Women's Writing in Early Modern England* (Cambridge: Cambridge University Press, 2008).

6 Debora K. Shuger, *Habits of Thought in the English Renaissance: Religion, Politics, and the Dominant Culture* (Berkeley: University of California Press, 1990), 6.

that investigated them in light of both doctrinal systems and cultural phenomena.[7] Margaret Ezell urged feminist scholars to set aside the anachronistic literary categories and values that marginalized religious writing, and Janel Mueller proposed that we recognize religion "as exercising a potentially determinate force in human life and its linguistic and social forms, just as race or ethnicity, class, and gender (and generation?) are already taken to do."[8]

Arguments such as these have prompted scholars to approach women's religious texts with different assumptions and to ask different questions of them.[9] Recent studies, for example, have developed reading strategies attentive to the interactions between religion (as belief, practice, politics, community, or institution), literary categories, gender politics (whether conventional or unconventional), and social class.[10] In particular, scholars have approached women's texts by locating them within specific literary, confessional, and kinship networks and by reading them in relation to a dense web of social and literary documents.[11] These studies have unearthed a wealth of information about women's education and religious alliances, and have enabled us to see that women were often deeply embedded within networks of textual production.

---

7 Kate Narveson, "Profession or Performance?: Religion in Early Modern Literary Study," in *Fault Lines and Controversies in the Study of Seventeenth-Century English Literature*, ed. Claude J. Summers and Ted-Larry Pebworth (Columbia: University of Missouri Press, 2002), 111–29.

8 Margaret J.M. Ezell, *Writing Women's Literary History* (Baltimore, MD: Johns Hopkins University Press, 1993); Janel Mueller, "Complications of Intertextuality: John Fisher, Katherine Parr, and 'the Book of the Crucifix,'" in *Representing Women in Renaissance England*, ed. Claude J. Summers and Ted-Larry Pebworth (Columbia: University of Missouri Press, 1997), 39. See also Suzanne Trill, "Feminism Versus Religion: Towards a Re-Reading of Aemilia Lanyer's *Salve Deus Rex Judaeorum*," *Renaissance and Reformation/Renaissance et Réforme* 25, no. 4 (2001), 67–80.

9 These shifts within feminist studies have played a role in a parallel "turn to religion" in early modern studies, although I believe that the impact of the study of women's religious writing on the broader field is often underestimated. For a discussion of the recent "turn to religion," see Ken Jackson and Arthur F. Marotti, "The Turn to Religion in Early Modern English Studies," *Criticism: A Quarterly for Literature and the Arts* 46 (2004), 167–90.

10 See especially the introductions to Danielle Clarke, *The Politics of Early Modern Women's Writing* (Harlow, England: Longman, 2001); Longfellow, *Women and Religious Writing*; Snook, *Women, Reading*; and Coles, *Religion.*

11 One example is Micheline White's "Women Writers and Religious and Literary Circles in the Elizabethan West Country: Anne Dowriche, Anne Lock Prowse, Anne Lock Moyle, Elizabeth Rous, and Ursula Fulford." *Modern Philology* 103.2 (2005): 187–214. Works by Queen Katherine Parr, Anne Askew, and Lady Elizabeth Tyrwhit have been read in light of Henrician religious networks; works by the Cooke sisters, Anne Lock, Dorcas Martin, Anne Dowriche, Elizabeth Melville, and Dorothy Leigh in terms of English and Scottish puritanism; works by Mary Sidney Herbert and Esther Inglis in terms of international Protestantism; and works by Margaret Roper, Mary Bassett, and Elizabeth Grymeston in light of Anglo-Catholic networks.

Scholars have also reframed women's texts by examining religious genres—psalm versifications, lyrics, translations, catechisms, spiritual diaries, and mothers' legacies—and exploring the kinds of literary and religiopolitical issues at stake in their development. Importantly, these studies have shed valuable light on the complex relations between genres, gender, and confessional concerns, and on women's contributions to the development of those relations.[12] Finally, scholars have begun to emphasize the dynamics surrounding the circulation and reception of female-authored works and the degree to which they had important public implications even if they appeared to address domestic or private concerns.

This collection is animated by the same commitment to recovering, historicizing, and theorizing women's religious writing. The contributors share a methodology that is attentive to the content of women's religious texts, their historical contexts, and the critical frameworks that make them legible, and their essays break new ground by addressing critical blind spots and examining little-known texts. Specifically, the collection seeks to advance scholarship by focusing on three areas of study: women and religious communities; intertextual prose genres such as prayers, meditations, and translations; and modes of textual production such as patronage, funeral monuments, and performative reading.

The first goal of this collection is to deepen our understanding of women's contributions to religious communities and their responses to shifting religious norms. As noted above, many studies have approached women's texts by positioning them within identifiable religiopolitical communities or movements. Many of the essays in this collection do the same and examine texts that engaged with the *devotio moderna*, the early Reformation, the Elizabethan Settlement, Anglo-Catholic recusancy, and English Franciscanism. Collectively, however, the essays invite us to take a closer look at the dynamics of religious culture itself and at the production of texts within a society animated by religious change, conflict, and factionalism. It is perhaps worth stressing that to write about religion as a woman in the Tudor and Jacobean periods was perforce to position oneself in relation to a range of "orthodox" and "heterodox" beliefs about theology, ritual, devotion, language use, ecclesiastical government, and female piety. During the century and a quarter covered in this book, there were several radical shifts in official religious policy, and religious dissent was often penalized with a heavy hand. Yet there remained a sizable body of beliefs, concerns, and texts that were shared by all Christians, and there was often room for moderate dissent on certain topics.

---

12 One example is Margaret P. Hannay's "'So May I with the *Psalmist* Truly Say': Early Modern Englishwomen's Psalm Discourse," in *Write or Be Written: Early Modern Women Poets and Cultural Constraints*, ed. Barbara Smith and Ursula Appelt (Aldershot: Ashgate, 2001), 105–34.

As the essays here demonstrate, women from different social classes, religious factions, and kinship networks used literary texts to respond to such a religiopolitical matrix in different ways: some explored widely shared Christian beliefs or elements of the official status quo; some cautiously explored new religious impulses or engaged in independent reflection; some challenged the authorities with acts of factional resistance and subterfuge; and others drew on religiopolitical markers in moments of strategic self-representation. Importantly, these essays remind us that women, like men, had multifaceted relationships to the official religious order and to their respective communities: that is, while some women can be identified as "activists" for specific causes, they also departed from their male and female coreligionists in independent and idiosyncratic ways, and they were often embroiled in intraconfessional conflict even as they struggled against religious opponents. In other words, we must be wary of rigidly classifying female writers as "puritan," "conformist," "Protestant," or "Catholic" and devote more attention to the ways in which they forged their own views. Finally, as the essays on Anne Howard and Katherine Parr remind us, we must not forget that there were religious texts that appealed to traditional and Reformed readers, and we must trace women's involvement in the production, editing, and circulation of such texts.

These essays also illuminate the varied ways in which gender and class inflected women's involvement in religious communities. For instance, while some women drew on distinctly female modes of piety and foregrounded their sex in their literary endeavors, others carefully used a genderless voice to promulgate their views. Of course, a woman's ability to participate in religious communities through texts was often directly tied to her social status, particularly if she sought to challenge official policy or serve as a patron. While most of the essays thus consider how titles, wealth, and connections enabled female literary activity, the essays on Elizabeth Evelinge, Anne Lock, and Anne Wheathill also shed light on the authorial strategies adopted by women who were not members of the landed, titled class.

In its investigation of religious communities and gender, this collection also seeks to make Catholicism (both pre- and post-Tridentine) more integral to our discussions of early modern women. To date, most scholarship has focused on how Protestant women responded to vernacular Bible reading, unmediated salvation, iconoclasm, print culture, prayer, marriage, household religion, monasticism, etc. By contrast, pre- and early Reformation women's activities and post-Reformation Catholic women's responses to these religious and literary changes have gone largely unexamined.[13] This collection thus includes essays on

---

13 There has been some recent scholarship on Margaret Roper, Mary Bassett, Margaret Clitherow, Elizabeth Grymeston, and Lady Elizabeth Cary, but Catholic women and literary traditions are often absent from discussions of Tudor and Jacobean women's writing. Essays on Stuart women are included in Robert Corthell, et al., *Catholic Culture in Early Modern England* (Notre Dame, IN: University of Notre Dame Press, 2007).

Margaret Beaufort, Katherine Parr, Anne Howard, and Elizabeth Evelinge, and these studies demonstrate that Eucharistic devotion, traditional Catholic prayers and meditations, militant recusancy, and monastic culture provided rich contexts for women's literary activities. The inclusion of these works asks us to think more carefully about the ongoing dialogue between "traditional" and "Reformed" religious practice and the way that dialogue disrupts a Protestant, Whiggish view of English history.

The second goal of this collection is to insist on the importance of intertextual prose genres such as prayers, meditations, compilations, and translations. Generic categories have always played a key role in the analysis of female writers, and several recent essay collections have focused on women's life-writing, manuscripts, letters, and poetry.[14] Some religious genres, however, have proved less amenable to feminist literary analysis than others, and this volume argues that women's prayers and meditations are in need of much more attention. The importance of prayer in this period is undeniable: monastics and the laity prayed throughout the day, prayer was the subject of heated theological debate, and prayers were a popular literary genre. Susan Felch observes that one hundred distinct titles of private prayer books were printed by 1600, and Jennifer Summit argues that prayer was a privileged literary genre for women.[15] It is surely striking, then, that at least thirteen women, from a range of social groups, produced or compiled prayers and meditations.[16] For the most part, however, these texts are unknown, and in cases where they have been discussed, scholars have often sidelined the prayers *per se* and have focused on the paratextual, organizational, or material dimensions of the volumes.[17]

The relative neglect of women's prayers and meditations may be explained by noting the confluence of several factors. One difficulty is that prayers and

---

[14] See Michelle M. Dowd and Julie A. Eckerle, eds. *Genre and Women's Life Writing in Early Modern England* (Aldershot: Ashgate, 2007); Victoria E. Burke and Jonathan Gibson, eds. *Early Modern Women's Manuscript Writing: Selected Papers from the Trinity/Trent Colloquium* (Aldershot: Ashgate, 2004); James Daybell, ed. *Early Modern Women's Letter Writing, 1450–1700* (Houndmills, UK: Palgrave, 2001); and Barbara Smith and Ursula Appelt, eds. *Write or Be Written: Early Modern Women Poets and Cultural Constraints* (Aldershot: Ashgate, 2001).

[15] Susan M. Felch, "The Development of the English Prayer Book," in *Worship in Medieval and Early Modern Europe: Change and Continuity in Religious Practice*, ed. Karen Maag and John D. Witvliet (Notre Dame, IN: University of Notre Dame Press, 2004), 132–61. To this figure we must add the untold number of manuscript prayer books produced between 1500 and 1625. Summit, *Lost Property*, 111.

[16] See works by Lady Jane Wriothesley, Queen Katherine Parr, Lady Elizabeth Tyrwhit, Lady Jane Grey, Queen Elizabeth I, Lady Frances Aburgavenny, Dorcas Martin, Anne Wheathill, Elizabeth Grymeston, Anne Jenkinson, Lady Grace Mildmay, Elizabeth Ashburnham Richardson, and Lady Elizabeth Hastings, Countess of Huntington.

[17] See, for example, recent scholarship on Anne Wheathill and Elizabeth Ashburnham Richardson. An exception is the scholarship on Parr by Janel Mueller, Kimberly Coles, and others.

meditations draw heavily on Scripture; consequently they have been seen as derivative works that yield little evidence of a woman's creative or political agency, or as works that acquiesce to conventional conceptions of female piety.[18] As Kate Narveson notes below, Lady Grace Mildmay "naturally writes in 'Scripture phrase,'" and it is precisely the apparent overlay of female voice and Biblical master-text that can frustrate a modern reader trained to focus on women's innovative reworking of male discourse. Studies of women's prayers and meditations may also have been hindered by the relative dearth of contemporary scholarship on the theological and literary evolution of prayer books,[19] and, indeed, scholars have sometimes lumped works with very different literary structures or political valencies under the vague rubric of "pious devotions."

This collection joins some very recent studies in focusing attention on prayers and prayer books and in analyzing women's important contributions to their literary and political development.[20] As the essays on Katherine Parr, Elizabeth Tyrwhit, Anne Lock, Anne Wheathill, and Grace Mildmay demonstrate, women who compiled or composed intertextual devotional works were engaged in complex forms of literary and religious expression: those who compiled prayer books created unique artifacts that register individual, and potentially risky, devotional choices, while those who composed new prayers elaborated on and recast well-known cultural material. These women adopted different strategies in assembling their volumes, and they composed works that differ in length, structure, affective tone, and medium; all of these distinctions should become part of our critical vocabulary. Women also self-consciously reflected on the act of writing devotional prose, and we must examine the terms they used to describe this activity and the way their texts responded to broader theological, political, and literary developments.

Women's religious translations have experienced a similar, albeit less pronounced, kind of neglect. At least fourteen women are credited with producing

---

18 See the introduction to *Anne Wheathill*, EME, Series I, pt. 1, vol. 9, selected and introduced by Patrick Cullen (Aldershot: Scolar Press, 1996); and Betty S. Travitsky, *Subordination and Authorship in Early Modern England: The Case of Elizabeth Cavendish Egerton and Her 'Loose Papers'* (Tempe: Arizona Center for Medieval and Renaissance Studies, 1999).

19 Many years ago, Cynthia Garrett observed that prayers have generally been ignored by theologians, historians, and literary scholars, and, indeed, not much has changed since then. "The Rhetoric of Supplication: Prayer Theory in Seventeenth-Century England," *Renaissance Quarterly* 46, no. 2 (1993): 328–57. The seminal works on prayer books were published during the 1950s (see chap. 6, n. 7). Meditations, by contrast, have received more attention (see chap. 8, n. 4), but there are very few discussions of women's meditations.

20 See Felch, "Development," and her introduction to *Elizabeth Tyrwhit's 'Morning and Evening Prayers,'* ed. Susan M. Felch (Aldershot: Ashgate, 2008). See also Pierre Janton, "Prayer in Prose as Literature and the British Reformers of the Sixteenth Century," *Cahiers élisabéthains* 66 (2004): 1–8; and Eamon Duffy, *Marking the Hours: English People and their Prayers 1240–1570* (New Haven: Yale University Press, 2006).

major religious translations between 1500 and 1625, with half of them producing more than one volume, yet these works have not loomed large in our assessments of the period.[21] Recent scholars have challenged an older view that translation was a marginal, imitative, and female activity in Tudor and Jacobean England, and have demonstrated that translation was a central, valued, difficult, and largely masculine mode of cultural production.[22] Yet, in spite of these arguments, women's translations are still rarely examined in detail and are often accorded only minor roles in our narratives about women's writing. This collection, by contrast, stresses the important work performed by women who produced, inspired, or patronized translations: the essays on Margaret Beaufort, Anne Bacon, Elizabeth Russell, Anne Howard, and Elizabeth Evelinge emphasize the religiopolitical dimensions of translations and their paratextual materials. As Patricia Demers has recently emphasized, however, translation is also a linguistic enterprise, an activity which can be viewed as "an inquiry into language in its grammatical, semantic, phonological complexity."[23] Indeed, a modern reader who encounters an early modern translation and its source text cannot help but appreciate the immense challenge of transferring complex religious ideas from one language to another, each language having its own syntax, grammatical idiosyncrasies, and cadences. Demers points out that Renaissance translators were celebrated for their facility with language and urges us to approach women's translations with what Alastair Hunter calls "a lexicographical sensitivity."[24] As the essays here on Margaret Beaufort and Anne Bacon demonstrate, a careful linguistic comparison of women's translations and their source texts enables us to reconstruct the richness of the moment of translation, to identify the linguistic choices and skills of the translator, and to interpret the relationship between those choices and the religious goals of the translators.

The final goal of this volume is to encourage further reflection on the intersection of diverse forms of textual production during this period. While literary scholars naturally tend to focus their attention on "finished" texts explicitly intended for

---

[21] See works by Lady Margaret Beaufort, Margaret Roper, Queen Katherine Parr, Queen Elizabeth I, Lady Anne Cooke Bacon, Queen Mary, Lady Mildred Cooke Cecil, Mary Bassett, Anne Lock, Dorcas Martin, Mary Sidney Herbert, Countess of Pembroke, Lady Elizabeth Cooke Russell, Anne Jenkinson, and Elizabeth Evelinge.

[22] See the succession of similar arguments made by Suzanne Trill, "Sixteenth-Century Women's Writing: Mary Sidney's *Psalmes* and the 'Femininity' of Translation," in *Writing and the English Renaissance*, ed. Suzanne Trill and William Zunder (New York: Longman, 1996), 140–58; Jonathan Goldberg, *Desiring Women Writing: English Renaissance Examples* (Stanford: Stanford University Press, 1997); Micheline White, "Renaissance Englishwomen and Religious Translations: The Case of Anne Lock's *Of the Markes of the Children of God* (1590)," *English Literary Renaissance* 29 (1999), 375–400; and Clarke, *Politics*, 13–14.

[23] Patricia Demers, *Women's Writing in English: Early Modern England* (Toronto: University of Toronto Press, 2005), 64.

[24] Ibid., 65.

broader readership (whether printed or in manuscript), many of these essays investigate women's involvement in other branches of the early modern literary system. Patronage, for example, was a vital part of literary production, and the essays on Anne Howard, Elizabeth Russell, and Margaret Beaufort examine wealthy, powerful women who sheltered illegal presses, commissioned legal printers, supported writers, and bought and distributed books. In addition, as the essay on Russell demonstrates, prominent, learned women of the Tudor period are often best approached with a methodology that reads their literary works as part of a lifelong intellectual enterprise that also included things like epistolary exchanges and elaborate funeral monuments. Finally, as the essay on Anne Clifford demonstrates, the act of reading was itself a mode of textual reproduction, and some early modern subjects used the reading of religious books in highly performative and politicized ways; indeed, this analysis of Clifford invites us to consider how religious books could signal religiopolitical positions of resistance, and how a woman might strategically represent reading in forms as diverse as a diary and a family portrait.

In the first essay, Patricia Phillippy makes an observation that serves as a perfect introduction to the first five essays on writing, religious communities, and religious norms: she notes that for a religious "activist" like Lady Elizabeth Russell, spirituality was "a social undertaking, intimately bound to conversation, debate, and conference" and a springboard for personal "expression, self-expression, and creation." The first two essays in this collection expand on this formulation and focus on powerful women who developed idiosyncratic perspectives on doctrinal questions even while working in heated confessional environments. Phillippy, for example, considers works by Lady Elizabeth Russell, a figure long associated with the activist Protestant circle surrounding the Earl of Leicester, and she posits that all of Russell's works are informed by a conception of "sacred conversation," a form of dialogue that addresses religious and secular concerns and seeks to facilitate reconciliation between religious factions or within the self. Phillippy illuminates this notion through a discussion of two previously overlooked works by Russell, both connected to the death of her nephew's wife: a consolatory letter to her nephew (Salis MS 175.92) and a Latin sestet that Russell appears to have written for him as he prepared his wife's funeral monument (Salis MS 140.82). Reading these new texts alongside Russell's more well-known contributions to funeral monuments, Phillippy demonstrates that they grapple creatively with Reformed attitudes towards mourning and showcase Russell's publicly crafted "twin identity" as humanist scholar and puritan activist.

Mary Trull also considers the relationship between poetry and confessional norms, examining how Lady Mary Sidney Herbert, Countess of Pembroke, creatively reworked doctrinal positions outlined by prominent ecclesiastical leaders. Here Trull examines Pembroke's *Psalmes* and challenges the longstanding view that these highly poetic works carefully avoided factional theological disputes. In fact, Trull demonstrates that Pembroke addresses the "knotty doctrinal problem of sacrifice" and develops a unique and independent Protestant position: in contrast to the Protestant commentators who spiritualized all Psalmic references to ritual sacrifice, she actually enhanced and reveled in the concrete and sensual details of such sacrifices. Pembroke is acutely aware, however, of the Protestant objections to Catholic views of sacrificial efficacy, and she thus stresses the radical asymmetry between divine and human gifts and makes sacrifice a "symbol for generosity on the part of both God and human." Pembroke's treatment of the relation between human and divine works also informs her dedicatory poems where she uses the logic of the gift to frame her claims to poetic authority.

The next two essays further enrich our understanding of women's responses to religiopolitical communities by emphasizing the importance of Anglo-Catholic culture and by examining the criss-crossing impulses of extra- and intra-confessional relations. Susannah Monta, for instance, draws our attention to the importance of wealthy laywomen in sustaining underground Catholic networks, but she also crucially emphasizes the tensions within the Catholic community and the movement of texts across confessional lines. Specifically, Monta reconstructs the risky patronage activities of Anne Dacre Howard, Countess of Arundel (1557–1630), including her sponsorship of illegally printed works by the Jesuit Robert Southwell, her material support of lay recusants and missionary priests, and her endowment of a Jesuit college in Ghent. Arundel's patronage is particularly instructive because it illuminates key conflicts within the Anglo-Catholic community. For example, Arundel sponsored texts by Southwell that advocated strict recusancy, a position that was rejected by other Catholics, including members of her extended family, and she supported the Jesuits in their struggles against secular priests. Her promotion of a separatist brand of Catholicism is complicated, however, by the fact that two of the Southwell texts she supported crossed and recrossed confessional lines, details that reveal the surprisingly wide reach of her patronage, as well as the limitations of an overly rigid conception of radically separated confessional communities.

Jaime Goodrich's essay on Elizabeth Evelinge complements Monta's study by examining the international significance of polemical works by English nuns and considering the forces that have led to their scholarly neglect. Elizabeth Evelinge (1597–1668), a Poor Clare nun from Gravelines, produced three translations of religious works between 1621 and 1635, yet the works have only recently been attributed to her with confidence and have not yet received detailed scholarly attention. Goodrich argues that Evelinge's strict Franciscan humility led her to "divest herself of public ownership of her work," a fact that has caused bibliographical uncertainty and has rendered her work less appealing to feminist studies that have privileged more subversive female texts. Goodrich argues, however, that Evelinge's anonymous or misattributed cloistered authorship was effective in allowing her to promote the ideals of her order while simultaneously engaging in a range of extra- and intraconfessional struggles. Specifically, she demonstrates that Evelinge's translations of 1621 and 1622 promoted Franciscan ideals and thereby contributed to local power struggles between the sisters, the Franciscans, and the Jesuits, as well as to broader initiatives to revive an

English Franciscan province and promote Franciscan piety in the struggle against Protestantism. This essay puts salutary pressure on current scholarly models by underscoring the vitality of monastic modes of female authorship.

Julie Crawford provides yet another vantage point from which to consider the relationship between female writers, personal beliefs, and religiopolitical communities. Lady Anne Clifford is famous for her land disputes, but is not often associated with religion or with religious conflict. Yet, as Crawford points out, her diary and the portraits she commissioned contain many references to religious texts by Catholics, conformists, and puritans. Crawford underscores the active nature of Clifford's relationship to these religious books and posits that it was intertwined with her land claims and her resistance to James's absolutist policies. Specifically, Crawford observes that while Clifford was a "Prayer Book Protestant" woman with apparently conformist views, she engaged with religious texts and polemic for multiple reasons: to receive encouragement from a Providential God, to develop skills of resolution and confrontation, and to publicly align herself with positions of religiopolitical resistance. Crawford reminds us that individuals, families, and social groups who were resistant to monarchical authority could find themselves in strategic alliances with oppositional religious factions, and she underscores the fact that women, like men, variously negotiated the relationship between their personal convictions, their sociopolitical allegiances, and the public performance of the two.

The next five essays continue to explore women's responses to religious communities and changing norms, but they also focus attention on the particular features of prayer books, meditations, and translations, and they provide models for interpreting these kinds of intertextual prose works. Janel Mueller's essay on Queen Katherine Parr, for example, explores the methodological challenges of interpreting a manuscript compilation of prayers produced during a time of complex religious upheaval. In this piece, Mueller demonstrates that the manuscript prayer book previously known as "Lady Jane Grey's Prayer Book" (British Library MS Harley 2342) was in fact compiled by Queen Katherine Parr for her own use and then given to Grey as Parr lay dying in 1548. Mueller initiates the investigation of this major new work by tracing Parr's many sources and examining her literary treatment of material from the Bible and from writers including Thomas More, Nicholas Shaxton, and John Fisher. She demonstrates that Parr's selection and adaptation of diverse devotional materials was a creative and theologically charged enterprise, and she concludes that, while the volume exhibits a "receptivity" to Reformed ideas, it also lays claim to the common ground shared by adherents of the old and new religions. This important archival discovery brings Parr's known oeuvre to four texts, and its private devotional character offers unique insight into Parr's personal responses to the dangerous religiopolitical crosscurrents of the mid-1540s.

In the next essay, Susan Felch focuses our attention on the little studied "psalm collages" and "psalm paraphrases" written or printed between the 1550s and the 1580s by Lady Elizabeth Tyrwhit, Anne Lock, and Anne Wheathill. Felch begins by making the important point that while Catholic primers include biblical Psalms printed in their entirety, Protestant prayer books feature pieces that may sound like direct quotations from the Bible, but are in fact creative compositions that encode considerable authorial agency. Felch carefully explores two such types of compositions, noting that psalm collages required sophisticated compositional skills and that psalm paraphrases enabled female writers to pursue didactic, theological, and political topics. This historical context is complemented by Felch's turn to Bakhtin's discussion of "heteroglossia," and "internally persuasive discourse," terms that alter our understanding of words like "originality" and creative "assimilation." Felch concludes that Bakhtin's analysis of the process through which words from "outside" become "ours" enables us to see early modern women's prayers as active texts that "engender authorial agency and 'originality' not despite, but because they borrow half their words from the Scriptures."

Kate Narveson addresses related questions about scripturalism and literary authority in her study of Lady Grace Mildmay's manuscript meditations. In this first detailed study of Mildmay's meditations, Narveson observes that many features of Mildmay's text point to Scripture as that which authorizes all that she writes, features including the manuscript's typography and *mis en page*, Mildmay's detailed marginal Biblical citations, and the meditations themselves. But Mildmay's use of Scripture is highly varied, and Narveson illuminates the multiple ways in which Mildmay engages with Scripture to develop her own ideas and motifs. Narveson instructively draws attention to the considerable difference between a modern interpretation of such biblically grounded writing and Mildmay's own account of her compositions. That is, while modern readers might see her internalization of a patriarchal discourse or her mastery of Bible-reading skills as that which produces her text, Mildmay explicitly points to the transformative power of the Word itself, and, in an unorthodox move, claims that her meditations are in fact directly inspired by God. The relationship between Mildmay's text and Scripture is thus more complex than we might first imagine, and even as she appears to subordinate her voice to God's, she creates a manuscript that foregrounds her own textual and religious authority.

The final two essays focus our attention on religious translations, and they return to some of the questions raised in Jaime Goodrich's political analysis of the pro-Franciscan translations by Elizabeth Evelinge. Both Brenda Hosington and Patricia Demers, however, focus on the act of translation as a linguistic enterprise, and they offer detailed analyses of the verbal choices, rhetorical skills, and religious goals of translators working in particular historical moments. Brenda Hosington, for example, provides the first detailed discussion of Lady Margaret Beaufort's *The Forthe boke of the folowynge of Jesu cryst* and *The mirroure of golde for the synfull soule*, two English translations from French versions of Latin works. Hosington notes that while Beaufort's volumes appeared without paratextual commentary, a comparison of her translations and their source texts reveals clear translating principles and strategies. For example, Hosington identifies strategies such as explicitation, inclusion, personalization, and intensification, arguing that they serve to clarify the source text and to encourage lay readers to prepare for the Eucharist. Beaufort's translations conform to late fifteenth-century theories of close translation, but they also display her desire to disseminate devotional works beyond clerical readers to a literate lay readership.

Patricia Demers similarly draws our attention to the literary complexity of Lady Anne Cooke Bacon's *An Apologie of the Churche of England* (1564), a translation that had international significance and that was produced at a time when questions about language use, the vernacular, and the accuracy of translations could be lethal. In this essay, Demers acknowledges that early modern polemical translations pose particular challenges for secular postmodern readers, yet she submits that such texts provide a unique means of observing the subtleties of early modern language. Demers foregrounds Bacon's literary prowess by offering the first detailed linguistic analysis of her important rendering of John Jewel's Latin text and comparing it with an anonymous earlier English translation from 1562. Demers highlights Bacon's grasp of the text's subtleties, her mimicking of Tridentine discourse, and her powerful verbal directness, and she concludes that this verbal *tour de force* records Bacon's angry reaction to the final session of the Council of Trent.

The essays in this collection address a wide range of genres, authors, and historical moments, yet they work together to advance the field of early modern women's writing in distinctive ways. They introduce previously unknown or little studied texts; they offer paradigms for incorporating these works into our interpretations of religious culture; and they explore the ways in which individual texts register the imprint of religion, gender, class, and modes of production. Moreover, they remind us that religion was never a neutral or private topic, and that women's religious activities always involved a conscious degree of strategic self-positioning and self-representation. Finally, the collection demonstrates that while women's texts emerged from a profoundly patriarchal culture, they made important contributions to England's religious development, and they are valuable today because they illuminate the dynamic interplay of beliefs, gender, political alliances, social status, generic conventions, and historical exigencies.

PART 1:
Women and Religious Communities

Chapter 1
Living Stones: Lady Elizabeth Russell and the Art of Sacred Conversation

Patricia Phillippy

When Robert Cecil met Elizabeth Brooke during the Christmas festivities at court in 1588, he fell in love at first sight. Married the following August, the couple went on to enjoy a happy but brief marriage. Elizabeth died in January 1597, after delivering her third child. Robert's grief was profound.[1] Six months after Elizabeth's death, Robert's aunt, Lady Elizabeth Cooke Hoby Russell, wrote to comfort her nephew and to exhort him to leave behind the "dissembling Devill," melancholy, which threatened to "make [him] a Sullen sharp, sowre plumme; and no better then in trewth a very malencoly moyle and a miseanthropos hatefull to god and man."[2] Russell's letter of June 1597 (Salis MS 175.92), attempts to ameliorate her nephew's grief with the commonplaces of consolation, but locates them in both spiritual and secular realms. As Russell encourages Robert to moderate his

[1] See BL, Lansdowne MS 101:28 fol. 127 and P.M. Handover, *The Second Cecil: The Rise to Power, 1563–1604, of Sir Robert Cecil* (London: Eyre & Spottiswoode, 1959), 148–9.

[2] Hatfield House, Salis MS 175.92. Reprinted in Royal Commission on Historical Manuscripts, *Calendar of the Manuscripts of the Most Honourable the Marquis of Salisbury Preserved at Hatfield House, Hertfordshire* (London: HMSO, 1883–1976), 7:281–2. Throughout this chapter, I have retained Russell's original spelling but expanded abbreviations. For a modernized edition of all of Russell's works, see Elizabeth Cooke Hoby Russell, *The Writings of an English Sappho*, ed. Patricia Phillippy (Toronto: University of Toronto Press, forthcoming). Salis MS 175.92 is included in the only previous edition of Russell's letters, Elizabeth Farber's "The Letters of Elizabeth Cooke Hoby Russell (1540–1609)" (PhD diss., Columbia University, 1977), 190–96, but it has received no critical attention. Russell's letter to Mary Talbot, discussed below (and see n. 28), escaped Farber's attention. She also did not include Russell's four manuscript poems, although she mentions the two to Robert Cecil in her introduction (53–4). In addition to Salis MS 140.82, discussed here, the poems are an elegy for Thomas Hoby, dated 1566 (BnF, Collections Dupuy 951, fol. 122v), an elegy sent to Thomas Egerton on the death of his eldest son in 1599 (Huntington, Ellesmere MS EL 11378), and verses from Horace sent to Robert Cecil to celebrate his appointment as Chancellor of the Duchy of Lancaster in 1597 (Salis MS 175.118). All are available with translations from Greek and Latin by Jaime Goodrich in Russell, *Writings*. All translations in this chapter are by Jaime Goodrich unless otherwise noted.

sorrow, she emphasizes doctrinal orthodoxy and political pragmatism equally. Similarly, in a manuscript poem written in February 1597 (Salis MS 140.82), Russell engages, without wholly endorsing, reformed proscriptions of immoderate mourning. The Latin sestet responds to Elizabeth Cecil's death, but instead of offering a conventional work of consolation, it seems to license Cecil's grief by stressing the affective bond between husband and wife, threatened but not severed by death.

Taking my cue from Russell's sole published work, her translation of John Ponet's *A Way of Reconciliation of the Good and Learned Man*, I view Russell's negotiation with religious discourse as a form of *reconciliation*, understood in the various secular and spiritual senses the term bore in the period.[3] "To reconcile," for Russell and her contemporaries, meant not only to mediate between disputing factions or individuals, but also to resolve an issue by establishing harmony between opposing sides; to cause an individual to accept an event or circumstance; to reconsecrate a desecrated church or cemetery; and, finally, to restore a penitent soul to communion within the church. Russell's "To the Reader," presents her translation and its argument under the dictum, "Blessed be the Peacemakers" (A1v), and the treatise itself energizes the multiple meanings of its title by attempting to bridge the gap between Catholic and Protestant views of the Eucharist; reconcile the apparently contradictory aspects of the sacrament itself; perform textual reconsecration of the sacrament desecrated by the false doctrine of transubstantiation; and unify the body of believers in a reformed understanding of the *corpus Christi*.

A critical approach alert to this polyvalent term and its nuances in Russell's writing highlights three characteristics of her works that suggest new directions for contemporary criticism of early modern women's religious writings. First, the fact that Russell engages the commonplaces of post-Reformation mourning and consolation in similar ways in a variety of genres and media, including manuscript poems, epistolary writings, funeral monuments, and a published translation, argues for the benefits of interdisciplinarity in addressing early modern women's writing. Recognizing a shared vocabulary between textual productions and those in other media illuminates the borders of unexplored categories and types of women's public (if not published) expression.[4] Second, Russell's inscription of the indelible mark of her own personality on her works in every medium—in part a product of the long periods of widowhood through which she lived, and in part the result of her self-awareness as one of the remarkable "Cooke sisters"—constitutes a persistent

---

[3] Elizabeth Russell, trans., *A Way of Reconciliation of the Good and Learned Man, Touching the Trueth, Nature, and Substance of the Body and Blood of Christ in the Sacrament*, by John Ponet (London, 1605), A1. Future references appear parenthetically.

[4] For an example of this turn toward interdisciplinarity, see Helen Ostovich and Elizabeth Sauer, ed. *Reading Early Modern Women: An Anthology of Texts in Manuscript and Print, 1550–1700* (New York: Routledge, 2003), 465–97.

program of self-authorship that extends throughout her adult life.[5] These gestures of self-authorship routinely involve independent interpretations of cultural and religious tropes, and they suggest that other women writers also utilized religious discourses independently, grounding them on personal beliefs and discretion.[6] Finally, Russell's manipulations of religious discourse often involve conflations of secular and spiritual concerns that defy the older scholarly wisdom relegating early modern women's texts primarily to the realm of religious writing, particularly to translations of religious works.[7]

Considering Russell's consolatory letter and manuscript poem to Robert Cecil in light of a reformed commitment to religious activism that informs virtually all of her undertakings, this essay examines the rich possibilities for personal expression, creation, and self-creation available to Russell through improvisations on the post-Reformation language and imagery of mourning and consolation. At the threshold between public performance and private grief, where these works reside, Russell explores and exploits an art of sacred conversation—invitations to speech intended to foster spiritual and secular reconciliation—which characterizes her encounter with the doctrinal voices governing the emotions in post-Reformation England.

Activism as Reconciliation

At the heart of Russell's writings, including her elegiac and consolatory works of 1597, is her commitment to promulgate the reformed faith and to protect and patronize its advocates at court, in the universities, at the pulpit, and in print. Russell's participation, and that of her sisters, in the Protestant circle surrounding Robert Dudley, Earl of Leicester, and Anne Dudley, Countess of Warwick (Russell's sister-in-law after her marriage to John Russell in 1574), has long been noted.[8] Her letters give further evidence of this commitment throughout her life.

5 See George Ballard, *Memoirs of Several Ladies of Great Britain Who have been Celebrated for their Writings Or Skill in the Learned Languages, Arts and Sciences* (Oxford, 1752), 198–208.

6 Although Mary Ellen Lamb sees "the interests of [the Cooke sisters'] close male relatives" (111) as a defining context for their literary works, I argue that Russell's writings during her widowhood reflect independent undertakings in defense of her beliefs and interests. See "The Cooke Sisters: Attitudes toward Learned Women in the Renaissance," in *Silent But for the Word: Tudor Women as Patrons, Translators, and Writers of Religious Works*, ed. Margaret P. Hannay (Kent, OH: Kent State University Press, 1985), 107–25.

7 This assumption is pervasive in the contributions to Hannay's *Silent But for the Word.* Micheline White, "Renaissance Englishwomen and Religious Translations: The Case of Anne Lock's *Of the Markes of the Children of God* (1590)," *English Literary Renaissance* 29 (1999): 375–400, argues that translation was not considered inferior to original writing. The front matter of Russell's translation broadcasts—actually, inflates—her rank, showing no sense of inferiority.

8 See Louise Schleiner, *Tudor and Stuart Women Writers* (Bloomington: Indiana University Press, 1994), 34–51, and White, "Renaissance Englishwomen," 386–9.

In 1571, Russell wrote to her brother-in-law, Secretary of State William Cecil, Lord Burghley, on behalf of Edmund Rockray, fellow of Queen's College, Cambridge, and former tutor to her four children, who, she reports, "is in trouble, for certaine woords spoken by him, for the defence of certain liberties."[9] In the sermon to which she refers, Rockray had condemned proposed Cambridge statutes which would increase the powers of the college heads, arguing that they violated both scripture and the liberty and privileges of the university. As a result, Rockray was expelled from the university the following April.[10] In his defense, Russell writes:

> having had no small tryall of him, both for religion, good nature, and disposition to learning, and other vertewes, during the tyme of his being skoolemaster in my howse: me thinkes I durst in my Conscience awnser in his behalf: that what fond woords soever passed him … they proceded not from a minde desirous of sedition, or otherwise less willing to shew him self a most trew subject, to his prince, then eny one of his Colledge.

The charge of Rockray's and other Cambridge scholars' sedition against the crown should be considered in light of the debate in the 1560s and 1570s, spearheaded by proto-Presbyterian Thomas Cartwright, a fellow at Trinity College since 1562, concerning the university's symbols of conformity to the Church of England. The proposed change in university statutes that Rockray opposed were devised by John Whitgift in order to remove Cartwright from the university's Lady Margaret chair, which he had held since 1570, and from which he had presented lectures condemning the Anglican Church's hierarchy and ceremonies. Following his dismissal from Cambridge in 1572, Cartwright (like Rockray) served in private households as a tutor, including in the household of Michael Hicks, secretary to the Cecils. Two decades later, when Cartwright was imprisoned following his implication in the Marprelate affair, Russell offered to intervene with Robert Cecil, Burghley's successor as Secretary of State, on his behalf. Cartwright thanked her in a letter dated August 13, 1591, addressed, "To the right honorable, the verie good Lady, the Lady Russell." Below this address, a note in Russell's hand to Robert, to whom she forwarded the letter, encourages her nephew, "Good my Lord, rede this thorow and do what yow can to the poor man."[11]

Russell's interventions on behalf of Rockray and Cartwright display her continuation in widowhood of a commitment to the Protestant cause which

---

9 TNA, SP Dom 12/77, no. 11. Russell's children by Thomas Hoby were aged eleven, nine, seven, and five when she wrote the letter.

10 Russell's appeal to Burghley was successful, and Rockray was restored to his post in July 1571.

11 BL, Lansdowne MS 68:58, fols. 131–2. On Cartwright, see Patrick Collinson, *The Elizabethan Puritan Movement* (Berkeley: University of California Press, 1967); A.F. Scott Pearson, *Thomas Cartwright and Elizabethan Puritanism, 1535–1603* (Cambridge: Cambridge University Press, 1925); and Farber, "Letters," 83–4.

her father, Anthony Cooke, and both of her husbands had supported.[12] When Cambridge scholar and suitor to Elizabeth Cooke, Walter Haddon, visited Sir Anthony Cooke's home in 1552, he reported, "And what a house I did find there, yea, rather a small university, in truth [where] the industry of the females was in full vigor."[13] Russell established similar universities in her adult households. Geoffrey Fenton praises Russell's "great charge to entertayne men of Artes and learned Faculties, by which your house [at Blackfriars] seemes an Universitie of learning."[14] Among those attached to her home may have been Fenton himself, who composed his 1574 *A Forme of Christian Policie*, dedicated to Burghley, "At my chamber in the Blacke Friers," perhaps supported by Russell.[15] As early as his first published work in 1567, Fenton demonstrated a "staunchly protestant faith" and attached himself, through his dedicatees, to Leicester's circle.[16] In 1571 and again in 1572, Fenton published works dedicated to Russell. His *Actes of Conference in Religion, Holden at Paris* shows affinities with Russell's *Way of Reconciliation* in that both works, translated from French into English, attempt to reconcile the doctrinal extremes of Catholicism and radical Protestantism, or as Fenton puts it, "the rude sophistrie of the Papistes, and milde simplicitie of the reformed side" (A3). Fenton applauds Russell's religious zeal and her support of notable figures of the English Reformation. Recalling Russell's "societie with publike Lectures and Sermons this last winter in London," Fenton commends her "vehement thirste after Gods worde, that even your boarde (which I did often assist) was seldome without the fellowship of deepe Devines and Preachers" (A2v). Russell's religious "societie," both within her household and beyond, Fenton argues, had a didactic goal, performed "to the ende, that as your example drew others to seeke God in Sermons abrode, so also your selfe by privie conference might be throughly resolved in every doubte touching your Christian opinion" (A2v). Russell's private resolution of spiritual doubts is rendered by Fenton as a "publicke monumente" to her Cooke heritage: "I have heard it often doubted whether your Reverend father hath had at any time more comfort in all his transitorie felicities, than in the successe of suche a daughter, by whose vertues his house is raysed into dignitie, and his aged yeres exercised in consolation" (A2v–A3).

12 See Marjorie Keniston McIntosh, "Sir Anthony Cooke: Tudor Humanist, Educator and Religious Reformer," *Proceedings of the American Philosophical Society* 119 (1975): 242–5.

13 Quoted in Stephen J. Barns, "The Cookes of Gidea Hall," *Essex Review* 21 (1912): 6.

14 Geoffrey Fenton, trans., *Actes of Conference in Religion, Holden at Paris, Betweene Two Papist Doctours of Sorbone, and Two Godlie Ministers of the Church* (London, 1571), A2v–A3. Future references appear parenthetically. On Fenton, see Andrew Hadfield, "Fenton, Sir Geoffrey," in *ODNB*, online ed., ed. Lawrence Goldman (Oxford: Oxford University Press), http://www.oxforddnb.com (accessed March 2008).

15 Geoffrey Fenton, *A Forme of Christian Policie* (London, 1574), 2v.

16 Hadfield, "Fenton."

In Fenton's delineation of the inward form and outward appearance of Russell's faith—her self-confident assurance in the reformed religion, on the one hand, and her exemplarity in leading others to spiritual truth, on the other—we can discern the chief features of Russell's own approach to religion in her writings. First, Fenton's emphasis on the "conversation," "societie," or "conference" attending private acts of devotion underscores the activism inherent in the reformed movement, a missionary and didactic approach to the Word. Fenton prefaces his account of the religious conference "betweene two papist doctours of Sorbone, and two godlie ministers of the Church" (A1) with the claim that:

> One cheefe frute of reading (Madame) is a confirmation of judgement, and therefore necessarie wee reade good things, to the ende, that with a vertuouse exercise in conversation, our conscience may also settle, and our selves reste supplied with wholesome instructions conducible to a happie state and direction of lyfe. (A2)

Spirituality is a social undertaking, intimately bound to conversation, conference, and debate. It resides in the threshold between the public and private spheres, and is inseparable from secular institutions, interlocutors, and concerns.

Second, if the goal of religious conversation is a reconciliation which moves in two directions (inward, to assuage private doubts, and outward, to unite factions in the Christian community), then the result of this reconciliation, for Fenton and for Russell, is consolation. While Fenton's first dedication to Russell casts his virtuous and erudite dedicatee as a consolation to her aging father, his dedication to a second translation, *Monophylo*, consoles Russell following the deaths of her two daughters, nine-year-old Elizabeth and seven-year-old Anne Hoby, in February 1571. Writing "To the Right vertuous Lady, the Lady Hobby," Fenton presents a work "whose argument albeit is not religious ... yet brings foorth a Phylosophie ... to assure our frayltie amydde many hidden miseries wherewith we stand envyroned by Gods necessary provydence."[17] Fenton's effort to reconcile Russell to her loss, and to reconcile classical philosophy with Christian consolation, finds its complement in Russell's Latin epicedium, inscribed on the Hoby girls' joint tomb in All Saints, Bisham, which must have been erected around the same time that Fenton was at work on his translation. On a ledger stone engraved with a classical urn, Russell's verses reveal their speaker's imperfect acceptance of God's providence. "By fate," the maternal speaker admits, the sisters lie entombed. "Your death was cruel" ("Mors tua crudelis"), she complains to Elizabeth, "it was much crueller / Because [your] younger sister Anne fell with you" ("multo crudelius illud, / Quod cecidit tecum junior ANNA soror").[18] In surrendering her daughters "dear

---

[17] Geoffrey Fenton, trans., *Monophylo*, by Etienne Pasquier (London, 1572), A2. Edgar Powell, *The Registers of Bisham, Co. Berkshire* (London: Parish Register Society, 1898), 27, records the burials of "[the worshipful] Elizabeth Hobbey" on February 17, 1572 (Old Style), and of "Agnis Hobbey" a week later on February 24.

[18] Schleiner, *Tudor and Stuart Women*, 210.

to God, hereafter [to] live" ("Chara Deo posthac filia vive") in death, Russell's speaker is resigned to her loss, but resistant to consolation. "[A]las my flesh and bone" ("eheu mia viscera!"), she exclaims in the poem's opening line, and the closing lines equate the "one stone" covering the sisters with the womb in which their mother carried them: "Et lapis hic unus corpora bina tegit. / Sic volui mater tumulo sociarier uno, / Una quas utero laeta genesque tuli" ("And here one stone covers two bodies. / Thus a mother, I wished I could unite in one tomb / Together those whom I bore in the womb, joyous and groaning"). Although she affirms the girls' immortality, the speaker derives no comfort from that certainty. Rather, the monument and its text mark the continuation of a conversation between mother and children that traverses the border between life and death. Mourning, and whatever consolation may be derived from it, is a form of conversation, one performed before and including the congregation of the church in which the monument is placed. Reconciliation, in the Hoby tomb, is difficult and resistant. The monument offers a memorial—permanent, but profoundly marked by temporality and transience—to its absent subjects and their mother's struggle to relinquish them.

Living Stones

When read alongside her commitment to the reformed faith, the funeral monuments erected by Russell for her parents, two husbands, four children, and, finally, herself, are acts of personal reconciliation and sacred conversation. Comprised of sculptural, architectural, and literary forms, these composite works understand texts as monuments and monuments as texts. Sir Anthony Cooke's monument in the Church of St. Edward the Confessor, Romford, of which Russell was probably chief author,[19] praises the expressive quality of tombs as speaking stones:

> For stones are doombe, and yet for mannes behove,
> God lends them tongues sometymes to rehearse
> Suche woords of worthe as worthiest wights may pearce.
> Yea, stones (oftymes), when bloode and bones be rott,
> Do blase the brute which ells might bee forgott.[20]

Conversely, Russell describes her published translation in monumental terms: "this booke … seemeth to be the worke of a good, learned, and modest man and one that hath bene long, and well exercised in the Monuments of our Fathers and Elders" (A3v–A4). This alignment of text and monument invites us to seek shared features, goals, and assumptions in Russell's writings in a variety of media.

---

[19] See Peter Davidson and Jane Stevenson, "Elizabeth I's Reception at Bisham (1592): Elite Women as Writers and Devisers," in *The Progresses, Pageants and Entertainments of Queen Elizabeth I*, ed. Jayne Elisabeth Archer, Elizabeth Goldring, and Sarah Knight (Oxford: Oxford University Press, 2007), 207–26.

[20] John Strype, *Annals of the Reformation and Establishment of Religion* (London, 1725), 2, Appendix, 108.

In its incomplete acceptance of orthodox Christian consolation, the voice of the grieving mother in Russell's epicedium for her daughters resonates in secular as well as spiritual registers. Recalling classical models in its material form (the engraved urn) and literary components (the Latin epicedium), the tomb showcases Russell's erudition, presenting her as the classically trained daughter of Anthony Cooke. This secular self-fashioning coexists, as it does throughout Russell's works, with the monument's spiritual aspects, including the speaker's affirmation of the girls' salvation, the tomb's location in the sacred space of the church, and the exemplarity of the speaker's ultimate, if imperfect, resignation. Consolation rests somewhere between the explicit satisfaction derived from the monument's material splendor and linguistic accomplishment, and the implicit (indeed, almost imperceptible) comfort afforded by its gestures toward spiritual reconciliation. In this work and others, Russell does not so much subvert traditional discourses of mourning and consolation but rather redirects them toward her self-representation as a humanist scholar and a committed activist for the reformed faith. Russell's writings consistently represent reformed devotion as a social event, inextricably bound to specific times, places, and individuals. Religious expression, like the erection of a family tomb, is at once an act of historiography and of autobiography.

Russell's letter of consolation to Robert Cecil (Salis MS 175.92) begins very much in the realm of autobiography:

> Mr Secretary if yow be so withowt comfort of worldly delight as yow seme, it is most ill to the helth of yowr both of body and sowle I speake by experience and know to well that to be trew which I say, and therfore bothe am I sory to Here it, and Besech the god of all Consolation and Comfort to remedy it.

Russell's correspondence with the Cecils, particularly with her nephew, is often marked by affection and intimacy, and her concern for Robert's well-being is evident here. As she begins by recalling her difficult acceptance of the deaths she has suffered, she closes by advancing companionship in sorrow as her reason for writing: "take this in good part, as a taste of what other yowr frends have ben acquaynted withal and felte, if the old verse be veryfied in yowr self *solatium est miseris socios habere poenarum* [it is a solace for the miserable to have companions in suffering]." This rationale lies behind many *ars moriendi* treatises published in post-Reformation England: the frequent experience of death in the period produced a burgeoning literature instructing readers in doctrinally sound approaches to the deathbed, from the point of view of both the bereaved and the dying. Thomas Playfere's *The Meane in Mourning* typifies the former kind, while among the latter, William Perkins's *Salve for a Sicke Man* was one of the most popular works of the period. Russell's compact treatise to her nephew shows affinities with both. Her effort to recall her nephew from the immoderate grief characterized by *melancholia* shares an insistence on moderation in mourning that was a touchstone of reformed approaches to death. Playfere's sermon, for example, claims that "immoderate weeping … [is] condemned *in nature; in reason; in religion*."

Yet, he admits, true faith requires some tears, "for we offend commonly in the want of weeping, seldome in the excesse." Playfere explains, "[T]he greatest work of love; towards our selves is *repentance*; towards our neighbour is *preaching*: towards God is *praier*. And al these require some tears. So that if we weepe so little as that we weepe not at all, we weepe too little."[21] Perkins's text shifts focus from the bereaved to the dying, presenting "general" and "particular" preparations for death, the former undertaken throughout the life of the Christian, the latter on the deathbed proper. Perkins's first particular preparation is "the dutie of reconciliation, whereby [the sick man] is freely to forgive all men, and to desire to be forgiven of all."[22] His fifth general preparation advocates a reformed activism similar to that espoused by Russell: "if any man be able to doe any good service either to gods Church, or to the Commonwealth, or to any private man, let him doe it with all speede & with all his might, lest death it selfe prevent him."[23]

For both Perkins and Playfere, the missionary zeal of their reformed beliefs leads them to emphasize unity and fellowship among Christians as the goal toward which the dying and the bereaved should strive throughout the potentially destructive, divisive processes of death and mourning. Thus Playfere describes preaching as the Christian's greatest duty to his neighbor, and Perkins insists that "because true faith is no dead thing, it must be expressed by speciall actions."[24] Among these actions, from Russell's point of view, are both the small sermon offered by her consolatory letter, intended to assuage her nephew's sorrow, and the service to which her letter recalls him. Surrender to the "*Daemonis meridianus*" (noontime devil) of *melancholia*, she warns him, "with pevish perswasions of good therby and solytary eiaculations it will bring foorth the Fruct of stupidytie Forgetfullness of yowr naturall disposition of swete and apt speches, fit for yowr place." Calling him, "a wise, Cownsayler and Cooning Coortier," Russell exhorts Robert:

> by fasting from Sinne, and prayer most devowt and ernest to god … study nothing more then *Letari, et bene facere* [to rejoice and to do good]; and to think no thinge better then to walk in [yowr] vocation: in yowr place a wise eloquent Orator; thogh *parum vehemens Dulcis tamen Ut patris discipulum possis agnosci* [a little ardent, but also sweet, so that you may be known as your father's disciple].[25]

---

21 Thomas Playfere, *The Meane in Mourning* (London, 1595), A3v and A7. Five editions appeared by 1616.

22 William Perkins, *A Salve for a Sicke Man* (Cambridge, 1595), 80. Eight editions appeared by 1638.

23 Ibid., 48.

24 Ibid., 89.

25 The first Latin tag is from Ecclesiastes 3:12; the second is adapted from Cicero, *De Officiis*, ed. and trans. Walter Miller (Cambridge, MA: Harvard University Press, 1913), 1.3.12.

If the avowed goal in Russell's epistle is to recall her nephew to his "vocation," her implicit argument is that his immoderate grief threatens his continued success as a counselor and courtier, heir apparent to his father's position at court and in the commonwealth. Russell's political pragmatism is cast in terms that echo the reformed conviction that the central duty of the dying and bereaved was to foster the health of the community of worshippers.

Characteristically, Russell's effort to reconcile her nephew to his wife's death also takes the occasion to display her credentials as spiritual advisor and humanist author. Her letter is marked by a self-conscious literariness, expressed in its artful use of English and Latin, and promotes itself not as a piece of private correspondence but as a textual monument, a work worthy of safeguarding and perhaps copying for readers other than her nephew. Russell uses a clear, mannered italic hand, while the care with which she sealed the letter reflects an artistry involved in early modern epistolarity that is often overlooked. Eight needle marks and the remainders of wax seals and silk threads on this and the majority of Russell's surviving letters indicate that she folded her folio sheets in an "accordion" fold before sewing them shut with embroidery threads and further sealing them with wax.[26] These material features suggest that Russell was creating not just a letter but a work of art. This fact may have prompted her to inquire, in another letter to Robert dated June 24, 1597, "Mr Secretary bicawse I never hering from yow … I now this way desyre to know whether you receaved eny from me … wherin I tooke a great deale of payne to mitigate yowr malencoly."[27]

Russell's consolatory letter is simultaneously a work of religious devotion and of pragmatic self-promotion, and the political service to which she recalls her nephew is marked by the same traits. As such, the letter expresses the centrality of conversation in Russell's approaches to secular and spiritual societies. Like those texts described by Fenton as promoting "the vertuouse exercise in conversation," the epistle demands a response. Russell's reaction to Robert Cecil's silence, her pointed inquiry as to whether he had received her letter at all, reveals the interactive nature of correspondence itself, and places letter writing, as a practice, in the category of reformed religious activity. An appropriate response to her letter might involve not only Robert's acknowledgment of its artistry, but also his resignation to his wife's death, the reconciliation urged by his aunt's beneficial advice.

Russell also initiates a conversation, and elicits a response, when she writes to Mary Talbot, Countess of Shrewsbury, in an effort to return her to the Church of England from Catholicism.[28] Presenting herself as an "affectionate Frend and owld acquaintance," Russell casts her spiritual counsel in the secular guise of a suit:

---

[26] Most of Russell's letters are sealed with silk threads. I am indebted to Heather Wolfe for drawing my attention to this.

[27] Hatfield House, Salis MS 52.52.

[28] Lambeth Palace, Talbot Papers, MS 3203, fol. 410. The Lambeth letter is not dated or endorsed, and I have as yet been unable to locate an inventory of Talbot's library. The letter must have been written after 1593, when Russell first added "Douager" to her

> Good Noble Lady I never made sute to yowr Ladisship in my life to my knoledge. Now I doe: I have sent yowr Ladishipp a little Booke wherby yow most Noble Lady may know what my religion is, and the grownds therof which I howlde and have ever taught to myne. Swete Lady Rede it, thorough. This is all my sute.

Appearing here as the countess's social inferior, Russell nonetheless plays the role of "a wise Cownsayler and Cooning Coortier," fully aware of the counselor's implied intellectual and moral superiority over her pupil ("prince" though she may be).[29] Russell stresses her function as the spiritual head of her household in introducing the doctrine she has "ever taught to myne," and thereby includes Talbot in the number of her children. As the letter progresses, she moves from counselor to parent to "charmer," encouraging the countess, "Be not good Madam like the Deafe Adder that stoppeth her eares and refuseth the voice of the Charmer." Russell concludes:

> Rede it, only I crave. God in whose Hands the Harts of princes be enlarge yowr Harte and Lighten the eyes of yowr mynde to here seke and follow his word and will in all obedience … So wishing yowr Ladyship as well as to myne owne sowle I end with swete Cowntess, Rede this. Yf yow fulfill not my request then shall yowr Ladyship's sowle be more beholdding to me then to yowr self. And so I rest.

Russell's letter and the volume accompanying it share Fenton's sense of reading as a conversation which may lead to spiritual certainty and religious reconciliation. It is tempting to imagine that the book Russell sent to the countess was her translation of Ponet's *Way of Reconciliation*: she sent a copy to Robert Cecil in May 1605, with a letter asking him to "Accept good Lorde a poore Widdowes myte, the Fruicte of my somers travell and I beseche yow to rede it thorowly yowr self at yowr Best leysor."[30] This letter to Robert Cecil displays none of the urgency of that addressed to the countess, however, and the responses elicited by the two letters clearly differ as well. From Robert, she seeks recognition of her skill as a translator and her wisdom as a spiritual advisor: her allusion to the text as a widow's mite—that is, modest, but praiseworthy because it is all she possesses—participates in a New Testament transvaluation in which the humble are exalted and the last become first. Russell thus adopts a position similar to that from which she addresses Mary

---

signature. The seal (one of three Russell used throughout her correspondence) consistently appears on letters dated after 1601, but was also used as early as 1594.

[29] Baldesar Castiglione's *Book of the Courtier*, trans. Charles Singleton (New York: Doubleday, 1959), 327–31, debates the conundrum that the effectiveness of the courtier's counsel may require his superiority over the prince. Russell had intimate knowledge of the text since Thomas Hoby published his English translation (London, 1561) during their marriage. The question of rank is vexed, since Russell pretended to the rank of countess throughout most of her second widowhood (as displayed here in her signature as "Douager"), despite the fact that John Russell predeceased his father, the Earl of Bedford.

[30] Hatfield House, Salis MS 197.53.

Talbot: at once inferior and superior, suitor and charmer. The response sought from the countess, however, is spiritual conversion; a reconciliation that would restore her penitent soul to communion within the true church.

This deployment of religious discourse as a provocation to speech is also clear in Russell's memorial program for her parents' tomb at Romford (Fig. 1.1). Following Cooke's death in 1576, his children erected a joint tomb for him and his wife, Anne Fitzwilliam, who had predeceased him in 1553.[31] In the central panel of the monument, effigies of Cooke and his wife kneel before a two-sided *prie-dieu*. Cooke is accompanied by his two surviving sons, while his four surviving daughters, from eldest to youngest, kneel behind their mother. Traces of paint remain on the marble figures, indicating that they were once brightly colored. The original monument must have presented a startling *tableau vivant*, capturing in stone the dynamics of the living family at the time of the parents' demise.

The desire to create this impression of immediacy and vitality may explain the monument's failure to recall the two sons who predeceased their father, while including in the central panel the ethereal image of a woman's face which may be a portrait of the deceased Cooke sister, Margaret. Although the division of the tomb into a triptych with the deceased parents in the central panel reflects the conceptual divide between the living and the dead, the resounding thesis of the monument is the persistent connection between the Cooke parents and their surviving children. This argument may reflect the family's reformed confidence in the literal resurrection of the visually identifiable body and in the immediacy of the soul's assumption to heaven at the moment of death. As Perkins summarizes this belief:

> [B]eing once certainly assured in conscience of our beeing in Christ, let death come when it wil, & let it cruelly part asunder both body & soule, yet shall they both remaine in the covenant; and by meanes thereof be reunited and taken vp to life eternall … Wherefore I say againe and againe, labour that your consciences by the holy ghost may testifie that ye are living stones in the temple of God.[32]

This tenet, which rests upon the Protestant rejection of Purgatory, precipitated a revised understanding of the function of funeral monuments. While pre-Reformation tombs were focal points for the recitation of masses and prayers for the soul of the departed, the Elizabethan view denied the intercessory power of prayer for the dead and, rather, protected monuments as repositories of personal and dynastic history.[33] Reflecting this reformed understanding of monuments and of the new relationship between the living and the dead that they symbolized, the sculptural and textual elements of the Romford tomb emphasize the immediate, affective relationships between the departed and the bereaved. The monument

---

31 See Royal Commission on Historical Monuments, *An Inventory of the Historical Monuments in Essex* (London: HMSO, 1921), 2:203–4.

32 Perkins, *Salve*, 28–9.

33 See Peter Sherlock, *Monuments and Memory in Early Modern England* (Aldershot: Ashgate, 2008), 165–96.

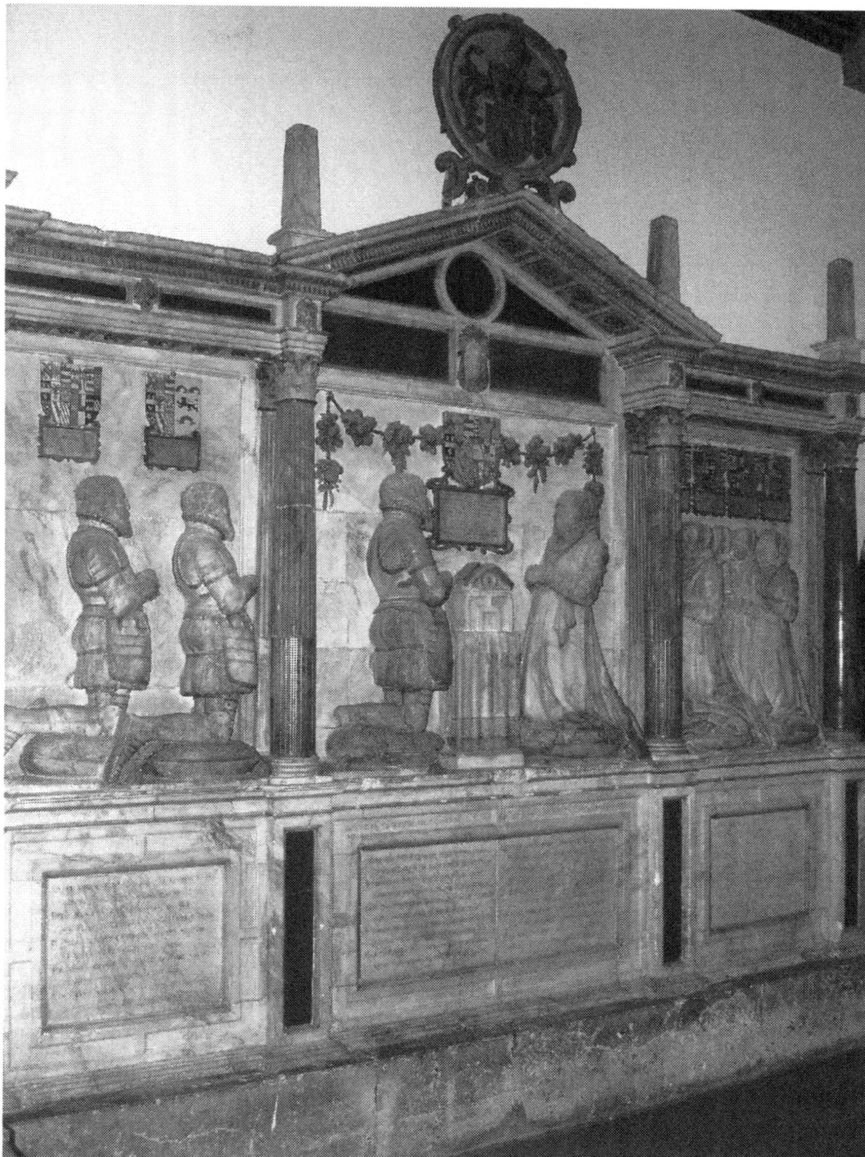

Fig. 1.1 Cornelius Cure. Monument for Sir Anthony Cooke and Anne Fitzwilliam Cooke. Parish Church of St. Edward the Confessor, Romford. Photograph by Patricia Phillippy.

gives visual form to the unity and Christian community that Playfere and Perkins advance as the goal to be sought in the face of death.[34] Each of the monument's three epitaphs presents a direct address of one speaker to another,[35] while the monument's effigies are material embodiments of the community of the faithful as "living stones in the temple of God."[36]

As living stones, effigies of the dead mark the absent-presence of the material body, removed from the body of worshippers by death but still included through interment in the physical space of the church. This continued fellowship, imagined in the Romford inscriptions as an ongoing conversation, is represented visually by the inclusion of effigies of the living alongside those of the dead. Russell's use of epitaphs at Romford and in later memorial projects to prolong the conversation between the mourner and the departed represents a reformation of the Catholic understanding of the funeral monument as a locus of continued spiritual activity and interchange across the border of life and death. Her reconciliatory view of effigies as figurative embodiments of the mystical Church body in which the spirits of the dead still participate—untransubstantiated signs, as her translation of Ponet puts it—sees the absent body as figured in the living Word.[37] When mourning and consolation are matters of conversation, dumb stones not only speak, but also live. It is under the banner of a continued conversation between Anthony Cooke's descendents, and in light of this desire for sculptural, if not spiritual, resurrection, that Russell's manuscript poem to her nephew should be read.

Sacred Conversation

In his profound sorrow, Robert Cecil commissioned a tomb for his wife, Elizabeth, in St. Nicholas' chapel in Westminster Abbey, the same chapel where Robert's father had erected a joint monument for his daughter, Anne Cecil de Vere, and his wife, Mildred. Mildred was, of course, Elizabeth Russell's sister, and the program

34 Nigel Llewellyn, *Funeral Monuments in Post-Reformation England* (Cambridge: Cambridge University Press, 2000), 42–59, describes social continuity as the primary function of post-Reformation monuments. I recast his observation in theological rather than societal terms.

35 A Latin inscription on the Cooke tomb directly addresses Cooke, and an English poem on a stone tablet adjacent to the tomb addresses, "You learned Men, and suche as Learninge love." The third textual element, Anne Fitzwilliam's memorial, is discussed below.

36 Perkins, *Salve*, 29. This image for the church, adapted from 1 Peter 2:4–5, is frequently deployed by reformed authors: "Ye also, as lively stones, are built up a spiritual house, an holy priesthood, to offer up spiritual sacrifices, acceptable to God by Jesus Christ" (Geneva Bible).

37 Ponet reconciles Catholic and Protestant views by confirming that the Eucharist is comprised of both substance ("trueth") and figure, while denying the real presence of the corpus Christi in the sacrament (*Way*, 7). Similarly, effigies figure the presence of the material body while marking the absence of the sanctified body already ascended as spirit.

of the Burghley tomb may have been influenced by Russell.[38] Robert's memorial for his wife stands within the gaze of his own effigy on the adjacent Burghley monument. The tomb is a modest alabaster and black marble sarcophagus devoid of figural sculpture. Two Latin epitaphs construct an affective conversation between the departed wife and her grieving husband.

WIFE:
Attendant of a Queen, Dear daughter of a Baron,
    Faithful wife of a Knight, I was *Elizabeth*:
One love was ours, one indivisible will,
    There was one heart, one inviolable faith.
He, if ever he were able to put aside his care for me,
    He would be unmindful of his own soul.
HUSBAND:
If love remains constant through tears, dearest Wife,
    Then tears will often attend your burial.
For how you, pious bride, were loved in return by me
    Your merit witnesses, known to me and to Him:
But neither love nor companionship allows sorrow to reign,
    And Christ draws you to himself with a greater love.
Thus that you, beloved, enjoy goodness and peace
    Gives hope to me that I may share your peace.[39]

An English inscription on the opposite side of the tomb identifies the female speaker in this moving dialogue and the husband who memorializes her:

A Brooke by name, the Baron Cobhams childe
A Newton was she, by her mothers side
Cecill her husband, this for her did builde
To prove his love did after death abid.

With the epitaph identifying Elizabeth and Robert turned discreetly away from circulation within the chapel, the tomb preserves the couple's privacy even in the highly public forum of Westminster Abbey. The monument—without effigy, with the quiet intimacy of its Latin inscription—memorializes marriage in and as a textual dialogue. Once again, mourning is cast as conversation.

The standard guides to the Westminster Abbey tombs state that Robert Cecil composed the epitaphs adorning his wife's tomb. This is only partially true. Shortly after Elizabeth's death, Robert consulted Latinist George Goodwin,

---

[38] Burghley authored the first-person inscription. See John Dart, *Westmonasterium: Or the History and Antiquities of the Abbey Church of St Peters Westminster* (London, 1742), 1:136–8.

[39] For the Latin text, see Dart, *Westmonsterium*, 1:130. The English translation is my own.

asking him to prepare epitaphs intended for the tomb.[40] In response, Goodwin sent 36 Latin epitaphs, and with them a note reminding Robert of his charge that they should be brief, simple, unaffected, and matronly ("solidam, simplisicem, sincerem, matronalem").[41] The last four lines of one of Goodwin's epitaphs ("Unus amor nobis, una indivisa voluntas, / Cor unum, una Fides inviolata fuit. / Ille mei si quando potest deponere curam / Ille potest anime non memor esse suae") are spoken by the "Uxor" on Elizabeth Cecil's monument: these lines, marked by an "X" in the left margin of Goodwin's manuscript, were copied intact. Her remaining two lines borrow phrases from several other poems in Goodwin's collection. The response by the grieving husband inscribed on the tomb seems to be Robert's own.

Around the same time that Goodwin sent his epitaphs to Robert Cecil, Elizabeth Russell sent a poem in Latin, "To the Right Honorable my Sorrowfull Nephew Mr Secretary at his Howse" (Fig. 1.2). One of Russell's four surviving poems in manuscript, the elegy, like those ultimately inscribed on Elizabeth Cecil's tomb, presents a partial—or more correctly, mutual—dialogue between husband and wife:

> My dear spouse, beloved for many years,
> Ah! My aid, mind, honor, and glory,
> With the body removed, only the divine things remain.
> By this part, you are perpetually present to me, Cecil.
> The more pleasing savor of Christ, death, mind, your words, griefs/labors—
> Stand as your monuments, which will not perish by day.
> **R** Cecil
> I have done what was permitted, I wish more were permitted to me.
> **R** C.[42]

---

[40] On Goodwin, see D.K. Money, "Goodwin, George," in *ODNB*, (see n. 14) (accessed March 2008). For a similar manuscript collection of epitaphs for Anne Cecil de Vere, see BL, Lansdowne MS 104, fols. 195–214.

[41] TNA, SP Dom 12/262, no. 53, "In obitum clarissima foemina Elizabethae Cecilae," fol. 1v.

[42] The Latin reads:

> Chara mihi multos Coniunx dilecta per annos
> Ah mihi praesidium Mens Honor atque Decus
> Corpore sublato tantum Divina supersunt
> Hac mihi Coecilio parte perennis ades
> Gratius odor Christi Mors Mens tua verba Dolores [Labores]
> Non peritura Die stant Monumenta tui.
> **R** Coecilius
> Quod Licuit feci vellem mihi plura Licere.
> **R** C.

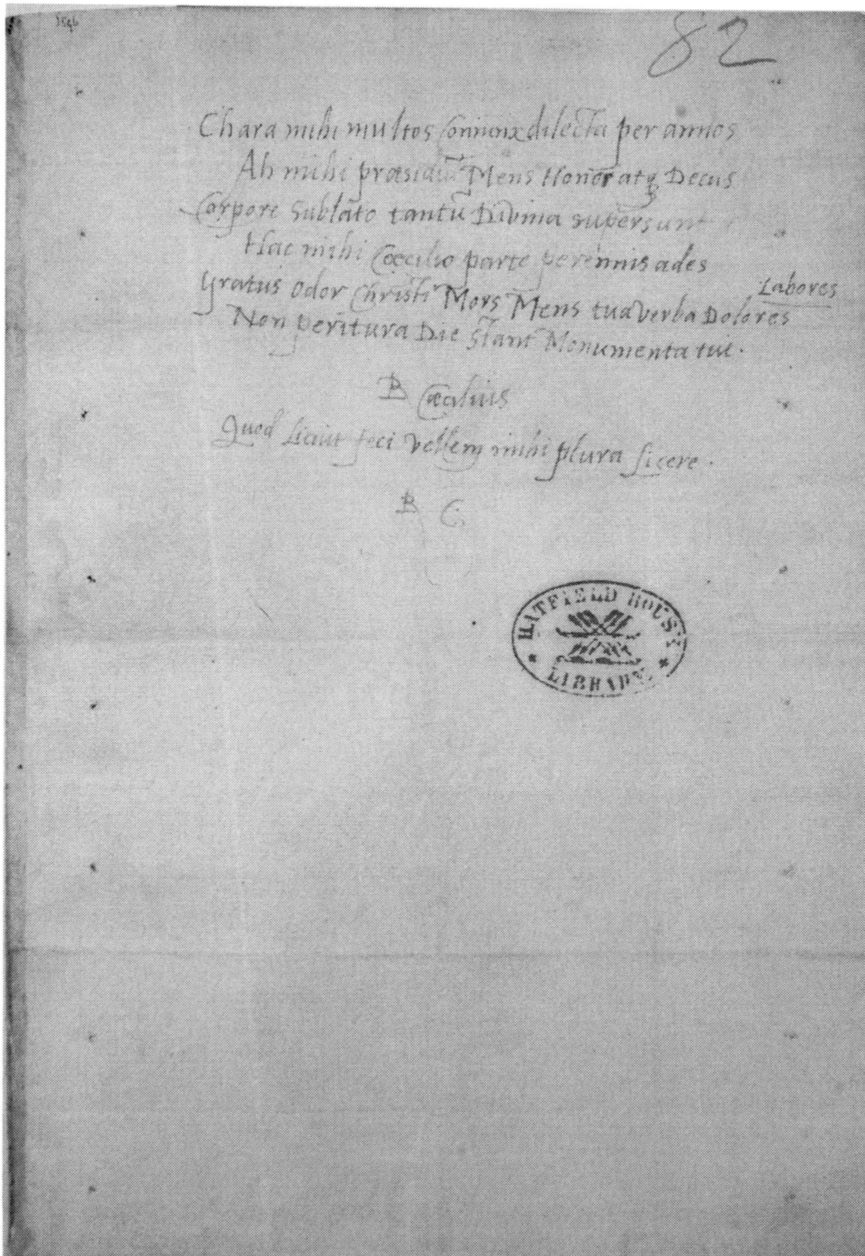
82

Chara mihi multos coniunx dilecta per annos
Ah mihi praesidium Mens Honor atque Decus
Corpore sublato tantum Divina supersunt
Hac mihi Caecilio parte perennis ades
Gratus odor Christi Mors Mens tua Verba Labores Dolores
Non peritura Die Stant Monumenta tui.

B Caecilius

Quod licuit feci vellem mihi plura licere.

B C

Fig. 1.2 Elizabeth Russell to Robert Cecil. Hatfield House, Salis MS 140.82. Reproduced by courtesy of the Marquess of Salisbury.

In this dense exchange, Russell exploits the inclusive gender of "conjunx" (spouse) to underscore the merger of husband and wife in marriage and in mourning: the speaker's address to "Coecilio" in line 4 and the superimposed initials, "E" and "R," make the point that this is a conversation that continues beyond the grave, in which the voices of the interlocutors may blend almost imperceptibly. The poem may be entirely in the voice of the grieving husband: thus Robert Cecil addresses Elizabeth as "Coecilio"—that is, as himself. Other elements, however, such as the emphasis on the traditionally masculine qualities of "mind" (mens) and "aid" (praesidium), suggest that Elizabeth speaks some portions of the poem. This coupling of masculine and feminine, life and death, may prompt the unresolved doubleness in the last word of line 5, simultaneously "Dolores" and "Labores."[43] Insofar as the superimposed initials concluding the poem serve as a mark of authorship, Russell must have been especially pleased that they signal not only Elizabeth and Robert Cecil, but also Elizabeth (Russell) Cooke.

The inclusion of two sets of superimposed initials, the first identified as Elizabeth and Robert Cecil and the second following the single line, "Quod Licuit feci vellem mihi plura Licere" (I have done what was permitted, I wish more were permitted to me), argues that Russell meant the second set to signify her authorship. The line, apparently a self-authored personal motto, was a favorite of Russell's. She had used it at least twice before. It first appears on the joint tomb she erected for her first husband, Thomas Hoby, and her brother-in-law, Philip, in 1566, where two Latin elegies by Russell describe the brothers' virtues. The line occurs in the middle of the elegy for Philip Hoby. It appears again on her second husband's tomb, erected in 1584 in St. Edmund's chapel of Westminster Abbey (adjacent to St. Nicholas's chapel, where the Cecil tombs would soon be built). An inscription on the tomb's base, spoken in the widow's voice, concludes:

> My husband deare more than this worlds light
> Death hath me reft: but I from death will take
> His memory to whom this tomb I make.
> John was his name, (ah, was) wretch must I say
> Lord Russell once, now my tear-thirstie clay.
> Quod licuit feci, vellem mihi plura licere.

In these two monuments, Russell affirms her control over her husbands' legacies and her fulfillment of the wifely duties of mourning and commemoration. Within these programs, the repeated Latin tag reflects Russell's reformed view of funeral rites and the relationship of the living to the dead. The question of what is allowed, and her wish for greater license to express grief, resonate with the encouragement she offers her nephew to ameliorate his melancholy by reconciling his will to God's: "Let Pacience have her perfect worke," she urges, "which is

[43] "Labores" is inserted at the end of line 5, above "Dolores," and seems to be offered as an alternative, the choice left to Cecil.

Antidotum vitae [the remedy for life]."[44] Russell's letter implies that Robert's prolonged sorrow is more than can be approved—spiritually, in his obdurate violation of the mean in mourning, and pragmatically, in his neglect of his duties to the commonwealth. As Russell's adaptation of the religious discourses of mourning in her epistle unfolds in both secular and spiritual registers and enables her gesture of self-authorship, the appearance of the Latin motto on these monuments serves a similar purpose. Introducing her voice and perspective into the commemorative program, the line affirms that Russell as author of the tombs has done, artistically, all that her abilities have allowed her to do.

The first line of Russell's Latin poem to Robert Cecil, like the last, refers the poem to an earlier family monument: the program at Romford provides the tantalizing source for the manuscript poem written some 20 years later. Strype describes the memorial for Anne Fitzwilliam (which has not survived) as follows: "Near the monument to Cooke, in the Chancel, on a flat stone, a brass plate, thus inscribed (being Sir Anthonies Farewel to his Wife deceased):"

> My dear spouse, beloved for many years,
> Mistress of the house, mother not without many offspring,
> Anna, farewell, dying, having understood that [your] melancholy husband
> Is deservedly not forgetful of your end.[45]

This imaginative address of the grieving husband to the dying wife once again understands mourning as conversation, and consolation in textual and monumental terms. Consolation is found not in spiritual reconciliation but in the labor of material commemoration, the fulfillment of one's duties to the dead. While Russell's later incorporation of this line into her elegy for her nephew places her in an immediate relation to the Romford epitaph, it cannot clarify whether her initial relationship to that text was as reader or writer. If the date of Anne Fitzwilliam's death is correct, it is possible that Anthony Cooke was the author of this epitaph and of the modest monument upon which is appeared. A slab or brass plate would have been an appropriate form with which to commemorate a woman, particularly if a joint tomb (such as the one ultimately erected in Romford) was projected upon her spouse's death. If the plaque was installed at her mother's death in 1553, thirteen-year-old Elizabeth would have learned from her father the formula which would so often be repeated in her adult writings, deriving from this ideal of erudite conversation between husband and wife a model for constructive self-representation in a variety of media.

The shared line also suggests a monumental function for Russell's manuscript poem. When considered in light of Russell's literary performances on the Cooke, Hoby, and Russell tombs, the elegy clearly carries the features of an epitaph prepared for inscription on a monument, where Russell's concessions to personal

---

44 A common proverb, "Antidotum vitae, patientia est" (Patience is the remedy for life). See, for example, in John Harmar, *Praxis Grammatical* (London, 1623), no. 301.

45 Strype, *Annals*, 2, Appendix, 108.

grief frequently threaten to overrun the limits of the orthodox mean in mourning. The poem may be a draft of an epitaph proposed for Elizabeth Cecil's tomb. We can only speculate as to whether the poem was written in response to a request from Cecil, like that issued to Goodwin. He may have consulted his aunt, renowned for her skill in epitaphs, on his program for the tomb. Alternatively, Russell may have learned of the plan and sent the epitaph uninvited.

Russell's citation in her manuscript poem of the epitaph addressed to her mother many years earlier and her transmission of this textual family heirloom to her nephew are characteristic of her lifelong project of self-representation as her father's daughter. Her translation of *A Way of Reconciliation* also participates in this project. Dedicating the work to her daughter, Anne, Russell presents the translation as an act of continued conversation with her departed father: she brings it to press, she explains, "fearing lest after my death it should be printed by the humors of other, and wrong of the dead, who in his life approved my Translation with his own allowance" (A2v). She expands this conversation, moreover, to include her nephew. In the letter she sent to Robert with the volume (Salis MS 197.53), she describes the book as a gift from grandfather to grandson: "in token yowr grandfather and moothers father doth thank yowr Lordshipp for so muche Honoring his Cookes Blood, he hath sent yow by me his Daughter yowr owld Aunt a Booke of his owne making in Germany, in the tyme of his pilgrimage." Here, as in her manuscript poem, Russell imagines material connections—between the tombs of Anne Fitzwilliam and of her granddaughter-in-law, Elizabeth Cecil, and between her father's manuscript translation and the printed volume offered to his grandson—that articulate and literalize the blood and affective ties among family members, living and dead. The monumental program eventually realized on Elizabeth Cecil's Westminster Abbey tomb responds to this intergenerational conversation, indebted to and completing the one-sided dialogue between the grieving husband and his wife initiated in the voice of Anthony Cooke in Romford.

The fact that Cecil chose Goodwin's, rather than Russell's, epitaph for his wife's memorial may imply that although Russell was considered a "wonder of the age,"[46] her credentials as a classicist could not compare with Goodwin's. At the same time, though, Russell's poem shares with the tomb's paired epitaphs a sense of the mutuality—even the interchangeability—of husband and wife, a sentiment also present in the one epitaph among Goodwin's numerous samples which appealed to Cecil. Similar sentiments are expressed in Russell's mournful epitaphs for John Russell, in which she grieves the loss of "my tear-thirstie clay," and for Thomas Hoby, whom she calls "Sweet husband, greatest part of one soul" ("O dulcis conjux, animae pars maxima nostrae"). Inspired by his aunt's dialogic and doctrinal model, Robert Cecil adapted Goodwin's text into the context of a reformed *sacra conversazione*, translating—as his aunt had taught him to do—the fragile bonds between loved ones into living, monumental stone.

---

46 Ballard, *Memoirs*, 198.

Chapter 2
“Theise dearest offrings of my heart”: The Sacrifice of Praise in Mary Sidney Herbert, Countess of Pembroke’s *Psalmes*

Mary Trull

The Hebrew Bible describes animal sacrifice in reverent detail, stipulating correct victims, locations, and gestures. Its reader learns of the priest’s hand laid on the head of the chosen animal, the blood splashed on the altar, the entrails precisely arranged, and the fat smoking on the fire (e.g., Lev. 1:1–9). With the highly orchestrated slaughter of carefully chosen, nearly perfect animal specimens, the Israelites hoped to glorify God and approach his presence. By the sixteenth century CE, however, Christian inheritors of these sacred texts found the concreteness of animal sacrifice profoundly disturbing. Protestants saw Hebrew animal sacrifice as an attempt to appease God and thus as a precursor to the Catholic doctrine on the sacrifice of the Mass. When English Protestants set their pens to creating new vernacular translations of the Book of Psalms, they also sought to replace the Catholic Mass with a more spiritual “sacrifice of praise,” and therefore translated psalmic references to sacrifice metaphorically. But the famous *Psalmes of David* by Philip Sidney (1554–1586) and Mary Sidney Herbert, Countess of Pembroke (1562–1621), are different. The psalms versified by the Countess of Pembroke highlight sacrifice, making it more concrete, more ceremonious, and grander than in the scriptures—more like a work of appeasement. Taking a direction different from any of her contemporaries, Pembroke engages the conflict over the meaning of the sacrifice of praise by imagining sacrifice not as a paltry return for God’s munificence, but as a marvelous gift. As in the gift theory of sacrifice described by anthropologists Henri Hubert and Marcel Mauss, Pembroke offers a counter-gift in response to God’s bounty.[1] In her dedicatory poems and the psalms themselves, she meditates on the problem of how to offer a gift to a divine being, and portrays sacrifice as a gift that draws human and divine beings together for a brief and sacred moment.

The Countess of Pembroke, a renowned early modern patron, editor, poet, and translator, has generally been depicted as stylistically innovative but reluctant to engage in theological controversy. This is surprising, since the project itself of translating the Book of Psalms bespeaks her Protestant mission, and her

---

[1] Henri Hubert and Marcel Mauss, *Sacrifice: Its Nature and Function*, trans. W.D. Halls (Chicago: University of Chicago Press, 1964).

dedicatory poem to Queen Elizabeth praises her sovereign's defense of the faith. For her contemporaries, psalm translation and commentary were favored venues for doctrinal polemics, but modern critics often remark that Pembroke avoids such areas of conflict; we see her as a scrupulous student thumbing through many volumes in order to arrive at the reading of each psalm most faithful to the scriptures.[2] G.F. Waller set the stage for this portrait by introducing Pembroke's readings as Calvinist, yet marked by an "aesthetic rather than doctrinal approach to the psalms,"[3] and Michael Brennan has suggested that her psalms are a work of doctrinal reconciliation, attempting to build a bridge between her family's Catholic past and Protestant present.[4] One exception to Pembroke's shying away from polemics might be seen in what Coburn Freer calls her portrayal of "devotion as a joyful game."[5] For Pembroke, worship is festive, celebratory, and often set to music—this despite the fact that her major sources considered the playing of music during worship services a sign of Catholic worldliness and idolatry. Moreover, her showcasing of poetry's sophistication and beauty through experiments in versification, diction, and imagery could seem an affront to Protestant suspicions of idolatry and works-righteousness.[6] However, this interest in aesthetics suits Pembroke's reputation for resisting the anti-Catholic polemics characteristic of Protestant psalm commentaries.[7] In addition, scholars have praised her ability to retain scriptural meaning while reflecting her own experiences through diction and imagery, a kind of artistry that Debra Rienstra and Noel Kinnamon call "particularizing the text."[8] Instead of doctrinal conflict, Pembroke highlights

---

2 On the evidence for and against Pembroke's use of Hebrew sources, see Mary Sidney Herbert, *The Collected Works of Mary Sidney Herbert, Countess of Pembroke*, ed. Margaret P. Hannay, Noel J. Kinnamon, and Michael G. Brennan (Oxford: Oxford University Press, 1998), 2:16–19; and Theodore L. Steinberg, "The Sidneys and the Psalms," *Studies in Philology* 92, no. 1 (1995): 1–17.

3 G F. Waller, "'This Matching of Contraries': Calvinism and Courtly Philosophy in the Sidney Psalms," *English Studies* 55 (1974): 23. See also his "A 'Matching of Contraries': Ideological Ambiguity in the Sidney Psalms," *Wascana Review* 9 (1974): 124–33.

4 Michael G. Brennan, "'First Rais'de by Thy Blest Hand, and What Is Mine / Inspired by Thee': The 'Sidney Psalter' and the Countess of Pembroke's Completion of the Sidneian Psalms," *Sidney Newsletter & Journal* 14, no. 1 (1996): 43–4.

5 Coburn Freer, *Music for a King: George Herbert's Style and the Metrical Psalms* (Baltimore, MD: Johns Hopkins University Press, 1972), 25, 73–108; *Collected Works*, Hannay, Kinnamon, and Brennan, 2:26–8.

6 Debra Rienstra and Noel J. Kinnamon, "Circulating the Sidney-Pembroke Psalter," in *Women's Writing and the Circulation of Ideas: Manuscript Publication in England, 1550–1800*, ed. George L. Justice and Nathan Tinker (Cambridge: Cambridge University Press, 2002), 50–72.

7 *Collected Works*, Hannay, Kinnamon, and Brennan, 2:20–28.

8 Rienstra and Kinnamon, "Circulating," 55. In contrast, Ramie Targoff thinks that Pembroke avoids doctrinal references in order to create a liturgical text for common prayer.

individual experiences of God, such as the difficulty or delight of faith,[9] and stresses themes familiar to an aristocratic woman, elaborating on images of pregnancy, childbirth, and children, and introducing aspects of Elizabethan court life into royal psalms like Psalm 45.[10]

In contrast to this critical consensus, I argue that Pembroke's verses reveal the action of an independent mind reflecting on the knotty theological problems of her day—particularly, the doctrinal problem of sacrifice. In interpreting one of the central themes of Protestant discourse, the "sacrifice of praise," Pembroke struck out independently of her sources, and in her idiosyncratic treatment of this key concept we can discern a unique theological position. While the major Protestant commentators minimized the importance of ritual sacrifice in the psalms and interpreted all references to sacrifice as metaphors for a spiritual state, Pembroke reveled in the concrete imagery of ceremonial Hebrew sacrifice. Despite her characteristically restrained translation methods and her deeply Protestant worldview, she made additions to the psalms emphasizing ritual aspects of sacrifice: the grandiosity of mass destruction, the magnanimous gestures of the officiant, and the smoke and incense of a mysterious performance. This is not the attitude toward lavish ceremony that we expect from sixteenth-century Protestants who were disturbed by the apparent congruency between these details and the ceremonies of the Catholic Mass. Nevertheless, the Countess of Pembroke's *Psalmes* demonstrate her comprehension of Protestant objections to sacrifice: by depicting sacrifice as a debt owed to God and emphasizing the asymmetry between God's munificence and what humans offer in return, she assuages the Protestant fear that talk of sacrifice will lead to works-righteousness. She makes sacrifice a symbol for generosity on the part of both God and the human sinner. Similarly, her dedicatory poems depict praise as a gift that miraculously breaches the gulf between herself as a mortal giver and its semi-divine recipient—respectively, Queen Elizabeth and Philip Sidney.

Common Prayer: The Language of Public Devotion in Early Modern England (Chicago: University of Chicago Press, 2001), 76–84.

9 For examples, see Beth Wynne Fisken, "'The Art of Sacred Parody' in Mary Sidney's *Psalmes*," *Tulsa Studies in Women's Literature* 8, no. 2 (1989): 223–39; Margaret P. Hannay, "'Unlock My Lipps': The *Miserere Mei Deus* of Anne Vaughan Lok and Mary Sidney Herbert, Countess of Pembroke," in *Privileging Gender in Early Modern England*, ed. Jean R. Brink (Kirksville, MO: Sixteenth Century Journal Publishers, 1993), 19–36.

10 *Collected Works*, Hannay, Kinnamon, and Brennan, 1:72–4; Margaret P. Hannay, "'House-Confinéd Maids': The Presentation of Woman's Role in the *Psalmes* of the Countess of Pembroke," *English Literary Renaissance* 24, no. 1 (1994): 44–71; and "'When Riches Growes': Class Perspective in Pembroke's *Psalmes*," in *Women, Writing, and the Reproduction of Culture in Tudor and Stuart Britain*, ed. Mary E. Burke, et al. (Syracuse, NY: Syracuse University Press, 2000), 77–97.

The Sacrifice of Praise in the Bible and Protestant Thought

The phrase "sacrifice of praise" attempts to reconcile a conceptual gap between inward and outward worship, between reverence itself and its expression in word and action. In the Hebrew Bible, blood sacrifice dominates outward forms of worship. Sacrifice is both the act most propitious to God and most open to error or subversion. Therefore, the prophets measure the people's standing in God's eyes by his willingness to accept their sacrifices. When the people hypocritically burn offerings in order to waft "a pleasing odor to the Lord" that covers their true iniquities, God turns his back on their altars, as Hosea, Isaiah, and Micah warn: "When Ephraim [Israel] multiplied altars to expiate sin / they became to him altars for sinning" (Hosea 8:11; NRSV). The Biblical prophets made sacrifice representative of ritual acts generally and thus a symbol for external gestures of worship, as opposed to inward reverence. In Micah, Hosea, Isaiah, and elsewhere, God rejects the sacrifices of a corrupted Jewish nation altogether or demands, in their stead, a more sincere expression of reverence—the "sacrifice of praise." Appropriately, the Book of Psalms applies the theme of figurative sacrifice to that activity the psalms enact: praise of God. In Psalm 40, the psalmist avers that God does not want sacrifice; instead, "I have told the glad news of deliverance … see, I have not restrained my lips … I have not hidden your saving help … I have spoken of your faithfulness and your salvation" (Ps. 40:9–10; NRSV).[11] The fact that a good sacrifice requires a faithful heart, as the prophets and the Book of Psalms maintain, does not diminish the significance of the sacrificial rites themselves, but underlines it—they are too important in Hebrew life to be undertaken irreverently.

The history of Christianity has been in part a long revision of the idea of sacrifice. With Christ's death on the cross, sacrifice became a divine act rather than a human one. But this substitution left a lacuna in the nature and meaning of worship, one that would be filled by spiritual acts. Paul urges the Romans to "present your bodies as a living sacrifice … which is your spiritual worship" (Rom.12:1–2; NRSV); in the Book of Hebrews, the sacrifice of praise substitutes for the old rituals. The writer dissuades the godly from observing Mosaic law too rigorously:

> We have an altar from which those who officiate in the tent have no right to eat. For the bodies of those animals whose blood is brought into the sanctuary by the high priest as a sacrifice for sin are burned outside the camp. Therefore Jesus also suffered outside the city gate in order to sanctify the people by his own blood. Let us then go to him outside the camp and bear the abuse he endured … let us continually offer a sacrifice of praise to God, that is, the fruit of lips that confess his name. Do not neglect to do good and to share what you have, for such sacrifices are pleasing to God. (Heb. 13:10–16; NRSV)

[11] Psalms 40, 50, 51, 69, 107, and 116 underscore that praise of God is better than sacrifice.

Since Christians participate freely in Christ's sacrifice, they will now replace ritual sacrifice with figurative sacrifices of praise and good conduct. As the medieval liturgy evolved, the Mass came to represent both a re-enactment of Christ's sacrifice at which Christ acts as victim and co-officiant and a sacrifice of praise accomplished through prayer.[12] Thus the sixteenth-century Reformation, with its call to replace the Mass with sacrifices of praise, did not so much reconceive the sacrifice of praise as place it at the center of doctrinal conflict. Early in his career, Luther used his commentary on the second Psalm as an example of the work of true priesthood. A true priest is one who replaces "abominations of the impious sacrifice of the papists" with teaching and writing on the Bible, by which he "not only does his neighbor a valuable service ... but he also offers to God in heaven Himself the most pleasant sacrifice and is truly called the priest of the All-highest."[13] Rejecting the sacrifice of the Mass united Reformers; with one voice, they accused the Catholic Church of falling, like the strayed Israel of the prophets' warnings, into hypocritical, soulless gestures of worship. Reformers indicted the sacrificial Mass as the ultimate expression of works-righteousness, one attempting to replicate and thus take the credit for Christ's crucifixion. If Christ's sacrifice could be repeated, Protestants argued, it could not have been sufficient to wipe out humankind's sin. Moreover, as a ceremonial gesture the Mass replaced inward reverence with outward rites and—perhaps the most serious charge—sought to broker with God by exchanging sacrifice for salvation. John Calvin writes with horror that "the sacrifice of the Mass is represented as paying a price to God ... And such is the most miserable ungratefulness of man that where he ought to have recognized and given thanks for the abundance of God's bounty, he makes God in this his debtor!"[14] Protestant Reformers generally ignored the longstanding Catholic view that the Eucharist accomplished a sacrifice of praise, and they represented the Mass as a heartless pretense of sacrifice and reformed worship as a thankful response to Christ's sacrifice.[15] This contrast captured the Protestant imagination and found expression in the acts which came to define public expressions of Protestant identity, such as hymn-singing, iconoclastic protest, Bible translation, and preaching.

---

12 See, for example, the fifteenth-century theologian Stephen Brulefer: "In every Mass celebrated by a priest we must distinguish a twofold work: first, there is the *opus operatum*, and that is Christ offering himself to the father for us; secondly, there is the *opus operantis*, and that is the celebration, prayers and ritual of the Mass." From *Reportata in IV S. Bonaventurae Sententiarum libros*, quoted in Francis Clark, *Eucharistic Sacrifice and the Reformation* (Oxford: Basil Blackwell, 1967), 527.

13 Martin Luther, *Luther's Works*, vol. 12, *Selected Psalms*, ed. Jaroslav Pelikan (St. Louis: Concordia Publishing House, 1955), 4–5.

14 John Calvin, *Institutes of the Christian Religion*, ed. John T. McNeill, trans. Ford Lewis Battles (Philadelphia: Westminster Press, 1960), 2:4.18.7.

15 See B.A. Gerrish, *Grace and Gratitude: The Eucharistic Theology of John Calvin* (Minneapolis: Fortress Press, 1993), 146–56.

A brief consideration of modern anthropological interpretations of sacrifice can help clarify some of the intellectual problems that animated Protestant theories of sacrifice. In 1871, for example, Edward Burnett Tylor advanced the theory that sacrifice involved a gift given to the gods in expectation of a return; by the logic of *do ut des*, "I give so that you will give," the value of sacrifice is primarily utilitarian.[16] Tylor thought that in more advanced societies, sacrifice attains a more spiritual meaning; in its most evolved form, not the material sacrificed but the reverence of the giver would determine the transaction's value. The transaction theory of sacrifice is not a modern invention: Plato implicitly draws upon it in the Socratic dialogue *Euthyphro*, in which Socrates asks, "what advantage could come to the gods from the gifts which they receive from us? Everybody sees what they give us. No good that we possess but is given by them. What advantage can they gain by what they get from us?"[17] As we have seen, this question struck Protestants with great force. In essence, Luther and Calvin accuse Catholics of viewing the Mass through the lens of *do ut des*. Like Tylor, Protestants preferred a more spiritual form of worship, one that called upon purer impulses: gratitude rather than greed. Unlike Tylor, however, they wished to forego the transaction model altogether, while preserving the role of human agency. Therefore, they conceived of the sacrifice of praise as a response to God's benefits, and of the Eucharist as a gift from God to his people, in no way reciprocal. Christians offer the sacrifice of praise as thanks for God's gift rather than as a gift; in fact, even the sacrifice of praise itself is a gift from God to human beings since it is therapeutic, easing the praiser's burdened heart and spreading God's message to others who will benefit.[18] Though Protestants assert that giving a gift to God is preposterous, they must, nevertheless, admit that God desires sacrifices of praise. Calvin, for example, writes that "God seketh no avauntage by us, as he hathe no nede: only he will that we do homage to hym for all the benefites that he geveth us."[19] However, the asymmetry between human praise and divine gifts assured Protestants that they were not, in presuming to make an offering to God, falling into the error

---

16 Edward Burnett Tylor, *Primitive Culture* (New York: Henry Holt & Co., 1889). For an overview of theories of sacrifice, see Gary A. Anderson, "Sacrifice and Sacrificial Offerings," in *The Anchor Bible Dictionary*, ed. David Noel Freedman (New York: Doubleday, 1992), 5:870–86.

17 Plato, *Euthyphro*, in *Plato: The Collected Dialogues*, ed. Edith Hamilton and Cairns Huntington (Princeton: Princeton University Press, 1961), 169–85; 14e–15a.

18 On Luther's attempt to sharply distinguish the gift metaphor of sacrifice from a transaction model of sacrifice, see William T. Cavanaugh, "Eucharistic Sacrifice and the Social Imagination in Early Modern Europe," *Journal of Medieval and Early Modern Studies* 31 (2001): 585–606.

19 John Calvin, "Sermons Upon the Songe That Ezekias Made," in *The Collected Works of Anne Vaughan Lock*, ed. Susan M. Felch (Tempe: Arizona Center for Medieval and Renaissance Studies, 1999), 50.

of *do ut des*.[20] Further, for Protestants it was crucial that the sacrifice would be solely spiritual or verbal and should never be imagined as concrete or "visible," as Antoine Marcourt writes: "by the great and wonderful sacrifice of Jesus Christ all outward and visible sacrifice is abolished and voided, and never is another to remain."[21] In the "sacrifice of praise," Protestants found a model that maintained the distance between God's power and human works by rejecting concrete human responses to God's gifts. Only praise would allow believers to approach the divine presence through an outpouring of gratitude.[22]

Luther and Calvin rejected the *do ut des* model, but in replacing the Mass with the sacrifice of praise, they offered no clear definition of the nature of this more inward form of sacrifice which was neither a gift nor a payment. In contrast, the model of sacrifice outlined by Henri Hubert and Marcel Mauss preserves the idea that sacrifice is a gift while rejecting Tylor's model of egoistic exchange. Hubert and Mauss argue that the consecration of the sacrificial object through destruction also consecrates the subject or "sacrifier" (the person on whose behalf the sacrifice is offered). The sacred gift is not a commodity but a mediator; it represents the subject and in its sacralization brings the subject closer to the divine presence. Furthermore, the incommensurability of the offered gift (such as a slaughtered animal) and what the subject receives from God (such as salvation) serves to establish the distinct roles of the human subject and divine recipient. In Mauss and Hubert's model, sacrifice brings the divine and the human into intimate relation yet clearly delineates their differences.[23] As we will see, such is the explicit function of the sacrifice of praise for Pembroke: while it is a gift, by definition it follows God's much greater gifts. Pembroke's solution captures and elaborates upon a distinction made by Thomas Cranmer in 1550 between "sacrifice propitiatory," or Christ's self-sacrifice which redeems sin, and "sacrifice gratificatory," the sacrifices of praise and good works which follow upon a believer's justification and show his or her thankfulness.[24] Pembroke's rich expansion of sacrifice and gift imagery implicitly revises the more rigid Protestant views of sacrifice by allotting to both the believer and God an ability to give worthy gifts. Human beings are drawn closer to God by sacrifice, while the asymmetry between their gifts underlines the difference between mortal and divine.

---

20 On asymmetrical reciprocity and Protestant theories of sacrifice, see Natalie Zemon Davis, *The Gift in Sixteenth-Century France* (Madison: University of Wisconsin Press, 2000), 100–123.

21 *Articles veritables sur les horribles, grandz et importables abuz de la Messe papalle* (Neuchâtel, 1534). Quoted in Christopher Elwood, *The Body Broken: The Calvinist Doctrine of the Eucharist and the Symbolization of Power in Sixteenth-Century France* (New York: Oxford University Press, 1999), 34.

22 On the Calvinist dichotomy between outward and inward acts, see ibid., 42–7 and 61–4.

23 Hubert and Mauss, *Sacrifice*.

24 See B.J. Kidd, *The Later Medieval Doctrine of the Eucharistic Sacrifice* (London: The Sidney Press Limited for the Church Historical Society, 1958), 16.

Pembroke's departure from the mainstream Protestant view of sacrifice also has important implications for the status of poetry as a means to devotion.[25] The Book of Psalms was the perfect context in which to claim that poetry could be a fitting gift to God, for the rejuvenated importance of the "sacrifice of praise," along with the emphasis on *sola scriptura*, created enormous interest among Protestants in verse translations of the psalms. Hannibal Hamlin has persuasively argued that psalm translation "substantially shaped the culture of sixteenth- and seventeenth-century England," and we can see its effects in themes and styles of poetry, in journals and life-writing, and in the spread of psalm imagery throughout early modern culture.[26] Miles Coverdale's 1535 prose translation of the psalms, the version used in the Book of Common Prayer, would have been a familiar echo to all churchgoers by the 1590s; meanwhile, translations in verse spread the psalms into every genre of Elizabethan letters. While Thomas Wyatt's 1549 verse meditations on the penitential psalms appealed to a courtly coterie who would understand his allusions to Henry VIII's reign, the sprightly common meter of the "Sternhold and Hopkins" versions (1549), each set to a popular tune, allowed congregational singing in churches. Anne Lock's verse paraphrase of Psalm 51 (1560) introduced the sonnet sequence into the English language while addressing a network of committed Protestant activists, many returning from exile. Through the proliferation of psalm translations, the themes and imagery of the psalms became a *lingua franca* for the expression of individual or collective praise or lamentation. These translations were not intended to exhaust the subject or to obviate the need for further translations; instead, readers seemed to thirst for a plurality of versions. Of the making of psalm translations, there should be no end, according to Joseph Hall: "It is a service to God and the church so much more carefully to bee regarded, as it is more common. For, who is there that will not challenge a parte in this labour?"[27]

Moreover, taking part in this labor was an act symbolizing one's participation in the "priesthood of all believers" envisioned by Luther and Calvin. By imitating the psalms, early modern writers took up the roles of priest and prophet attributed to David, who was supposed to have authored most of the psalms. The Bible depicts David officiating as a priest in performing sacrifices, a privilege assumed by ancient near Eastern kings; his creative power and his right to act as a priest are

---

25 For detailed studies of the liturgical, musical, and literary uses of sixteenth-century verse psalters and the conceptual differences among them, see Beth Quitslund, "Teaching Us How to Sing?: The Peculiarity of the Sidney Psalter," *Sidney Journal* 23 (2005): 83–110; Targoff, *Common Prayer*.

26 Hannibal Hamlin, *Psalm Culture and Early Modern English Literature* (Cambridge: Cambridge University Press, 2004), 1. See also Hamlin, "'The highest matter in the noblest forme': The Influence of the Sidney Psalms," *Sidney Journal* 23 (2005): 133–57; and Rivkah Zim, *English Metrical Psalms: Poetry as Praise and Prayer, 1535–1601* (Cambridge: Cambridge University Press, 1987).

27 Joseph Hall, *Holy Observations. Lib. 1. Also Some Fewe of Davids Psalmes Metaphrased* (London, 1607), G1r.

appropriate to his singular status as king and prophet.[28] Since Luther and Calvin had assured Protestants that they all bore the right and responsibility to perform offices of worship, each and every godly person could identify with David as poet and priest, a link we find in several English Renaissance works.[29] For example, in 1589 George Puttenham praised poetry by deriving its origins from ancient worship rites:

> And these hymnes to the gods was [sic] the first forme of Poesie and the highest and the stateliest, and they were song by the *Poets as priests*, and by the people or whole congregation as we sing in our Churches the Psalmes of David, but they did it commonly in some shadie groves of tall tymber trees: In which places they reared aulters of green turfe, and bestrewed them all over with flowers, and upon them *offred their oblations and made their bloudy sacrifices*, (for no kinde of gift can be dearer than life) of such quick cattaille, as every god was in their conceit most delighted in .... (italics mine)[30]

While attempting to defend poetry, Puttenham rather surprisingly turns to pagan sacrifice, even though for Protestants "bloudy sacrifice" exemplified godless superstition. Puttenham not only links the singing of psalms in church to animal sacrifice, but remarks that such sacrifice was the dearest of all gifts. His analogy shows that Protestants' understanding of the psalms as a sacrifice of praise was both deeply held and potentially contradictory. By linking poets to priests, writers like Puttenham suggested that divine poets represent the community in God's presence by offering poetry as a sacrificial gift. Martin Luther's conception of the priesthood of all believers supports this apparently hubristic view since for him every effort to communicate the word of God to others constitutes the highest form of worship: "they which teach, reade, write or heare the holy Scriptures, are Gods true priestes."[31] Likewise, for John Calvin the sacrifice of praise makes believers priest-kings like David: "From this office of sacrificing, all Christians are called a royal priesthood."[32]

---

[28] See Gen. 14:18; 2 Sam. 6:13–14 and 8:18; 1 Kings 3:15 and 9:25; and Ezek. 45:17.

[29] See Anne Lake Prescott, "King David as a 'Right Poet': Sidney and the Psalmist," *English Literary Renaissance* 19 (1989): 131–51.

[30] George Puttenham, *The Arte of English Poesie*, in *Elizabethan Critical Essays*, ed. G. Gregory Smith (London: Oxford University Press, 1904), 2:31. See also Thomas Lodge, "Defence of Poetry," in *Elizabethan Critical Essays*, 1:70–72; Philip Sidney, *An Apology for Poetry: Or, the Defence of Poesy*, ed. Geoffrey Shepherd and R.W. Maslen, 3rd ed. (Manchester: Manchester University Press, 2002), 84.

[31] Martin Luther, *Commentarie Upon the Fiftene Psalmes*, trans. Henry Bull (London, 1577), iv–v.

[32] Calvin, *Institutes*, 2:4.18.16–17.

The Sacrifice of Praise in the Sidney *Psalmes*

Given the Sidney-Dudley family's history of Protestant support, it is not surprising that the Countess of Pembroke and Philip Sidney joined their labors to the international Protestant movement to translate and disseminate the psalms. Public acts of Protestant solidarity and their often personally devastating consequences defined a vigorously Protestant political and religious identity for the Sidney and Dudley clans throughout the sixteenth century. Philip and Mary Sidney represented the third generation of their family's commitment to the "new religion."[33] Nevertheless, it is often difficult to discern the outlines of Mary's or Philip's personal understanding of theological issues against the vivid backdrop of domestic and international political crises in which their family took part.[34] The origins and individual coloring of Philip's religious beliefs have been the subject of investigations into his *Defense of Poesy*, *The Countess of Pembroke's Arcadia*, and the diverse Protestant and Catholic personages and philosophies he encountered on his youthful Grand Tour.[35] Similarly, while Pembroke's support for the Protestant cause is well-established, the specific shape of her beliefs remains vague. Her choice of works for translation suggests her interest in the Protestant Neo-Stoicism espoused by the Huguenots of her brother's circle. Margaret Hannay has argued that Pembroke's version of Philippe de Mornay's *Excellent discourse de la Vie et de la Mort* (1577) "was part of a series of translations undertaken by Sidney and his Continental friends to support … the Protestant cause."[36] In preparing her *Psalmes* she compared psalm commentaries by John Calvin and Théodore de Bèze and imitated verse forms from the 1562 Huguenot verse psalter by Bèze and Clement Marot.[37] Moreover, the two dedicatory poems she added to a copy of the *Psalmes* intended for presentation to Queen Elizabeth link the psalms to Elizabeth's role as Protestant sovereign ("the foes of heav'n no lesse have beene thy foes"), and her brother's role as slain Protestant hero.[38]

---

33 See Margaret P. Hannay, *Philip's Phoenix: Mary Sidney, Countess of Pembroke* (New York: Oxford University Press, 1990), 3–58.

34 Jennifer Richards argues that Philip was "willing to compromise his religious and political position" in his literary works. Robert E. Stillman argues that he followed Melanchthon's views encouraging "freedom from theological disputation," while William Craft interprets Philip's works as expressing orthodox Protestant beliefs. See Richards, "Philip Sidney, Mary Sidney and Protestant Poetics," *Sidney Newsletter & Journal* 14, no. 1 (1996): 33; Stillman, "Deadly Stinging Adders: Sidney's Piety, Philippism, and the *Defence of Poesy*," *Spenser Studies* 16 (2002): 234; Craft, *Labyrinth of Desire: Invention and Culture in the Work of Sir Philip Sidney* (Newark: University of Delaware Press, 1994).

35 On Sidney's friendships, see Edward I. Berry, *The Making of Sir Philip Sidney* (Toronto: University of Toronto Press, 1998).

36 Hannay, *Philip's Phoenix*, 61.

37 *Collected Works*, Hannay, Kinnamon, and Brennan, 2:20–42.

38 Ibid., 1:102–4, line 70. All citations of Pembroke's works will refer to this edition.

Clearly, Pembroke dedicated her works to the cause of the "new religion." Yet her thoughts on such essential Protestant topics as grace, the experience of sin and redemption, and the dangers of idolatry and works-righteousness remain relatively unexplored.

In at least one major area of Protestant thinking, Pembroke's psalm translations reveal the shape of an idiosyncratic theology: in opposition to her sources, her verses draw attention to the theme of sacrifice. In psalms that provided proof texts for the Protestant interpretation of the "sacrifice of praise," Pembroke makes sacrifice a concrete ceremony rather than, as her sources stressed, a spiritual or inward process. For example, in Psalm 50 the voice of God asserts that "Those who bring thanksgiving as their sacrifice honor me" (Ps. 50:23; NRSV). The editors of the Geneva Bible are so concerned to spiritualize sacrifice—even in a psalm that relegates it to a metaphor—that they translate the verse with "He that offreth praise, shall glorify me" and, lest the word "offreth" suggest some sort of propitiation, gloss it: "under the which is conteined faith and invocation" (Ps. 50:23; Geneva). In Pembroke's version, God declares that "my deerest worship I / in sweete perfume of offred praise doe place" (61–2). Adopting from Leviticus the priestly formula that burnt offerings emit a "pleasing odor to the Lord" (Lev. 1:9 and *passim*), Pembroke revels in the imagery of sacrifice even when she affirms that praise replaces the rite. The most important psalm for defining both the sacrifice of praise and the concept of *sola fides*, Psalm 51, provides another striking example. Protestants relied heavily on the rejection of ritual sacrifice in this psalm to support justification by faith alone: "The sacrifices of God are a contrite spirit: a contrite & a broken heart, o God, thou wilt not despise" (Ps. 51:17; Geneva). However, in the next breath the psalmist promises that when the temple of Jerusalem is rebuilt, ritual sacrifice will again take place and "then shal they offer calves upon thine altar" (Ps. 51:19; Geneva). In Anne Lock's interpretation of Psalm 51, which may have influenced Pembroke, this verse ingeniously puns on "hart/heart" to make the sacrifice a spiritual one: "Thou shalt behold upon thine altar lye / Many a yelden host of humbled hart" (371–2).[39] Pembroke clearly regarded such intervention as unnecessary, for in her phrasing the image of animal sacrifice is more concrete than it is in the Bible:

> then shalt thou turne a well-accepting face
> to sacred fires with offred guiftes perfumed:
> till ev'n whole calves on alters be consumed. (53–5)

This sacrifice is a sensuous ("perfumed") and extravagant act destroying "ev'n whole calves," a motif Pembroke adopts from elsewhere in the scriptures (e.g., 1 Kings 8:5). She adds the same concepts to the figure of sacrifice in Psalm 66,

---

[39] Anne Lock, "A Meditation of a Penitent Sinner," in *Collected Works*, Felch, lines 371–2. See Mary Trull, "Petrarchism and the Gift: The Sacrifice of Praise in Anne Lock's 'A Meditation of a Penitent Sinner,'" *Religion and Literature* 41.3 (2009): 1–25. On Pembroke as a reader of Lock, see Hannay, "Unlock My Lipps," 19–36.

where the speaker promises to "offer unto thee the burnt offerings of fat rams with incense: I will prepare bullockes and goates" (Ps. 66:15; Geneva). Again, she expands the theme of munificence, declaring her intention

> to offer whole burnt sacrifices,
> the fatt of Ramms with sweete perfume:
> Nay goates, nay bulls, of greater sises,
> and greater prices to consume. (45–8)

As in Pembroke's Psalm 51, the speaker glories in the splendor of ritual sacrifice, particularly its sensory pleasures and its extravagance. Her grammatical construction also mirrors the theme of bounty through rhetorical amplification, using the figure known as *correctio*: "Nay goates, nay bulls, of greater sises, / and greater prises." In contrast, Calvin comments that this verse alludes to Christ's self-sacrifice and that under the new covenant the "true spiritual service" has replaced such acts.[40]

In another psalm cited by Protestants in support of "the true spiritual service," Pembroke inserts the imagery of ritual sacrifice where the scripture avoids it. The speaker of Psalm 116 mentions only the sacrifice of praise and vows, "I wil take the cup of salvacion, and call upon the Name of the Lord" (Ps. 116:13; Geneva). The Geneva editors, alert to sacrificial connotations, assert that this action would take place at a banquet—not at an altar. Théodore de Bèze also portrays the action as an opportunity for praise: "Verily I will take in my handes the cup of thankfull sacrifice, & calling upon thee by name O Lord, I will testify openly, that I knowledge this deliverance to be of thee."[41] By inserting a reference to destruction by fire, Pembroke calls up sacrificial rather than banquet imagery:

> My cup with thancks shall flow
> for freedom from my thrall:
> which I in flames will throw,
> and on thy name will call. (33–6)[42]

The "cup of salvation" becomes a drink offering like those described in Genesis 35:14, Exodus 29:40, and Leviticus 23:13, which accompany animal or grain sacrifices. For Pembroke, ritual annihilation seems to heighten the beauty and significance of praise. Far from being troubled by ritual acts, she finds figurative sacrifice more compelling if accompanied by the concrete imagery of animal flesh, perfumed smoke, and the grand gesture of casting a valuable object into the flames.

---

40 John Calvin, *Commentary on the Book of Psalms*, trans. James Anderson (Edinburgh: The Calvin Translation Society, 1845), 2:476.

41 Théodore de Bèze, *The Psalmes of David Truely Opened and Explaned by Paraphrasis*, trans. Anthony Gilby (London, 1590), 280.

42 Pembroke's editors note that her additions might allude to the drink offering described in Exodus 29:40–41. *Collected Works*, Hannay, Kinnamon, and Brennan, 2:423.

In Pembroke's translations, sacrifice becomes a figure for plenty—for unstinting generosity either from God or human beings. Marcel Mauss's transcultural analysis of gift-giving produced a similar image with the potlatch, a "purely sumptuary destruction of wealth," often sacrificed to the gods or spirits.[43] In the potlatch, the more lavish the obliteration of one's wealth, the higher the social status one attains. While Mauss observed an essentially agonistic practice reflecting each participant's drive to best the others at prodigal expenditure, in Pembroke, generosity is not competitive. In fact, she inserts sacrificial imagery into a joyous psalm celebrating God's generosity to his creatures in making the earth fruitful. Psalm 65, a psalm of communal praise celebrating the bounty of creation, uses harvest and feast imagery to convey the pleasure each part of creation takes in God's plenty. The original contains no sacrificial imagery, and at first glance such a motif hardly suits the psalm. In Pembroke, however, generation and generosity are closely linked; the earth's fertility demonstrates God's power and his kindness to humans. Since the earth's fecundity reveals God's creative power, it becomes a symbol for the universal praise of God:

> Drunck is each ridg of thy cupp drincking;
> each clodd relenteth at thy dressing:
> thy cloud-born waters inly sincking
> faire spring sproutes foorth blest with thy blessing.
> the fertile yeare is with thy bounty crown'd:
> and where thou go'st, thy goings fatt the ground.
>
> Plenty bedewes the desert places:
> a hedg of mirth the hills encloseth:
> the fieldes with flockes have hid their faces:
> a robe of corn the valleies clotheth.
> Desertes, and hills, and fields, and valleys all,
> rejoyce, showt, sing, and on thy name doe call. (37–48)

As in the Biblical text, praise is a natural response to the pleasure of abundance.[44] Pembroke therefore depicts praise as mirroring that bounty: while in the scripture pastures and valleys shout for joy and sing, Pembroke multiplies the praisers and kinds of praise by *accumulatio*: deserts, hills, fields, and valleys rejoice, shout, sing, and invoke God.

Likewise, Pembroke's introduction of the idea of sacrifice into the first stanza responds to the theme of God's bounty. The scripture states that "Wicked deeds have prevailed against me: but thou wilt be merciful unto our transgressions" (Ps. 65:3; Geneva). Pembroke follows the Genevan editors by interpreting "wicked deeds" as the speaker's own sins, but she diverges from her sources by figuring God's mercy through ritual sacrifice: "thou my sinns prevailing to my shame / dost turne to smoake of sacrificing flame" (5–6). Here again, sacrifice stands for bounteous

---

[43] Marcel Mauss, *The Gift: The Form and Reason for Exchange in Archaic Societies* (London: Routledge, 2000), 6.

[44] See also Ps. 96:11–12, 98:7–8, and 148:1–10.

generosity; in this case, God and not the sinner performs the sacrifice that purges sin. As in Psalm 116, sacrifice is a figure for plenty—this time, the plenty of God's mercy rather than that of human gratitude. Moreover, as in "To the Angell Spirit," Pembroke imagines sacrifice as a closed circle of gift exchange: the recipient of sacrifice is also its source. Far from avoiding the representation of the sacrifice of praise as a reciprocal exchange between the sinner and God, she draws strong connections between the sinner's promise of sacrifice and God's benefits: the "smoake of sacrificing flame" is a powerful gesture calling upon a response from God. She delights in the ritual aspects of sacrifice while maintaining that no human work can compare with God's all-sufficing grace.

Despite her willingness to deploy ritual sacrifice as an image for worship, Pembroke maintains a Protestant concern with works-righteousness and the tenet that good works must follow justification rather than precede it. John Calvin often stresses that believers must call upon God's promises, and Pembroke insists that this is the role of sacrifice; thus, the sacrificer responds to God's previous gifts.[45] Moreover, the sacrifice is not commensurate with God's past and future gifts; thus, though she readily calls sacrifice a "payment," she stresses that it does not fully reciprocate for God's benefits. In Psalm 119 (in Pembroke, marked as "O") the narrative of exchange begins with God's promise:

> lord raise me by thy word,
> as thou to me didst promise heretofore.
> and this unforced praise:
> I for an offering bring, accept ô lord,
> and show to me thy waies. (8–12)

Her sacrifice of praise is "unforced," arising from gratitude, calling freely upon God's vow and claiming from him a promised enlightenment. Thus, God initiates the chain of exchange, but it is still clearly an exchange. In Psalm 56:12–13, the scripture depicts praise as a response to God's gift of salvation, and Pembroke stresses the transaction motif by adding the word "payment" and repeating it to underline the point.[46] But this addition also allows her to show that praise is a response to a debt incurred by the sinner. Furthermore, she is at pains to show that such exchanges are unequal, although God chooses to accept sacrifice as though it were sufficient. The speaker laments the inadequacy of human works, comparing them with the glorious promises God has made:

> For this to thee how deeply stand I bound
> lord that my soule dost save, my foes confound?
> ah I can no paiment make,
> but if thou for payment take,
> the vowes I pay, thy praises I resound. (36–40)

[45] Calvin, *Commentary on the Book of Psalms*, 4:114.

[46] Pembroke might have been inspired by Bèze's use of "pay" in paraphrasing this verse, but she develops the term into a richly meaningful motif. Bèze, *Psalmes of David*, 125.

God is appeased by sacrifice, but only as the fulfillment of his promise and only because he overlooks the inequality between the human work he receives and the grace he gives.

Though Pembroke makes sacrifice an elaborate ceremony that invests human gratitude towards God with a level of grandeur that might have troubled an astute Protestant reader, she shows that the sacrifice of praise is itself a gift given to human beings. In her reading, Psalm 145 is an ecstatic declaration of the speaker's vocation to praise that frames an inset hymn of praise. Pembroke works a motif of breath into the hymn in order to depict the moment-by-moment dependence of all creatures upon the divine hand for life itself.[47] Where the scripture has "The eyes of all waite upon thee, and thou givest them their meat in due season," Pembroke introduces divinely given breath: "then all that on the aire do feede, / receave besides what food they neede" (Ps. 145:15; Geneva; *Coll. Works*, lines 48–9). She repeats the motif in the final stanza, where the speaker gratefully promises eternal praise:

> He will his lovers all preserve:
> he will the wicked all destroy:
> to praise him then as these deserve,
> ô thou my mouth thy might employ:
> nay all that breath, recorde with joy
> his sacred names eternall praise,
> while race you run of breathing daies. (57–63)

Pembroke reintroduces the idea of breath in order to link praise to God's benefits: praise is joyous and eternal, but possible only through God's continuous inspiration. He "feeds" all creatures with air and food, giving them the wherewithal to return that breath in the form of praise. Pembroke privileges a closed circle of gift exchange, in which the magnitude of God's grace virtually effaces the human role in the work of praise. She preserves praise as an exalted human work while giving all the credit to God.

Moreover, Pembroke's psalms explicitly draw attention to the poetic form of her praise. As critics have noted, both Sidneys' psalms deviate from their sources by emphasizing the power and delight of poetry.[48] Though the psalms themselves were known to have been composed in Hebrew verse, Protestant translators often minimized the lyrical qualities of praise as depicted in the psalms.[49] In Psalm 40, one of the defining psalms for the "sacrifice of praise," God hears the psalmist's

---

47 On the theme of breath or "ruah" in the psalms, see Hans-Joachim Kraus, *Theology of the Psalms*, trans. Keith Crim (Minneapolis: Augsburg Publishing House, 1986), 146.

48 On Pembroke's stress on the poetic nature of psalmic tribute, see Debra Rienstra, "The Countess of Pembroke and the Problem of Skill in Devotional Writing," *Sidney Journal* 23 (2005): 37–60; Suzanne Trill, "Sixteenth-Century Women's Writing: Mary Sidney's *Psalmes* and the 'Femininity' of Translation," in *Writing and the English Renaissance*, ed. William Zunder and Suzanne Trill (London: Longman, 1996), 140–58.

49 As William Craft argues, Sidney's comparison of the poet's creative power to God's work was not necessarily unorthodox. *Labyrinth of Desire*, 23.

lament, delivers him from misery, and inspires him with song: "And he hathe put in my mouth a new song of praise unto our God: manie shal se it and feare, and shal trust in the Lord" (Ps. 40:3; Geneva) The Geneva editors discount the importance of the song as music or poetry, glossing divine inspiration as "a special occasion to praise him"; Calvin too understands the passage to mean that God's benefits toward the speaker will be "proofs of the goodness which he constantly exercises."[50] But for Philip Sidney, what God gives the speaker is creative power, truly a song or poem; that is, not only a reason for praise but a marvelously crafted work: "So in my mouth he doth a song afford, / New song unto our God of prayse" (11–12).[51] Like her brother, the Countess of Pembroke interprets many psalms so as to emphasize the beauty and joy of praising God in verse. Psalm 93 praises God as an all-powerful king, glorifying his eternal might: "Thy testimonies are verie sure: holiness becommeth thine House, o Lord, for ever" (Ps. 93:5; Geneva). Bèze's paraphrase applies the psalm to confessional conflict, for he notes that "howsoever the world do freat [sic], and how great stormes soever it doe stir up against thy house oh Lord," the "assemblie of the saints" remains constant.[52] Pembroke rejects this opportunity and instead inserts the idea that human worship participates in God's immortality: "Now and still, as heretofore: / holy worship never dies / in thy house where we adore" (14–16). The writer of psalm 135 directs his audience to "sing praises unto his Name: for it is a comelie thing" (Ps. 135:3; Geneva). Pembroke makes the praises as well as the name of God comely: "praise god, right termed god, for good is he: / o sweetly sing / unto his name, the sweetest, sweetest thing." In a move reminiscent of her brother's works, she asserts poetry's divine nature by linking the sweetness of song to the ultimate sweetness of the name of God. Likewise, in Psalm 138 Pembroke changes the simple "praise" of the original to "harty tunes" performed by an exulting speaker. She begins stanzas two and three with the declaration, "There will I sing," and expands the Bible's terse "When I called, then thou heardest me" (Ps. 138:3; Geneva) to remind her readers of God's responsiveness to lament:

> There will I sing, how when my carefull cry
> mounted to thee, my care was streight released,
> my courage by thee mightily encreased. (10–12)

Her speaker thus evokes the psalms' recurring narrative of lament and praise, highlighting the special power of David's poetry to elicit a divine response.

While Pembroke exalts poetic tributes, she also distinguishes between elect and reprobate poetry and thus suggests that the power of lyrical praise is a gift from God to his chosen people. The satisfaction in authorship expressed by the assertive "I" of the speaker in Psalm 138 contrasts with the view of others' poetic efforts in

---

[50] Calvin, *Commentary on the Book of Psalms*, 2:92.

[51] Philip Sidney, *The Poems of Sir Philip Sidney*, ed. William A. Ringler Jr. (Oxford: Oxford University Press, 1962), 330–32.

[52] Bèze, *Psalmes of David*, 218.

Psalm 75. There, the scripture admonishes the wicked to "Lift not up your horne on high, nether speake with a stiffe necke" (Ps. 75:5; Geneva). For Pembroke, the wicked express their bad attitudes specifically in verse: "lift not lewd mates: no more with heav'ns scorne, / daunce on in wordes your old repyining measure" (11–12). She contrasts the hackneyed and disingenuous rhythms of the wicked with the speaker's sincerely celebratory singing:

> And I secure shall spend my happie tymes
> in my, though lowly, never-dying rhymes,
> singing with praise the god that Jacob loveth. (25–7)

The phrase, "though lowly, never-dying rhymes," seems paradoxical: How can verse be both immortal and humble? Moreover, Pembroke makes the speaker anything but lowly, for following Bèze's interpretation of this psalm rather than Calvin's, she strongly identifies David as the speaker.[53] Her attribution of the psalm to David seems clear in her allusions to a king's authority: the speaker plans to "denounce my uncontrolled pleasure" on the wicked and his "princly care shall cropp ill-doers low" (9, 27). Pembroke dramatizes the contradiction implicit in the sacrifice of praise: the highest and most worthy, even immortal, praise is nevertheless a merely human work. Her distinction between elect and reprobate verse suggests that worthy praise follows justification; moreover, only as divine praise can poetry stake a claim to immortality.[54]

The Sacrifice of Praise in Pembroke's Dedications

Pembroke also explores these difficult questions in her dedicatory poems as she creates a complex choreography in which her dedicatee at times takes the place of God as recipient of the "sacrifice of praise" and at times becomes a third party in the gift-exchange relationship. The poems weave together both her celebration of poetry as a "sacrifice of praise" and the careful logic with which she draws distinctions between human and divine works. "Even now that Care," the poem addressed to Queen Elizabeth, dwells on the problem of how an inferior may offer an appropriate gift to a higher order of being.[55] The first two stanzas introduce the theme of fitness or suitability, as Pembroke appeals to a "thrice sacred Queene" perfectly matched to her role:

---

[53] Bèze, *Psalmes of David*, 170. Calvin, *Commentary on the Book of Psalms*, 3:183.

[54] Calvin writes that God only accepts the sacrifice of praise from "those whom he has reconciled to himself by other means, after they have received forgiveness of sins, and he has therefore absolved them from guilt." *Institutes* 2:4.18.16.

[55] On this poem's political import, see Beth Wynne Fisken, "Mary Sidney's *Psalmes*: Education and Wisdom," in Hannay, *Silent But for the Word*, 166–83; and Margaret P. Hannay, "'Doo What Men May Sing': Mary Sidney and the Tradition of Admonitory Dedication," ibid., 149–65.

What heav'nly powrs thee highest throne assign'de,
assign'd thee goodness suting that Degree:
and by thy strength thy burden so defin'de,
To others toile, is Exercise to thee. (13–16)

She expresses exactitude through verbs such as "assigned," "defined," and "suting"; likewise, the speaker's assessment of the queen is itself an exercise in precise definition: "not waighing less thy state, lighter thy Care, / but knowing more thy grace, abler thy minde" (11–12). Nevertheless, Pembroke suggests that despite her fastidious tone the speaker lacks the divine propriety that surrounds the Queen and overreaches by offering her work as a gift. The speaker alone is out of place, unfit: "my Muse offends, / and of respect to thee the line outgoes" (4). Implicitly, she sums up the problem faced by Protestant interpreters of the sacrifice of praise: how can the unworthy give a worthy gift to a being of surpassing perfection? She answers the question by matching her praise of Elizabeth with praise of David, who alone is a fit tribute to the Virgin Queen: "A King should onely to a Queene be sent. / Gods loved choise unto his chosen love" (53–4). After elaborating on the matched excellencies of the two rulers for a few stanzas, Pembroke turns the language of fitness on its head by pointing out that the role for which Elizabeth is so beautifully suited has knocked the rest of the world off kilter—to its benefit:

Kings on a Queene enforst their states to lay;
Main=lands for Empire waiting on an Ile;
Men drawne by worth a woman to obay;
one moving all, herselfe, unmov'd the while .... (81–4)

Now Pembroke seems to undercut her own carefully constructed ideal of fitness, for she celebrates the irony that the ideal, "unmov'd" Elizabeth embodies multiple violations of the traditional order. Pembroke relies on the common representation of Elizabeth as the Phoenix: as a woman and a Protestant, she is unique and therefore a rule unto herself and an object properly of wonder rather than judgment from the lesser beings around her. Her miraculous singularity overthrows the usual order of causality and in her reign there is "wealth sprung of want, warr held without annoye" (85–6). By the same logic, Pembroke implicitly justifies her authorship. By ordinary standards, her work would be presumptuous, but in Elizabeth's regime such prodigies are to be expected: now a female author can conjure up King David's company for a monarch. Though Pembroke's work is a gift, it is only adequate to Elizabeth's high status by a miraculous overturning of the natural order.[56]

While Pembroke's address to Queen Elizabeth tackles some of the problems of praise as a gift, her poem to her brother more straightforwardly investigates

[56] Jane Donawerth describes the language of gift in this poem as a counter-gift. "Women's Poetry and the Tudor-Stuart System of Gift Exchange," in *Women, Writing, and the Reproduction of Culture*, Burke, et al., 3–18.

the sacrifice of praise as it appears in the psalms.[57] In "To the Angell Spirit of the most excellent Sir Phillip Sidney," Pembroke describes her *Psalmes* as a sacrifice that avoids obligating its recipient. She implies twinship with her brother in the opening apostrophe:

> To thee pure sprite, to thee alone's addres't
> this coupled worke, by double int'rest thine:
> First rais'd by thy blest hand, and what is mine
> inspird by thee, thy secrett power imprest.
> So dar'd my Muse with thine it selfe combine,
> as mortall stuffe with that which is divine,
> Thy lightning beames give lustre to the rest .... (1–7)

The title and Pembroke's first epithet of "pure sprite" establish the topos of address to a heavenly being, while her description of their joint project, "this coupled worke, by double int'rest thine," by metonymy figures not the work but its authors as twins. Her image of one immortal and one mortal twin in line 6 suggests the Dioscuri, twin sons of Leda: Castor, the mortal son of her husband Tyndareus, and Pollux (or Polydeuces), the immortal son of Zeus. When Castor is killed in combat Zeus allows him to share immortality with his brother: each will spend half his days on earth, half in heaven, visible in the constellation Gemini. The Gemini allusion makes sense of Pembroke's description of her brother's "lightning beames"; later, she makes a clearer allusion to Philip as a star "above," "Where thou art fixt among thy fellow lights" (57). Pembroke executes a turn on the myth by giving herself, the mortal "twin," the role of instigator, though in Homer, Zeus is the grantor of this shared immortality and in Pindar, Pollux chooses to share his immortality with his brother.[58] By co-authoring the *Psalmes*, she writes, she "dar'd" to transgress the line separating her from divinity. Pembroke's choice to "combine" her mortal with Philip's heavenly Muse creates a work "coupled" not only by joint authorship but by its liminal status between heaven and earth, for Philip continues to inspire the work from heaven, where his "lightning beames give lustre to the rest." The Countess of Pembroke expresses a wish to join her twin in heaven as Castor did, but she doubts her own deserving (89–90). Stressing her inadequacy to match Philip's wit, Pembroke lends her act of authorship mythic grandeur while belying her use of the humility topos by her carefully crafted rhetoric.[59]

---

57 On the poem as an imitation of psalmic themes of faith and doubt, see Suzanne Trill, "Spectres and Sisters: Mary Sidney and the 'Perennial Puzzle' of Renaissance Women's Writing," in *Renaissance Configurations: Voices, Bodies, Spaces, 1580–1690*, ed. Gordon McMullan (New York: St. Martin's Press, 1998), 191–211.

58 *The Odyssey* 11.300–304; Pindar, *Nemean* 10.

59 On Pembroke and the humility topos, see Helen Wilcox, "'My Soule in Silence'? Devotional Representations of Renaissance Englishwomen," in *Representing Women in Renaissance England*, ed. Claude J. Summers and Ted-Larry Pebworth (Columbia: University of Missouri Press, 1997), 9–23.

The theme of Philip's divinity allows Pembroke to progress from her initial description of the "coupled worke" to a new metaphor in which the work is a sacrifice expressing gratitude. She first establishes the theme of gratitude: Philip's goodness was such as to create a burden of indebtedness which her powers are inadequate to repay. Philip's works are a great sea, while her contributions are mere "tributes" in two senses: both tributary streams and thankful memorials to Philip's achievements.

> As little streames with all their all doe flowe
> to their great sea, due tributes gratefull fee:
> so press my thoughts my burthened thoughts in mee,
> To pay the debt of Infinits I owe
> To thy great worth; .... (32–6)

Several aspects of Protestant rhetoric on the psalms appear here. Pembroke asserts that her tribute is a counter-gift and stresses the asymmetry between the original gift—the "great sea"—and her payment of the "debt of Infinits." For Protestants, praise of divinity arises from the believer's thankfulness, but fails to weigh in the balance against human sin; similarly, Pembroke's offering to her brother is insufficient to pay her debt to him. Had Pembroke used these images in a poem unrelated to the psalms, they might have seemed typical of the dedicatory genre; here, they resonate strongly with the "sacrifice of praise."

Functioning as a proem to the psalm translations, "To the Angell Spirit" mirrors psalmic language while casting Philip in the role of God and Mary as the lamenting David.[60] Early in the poem she sharply distinguishes between the Sidney psalms and David's poetry; she confesses to God that their poems are only a new dress, "superficial tire," adorning the "sacred Hymmes thy Kinglie Prophet form'd" (10, 14). The Sidney psalms do not attempt to replicate David's, but serve "to praise, not to aspire / To, those high Tons" (10–11). In this case, the sacrifice of praise is a double movement since the Sidney translations praise the original "sacrifice of praise." However, Pembroke allows the subject being praised to slip from the psalms to Philip himself; in the process, Philip's authorship is obscured and she appears as sole author. In this shift, Pembroke does indeed "aspire to"—at least to the extent of imitating—psalmic themes. While the psalms are "sacred Hymmes," the Sidney translations are "theise Hymnes, these obsequies" (85). The dedicatory lament, "this Audit of my woe," invokes Truth to create a ritual memorializing Philip Sidney: "Thee sole to solemnize / Those sacred rights well known best minds approve" (52–3). Pembroke continues her subtle puns here, since "rights" implies both her special role as Philip's "twin" and the funeral "rite" that is the poem; in fact, the variant published in Samuel Daniel's *Works*, presumably an earlier draft of the poem, works the pun further: "Nor be my weakness to thy

[60] Some critics have found in the figure of David an opportunity for women writers to inhabit masculine roles such as prophet, priest, or king. See Fisken, "Art of Sacred Parody," 226–7; Wilcox, "'My Soule in Silence'?" 14.

rites a staine / Rites to aright, life, bloud would not refraine" (26–7).[61] The rites that Mary claims best right to perform are, moreover, linked to the sacrifice of praise that David's psalms dedicate to God. She consecrates the poems to Philip's "ever praised name":

> To whiche theise dearest offrings of my hart
> dissolv'd to Inke, while penns impressions move
> the bleeding veines of never dying love:
> I render here: these wounding lynes of smart
> sadd Characters indeed of simple love
> not Art nor skill which abler wits doe prove,
> Of my full soule receive the meanest part.
>
> Receive these Hymnes, theise obsequies receive;
> if any marke of thy sweet sprite appeare,
> well are they borne, not title else shall beare. (78–87)

The repetition of the command "receive" (line 85) imitates the psalms' insistent pleas for God's attention. The humility topos evident in line 83 evokes the idea of the counter-gift, for as an unworthy supplicant she offers sacrifice not as satisfaction of a debt, but as thanks for benefits freely given.

In this poem, Pembroke's identification with David is tentative, temporary, and compromised by the humility topos. Reluctant to allow her self-portrayal as priest-poet to govern the poem, she evinces the Protestant concern that the sacrifice of praise may too easily glorify the speaker, elevate his or her works, or claim to compensate for sin. While the poems are obsequies or funeral rites in Philip's honor, she also humbly insists that they are actually his own work; her offerings return to him what is his own. In line 87 the countess transforms the image of offering into one of childbirth: if the Sidneys' joint work bears the "marke" of Philip's paternity, it will be "well-born." Pembroke is both a priest-poet performing the sacrifice of praise and a mother delivering a child that bears the marks of its father.[62] In both cases, Pembroke imagines her own authorship as an intermediary function, though the connection to David elevates the role of mediator to that of "Kinglie Prophet." With this turn, Pembroke has come full circle, portraying the psalms first as a joint work, then as her memorial rites in Philip's honor, then as the child of their union, then again as a joint work distinguished by Philip's contribution. The Tixall dedicatory poems use the logic of the gift to balance Pembroke's claim to authority against the humility topos and to magnify the distance between her dedicatees' status and her own. Nevertheless, Pembroke uses the gift motif to define authorship as a multivalent, transgressive, but also powerful role via two

---

61 *Collected Works*, Hannay, Kinnamon, and Brennan, 2:110–12.

62 Wendy Wall highlights the sexual nature of this image and links it to Petrarchan discourse. *The Imprint of Gender: Authorship and Publication in the English Renaissance* (Ithaca: Cornell University Press, 1993), 310–19.

symbols: the overreaching client in "Even now that Care," and the semi-divine twin, mother and priest-poet in "To the Angell Spirit."

In her interpretation of the sacrifice of praise, Pembroke balances several competing impulses. As a poet, she preferred to convey spiritual ideas through concrete imagery; as a reader of the Bible, she recognized the power of animal sacrifice as a symbol of marvelous largesse; as a Protestant, she strove to avoid aggrandizing human works. She emerges as an author deeply cognizant of doctrinal conflict and capable of rising above the fray to arrive at her own conclusions. She creates an important role for herself by taking seriously the notion that Christians should imitate David by becoming, as Puttenham suggests, poet-priests.[63] While Luther, Calvin and Bèze conceived of reformed priests primarily as preachers rather than as officiants in a divine ceremony, Pembroke's psalms evoke a hieratic impresario of grand gestures, a heroic figure whose magnificence reflects the greater glory of God. Thus poetry's beauty, its elaborateness, and its glorification of the created world needs no defense, for Pembroke suggests that the sacrifice of praise should be performed with brio, like a priest tossing a cup into the flames or piling ever greater and more precious "whole burnt sacrifices" on the altar to rise into the air as "sweete perfume" (Ps. 66). If her Protestant contemporaries paused to register this imagery, perhaps they were taken aback. But Pembroke's unorthodox imagery makes a point central to the Protestant mission: that the believer achieves communion with God through a sacrifice of praise.

63 On Pembroke and the priesthood of all believers, see Rienstra and Kinnamon, "Circulating the Sidney-Pembroke Psalter."

Chapter 3
Anne Dacre Howard, Countess of Arundel, and Catholic Patronage

Susannah Brietz Monta

Catholic women's patronage in the late sixteenth and early seventeenth centuries took many forms as increasingly harsh recusancy laws and penalties pushed many expressions of Catholicism underground and overseas. Although patronage has been a major topic of study in recent years, the varied patronage networks of English Catholics (howsoever one defines them) have only begun to be traced.[1] Research into Catholic patronage networks is extremely promising, however, for what it can tell us about the complex forms Catholicism took beyond seemingly straightforward, even reckless recusancy and more ambiguous church-papist conformity. The study of Catholic women patronesses, which has hardly begun, also promises to tell us much about the ways gender and social status inflected Catholic patronage networks and the religious and political uses to which they were put.[2] This essay takes as a case study the patronage activities of Anne Dacre Howard, Countess of Arundel, who contributed in material and intangible ways to the dissemination of texts Elizabeth I's government deemed dangerous and to the fortification of a staunchly recusant strand of English Catholicism both in England and abroad. The varied materials surviving about her patronage activities also highlight fault lines within English Catholic communities that complicate the notion of confessional cultures—that is, of cultures firmly divided by and made to cohere through clearly defined sets of religious beliefs and practices—even as her early modern biographer promotes such a culture for English Catholics with the help of the materials her life affords him.

In what follows, I focus on four of these fault lines. The first has to do with the wide audiences for the texts written or published under her patronage, texts

---

1 See, for instance, Thomas F. Mayer, "When Maecenas was Broke: Cardinal Pole's 'Spiritual' Patronage," in *Sixteenth Century Journal* 27, no. 2 (1996): 419–35; Donna Hamilton's work on patronage networks in *Anthony Munday and the Catholics, 1560–1633* (Aldershot: Ashgate, 2005); and especially Michael C. Questier, *Catholicism and Community in Early Modern England: Politics, Aristocratic Patronage and Religion, 1550–1640* (Cambridge: Cambridge University Press, 2006).

2 My essay is prompted by earlier work on religious patronage networks, including John N. King's seminal work on Catherine Parr's patronage of reform-minded writers. See "Patronage and Piety: The Influence of Catherine Parr," in *Silent But for the Word*, Hannay, 43–60.

intended for Catholic readers but sometimes becoming bestsellers in the legal print market as well. The second fault line is more of a gently meandering crack, and has to do with the relationship between pre- and counter-Reformation forms of pious patronage. The third is a messy, often inconsistent division within English Catholic culture between Jesuits and their supporters among the secular priests and those secular priests who opposed them. Such intra-Catholic politics were far from stable, and through the Countess's life and activities we can begin to limn women's contributions to these shifting allegiances. The fourth has to do with fault lines within her immediate family over questions of religious conformity. As is evident from the many textual traces that survive about her—in government records, manuscript letters, her receipt (recipe) book, polemical treatises, and a seventeenth-century manuscript biography, to name a few—her activities have much to teach us about the often blurry boundaries of so-called confessional culture. While she has long been recognized as an important but shadowy figure in the poet-martyr Robert Southwell's mission, I hope here to bring her into the spotlight, and in so doing, to illuminate the complex contours of English Catholic communities.

Although a modern biography of Anne Dacre Howard has yet to be written, the broad outlines of her life are fairly clear.[3] Anne Dacre was born March 31, 1557, in Carlisle to Thomas Lord Dacre and his second wife Elizabeth. Confirmed by Cuthbert Tonstal, Bishop of Durham, she was instructed as a child by a priest in the household of her grandmother, Lady Mounteagle. Her seventeenth-century biographer writes that from her grandmother she learned "a high esteem and affection, for Catholick Religion … great compassion of sick, or otherwise afflicted persons … and a great Kindness for the Society of Jesus."[4] After her father's death,

---

[3] See Nancy Pollard Brown's thorough "Howard [Dacre], Anne, countess of Arundel (1557–1630)," in *ODNB* (see chap. 2, n. 14) (accessed August 25, 2009).

[4] Arundel Castle Archives, "The Life of the Right Honourable & Virtuouse Lady, the Lady Anne Late Countesse of Arundell & Surrey," 3. All subsequent parenthetical references are from this manuscript. This biography is one of two surviving manuscript biographies held at Arundel Castle. It comprises 104 pages, and it is more complete than the 97-page manuscript containing the lives of the Countess and her husband Philip Howard, Earl of Arundel. C.A. Newdigate argues that the single biography predates the dual biography. "A New Chapter in the Life of B. Robert Southwell, S.J.," *The Month* 157 (1931): 246–54. Though Newdigate confuses the two texts somewhat, I agree with his conclusions, and would add only that the hand in which the single biography is written appears to be an earlier hand, perhaps mid-seventeenth-century, than that of the dual biography's scribe. The dual biography forms the basis for the printed text edited by Henry Granville Fitzalan-Howard, *The Lives of Philip Howard, Earl of Arundel, and of Anne Dacres, His Wife* (London: Hurst and Blackett, 1857); that printed text omits some passages from its copy text. For that reason, and given the probable earlier date of the single biography, I cite the single biography manuscript alone. Brown, "Howard, Anne" notes that the biography "is clearly a compilation of reminiscences, some of which represent [Howard's] attempts to recall early stages in her life, while others record the

when she was nine years old, her mother married Thomas Howard, fourth Duke of Norfolk. At the age of twelve, she was married to the Duke's eldest son and heir, Philip Howard, then Earl of Surrey. Although her early modern biographer claims she always inclined toward Catholicism, her formal reconciliation, at the hands of a Marian priest, did not occur until 1582 or 1583. Within a short time she was presented for recusancy by the inhabitants of Arundel and the man who had procured the priest for her reconciliation, Richard Bayly, was banished. Bayly remained her beneficiary: throughout her life she sent him "relief" out of gratitude for his services (13).

As a result of her reconciliation, she was placed under house arrest in the home of Sir Thomas Shirley. Her biographer claims that she was pregnant at the time she was arrested; when her child, a daughter, was born in 1583, she was baptized a Protestant against her mother's wishes (15). A manuscript record of the Countess's interrogation at Wiston on April 9, 1584, survives, in which she denies speaking ill or indeed at all about Elizabeth's government, denies having had conference with any seminary or Jesuit priest, denies having heard Mass, been shriven, or reconciled, and denies knowledge of or assistance to those "evil affected" toward the state's religion and wishing to leave the realm.[5] She affirms that she has not gone to any church or chapel where the established service is used for two and a half years and states that her change of mind came about not by the persuasion of any single person but through reading books of controversy, a point her biographer corroborates (12).[6] It is clear from her correspondence with Walsingham that she was at liberty by September 1584 as a result of his intervention.[7] In September of 1584, her husband was received into the Roman Catholic Church by the Jesuit William Weston; the Earl then attempted to flee the realm in April of 1585 but was caught and arrested. The Countess would turn to Walsingham again in August 1585 to request permission to live in some of her husband's houses, a request Walsingham seems to have endorsed.[8] Her biographer writes that she, her friends, and her servants were "several times before the Council, where they were very

day-to-day life in her household"; it would seem, then, that large portions of the biography were written with the Countess's cooperation.

5 At the editor's request, I refer to Anne Howard, Countess of Arundel as "the Countess," a title that reflects the social status so important to her activities in support of Catholic causes. After her son Thomas's marriage to Lady Aletheia Talbot in 1605, her title would properly have been "Dowager Countess," but for clarity's sake I refer to her as "the Countess" throughout.

6 Pollen and MacMahon print a statement from George Law which seems to have been the basis for the questions posed to her. She denies Law's claim that she has material aids to Catholic piety: martyrs' stained linen, a papal bull, hallowed grains. See John Hungerford Pollen and William MacMahon, eds., *The Ven. Philip Howard, Earl of Arundel, 1557–1595* (London: Catholic Record Society, 1919), 52–5.

7 See her letter to Walsingham dated 10 June 1584. Ibid., 56.

8 Ibid., 134–5.

strictly examin'd" (18). Her son, Thomas Howard, Earl of Arundel, was born in July of 1585 and would become a famous collector and patron of the arts.[9]

From the time of her arrest through the end of Elizabeth's reign, she faced numerous financial difficulties arising from the crown's seizure of lands and incomes belonging to her husband or to her (17–18).[10] The Queen did not allow her to see her husband again after his 1585 arrest. Some of her correspondence survives, including a letter from Mary, Queen of Scots, to the Countess, an apparently unsuccessful attempt to draw her into Mary's circle of confidants and assistants; according to Betty Travitsky, she was a friend to Elizabeth Cary as well.[11] Other letters suggest associations along the lines of her noble status rather than her religious inclinations: she corresponded, for instance, with Elizabeth Stuart, and members of her family went out of their way to show respect to the "Winter Queen" during her long exile in The Hague (72).[12] Upon Elizabeth I's death, her situation seems to have improved. Her jointure estates, which had been seized by the crown upon her husband's death, were restored to her.[13] Her biographer records

---

9 See David Howarth, *Lord Arundel and His Circle* (New Haven: Yale University Press, 1985), and Christopher White, *Anthony Van Dyck: Thomas Howard the Earl of Arundel* (Malibu: Getty Museum Studies on Art), 1995, though I qualify White's statements about the Countess below.

10 Brown, "Howard, Anne."

11 See the prefatory notes to "Elegy," in Betty Travitsky, ed. *The Paradise of Women: Writings by Englishwomen of the Renaissance*, 2nd ed. (New York: Columbia University Press, 1989), 33–4. I believe it quite unlikely, however, that the Countess is the author of the poem Travitsky entitles "Elegy" (the first line of which is "In sad and ashy weeds"). The poem appears on the reverse of Letter 218 in Arundel Castle Archives; the Countess is neither the addressee nor the author of the letter, and the poem is not in her hand. Markings on the back of the letter suggest that the poem was inscribed prior to the sending of the letter. Thus, although the most recent edition of Alistair Fowler's *The New Oxford Book of Seventeenth Century Verse* (Oxford: Oxford University Press, 2008), 10–11, continues to identify the poem as hers, I find no basis for that identification, especially as the poem is nearly identical to a popular early seventeenth-century ballad entitled "The good Shepherds sorrow for the death of his beloved Sonne" (Pepys 1.352–3; http://emc.english.ucsb.edu/oldebba/index.asp; accessed June, 2010). The ballad is printed in Richard Johnson, *The Crown Garland* (London, 1631), and in subsequent editions. An adaptation of the ballad for the death of Queen Anne, which occurred in 1619, is published in the 1659 edition of *The Crown Garland*; if the purported occasion of the adaptation may be trusted, it may suggest that the ballad was circulating widely prior to the writing of Letter 218, which is dated 25 July 1617. The attribution of another poem to the Countess is nearly as controversial; see Micheline White, "Recent Studies in Women Writers of Tudor England, 1485–1603," *English Literary Renaissance* 30:3 (2000): 479–80. I have therefore chosen to focus exclusively on the Countess's patronage activities, for which there is much evidence.

12 On the trip to The Hague, see the *ODNB* entry for Aletheia Howard, Anne Howard's daughter-in-law, and "The Life," 52–3.

13 See J.G. Elzinga, "Howard, Philip [St Philip Howard], thirteenth Earl of Arundel," in *ODNB* (accessed August 25, 2009).

an unsuccessful attempted wooing by one of the many Scottish noblemen who accompanied James I at his accession, and she appeared at court (though dressed very modestly, her biographer writes) for James and Queen Anne's reception (31, 75). In 1624, she requested and was granted permission from James I to rebury her husband's remains, moving them from the chapel of St. Peter ad Vincula at the Tower to West Horsley, Surrey, and then to Arundel Castle.[14] A portrait of the Countess was authenticated in late 2007 and is reproduced in Fig. 3.1.

Sara Rodger, an archivist for Arundel Castle Archives, notes that "in the portrait, which is by an unknown painter, she is wearing a pendant showing the Madonna of the Assumption surrounded by angels, which appears in a catalogue of gems belonging to her son the 14th (Collector) Earl of Arundel." The pendant is described in the manuscript biography (76), and indeed the portrait was authenticated partly on the basis of its description in the biography and in her son's catalogue.[15] She lived to see two Catholic queens on England's throne, dying in April of 1630. The traces of her life in various manuscript and print sources give us a picture of a woman who used patronage, expressed in a variety of forms, to further the Catholic cause as she saw it, in the process intervening significantly in the histories of early modern religious literature, confessional conflict, and intra-Catholic politics.

Patronage and Print: Popularizing "Catholic" Writing

The Countess's most readily visible patronage activities are those in support of the missionary Jesuit priest and poet Robert Southwell. Southwell's relationship with her began shortly after her previous chaplain, a seminary priest named Martin Array, was arrested in June 1586 and banished a month later.[16] The evidence for her relationship with Southwell is considerable. Her biographer dedicates a chapter to it, indicating it was one of deep mutual respect.[17] In a dispatch to Richard Verstegan dated early December 1591, Southwell gives details about financial hardships facing a particular Catholic family as an instance of English Catholics' suffering, more grist for Verstegan's propaganda mill. In the letter Southwell

[14] Ibid. In 1971, his remains were moved again to the Roman Catholic cathedral in Arundel.

[15] Sara Rodger, personal communication, 20 January 2010. I am deeply grateful to Ms. Rodger and to her colleagues Margaret Richards and Heather Warne for their assistance.

[16] Brown, "Howard, Anne."

[17] The chapter appears in the earlier, single biography (the author indicates the biography was written in 1635, though the manuscript I cite is of a later date) but not in the later, dual biography of her and her husband (copied sometime after 1660, as Newdigate argues). The chapter on her relationship with Southwell was not included in the 1857 printing, presumably because that printing was based on the later dual biography. See Brown, "Howard, Anne," for the theory that the manuscripts were prepared for an eventual Latin text intended for presentation in Rome.

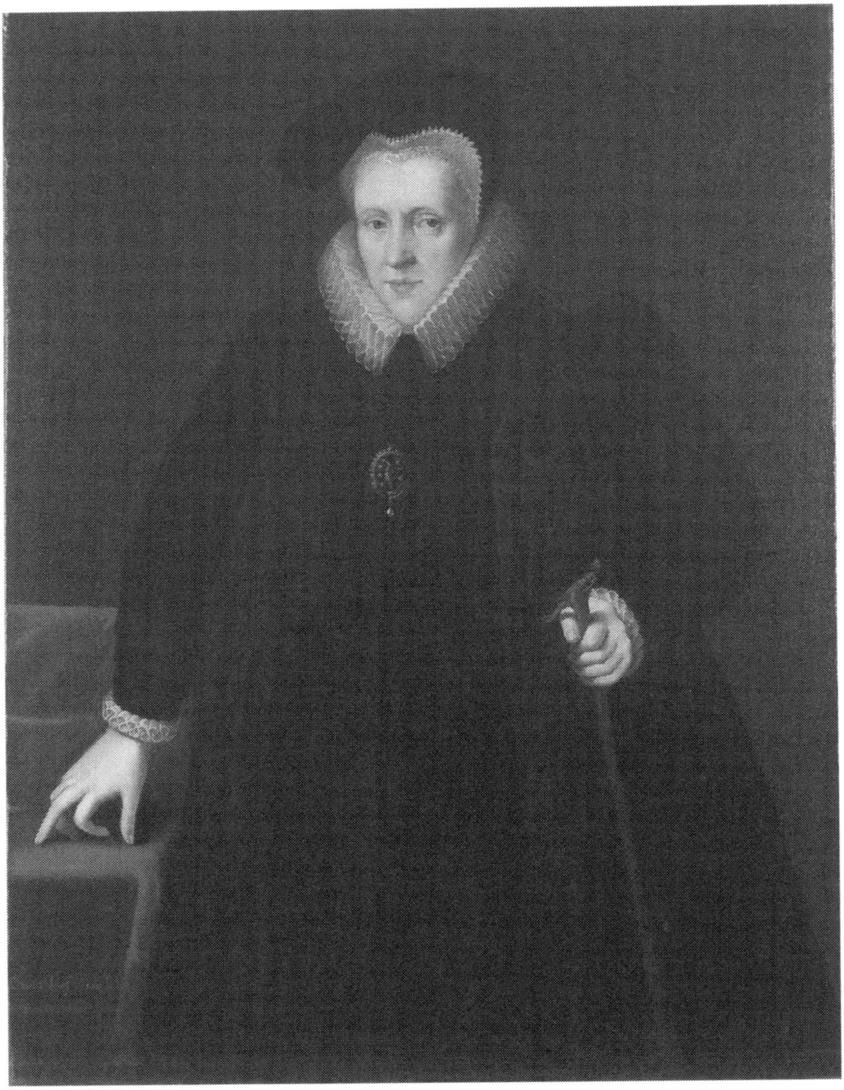

Fig. 3.1 Anne Dacre Howard, Countess of Arundel (1557–1630), widow of Philip Howard, 13th Earl of Arundel. Reproduced by kind permission of His Grace The Duke of Norfolk, Arundel Castle.

alludes to the Countess's financial difficulties in some detail. He also supplies details about Martin Array's banishment, knowledge he almost certainly got from her.[18] In his autobiography, the Jesuit John Gerard describes the difficult situation facing Jesuit missionary priests in the later 1580s, remarking upon Southwell's relationship with the Countess as the only bright spot: "We then had few friends in a position to help us. Father Southwell alone had a great benefactress, and while we had him with us, he was able with her help to maintain himself and some other priests as well as keep a private house where he usually received the Superior on his visits to London. It was there that I first met them both; there, too, that Father Southwell had his printing press, where his own admirable books were produced."[19] Gerard's remark tells us that despite the Countess's difficult financial situation, she supported Southwell's missionary activities, including, significantly, his first foray into print.

That foray was Southwell's *Epistle of Comfort*, published in 1587 on a press hidden on one of her properties, probably her house at Spitalfields.[20] In this area were also sheltered a number of Catholic families and Catholic manuscript copyists; Nancy Pollard Brown has demonstrated that the Countess of Arundel's rank was "sufficient … to provide some security" to Catholic families living in the Spitalfields or nearby, protection which enabled a scriptorium that produced manuscript copies of a number of devotional works, including one of two surviving manuscript copies of Southwell's "Saint Peter's Complaint" and his "Epistle to His Father."[21] Gerard's remark that the Countess allowed Southwell to operate a press from her home is corroborated by an unlikely source: Martin Marprelate (though Martin appears to be incorrect about the particular location of the press). In *The Epistle* (1588), the first of the Martin Marprelate tracts, Martin complains that "popish printers" are favored while Puritan printers like Robert Waldegrave, the printer of the first four Marprelate tracts, are persecuted; Martin gives two examples of such "popish" printing, one of which is relevant to the Countess: "I do now remember my selfe of another printer that had presse and letter in a place called Charterhouse in London (in Anno 1587, neere about the time of the Scottish Queenes death) intelligence was given unto your good grace of the same by some for the Stacioners of London … what worke was in hand what letter the booke was on what volume vz. in 80 i. halfe sheetes what workemen wroght on the same: namely J. D. the Earle of Arundels man and three of his servants with their severall names … Your grace gave the Stacioners the hearing of this matter but to this daye

---

[18] See Anthony Petti, ed., *The Letters and Despatches of Richard Verstegan* (London: Publications of the Catholic Record Society, 1959), 1–33, esp. 2, 4.

[19] *John Gerard. An Autobiography of an Elizabethan*, trans. Philip Caraman (London: Longmans, 1951), 26.

[20] Nancy Pollard Brown, "Paper Chase: The Dissemination of Catholic Texts in Elizabethan England," *English Manuscript Studies, 1100–1700* 1 (1989): 120–43.

[21] Ibid., 125–7.

the parties were never cald in Coram for it."[22] The "Earl of Arundel's man" was probably also under the Countess's direction at this point, as the Earl was held in the Tower with restrictions on his communications; the decision to permit the printing of this "popish" treatise on a press hidden on Arundel property—probably Southwell's *Epistle of Comfort*, first written for the Earl—may well have been a collaborative one. Nor was Southwell's the only Catholic treatise published under her auspices; one H.B.'s *A Consolatory Letter to All the Afflicted Catholikes in England* was likely published one year later, in 1588, on a secret press on one of her properties.[23] Much is known about other Catholic clandestine presses in England such as that of Richard Verstegan (used for the 1581 printing of the first English Catholic martyrology, Thomas Alfield's *A True Report*), of Robert Persons (on which was printed, *inter alia*, Campion's *Rationes decem*), and of Henry Garnet (on which Southwell's *Short Rule* would be printed posthumously, in 1597).[24] The Arundel press used for Southwell's *Epistle of Comfort* is arguably as important, since Southwell's *Epistle of Comfort* is a key treatise in support of strict recusancy at a moment when the wisdom of such a policy was yet again under debate within the Catholic community and had in fact been recently debated within the Countess's own extended family.

Indeed, within that extended family we can trace a complicated division over the question of outward religious conformity. Through her aunt Lady Magdalen Browne's marriage, the Countess was related to the powerful Catholic magnate Anthony Browne, the first Viscount Montague, who maintained his position and authority within Elizabeth I's regime through occasional (but by no means uniform) religious conformity. His intermittent and yet rather vexed conformity was urged by his chaplain, Alban Langdale, who wrote a treatise arguing that the best way to preserve Catholicism in England was through occasional conformity combined with dedicated Catholic devotion—not to exterminate the Catholic community by

---

22 Martin Marprelate [pseud.], *The Epistle* (East Molesey, 1588), 24. See also my "Martyrdom in Print in Early Modern England: The Case of Robert Waldegrave," in *More Than a Memory: The Discourse of Martyrdom and the Construction of Christian Identity in the History of Christianity*, ed. Johan Leemans (Leuven: Peeters, 2005), 271–95, on Waldegrave's 1599 edition of Robert Southwell's poetry.

23 See the information in the *STC* about this press's location. A secret press also printed, in 1595, Philip Howard's *An epistle in the person of Christ to the faithfull soule*, a translation of a treatise by Johannes Justus Lansperger completed while Howard was in the Tower; it bears a false imprint indicating place of publication as Antwerp. For a discussion of the second printing of this text, see the essay by Jaime Goodrich in this collection. Philip Howard's *A Foure-fold Meditation of the Foure Last Things*, incorrectly attributed to Robert Southwell (likely for purposes of marketing) in its 1606 printing, was printed in England on a legal press and published by Francis Burton, who also published many anti-Catholic materials. Whether the Countess had any hand in these publications is uncertain.

24 On Robert Persons, see Victor Houliston, *Catholic Resistance in Elizabethan England: Robert Persons's Jesuit Polemic, 1580–1610* (Aldershot: Ashgate, 2007).

running headlong onto recusancy penalties.[25] Given the heated debate in the 1580s within the Catholic community on just this point, Southwell's *Epistle* is all the more striking. The *Epistle* was based, Southwell implies in his address "To the Reader," on letters Southwell wrote to Philip Howard.[26] The *Epistle* allows no quarter for those who, like Langdale and the Countess's powerful uncle, would engage in what Southwell saw as temporizing: "to saye that goinge to churche at suche tymes as theyre service and sacramentes are mynistred, theyre doctrine preached, or the rites of theyre secte practised, is not a spiritual, but a civile action, is against all sense and reason … the Pastores yea al the Catholikes of this time [are] bound to endure the pinchinge and freesinge colde of what adversitye soever … rather then to suffer … Christes flocke ether to be scandalized by our example, or destitute of our necessarye endevours."[27] The Countess's likely support of the printing of Southwell's treatise positioned her against the more nuanced view adopted by her powerful uncle and with the hard line of the Jesuit author who encouraged her husband in his sufferings by brooking no compromise with an heretical regime.

In addition to the *Epistle*, the Countess played roles of varying importance with respect to three of Southwell's other prose works: *Triumphs over Death, Short Rule for a Good Life*, and, probably, *An Humble Supplication to Her Majestie*, which Southwell wrote late in 1591 while he was likely living in the Countess's Spitalfields house.[28] Yet here other fault lines begin to emerge. One of these works, the *Humble Supplication*, was printed posthumously, in 1600 on a secret press, probably in order to compromise the Jesuits during the archpriest controversy between Jesuits and secular priests in the later sixteenth and early seventeenth centuries; its publication history points to significant debates within the Catholic community on which the Countess took a definitive stand, as I discuss below. The other two works—*Triumphs over Death* and *Short Rule for a Good Life*—crossed over into the legal print market and to broad Protestant readerships. These works suggest the reach that Catholic patronage could have to readerships beyond the committed recusant Catholic community whom Southwell addresses and indeed helps to constitute through his *Epistle*. Southwell's *Triumphs over Death* was written for Philip Howard's consolation after the death of his half-sister Lady Margaret Sackville; the Countess's biographer notes that she too experienced deep grief at Lady Margaret's death (28–9).[29] Written for the Earl of Arundel,

25 Alban Langdale, *Reasons why Catholics may go to Church* (London, 1580). See Questier, *Catholicism and Community*, for an excellent discussion of the complexities of this sort of conformity.

26 Robert Southwell, *An Epistle of Comfort* (London, 1587), A2.

27 Ibid., 171r; 98v.

28 Brown, "Paper Chase," 132–3.

29 The Countess's biographer emphasizes Lady Margaret's conversion to Catholicism (as against mere survivalism or increasingly private enclosure of Catholicism as some historical models have it), and it is this dynamic Catholicism that helped endear her to the Countess (14).

the treatise also became a sensation in the legal print market, spurred in part by Southwell's 1595 execution. Three editions were printed in rapid succession, in 1595, 1596, and (probably) 1600. The Countess was the direct inspiration for Southwell's *Short Rule for a Good Life*, a guide to practical domestic piety first printed on the Jesuit Henry Garnet's secret press in 1597. Her biographer writes that the treatise was "written at first by him only for her direction" and that she closely followed its advice on daily godly living: "in the observance whereof she was always as carefull and diligent, as others are remisse, carelesse, and negligent" (23). Southwell's manuscript treatise adapts the spirit of daily monastic devotion and the intellectual foci of Loyola's *Spiritual Exercises* to life in a busy Elizabethan household. While it makes practical accommodation to the demands of running a large household, it also bears the imprint of the *Epistle of Comfort* in its insistence on Catholic devotional separation. Repeatedly, Southwell asks his reader to think about the "signs" and "badges" she gives to others about her religious opinions and commitments; the emphasis of the text is on daily, faithful witness to those commitments.[30]

While the Countess is clearly the treatise's first audience and inspiration, there is manuscript and print evidence suggesting it eventually reached religiously diverse audiences, audiences who might not have given quite the same "signs" and "badges" that Southwell hoped for. Some manuscripts prepared for Catholic readers indicate that the treatise was thought particularly appropriate for women. In 1600, one R.C. made a copy of the text followed by a preparation for confession targeting women; the text contains, for instance, a form for confessing attraction to men other than one's husband: "I have hed many uncleane thoughts, touchinge others then my husband, which I doute I have not so soone expelled as I ought."[31] This order is included in manuscript copies held at Gonville and Caius College, Cambridge, and at the Warwickshire Public Record Office; in a fourth manuscript copy, held at Durham Cathedral Library, there is a table of contents in which this confession is included, though much of the order for confession was ripped out after the table of contents was organized.[32] Most strikingly, in R.C.'s copy the text and the preparation for confession are followed by a copy of the latter part of John Mush's *Life* of the Yorkshire housewife and martyr Margaret Clitherow, such that the manuscript pieces together a recusant Catholic handbook for ideal wives: a manual for daily

[30] Gonville and Caius College, Cambridge, MS 218/233, fol. 133. The textual history of the *Short Rule* is vexed; the edition printed in 1597 shows evidence of a number of small revisions. Nancy Pollard Brown deems the Gonville and Caius manuscript "most authoritative," though she gives no further explanation. "Robert Southwell: the Mission of the Written Word," in *The Reckoned Expense: Edmund Campion and the Early English Jesuits*, ed. Thomas M. McCoog (Woodbridge: Boydell Press, 1996), 209. In the passages I cite, the Gonville and Caius text does not differ significantly from other surviving manuscript copies I have consulted.

[31] York Minster Add MS 151, 44r–v.

[32] Warwickshire PRO, Throckmorton Papers, CR 1998/Tribune/Chest of Drawers/Drawer 4; Durham Cathedral Hunter MS 112.

devotion, a practice for regular self-examination, and a contemporary hagiography. These manuscripts suggest that the treatise inspired initially by the Countess was thought to be a good guide for Catholic women more generally.

Other manuscript copies suggest a broad Protestant readership as well, such that the Countess seems to have inspired a text capable of sustaining both recusant Catholic women intent on maintaining a definitively separate confessional culture and Protestant readers attracted by its practical spirituality. The provenance of a manuscript copy held at the Folger, for instance, suggests the treatise's ability to cross and recross confessional lines. The treatise seems to have been copied by a Catholic scribe from another copy silently amended by a Protestant. That Protestant copyist removes many (though not all) of the text's distinctions between mortal and venial sins, and many (but not all) references to the accumulation of merit; the Catholic copyist seems unaware of these rather erratic emendations.[33] The Folger manuscript's attestation to the cross-confessional circulation of this work is bolstered by the Gonville and Caius College manuscript. In this manuscript, the *Rule* is copied without any of the emendations that the copyist of the Folger manuscript's source felt necessary, and yet the text appears in a commonplace book among decidedly Protestant textual excerpts: speeches from several of Foxe's most prominent Protestant martyrs, such as Thomas Cranmer, and anti-Catholic and anti-Spanish propaganda. The copyists for the Foxean and Southwellian material are distinct; the Southwell material begins, however, on the last page of the gathering containing the Foxe material, such that the Southwell copyist would have seen the Foxean excerpts, and the material contained within the commonplace book can be dated no earlier than 1563 and no later than 1600.[34] The manuscript may imply cross-confessional exchange at some early point in its history. It may also suggest that the later Catholic copyist seized the opportunity to use the Foxean material to disguise the Southwell treatise, though that suggestion must remain a hypothesis.[35] The text also enjoyed a printed life in both Catholic editions (printed at Saint-Omer) and a collected edition of Southwell's works printed in London in 1620, in which the work was emended to remove the most obvious Catholic references, though again some of these emendations are not entirely consistent.[36] This brief textual history tells us much about the reach of Catholic women's patronage activities: a text originally produced for a Catholic recusant noblewoman eventually finds audiences both like and unlike her.

---

[33] See the edition of the Folger manuscript printed in Robert Southwell, *Two Letters and Short Rules of a Good Life*, ed. Nancy Pollard Brown (Charlottesville: The University Press of Virginia, 1973).

[34] Gonville and Caius MS 218/233; 1563 is the date of Foxe's first edition of *Actes and Monuments*; the last item in the commonplace book refers to a political event of ca. 1600.

[35] See Brown, "Paper Chase."

[36] I discuss this emended edition, printed by William Barrett, in an article forthcoming on Southwell's *Short Rule*.

Indeed, the broad readerships eventually reached by the texts she inspired caution us against overly rigid conceptualizations of confessional culture. Although it is clear from Southwell's literary efforts that he sought to create a firmly separated Catholic religious culture, and it is clear from her support of these efforts and her own patterns of behavior that she concurred with his basic position, the texts themselves moved fairly easily into the legal print market and into Protestantizing manuscript circulation. If the fruits of the Countess's literary patronage are any measure to go by, so-called Catholic patronage has repercussions far beyond the so-called Catholic community and indeed can help recent scholarly efforts to render both more precisely and more fluidly the boundaries and contours of that community.[37]

Pious Patronage and Post-Reformation Exigencies

What counts as patronage activity according to our modern definitions, and in what ways might our definitions obscure some facets of early modern practices? In a magisterial article on literary patronage in the English Renaissance, Graham Parry notes that "following the suppression of the monasteries and the turmoil in the church in the 1530s, the patronage of writers became almost exclusively secular, with the monarch and the nobility broadly accepting that the encouragement of learning was one of the functions of power and authority."[38] Reformation scholars have commented on other, more humble forms of what I am calling pious patronage disrupted or rearranged by monastic dissolution, namely activities in support of the poor and the offering of shelter.[39] The Countess's activities encompass both aspects of patronage affected by the monastic dissolutions. Her biographer expounds upon her many charitable activities, and in this he resembles other Catholic authors who wrote in praise of English Catholic wives' pious and charitable activities.[40] While such activities have been explored in terms of the devotional habits of Catholic wives, they could also be used to broaden conceptions of patronage within English Catholic communities, extending pre-Reformation models of charitable patronage to post-Reformation legal and ecclesiastical realities. To the extent that these pious activities helped to sustain and shape networks within the recusant Catholic community, they are worth examining as patronage.

[37] See, for instance, Questier, *Catholicism and Community*, and Ethan H. Shagan, ed., *Catholics and the 'Protestant Nation': Religious Politics and Identity in Early Modern England* (Manchester: Manchester University Press, 2005).

[38] Graham Parry, "Literary Patronage," in *The Cambridge History of Early Modern English Literature*, ed. David Loewenstein and Janel Mueller (Cambridge: Cambridge University Press, 2002), 117.

[39] See for instance Timothy G. Fehler, *Poor Relief and Protestantism: The Evolution of Social Welfare in Sixteenth-Century Emden* (Aldershot: Ashgate, 1999).

[40] On these biographies, see Frances E. Dolan, "Reading, Work, and Catholic Women's Biographies," *English Literary Renaissance* 33, no. 3 (2003): 328–57.

The Countess's biographer gives her pious patronage activities both biblical and hagiographical warrant. Citing a passage from Tobias in which the angel Raphael gives Tobias and his son a document "concerning the Joining together of prayer, fasting and Almes" (36), he claims that the Countess exemplified this biblical ideal.[41] Her actions are also modeled on a group of saints, including St. Lucy, "by whose words spoken to her Mother about the distributing in her life time her money to the poor, as it is related in her life, she was moved efficaciously to put in practise that point of great wisdome, which few do learn, of not deferring till their death such good deeds as God moves them unto" (92–3). This *imitatio sanctorum* extends itself through the Countess to others. Her biographer notes that her example moved another person to give significant sums to an unspecified religious order and to the Society of Jesus, and to leave money after his death to "pious uses." Significantly for the biographer, his death was on "the Vigil of S. Lucy his Patronesse within the Compasse of her feast, whose worthy example he had follow'd by the good advice of his noble and pious Lady" (94).

This unnamed benefactor had plenty to imitate in following the Countess. Her biographer details numerous activities that both resemble and extend the traditional seven corporal acts of mercy: feeding the hungry, giving drink to the thirsty, sheltering travelers, providing clothes for the needy, redeeming prisoners, attending the sick, and burying the dead.[42] He writes that she gave "meat, Drink, Cloathes, medicines and money" to "ordinary poor people," and that while these gifts were "known unto many" she also performed "divers others … whereof very few took notice … such were the providing for orphans, the putting poor men's Children to be apprentices, the relieving of Prisoners, giving of portions towards the marriage of some young women whose friends either had not will or ability to do it" (36). She offered her house as a refuge for those despairing of physical recovery, and her biographer says that she made salves and medicines for them with her own hands: "Others again I have known, who being dismiss'd from the hospitals as incurable, she out of compassion has taken again to her house, and in the end hath cured them, God particularly assisting and blessing her endeavours therein" (40). He returns several times to her work in medicines and her skill in healing, calling her work in this area "another kind of almes" (38) and remarking that he has heard "her Judgement much commended by persons skilfull in … the knowledge of the nature and qualities of hearbs, to be [more] than ordinary knowing" (78). A 1679 manuscript copy of her receipt book, made at

41 Richard Smith, author of the Lady Magdalen Browne biography, describes her future husband Anthony Browne as "another Tobias" who seeks out the service of God "practiced by his parents." *An Elizabethan Recusant House, Comprising the Life of the Lady Magdalen Viscountess Montague (1538–1608)*, trans. Cuthbert Fursdon (1627), ed. A.C. Southern (London: Sands & Co., 1954), 18. The particular reference to Tobias may be meant to indicate historical continuity in pious practice and patronage.

42 For evidence of the persistent association of these activities with religious life, see the "House of Holiness" episode in Spenser's *Faerie Queene*, wherein seven beadsmen undertake a slightly modified version of these tasks.

the instigation of her great-grandson Charles Howard, indicates her skill in these areas as well. On the dedicatory page, Charles Howard writes that he has made "an exact Coppie" of her receipt book (containing 103 pages of medicinal recipes and diagnostic guidelines) as a gift for his niece, a book first inherited by the Countess's daughter-in-law Aletheia Howard, "who kepte it as long as she lived as a greate tresor."[43] In the portrait of charitable activities her biographer provides, the Countess both extends the traditional works of mercy practiced by monastics and suits those works to her circumstances and training as a peer and a woman.

Her biographer also writes of her activities in support of recusant Catholics and their priests, carried out under circumstances no medieval religious could have foreseen. The Countess assisted in the honorable burial, for instance, of Anne Line, one of three early modern Catholic Englishwomen judicially executed for assisting priests.[44] The Countess supported other Catholics' attempts to bury Line reverently: "understanding that certain resolute Catholicks intended to take up her body in the night time out of the place where it was dishonourably buried in the same grave and under the bodies of diverse malefactors, she sent her Coach with them and in it brought the body to her own house, where it was kept with reverence untill it could be conveniently disposed of by those who had more interest therein" (89). Here, the Countess extends the traditional work of burying the dead to the much riskier, more defiant action of honorably reburying an executed traitor.

The traditionally pious act of relieving prisoners also takes on a defiant tinge in the circumstances of post-Reformation England. The Countess, like Line, provided shelter and support to priests, though from a position of considerably greater social advantage. Her biographer enumerates deeds in support of priests and religious: "the relieving of Priests in prison, or otherwise in trouble, danger, or necessity, for the profession of the catholick Religion: The furthering and furnishing of some who had a desire, but wanted means to be religious: The helping of colledges and religious houses in their temporal necessitys. The concurring to such things as were convenient or necessary for the advancement of Religion" (40–41). Corroboration for his statement appears in two Jesuit priests' autobiographies. Arrested in 1586, William Weston records that "others" tried to use wealth to procure his pardon or, alternatively, his banishment from the realm; upon hearing of such attempts Weston "wrote immediately to Father Robert Southwell asking him to use every means he knew to stop it."[45] It is clear from the mention of Southwell's influence that the Countess was the person behind these attempts.[46] John Gerard

[43] Arundel Castle Archives MS, p. 1.

[44] John Gerard discusses Line's activities as manager of a safe house he established in London. *Autobiography*, 84–5. On Line's execution, see ibid., 85–6, and the Historical MSS commission, Rutland MSS, i, 370, cited by Caraman, ibid., 86.

[45] *An Autobiography from the Jesuit Underground, by William Weston*, trans. Philip Caraman (New York: Farrar, Straus, and Cudahy, 1955), 125. As noted above, Weston is the priest who reconciled Philip Howard.

[46] The Earl of Arundel's biography corroborates this as well.

records that he found shelter at her house just prior to his arrest. Gerard's remarks suggest both the protection that her status could provide and its limitations. On returning to London in the spring of 1594, Gerard stayed "with a person of high rank and was completely safe"; he later specifies that this person was the same person who had protected Southwell until a year before his arrest, the Countess herself. While Gerard was "completely safe" in her home, he felt he could not conduct his "business" (his mission work of reconciliation and ministry) from that house, remarking on the difficulty of doing so in someone else's home "and particularly in the one where I was staying."[47] Later comments make clear that Gerard feared drawing attention to the Countess's home: at the moment of his arrest "I was very concerned about the lady's house, which I had left that night to return to my apartment—they might have seen me come out and shadowed my steps and I was afraid that very illustrious family might suffer for my sake."[48] Gerard's comments imply his understanding that priests hidden in her home could rest with safety provided they did not carry on the "business" of active ministry, and that if proof of such active ministry were found, the Countess's status would not shield her.

It is clear from these autobiographies and from her biographer's comments that the Countess's pious patronage activities were well known and helped establish a community of like-minded Catholics around her. It is also clear that her activities were crucial for Jesuit missionary priests who relied upon her for protection, despite its acknowledged limitations. Her activities as described by her biographer connect her to traditions of Catholic piety, while suggesting that such traditional piety could produce a community of like-minded Catholics operating in much altered, straitened circumstances. Expanding the range of patronage activities to include those both charitable—offering shelter to the needy—and treasonous—offering shelter to priests—makes more visible the adaptations of traditional piety post-Reformation English Catholics undertook, as well as the ways in which those activities were used to create a network of connections capable of creating Catholic subcultures.[49]

Intra-Catholic Politics: The Countess and the Jesuits

The Countess's patronage activities can refine our notions of confessional culture in another way, insofar as they highlight divisions within the English Catholic community. These included disagreements over the policy of strict recusancy and over the best forms of ecclesiastical organization in England. The Countess's activities make clear her alignment with the Jesuit faction, firmly behind the strict

47 Gerard, *Autobiography*, 64.

48 Ibid., 65.

49 For an up-to-date historical account of similar sorts of adaptations in Catholic devotional practices, see Lisa McClain, *Lest We Be Damned: Practical Innovation and Lived Experience Among Catholics in Protestant England, 1559–1642* (New York: Routledge, 2004).

recusancy Southwell advocated in his *Epistle* and against the appointment of a bishop for England.[50] The Countess's patronage activities, often not in perfect alignment with those of other Catholic members of her prominent family, lent their considerable weight to the Jesuit cause. Her life provided her biographer with an opportunity to promulgate a model for other would-be patrons and patronesses of English Jesuits.

As scholars have increasingly recognized, biographies of early modern Catholic Englishwomen were used, *inter alia*, as instruments for intra-Catholic maneuvering. For instance, the famous *Life* of the martyr Margaret Clitherow was written by her confessor, John Mush, at least in part as a reproach to those Yorkshire Catholics unwilling to take the risks Clitherow did to shelter priests.[51] The Countess's biographer praises her in similar terms: she "not only passed through many boisterous blasts of persecution, which happened in those times, without ever shewing any frailty, when many strong stoutharted men of of [sic] the Laity and Clergy were blown down, but animated moreover and encourag'd several by her words and example to the like, who otherwise by fear were in great danger of falling" (88–9). In addition to rebuking weaker-willed Catholics, her biographer provides nearly unique information about her patronage activities in support of religious orders and of the Society of Jesus specifically.

The intra-Catholic politics of this alignment are evident when her biography is compared with that of her aunt Lady Magdalen Browne, Viscountess Montague and wife of the important Catholic patron Anthony Browne. The Viscountess's biography was first written in Latin by Richard Smith, the priest who would become Bishop of Chalcedon and England's top-ranking Catholic ecclesiastical figure in 1625.[52] The Countess's biographer praises Browne's biography and its noteworthy subject: "her life has been written, for an Example to others, and afterwards printed and publish'd" (7–8). Still, there are subtle differences in emphasis between the Viscountess Montague's and the Countess's biographies, for the Viscountess's biography tends to align her with the cause of Smith's faction, those secular priests who sought to mitigate Jesuit influence in England. First published in 1609, Smith's biography appeared just after the appointment of the second archpriest, George Birkhead, a close associate of Smith and a patient, if timid, advocate for those seculars interested in the appointment of a bishop.[53] According to Smith,

---

50 On the ecclesiastical politics behind this position, see Michael C. Questier's introduction to *Newsletters from the Archpresbyterate of George Birkhead* (Cambridge: Cambridge University Press, 1998).

51 On intra-Yorkshire Catholic politics and Mush's *Life*, see Peter Lake and Michael C. Questier, "Margaret Clitherow, Catholic Nonconformity, Martyrology, and the Politics of Religious Change in Elizabethan England," *Past and Present* 185, no. 1 (2004): 43–90.

52 The first Bishop of Chalcedon, the appropriately named Father William Bishop, was appointed in 1623.

53 On the politics of the Birkhead appointment, see the introduction to Questier, *Newsletters*.

Birkhead praised the Viscountess as "the worthy patroness of the holy faith and the singular ornament of the Catholic religion in England."[54] At Smith's request, the biography was then translated into English and published in 1627, two years after Smith's appointment as Bishop of Chalcedon. While much of Smith's account of the Viscountess's life reads like the pious hagiography it is, Smith also emphasizes her support for secular priests. She sheltered three in her house, including Thomas More's great-grandchild, another close associate of both Smith and Birkhead.[55] Smith praises her for her reverence of priests in a passage that also boasts of the "above one hundred and twenty secular priests" who have within thirty years been "crowned with martyrdom in England," conspicuously omitting a similar tally for Jesuit priests.[56] Perhaps partly in gentle response to Smith's biography, the Countess's Jesuit biographer stresses her pro-Jesuit patronage activities.[57] The biography's account of these activities thus indicates another fault line in confessional culture: that within the multifaceted Catholic community over the relative merits and importance of Jesuits to the English mission.

Through accounting for her patronage to Jesuits, her biographer gives plenty of detail about intra-Catholic tensions. He writes that her support for Jesuits began in her youth, when she heard "good reports" of Campion and Persons (44), and had a brief acquaintance with Jasper Heywood, John Donne's Jesuit uncle. She was briefly affected by intra-Catholic controversies over the Jesuits and later attempts were made to draw her away from her support for Jesuits:

> meeting with some who buzz'd many things against them, she was not a little alienated (as her self has often told me) until being inform'd of the truth partly by Father William Weston who reconciled the Earle her husband, but Chiefly by Father Southwel, she remain'd so well satisfy'd, that ever after she continued a most constant friend and perpetual Benefactresse to them, notwithstanding that such means were us'd to avert her, that some doubted not to cause it to be publish'd in the Gazetts at Rome, that now she had left and lost her opinion and affection towards them: but how far she was from that, appear'd best by her works already mention'd and continued to her end, in which (the very last night of her life) she told me that nothing did then more comfort her, than what she had done for the Society (45).

---

54 Smith, *Elizabethan Recusant House*, 65.

55 Ibid., 43.

56 Ibid., 49.

57 Brown, "Howard, Anne," speculates that the Countess's biography "may have been written originally in Latin, to be sent to Rome"; if she is right, the case for examining the Browne and Howard biographies together is strengthened. The political differences I note here between the two biographies are nuanced. Browne apparently conformed for a time, but Smith makes clear that after proper instruction she no longer attended Church of England services. *Elizabethan Recusant House*, 41. It is also clear that Anne's biographer respects her "noble Aunt" even as he indicates that Anne rejected her advice not to make a vow to remain a celibate widow (29), thereby implying the depth of Anne's piety.

The biographer's refutation of misinformed Catholic news reports indicates how valuable this noblewoman's patronage was, and how important it was that he help set the record straight. Her biographer claims that she sheltered Jesuits in her home for over forty years and relieved Jesuits numerous times with financial assistance. Evidence from other sources supports his claims. In addition to assisting particular Jesuits such as Weston, Gerard, and Southwell, her biographer writes that "she gave yearly a very great almes to their community here in England and continued it till her death" (42). Her support was recognized in high places: she was sent "a plain pair of beads" as a gift from Father Claudius Aquaviva (76), General of the Society of Jesus from 1581 to 1615.

At several points, the strain of intra-Catholic politics becomes clear: the Countess's biographer wants both to extol her support for Catholics more generally and to claim her patronage for the Jesuits. He writes rather backhandedly that she supported secular clergy and would have done more had she not heard of some vague indiscretions: "altho she had little or no acquaintance with any of the secular Clergy, yet at several times to my knowledge, she has given good summs of money for their relief, and would have done more, had not the less discretion of some, cool'd her Charity in that kind" (41). She even assists George Blackwell at one point, the controversial first archpriest suspected of too much closeness with Jesuits, which her biographer cites as evidence of her good will towards secular priests (those secular priests suspicious of Blackwell would not have concurred with this reading).[58] Still, he emphasizes that her political views and most of her patronage activities position her firmly behind the Jesuits. For instance, her biographer situates her with respect to the Jacobean Oath of Allegiance. Secular clergy were divided over whether to take it, while Jesuits strongly opposed it. Her biographer writes that the Countess took the Jesuit view, "easily perceiving the craft therein contain'd and the pernicious drift of those who contriv'd it" (78).

These intra-Catholic struggles held implications for extra-Catholic politics as well, as is evident once the reach of her pro-Jesuit and pro-religious activities is traced beyond English shores. As exile communities of English religious and English Catholic colleges developed on the continent, she lent her support to them:

> there was not one Order in England whereof she had notice, but at one time or another, receiv'd some considerable almes from her; nor scarce any Colledge or religious house of our nation in Flanders, that did not the like, and some of them oftentimes as their necessitys did require, twenty, forty, and threescore pounds at a time. And not only to those in Flanders, and of our own nation, but to others also in more remote Countrys, as Italy and Spain, he [sic] did extend her Charity. (42)

[58] After the Countess bribed an official searching for Blackwell, she apparently sheltered Blackwell at her house for a few days and then assured his safe transport to his next hiding spot (41–2).

Her largest bequest to the Jesuits also had international implications. In 1612 she gave 2500 pounds into the safekeeping of the Jesuit Richard Blount, whom her biographer tactfully leaves unnamed; he was to invest the money and use the interest for continuing support of the Society.[59] Instead, he mishandled it and lost it. Her biographer writes that her response was to continue in her efforts to support English Jesuits by:

> buying a house at the Citty of Ghendt in Flanders, where such as had ended their studies might make their third probation, and better prepare themselves to labour in God's vineyard according to their Institute; She furnish'd it with all things necessary for their use; maintain'd it dureing her life, and left competent means for the perpetual maintenance thereof, with order that when ever England shall be converted, that house should be transferr'd thither and placed in the Citty of Carlile where she was born to the end that not only those of that Citty and her tenants thereabouts, but all the whole Country thereto adjoyning might receive some spiritual good, by the teaching, preaching and other pious labours and endeavours of those Religious, whom she intended should be maintained therein. (43)

Her support of the College was imitated by her steward, who both in life and death was "very bountifull" to the Society, ultimately supporting the College at Ghent with a bequest (57); his wife, too, gave the Society an annuity out of her inheritance (58). At her death, the Countess left some ornaments to be finished and sent "to her house at Ghendt for the service of a Chapel there dedicated to the memory of the Holy Virgin and Martyr S. Lucy to whom she was particularly devoted" (44). Through this Jesuit College of Ghent, John Gerard again enjoyed her patronage; he served as rector from the founding of the College till 1627, when he took up his final post as confessor to the English College at Rome.[60]

To her biographer, the Countess's support for the College represents the ultimate testimony to her Catholic commitments. Through the College, her patronage extended beyond England's borders to an institution capable of training future generations of English Jesuits and of serving and proselytizing Englishmen and women abroad. Given the College's location, in Spanish Flanders, the Countess's patronage also reached into the shadow war between England and Spain carried out on Flemish soil. The sort of work the College supported is made clear through its first annual letters reporting on its activities; her funds would have supported overt proselytizing efforts among English soldiers fighting on both sides of the confessional divide in the Low Countries.[61] Her patronage of Jesuits thus helps us

---

59 Brown, "Howard, Anne."

60 See Gerard, *Autobiography*, 277.

61 Such efforts are described in the annual letters from the Ghent college. See Henry Foley, *Records of the English Province of the Society of Jesus* (London: Burns and Oates, 1883), vol. 7, pt. 2, 1195 ff; see also Foley's comment on her: the "House of the Third Probation was opened about the middle of the month of August, 1621 … [and] founded by

mark and nuance extra- and intraconfessional conflicts, conflicts limned more clearly in the glare of international warfare and made murkier by the intraconfessional differences emerging in the pages of her biography and in that of her aunt.

A Patroness's Legacy: Family and Faith

While it is clear that the Countess's social status protected her to some extent and enabled her service to the Catholic community as she construed it (in the senses both of understanding and shaping), she also suffered—and, it seems, protested—the deprivation of honors due to her and hers. For instance, Philip Howard was, infamously, denied a funeral befitting his status. His funeral expenses amounted only to five pounds; his coffin was wrapped in a mere three yards of black cloth—both indications of a funerary insult to the imprisoned Catholic Earl deemed a traitor to the state.[62] The Earl's curtailed burial contrasts markedly with the funerary commemoration afforded to the Countess's uncle, Anthony Browne, first Viscount Montague, just three years prior: "He was buried at Midhurst on 6 December [1592], under a splendid tomb of marble and alabaster, surmounted by a kneeling figure of himself and recumbent effigies of his two wives."[63] Not until 1624, the last year of James I's reign, and after considerable labors did the Countess win the right to rebury the Earl with some funereal honors.

As her persistence over the matter of her husband's burial indicates, the Countess worked to preserve her family's honor; she also sought its unity in religion, a unity threatened by some of her descendants' willingness to conform rather than risk the fate her husband suffered. The Countess's patronage to the Jesuit College in Ghent, for instance, would play into intrafamilial struggles over the question of conformity. The Countess sought to ensure that the causes she endorsed would continue to receive support after her death. She thus needed the cooperation of her heirs, something not, from her point of view, always forthcoming. Overheated anti-Catholic polemicists and sympathetic historians alike have recognized that Catholic women were crucial to the sustenance of the faith, in part through their roles in educating their children. The Countess had one child who survived past the teen years, the prominent collector and powerful nobleman Thomas Howard, Earl of Arundel. Scholars are divided over the nature of their relationship.[64]

---

the pious bounty of Anne Dacre, Countess of Arundel and Surrey, a warm and sincere friend of the Society of Jesus." Ibid., vol. 7, pt. 1, liii.

62 Elzinga, "Howard, Philip," (see n. 13).

63 J.G. Elzinga, "Browne, Anthony, first Viscount Montagu (1528–1592)," in *ODNB* (accessed August 25, 2009).

64 Compare, for instance, Brown's remarks on the Countess's role in reclaiming Arundel House for her son with Malcolm Smuts's claim that the recovery was Thomas Howard's own doing: Brown, "Howard, Anne" and Malcolm Smuts, "Howard, Thomas, fourteenth earl of Arundel, fourth earl of Surrey, and first earl of Norfolk (1585–1646)," in *ODNB* (accessed August 25, 2009).

Perhaps predictably, some scholarly assessments of the education he received at his mother's instigation still reflect the lines of old confessional battles. In a recent history of Anthony Van Dyck's portrait of Thomas Howard, Christopher White notes that "because of his father's fate his education had become the responsibility of his mother … she subjected him to an austere and rigid upbringing with strict observance of the Catholic faith, which, for political reasons, he later repudiated in favor of the Church of England."[65] The Countess's biographer paints a different portrait, praising the education she procured for her children, including religious instruction primarily by example, and suggesting that despite their evident religious differences the Earl continued some of her charitable activities "in remembrance of his blessed Mother, for so he stiled her when ever occasion was offer'd to mention her" (38). Despite this anecdote, it seems reasonable to infer that their relationship was not always serene, largely because of his public conformity to the Church of England from 1616 till the last years of his life when he was reconciled to the Catholic Church. Her biographer writes that she did all

> that was necessary for his Education and continuance in the catholick Religion, in which he did remaine some years after his marriage and departure from her government, till partly through fear, partly through desire of the King's favour (meeting also with some bad Counsellors) he accommodated himself by degrees to the times more than he ought to have done, to the incredible sorrow of his Good Mother, who in all convenient occasions did ever give him the best Counsell she could for the safety of his soul and return to Gods true church. (48)

Thomas Howard's conformity furthered his political career but was from his mother's point of view a spiritual disaster; she was apparently not mollified by the fact that the Earl's political sympathies often remained with his former coreligionists.[66]

Her regret over what she saw as his apostasy is evident in a letter her biographer preserves, addressed to her son and to be delivered after her death. The letter, if authentic, is both a mother's legacy (a genre comprising advice from a dead mother) and a feminine, much shorter version of a well-circulated letter Southwell wrote to his father urging him to strict recusancy. In her letter, the Countess presses her son to "think seriously upon your present state, and consider how little you have gained either of honour, wealth, reputation or true contentment of mind by the course which now many years you have followed, contrary to the breeding and Education I gave you, and to the worthy example your Blessed Father left

---

65 White, *Anthony Van Dyck*, 5. Smuts notes the common assumption that Thomas Howard was educated at Westminster school under Camden and then at Cambridge. In his otherwise very helpful entry on Thomas Howard, Smuts follows the Earl of Clarendon, who held little affection for Howard, in his assessment that he "was a man supercilious and proud" and attributes that pride and aloofness to "the influence of an embittered mother." Smuts, "Howard, Thomas."

66 On his political sympathies, see Smuts, "Howard, Thomas."

you, and the true Judgment of all those that wish best unto you." She urges him to "speedily return to that safe harbour of God's Holy Church, out of which you can see nothing but confusion, nor any that are not wholy ignorant, can prudently expect salvation" (49).[67]

Her biographer indicates that she wrote another letter, which he did not transcribe, to her grandson, the eldest son of Thomas Howard, urging him to discover the truth about religion and asking him, if he lived to see Catholicism restored in England, to "favour and further the house she had set up at Ghendt (tho not nameing it) for the Society, and that he would leave the like order to his Children and Posterity" (51). Her concern for her familial legacy thus includes a concern for a continuation of her patronage activities. The grandson to whom she wrote, James Howard, died in Ghent in July 1624 at the age of 18. While traveling with his family through Ghent on the way to Elizabeth Stuart's residence in The Hague, James contracted smallpox, which proved fatal. But in this death her biographer sees a providential reward:

> before his death [he] was so fortunate as to be visited by Father John Gerard a Priest of the Society, who together with others lived there in the house, which his Grandmother a little before had newly erected, though neither he nor any of his company, nor perhaps any one of those who lived ther at that house, did know that it was set up and maintain by her, so secret was it kept. He was at last reconciled by that Father to the Holy church, haveing never been a Catholick before, nor known to be so much as any thing affected that way, because he had for Tutor both in England and Italy a Protestant Minister. At the hands of the same Father he receiv'd all the Holy Sacraments necessary to a due preparation for death, and with so good a disposition that he left no smal hopes, in those who observ'd it, of his going to a better life. whereof when notice was given to his good Grandmother, she instead of lamenting the losse as parents in such cases are wont to do, gave thanks to God rejoyceing that he made so good an end. and when considering that if he had either come into England, or dyed in Holland or any other Citty almost of Flanders, France or Italy, he either could not at all, or not so conveniently have had the like means of dyeing well as he had at Ghendt, she not only admired the providence of God therein, but took it as a special favour from him and as a sign that he was pleased with the work she then had begun and therby was not a little animated for the finishing thereof. (52–3)[68]

The biographer prayerfully envisions a continuing legacy for her, one firmly grounded in the intercession of saints; he hopes that "she now enjoying everlasting happyness, and being nothing decreased in her Charity, by her holy prayers and intercession may and will obtaine for them of Almighty God abundant grace to imitate her vertues here, that thereby at length they may come to be partakers of

67 Compare with Southwell's "Epistle to his Father," in Southwell, *Two Letters*.

68 Her descendants seem to have returned to the Catholicism towards which she urged her son: her grandson, William Howard, was executed during the Titus Oates plot; a great-grandson, Philip Howard, became a cardinal.

the Glory which she doth possess in heaven" (104). He imagines her intercession as supporting familial continuance of her patronage activities, across the entire range of work I have traced here.

The intra- and extra-confessional struggles to which the Countess contributed are visible in the history of the secret Arundel press, the complex manuscript inheritance of the *Short Rule*, her charitable patronage activities, the subtle differences between her affiliations and those of the Browne family, and the proselytizing of the College of Ghent, including efforts directed at her own family. Her activities both witness to a longed-for continuity in religious practice and manifest the pressures of post-Reformation exigencies. Her example implies what is to be gained from the study of Catholic women patronesses, for the impact of her work extends beyond and calls into question boundaries between nations, confessions, and manuscript and print cultures. If this example is instructive, then the study of Catholic women patronesses can help greatly as we complicate and nuance our mappings of confessional culture and religious conflict in the early modern period.

Chapter 4
"Ensigne-Bearers of Saint Clare": Elizabeth Evelinge's Early Translations and the Restoration of English Franciscanism[1]

Jaime Goodrich

During the sixteenth and seventeenth centuries, Catholic Englishwomen established over 20 Continental convents in order to pursue religious beliefs that were illegal in their home country.[2] By placing themselves at such a physical remove from England, these women may appear to have withdrawn into an apolitical sphere where their privacy was only heightened by their enclosure.[3] However, recusant nuns provided spiritual and material aid meant to hasten the conversion of England. As Claire Walker has shown, these convents became beacons of English Catholicism, and the nuns' very survival represented the future restoration of their religion.[4] Yet while recent critics have documented the importance of Catholic laywomen, early modern English nuns have received scant attention and no group of these women is as overdue for recognition as the Franciscan nuns.[5] Scholars

1 The research for this essay was made possible by generous grants from the American Association of University Women, the Renaissance Society of America, and the Catholic Record Society. Sister Chiara of Jesus, archivist at the Poor Clare monastery in Much Birch, provided much kind assistance.

2 Claire Walker, *Gender and Politics in Early Modern Europe: English Convents in France and the Low Countries* (Hampshire: Palgrave Macmillan, 2003); Peter Guilday, *The English Catholic Refugees on the Continent 1558–1795*, vol. 1 (New York: Longmans, Green, and Co., 1914).

3 Marie B. Rowlands reads enclosure as "an essentially private setting," since it restricted the nuns' contact with the outside world. "Recusant Women 1560–1640," in *Women in English Society 1500–1800*, ed. Mary Prior (London: Methuen, 1985), 168.

4 Walker, *Gender and Politics*, 117–18.

5 Influential discussions of Catholic laywomen include: Arthur F. Marotti, "Alienating Catholics in Early Modern England: Recusant Women, Jesuits and Ideological Fantasies," in *Catholicism and Anti-Catholicism in Early Modern English Texts*, ed. Arthur F. Marotti (New York: St. Martin's Press, 1999), 1–34; and Frances E. Dolan, *Whores of Babylon: Catholicism, Gender, and Seventeenth-Century Print Culture* (Ithaca: Cornell University Press, 1999). The only critical assessment of works by Franciscan nuns is found in volumes in the series Early Modern Englishwoman: A Facsimile Library of Essential Works—

such as Dorothy Latz and Heather Wolfe have already outlined the importance of literature written by Benedictine nuns at the English convent in Cambrai.[6] Father Augustine Baker, the unofficial spiritual confessor at Cambrai, drew on the traditional association of Benedictinism with learning to create an environment that uniquely fostered literary composition. Following Baker's ideal of using reading to facilitate piety, the Cambrai nuns composed, translated, and transcribed a wealth of important literary works.[7] The state of learning at other Continental convents for Englishwomen remains less well documented, particularly for those orders which were not historically known for scholarship.[8] This essay seeks to fill in one such gap by examining two translations only recently attributed with confidence to Catherine of Saint Magdalen (Elizabeth Evelinge, 1597–1668), a Poor Clare from the English convent at Gravelines. One of the most published female translators of the early seventeenth century, Evelinge's considerable spiritual and literary contributions to English Catholicism merit scholarly attention.[9] Not only do Evelinge's works illuminate the ways Franciscan spirituality informed learning at Gravelines, but they also participated in contemporary attempts to restore and define English Franciscanism both at Gravelines and beyond.

Printed Writings, 1500–1640 (referred to as EME hereafter). See *Elizabeth Evelinge I*, EME, Series 1, pt. 3, vol. 3, selected and introduced by Frans Korsten (Aldershot: Ashgate, 2002); *Elizabeth Evelinge II*, EME, Series 1, pt. 3, vol. 4, selected and introduced by Jos Blom and Frans Blom (Aldershot: Ashgate, 2002); *Elizabeth Evelinge III*, EME, Series 1, pt. 3, vol. 5, selected and introduced by Claire Walker (Aldershot: Ashgate, 2006); and *Catherine Greenbury and Mary Percy*, EME, Series 1, pt. 4, vol. 2, selected and introduced by Jos Blom and Frans Blom (Aldershot: Ashgate, 2006). For a consideration of Catherine Greenbury's work, see Jaime Goodrich, *Early Modern Englishwomen as Translators of Religious and Political Literature, 1500–1641* (PhD diss., Boston College, 2008).

6 Dorothy L. Latz, *"Glow-Worm Light": Writings of 17th Century English Recusant Women from Original Manuscripts* (Salzburg: Institut für Anglistik und Amerikanistik, 1989); Dorothy L. Latz, ed. *The Building of Divine Love as Translated by Dame Agnes More* (Salzburg: Institut für Anglistik und Amerikanistik, 1992); Heather Wolfe, ed. *Elizabeth Cary, Lady Falkland: Life and Letters* (Cambridge: Renaissance Texts from Manuscript, 2001).

7 Heather Wolfe, "Reading Bells and Loose Papers: Reading and Writing Practices of the English Benedictine Nuns of Cambrai and Paris," in *Early Modern Women's Manuscript Writing: Selected Papers from the Trinity/Trent Colloquium*, ed. Victoria E. Burke and Jonathan Gibson (Aldershot: Ashgate, 2004), 135–56.

8 Nicky Hallett has recently published two important books on the English Carmelites: *Witchcraft, Exorcism, and the Politics of Possession in a Seventeenth-Century Convent: "How Sister Ursula Was Once Bewitched and Sister Margaret Twice"* (Aldershot: Ashgate, 2007) and *Lives of Spirit: English Carmelite Self-Writing of the Early Modern Period* (Aldershot: Ashgate, 2007).

9 Critics have traditionally chosen to refer to Evelinge by her secular name.

The Complications of Evelinge's Cloistered Authorship

When Elizabeth Evelinge professed at the Poor Clare convent in Gravelines under the name Catherine of Saint Magdalen in 1620, she joined a house already famous throughout England for its preservation of English Catholicism. Mary Ward founded the convent at Gravelines in 1608/1609, establishing the first Franciscan convent for Englishwomen—and only the second English convent—on the Continent.[10] As a result, the Gravelines house gained a special reputation as an embodiment of English piety. In 1610, for example, John Wilson described the convent as a repository of nearly extinguished Catholic fervor: "some little sparkes of piety may be conserved alive, within the embers of your Religious breasts."[11] One way the Poor Clares "conserved" English Catholicism was through their unusual emphasis on scholarship. The distinguishing element of the Poor Clares is their commitment to strict poverty, but the Gravelines convent also embraced a devout learning not historically associated with their order. Unlike the Cambrai Benedictines, the initiative for making scholarship part of daily piety appears to have arisen from the nuns themselves rather than their confessors. First abbess Mary Stephen Gough assiduously educated choir nuns so they could pronounce Latin properly when singing the offices. The *Gravelines Chronicle* records that some choir sisters even learned Latin grammar ("accidents") as part of their training: "three or four that were most apt were put to learn their accidents, a Religious being appointed at certain hours to heare their lessons."[12] Although this "Religious" overseer may have been a priest, it is also possible that more learned nuns taught the novices Latin. Gough's stress on learning Latin is not surprising, since many of the nuns probably came from recusant gentry families, which often taught their daughters Latin to enhance their piety.[13] Well before the Cambrai Benedictines were founded in 1623, then, the Gravelines Poor Clares made learning an important element of cloistered devotion. Yet while the Cambrai Benedictines encouraged all of their community to study for pious purposes, the Gravelines convent only promoted the educational progress of those women who showed scholarly aptitude. This difference may very well account for the fact that out of all the Gravelines Poor Clares, only Evelinge has been recognized as an author, in contrast with the numerous writers at Cambrai.

For Evelinge, literary work was an important means of serving her cloister, first at Gravelines and then at a new filiation in Aire. As her obituary indicates,

10 For the convent's history, see Guilday, *English Catholic Refugees*, 297–301 and William Martin Hunnybun, ed. "Registers of the English Poor Clares at Gravelines," in *Miscellanea* (London: Catholic Record Society, 1914), 9:25–31.

11 John Wilson, preface to *An Epistle or Exhortation of Jesus Christ to the Soule …*, by Johannes Lansperger (Saint-Omer, 1610), *2v–*3v.

12 Monastery of Poor Clares, Much Birch, MS *Gravelines Chronicle*, 36.

13 Jane Stevenson, "Women Catholics and Latin Culture" in *Catholic Culture in Early Modern England*, ed. Ronald Corthell et al. (Notre Dame: University of Notre Dame Press, 2007), 52–72.

Evelinge was legendary among the nuns at her Poor Clare convent at Aire for both her scholarship and leadership:

> the Venerable Mother, Sister Catherine Magdalin Evelinge,—for 25 years a most deserving Abbess; who haveing with great praise Discharged the office of Portress, & Mistress of Novices, for the admirable guifts of her Soul, also a more polish'd way of writing above her Sex, prefer'd at Length to the Government of the above sayed Convent, and hath peacefully governed the same not with Less prudence, than general Satisfaction of all, leaving behind her a great Example of a most perfect Poverty, which she delighted in. She was most Loveing & tender to all: & very austere to her self.[14]

This obituary reveals that Evelinge played a vital role in assuring the success of the Aire convent, no small feat in an age when resources for English Catholicism were meager. Since the portress oversaw the convent's gate, Evelinge served as the Aire house's representative to the outer world. Evelinge's successful tenures as mistress of novices and abbess also indicate her aptitude for leadership. Yet the obituary suggests that Evelinge served her community in another way: by composing literature. It appears that Evelinge was "prefer'd," or promoted to abbess, due to the "great praise" accompanying her previous offices, "the admirable guifts of her Soul," *and* "a more polish'd way of writing above her Sex." The *Aire Register* furthermore praises the "many choice monuments of her Laborious industry and great abilities admirable in human Lerninge."[15] Evelinge's fellow nuns clearly valued her literary work, viewing it as central to the piety that made Evelinge so exemplary. However, her work was not confined to the cloister. Three of these "monuments," all translations into English, were published in her lifetime. Evelinge translated two works from French: *The Admirable Life of the Holy Virgin S. Catharine of Bologna* by Dionisio Paleotti (Saint-Omer: English College Press, 1621; *STC* 5350.7; Saint-Omer, English College Press, 1622; *STC* 5350) and *The History of the Angelicall Virgin Glorious S. Clare* by François Hendricq (Douai: Martin Bogard, 1635; *STC* 24924). In addition, she translated *The Declarations and Ordinances Made upon the Rule of our Holy Mother S. Clare*—Saint Colette's revision of Saint Clare's *Rule*—from either Latin or French (Saint-Omer: English College Press, 1622; *STC* 5349.8).[16] Evelinge's unusual decision to publish these works suggests that she sought an audience outside the walls of her convent.

14 Hunnybun, "Registers," 52.

15 Monastery of Poor Clares, Much Birch, MS *Aire Register*.

16 Evelinge translated N. de Soulfour's French version of Paleotti's Latin text: A.F. Allison and D.M. Rogers, *Contemporary Printed Literature of the English Counter-Reformation Between 1558 and 1640: An Annotated Catalogue* (Aldershot: Scolar Press, 1994), 2:29. Evelinge also wrote three MS poems, which I recently discovered in the Durham University Special Collections: a life of Saint Euphrosina and two Psalms (PCD MS 28). I intend to edit these poems for publication.

Yet Evelinge's melding of scholarship and Franciscan piety has resulted in critical neglect of these translations and their public agendas. Evelinge assumed an extreme modesty for the purpose of publishing, which has created serious bibliographical and critical issues. Evelinge published her translation of the *Rule* anonymously, and the title pages to her versions of Paleotti and Hendricq attribute the work to another Poor Clare at Gravelines: Magdalen of Saint Augustine (Catharine Bentley). Luke Wadding, a contemporary Franciscan bibliographer, nevertheless asserts that Evelinge translated all three works in an appendix to his bibliography of Franciscan authors:

> Catherine of Saint Magdalene, a Poor Clare of the English monastery at Aire, translated from French into the English language *The Life of her Foundress Saint Clare*, Douai by Martin Bogard, 1635, & *The Life of Blessed Catherine of Bologna*, and also *Some Declarations on the Rule of Saint Clare*, St. Omer.[17]

Many critics have accepted his attribution on the basis of the scholarly achievements mentioned in Evelinge's obituary and the *Aire Register*.[18] The obituary for Catherine Bentley, by contrast, gives no hint of literary ambitions, describing her as "vertuous, Charitable, and Devout."[19] This decision in Evelinge's favor raises the question of why Evelinge attributed them to Bentley in the first place. Both A.F. Allison and Olga Valbuena suggest that the two nuns may have collaborated.[20] Still, one would think that Wadding would have been aware of any collaboration, especially since Hendricq's work was a translation of Wadding's own *Annales ordinis minorum*. An avid bibliographer, Wadding would have probably paid special attention to a translation of his own work. Frans Korsten cites Evelinge's extreme youth, a point worth taking as she had only professed in 1620, a year before her first translation was published, while Bentley had been at Gravelines since 1610.[21] In addition, Claire Walker has argued that the misattribution of her first translation may be an attempt to mirror the extreme modesty of its subject

17 "Catharina à S. Magdalena Clarissa Monasterii Anglicani Æriae, transtulit è Gallico in Anglicum idioma Vitam suae Institutricis S. Clarae. Duaci apud Martinum Boggardan. 1635. & Vitam B. Catharine Bononiensis, nec non Declarationes aliquot in Regulam S. Clara. Audomari." Luke Wadding, *Scriptores Ordinis Minorum* (Rome, 1650), Fff1v, my translation.

18 A.F. Allison, "Franciscan Books in English, 1559–1640," *Biographical Studies, 1534–1829* 3, no. 1 (1955): 23.

19 Hunnybun, "Registers," 39. Also see Claire Walker, introductory note to *Elizabeth Evelinge III* (see n. 5), xi.

20 Allison, "Franciscan Books," 49; Olga Valbuena, introduction to Sister Magdalen Augustine, trans., *The History of the Angelical Virgin Glorious S. Clare* (Douay, 1635). *Renaissance Women Online*, Women Writers Project. Brown University. 12 May 2008 <www.wwp.brown.edu/rwoentry.html>.

21 Frans Korsten, introductory note to *Elizabeth Evelinge I* (see n. 5), x.

matter, Saint Catherine of Bologna.[22] I believe, however, that Evelinge's refusal of an authorial voice was most likely due to her own deep humility. As we have already seen, her obituary notes that Evelinge was "very austere to her self," and the *Aire Register* further describes her as "a rare mierour of profound humility."[23] Given Evelinge's reputation for extreme "Poverty," it seems that Evelinge probably refused to take public authorship of her work because it interfered with her own personal conception of the poverty appropriate to her order. Just as Saint Clare had advised her followers to give away all their worldly goods, so Evelinge divested herself of public ownership for her translations of Paleotti and Hendricq. While insiders like Wadding knew of her authorship, outsiders could have still associated the work with the English Poor Clares. Evelinge consequently could speak for her convent and order without violating her remarkably stringent modesty.

Unfortunately, Evelinge's efforts to comply with the humility of her order have resulted in scholarly neglect of her work. On a practical level, the uncertain attribution of these translations has long prevented scholarly discussion. Now that Evelinge's authorship has been generally accepted by her most recent editors, one stumbling block remains: Evelinge's dogged evasion of public authorship. Evelinge does not fit with the prevailing tendency in early modern women's studies to champion those women who actively resisted the patriarchal nature of their society. Many of the earliest scholars who worked to restore women to the canon privileged women who appeared to be quasi-feminists, claiming these women as forebearers of modern feminism. Catholic women who overtly challenged the status quo, such as Elizabeth Cary, have therefore garnered the most critical attention. However, Margaret Ezell has critiqued the limitations of this trend to valorize women who "have gone *our chosen way*": "What of those early women who went quite another way—their own ways—ways which we may not understand or perhaps with which we may not identify or sympathize?"[24] Evelinge's unusual approach to authorship provides a salutary example of how women went their own way. Post-Romantic paradigms of authorship may value the author's creation of an independent and identifiable voice, but Evelinge chose to obscure her voice with several gestures: anonymity, misattribution, and translation. Her denial of authorship befitted her piety, which clashed with any apparent flaunting of her literary accomplishments, and translation allowed her to portray herself as an anonymous entity limited to the cloister even as she publicly linked her house with Franciscan exemplars like Saint Clare, Saint Colette, and Saint Catherine of Bologna. Indeed, while translation has long been denigrated

[22] Walker, introductory note, xii.

[23] *Aire Register*. Walker also notes the "culture of self-abnegation" at Gravelines. Introductory note, xii.

[24] Margaret J.M. Ezell, "Re-Visioning the Restoration: Or, How to Stop Obscuring Early Women Writers," in *New Historical Literary Study: Essays on Reproducing Texts, Representing History*, ed. Jeffrey N. Cox and Larry J. Reynolds (Princeton, NJ: Princeton University Press, 1993), 143–4, her emphasis.

for its supposed subordination of women's voices, recent critics have drawn attention to women's use of translation for political and religious purposes.[25] As the remainder of this essay will show, Evelinge's early translations of Paleotti and the Colettine *Rule* advanced English Franciscanism, serving both her house at Gravelines and the English Franciscan community.[26] While a more traditional form of ascription would have impeded her spiritual progress, Evelinge's evasion of authorship facilitated both her spiritual and political goals: by obscuring her literary voice, she crafted a cloistered authorship that was compatible with her profession and allowed her a form of public speech with political applications.

Conflicts Over Franciscanism and Jesuitism at Gravelines

In the early 1620s, Elizabeth Evelinge published translations of Paleotti and the Colettine *Rule* in order to promote English Franciscanism at her convent and beyond. In doing so, Evelinge intervened in disputes over the roles of poverty and Franciscan jurisdiction at the Gravelines convent. Although the conflict over Franciscanism might appear to have been confined to Evelinge's cloister, it had larger repercussions for both English Franciscans and English Catholicism. The survival of Catholicism in England had depended on the arrival of missionary priests trained in Continental seminaries for English Catholics during the 1570s. Yet while the mission succeeded in preserving English Catholicism, its very success created a power struggle among regular and secular priests over control of the English church.[27] Each group of regular priests (any priest belonging to a religious order) advanced distinct spiritual modes that might strengthen their authority among the laity. As a result, spiritual modes like Jesuitism and Franciscanism gained a political symbolism highly relevant to the larger ongoing battle over the future of English Catholicism. Jesuitism in particular was fiercely debated within the Continental convents for Englishwomen, where many nuns were ardently devoted to Jesuit confessors. However, some contemporaries like Gertrude More of the Cambrai Benedictines felt that Ignatian spirituality was unsuitable for

---

25 For a classic version of the older argument, see Mary Ellen Lamb, "The Cooke Sisters: Attitudes toward Learned Women in the Renaissance," in *Silent But for the Word*, Hannay, 107–25. However, see Micheline White, "Renaissance Englishwomen and Religious Translation: The Case of Anne Lock's *Of the Markes of the Children of God* (1590)," *English Literary Renaissance* 29 (1999): 375–400, and Goodrich, *Early Modern Englishwomen*.

26 For a discussion of Evelinge's final translation, see Goodrich, *Early Modern Englishwomen*.

27 For the complex history of disputes over Jesuitism, see Arnold Pritchard, *Catholic Loyalism in Elizabethan England* (Chapel Hill: University of North Carolina, 1979). For considerations of the archpriest controversy and the Bishop of Chalcedon, see respectively Patrick McGrath, *Papists and Puritans under Elizabeth I* (London: Blandford Press, 1967); and A.F. Allison, "A Question of Jurisdiction: Richard Smith, Bishop of Chalcedon, and the Catholic Laity, 1625–31," *Recusant History* 16 (1982): 111–45.

convent life.[28] Seventeenth-century Ignatian modes aimed to stir the penitent to action, whether internal or external, through frequent confession, analysis of the conscience, discursive (meditative) prayer, and methodical set prayers that used all the senses to recreate pivotal biblical moments.[29] This activation of the will could conceivably conflict with the nuns' submission to a religious rule based on the subordination of the will, yet many nuns clung fiercely to their Jesuit confessors. While such matters might seem to belong to the confessional alone, the Continental convents had a special significance as emblems of English Catholicism, meaning that the nuns' piety could be read as endorsements of politically charged spiritual modes. Both Evelinge and the Franciscan friars therefore printed works that framed the Gravelines house as a symbol of English Franciscanism in order to aid the restoration of the English Province.

Such a publicity campaign was necessary because the Gravelines Poor Clares already had many strong ties to Jesuits. The convent had been established under Jesuit authority in 1608 as their monastic order had not yet been revived. Founder Mary Ward had relied on Jesuit assistance to find land as well as to form the initial group of sisters.[30] Ward herself was a firm supporter of Ignatian spirituality and left Gravelines in 1609 to found an uncloistered order of nuns with a philosophy of active service similar to Jesuit ideals: the Institute of the Blessed Virgin Mary. In the wake of Ward's departure, Jesuitism remained strong at the convent, which had relied on Jesuit confessors from the outset.[31] In addition, many of the nuns themselves had Jesuit connections. Second Abbess Clare Mary Ann (Elizabeth) Tyldesley, for example, had intended to join the Brussels Benedictines, notorious for their Jesuit leanings,[32] and contemporaries viewed the Gravelines convent as a haven for relatives of those involved in the Gunpowder Plot, a conspiracy tinged with Jesuit associations.[33] These links were bolstered by the dedication of several works to the convent by the Jesuit John Wilson; one such preface to Abbess Tyldesley mentioned "the many benefits I have receaved from your selfe, and your holy Family."[34] It nevertheless appears that many members of this "holy Family"

[28] More adopted the attitude of Augustine Baker, who remarked of Jesuit practices: "the exercises of those men cannot be trulie Contemplative and spirituall, nor they be internall and Contemplative livers: But their exercises and living must be in the active life." Augustine Baker, *The Life and Death of Dame Gertrude More*, ed. Ben Wekking (Salzburg: Institut für Anglistik und Amerikanistik, 2002), 66.

[29] Joseph De Guibert, *The Jesuits: Their Spiritual Doctrine and Practice*, trans. William J. Young (Chicago: Institute of Jesuit Sources with Loyola, 1964), 282.

[30] Hunnybun, "Registers," 25.

[31] Two such Jesuits were Father George and Father Roger Lea. The convent was also served by Irish Recollects. *Gravelines Chronicle*, 26, 142.

[32] Ibid., 14.

[33] Guilday, *English Catholic Refugees*, 297.

[34] John Wilson, epistle dedicatory to *The Practise of Christian Workes*, by Francisco de Borja, trans. John Wilson (London, 1620), *4r–*4v. Walker reads this moment as indicative of Tyldesley's Jesuit leanings. *Gender and Politics*, 115.

saw no conflict between Franciscanism and Jesuitism. As the *Gravelines Chronicle* records, Abbess Tyldesley played a leading role in founding a temporary friary at Gravelines in 1616 to aid the newly reconstituted English Franciscan friars:

> Reverend Mother Tildesly being a person of great courage thought it a work worthy of her labour, to advance the setting up of a house for English Friars as much importing the honour of God, the good & spiritual happiness of that convent & the benefit of her Country; & in order to its beginning she writt to all her friends in England, she employ'd all the power of those she knew in Flanders, she added unto it all the money she was able to give or procure from others for their building of their house at Douay, she procured members out of England to furnish it with, & was at a part of the charges of setling them therin, & many of them made their noviship upon her account & at her charges, & was professed in their Church.[35]

This account emphasizes the active nature of Tyldesley's "labour," which included networking for funds within England and Flanders, providing material assistance for the fledging friars herself ("upon her account & at her charges"), and locating suitable novices ("she procured members"). Clearly Tyldesley and her fellow nuns expected their pious works to have beneficial effects for their "Country" as well as their "convent," both of which would profit from revived Franciscan spirituality. While the Gravelines convent was at this point under Jesuit jurisdiction, the house still maintained a distinctly Franciscan character.

The convent's mixture of Franciscan and Ignatian spiritual modes only became a source of discord after the English Franciscan friars gained jurisdiction of the Gravelines convent in 1618.[36] The English Franciscan friars had dwindled greatly in number since Elizabeth abolished their order in 1559, but the early seventeenth century saw a resurgence of Franciscan spirituality.[37] Father William Staney, Superior of the English friars and a member of the Marian reconstitution of the order, hoped to revive the English Franciscan Province. In 1614 he received John Gennings into the order with the express aim of fulfilling that goal, and Gennings' enthusiasm inspired many promising young men to join the order, including Franciscus à Sancta Clara (Christopher Davenport). By 1616, Gennings had enough recruits to open a temporary friary in Gravelines, thanks to Tyldesley's aforementioned assistance. At the 1618 General Chapter, the Franciscans took the first steps toward recognizing an English province by naming Gennings Vicar of England and approving an English friary, Saint Bonaventure's College, in

---

35 *Gravelines Chronicle*, 142–3.

36 For Franciscan jurisdiction over the Poor Clares, see Francis Borgia Steck, *Franciscans and the Protestant Revolution in England* (Chicago: Franciscan Herald Press, 1920), 223–4, and Guilday, *English Catholic Refugees*, 302–6. For Sancta Clara's role, see John Berchmans Dockery, *Christopher Davenport, Friar and Diplomat* (London: Burns & Oates, 1960), 117.

37 Steck, *Franciscans*, 215.

Douai. At the same time, the English Franciscans gained jurisdiction of spiritual direction at the Poor Clare convent in Gravelines, and in 1619 they founded another Franciscan convent: a Third Order house at Brussels. The friars naturally viewed the Poor Clares at Gravelines as a source of spiritual authority that could help their efforts to restore the English Franciscan Province. Anthony Parkinson, a late seventeenth-century Franciscan historian, noted that the swelling numbers of the English Franciscans led to the reestablishment of the English Province in 1630: "The English Franciscans [were] now sufficiently numerous, … having a noviceship and schools of both philosophy and divinity, and also two convents of nuns under their obedience and direction."[38] However, the nuns at Gravelines were actually divided over their allegiance to Franciscan jurisdiction, and in 1626, Sancta Clara, who had benefited from Tyldesley's financial assistance, sought to eliminate Jesuit influence at the convent by deposing Tyldesley.[39] This action precipitated a final rift in 1629, leading to the establishment of a small group of pro-Franciscan nuns, including Evelinge and Bentley, at a new convent at Aire, where Evelinge composed her final translation.

During the first five years of Franciscan jurisdiction, however, Sancta Clara attempted to reclaim the convent's spirituality more subtly with a major publication that represented Gravelines as an exemplar of Franciscan piety. In 1618, Sancta Clara dedicated William Cape's translation of a text by Marcos da Silva, *The Chronicle and Institution of the Order of the Seraphicall Father S. Francis* (*STC* 11314.2), to the English Poor Clares. This expensive, 800-page folio edition invoked the Gravelines convent in order to legitimate English Franciscan spirituality and so promote the reinstatement of the English Franciscan Province.[40] Cape's translation consists of documents relating to the earliest Franciscan saints and martyrs, and Sancta Clara's preface to the reader makes clear the importance of returning to Franciscan roots: "the life and examples of the Frier Minors the especiall servantes of God … point out unto us the true rule and observance of the tree instituted by the said Father S. Francis, procuring many in these dayes to blush att their faultes and transgressions."[41] His emphasis on "the true rule and observance" of Franciscan piety indicates the importance of maintaining a Franciscanism undiluted by other spiritual modes, such as those of Jesuitism. Sancta Clara indicates that the Gravelines convent requested the translation of this material, implying that the English Poor Clares support his agenda of restoring Franciscanism: "Which earnest desire or longings it pleased you (Right worthyly Religious) to manifest

---

38 Qtd. in Thaddeus, *The Franciscans in England, 1600–1850* (London: Art and Book Company, 1898), 46.

39 According to the *Gravelines Chronicle*, "The Abbess [Tyldesley] had been at the chief expense of his education," 143.

40 Allison discusses the book's cost. "Franciscan Books," 47.

41 Franciscus à Sancta Clara, preface to *The Chronicle and Institution of the Order of the Seraphicall Father S. Francis*, by Marcos da Silva, trans. William Cape (Saint-Omer, 1618), C1v.

by your zealous importuninge me to prevayle with a third [Cape], that could and would undertake the Translation of this worke from French."[42] Since the nuns themselves have actively facilitated Cape's work (through their "earnest desire or longings" and "zealous importuninge"), they exemplify the original spirit of Franciscanism praised by Sancta Clara. He furthermore describes Cape as

> an extraordinary devote of your order, and particularly of your co[n]vent, whose will it also is that by reason you were only in cause of the Translation, & through your entreatie only it was provided for in the impression, that the whole volume of his labors shold be shadowed under your matronadge.[43]

Sancta Clara invokes Cape as a witness to the Poor Clares' interest in this translation, citing his intimacy with their "order" and "convent" as proof that the values of the translation coalesce with the spirituality of the Gravelines house. Cape's "impression" that his work will be protected by the "matronadge" of the Poor Clares suggests the translation is truly the spiritual child of their great piety, and by locating the nuns as the inspiration for this authoritative expression of Franciscan spirituality, he places their convent at the center of efforts to restore the Franciscan province.

Sancta Clara's dedication also heightens the reputation of the English Poor Clares as agents of spiritual conversion, a gesture emphasizing the political nature of Cape's translation. The convent's spiritual importance is evident from Sancta Clara's initial salutation: "To the most religious ensigne-bearers of S. Clare, the Englishe Poor Clares in Gravelinge, the author wisheth victorious triumph."[44] As "ensigne-bearers of S. Clare," the Poor Clares have a representative role as symbols of Franciscanism even as they participate in spiritual warfare against evil. The "victorious triumph" Sancta Clara mentions is probably the conversion of England, since contemporary Catholics viewed their spiritual struggles in England as part of a holy battle. The publication itself plays a role in this "triumph," as it will provide England with a model of spiritual renewal. Sancta Clara therefore urges the nuns to pray for the work's success: "Your office therefore in matronizinge [it], is but with your wonted simplicitie to offer the translatours labours to god almightie for successe."[45] Paradoxically, in order for the nuns to embody the humility of their order, they must show a "simplicitie" that might preempt any public acknowledgment of their role in authorizing this work. Sancta Clara therefore praises the nuns for their great modesty, which might cause them to deny any responsibility for inspiring Cape: "neyther lett the title of patronesses deterr you, as if it savoured of the world which ye have abrenunciated, or as if it did not correspond with your Religious simplicitie which ye have embraced; for the great affinitie of the worke with your truly simple dispositions, of it selfe did

---

42 Ibid., A2r.

43 Ibid.

44 Ibid.

45 Ibid., A2v.

challenge you."[46] Sancta Clara stresses the nuns' pious removal from the world ("abrenunciated"), linking it with the "Religious simplicitie" that is the hallmark of their order, and he enhances the Poor Clares' pious reputation even as he asserts that their modesty makes them reluctant "patronesses." This move brilliantly associates the nuns' renunciation of the world with their spiritual victory against the agents of English Protestantism. Sancta Clara suggests, moreover, that only Franciscanism can successfully restore English Catholicism and publicizes the newly revitalized English Franciscan friars by way of their newest sphere of influence, the Gravelines Poor Clares.

Evelinge's *The Admirable Life* and *Declarations* and Franciscan Revival

Elizabeth Evelinge's early translations were closely connected with Sancta Clara's efforts to bolster Franciscan spirituality inside the Gravelines convent and beyond.[47] Her rendition of Paleotti's *The Admirable Life of the Holy Virgin S. Catharine of Bologna* was directly applicable to simmering concerns over the spiritual jurisdiction of the Franciscan friars at Gravelines in that it addressed cloistered disputes over Franciscanism and monastic order experienced by Saint Catherine of Bologna (1413–1463). This text includes three sections: "The Admirable Life" (83–150), "Divers Miracles Wrought by S. Catharine" (151–92), and "The Admirable Instructions of S. Catharine" (193–394).[48] The first two sections are fairly standard hagiographic fare detailing Saint Catherine's exemplary life and the miracles performed after her death. The final treatise is Saint Catherine's own book of spiritual advice written for novices at her convent: *Le sette armi spirituali* (or *Libro devoto*). Not only does this text guide readers toward proper cloistered piety and monastic obedience, but it also serves as Saint Catherine's spiritual autobiography. The "Instructions" are the heart of *The Admirable Life*, testifying to Saint Catherine's unending fidelity to the Franciscan cause despite the obstacles she faced within her own convent.

As a result, Saint Catherine's "Instructions" likely provided the pro-Franciscan sisters at Gravelines with a model of resistance to monastic authority that was based in Franciscan spirituality. Although Saint Catherine's convent had originally begun as a loose-knit community of laywomen, a rich patroness named Verde Pio da Carpi transformed the group into a Poor Clare convent which her sister and niece could govern. This change left Saint Catherine with a great dilemma, because while she herself had always been drawn to Franciscanism, the community's leader

---

46 Ibid.

47 Walker notes the relationship of these translations to Cape's translation and the debate over Franciscan spirituality, but she does not discuss how these works reshape English Franciscanism. See Walker, introductory note, xvii.

48 Elizabeth Evelinge, trans., *The Admirable Life of the Holy Virgin S. Catherine of Bologna*, by Dionisio Paleotti (Saint-Omer, 1621) in *Elizabeth Evelinge III* (see n. 5). All parenthetical references are from this text.

vigorously opposed Carpi's alterations. Mary Martin McLaughlin reads *Le sette armi spirituali* as a submerged account of this conflict, in which Saint Catherine is torn between her own incipient Franciscanism and monastic obedience.[49] The treatise describes the convent as a place of spiritual warfare, where the nuns must be armed with seven devotional weapons to repel the devil in "the spirituall combat of Religious life" (347). Saint Catherine presents this battle as a perpetual struggle on behalf of Christ:

> whosoever undertaketh this Combat must not at any time lay aside his weapons, knowing that he fights agaynst enemyes that never sleepe, and that doe nothing but watch for advantage agaynst us. Go too then, let us march on with great fervour of spirit, let us with confidence and courage undaunted take into our handes these weapons to the prayse of Jesus Christ. (200)

This dramatic presentation of monastic life as a battle against Satan must have held great resonance for the English convent at Gravelines, considering that contemporaries like Sancta Clara portrayed their convent as a linchpin in the Catholic struggle against Protestant heresy within England. The translation may even have reminded the nuns of Sancta Clara's depiction of the Gravelines convent as full of "ensigne-bearers" from Christ's army. As a result, the "Combat" alluded to by Saint Catherine may have been read as an oblique comment on the need for "great fervour of spirit" to defeat the "enemyes" of Catholicism within their native country. *The Admirable Life* therefore appeals to the nuns' pre-existing reputation as conservers of English Catholicism and their interest in using piety as a spiritual "weapon" that could advance their battle on behalf of Catholicism.

Evelinge's translation also had an intra-Catholic partisan edge, since it presents Franciscanism as the best possible means of waging the battle against heresy. Saint Catherine's primary complaint against her superiors was their failure to adhere to the new Franciscan orientation of their convent: "the little account which they make of the observance of their Rules and Institution" (364). She faced spiritual temptations from the devil, who suggested that she resist Franciscanism by either obeying her superior or leaving the convent. Appearing as Christ, the devil urges, "take thy memory, understanding & will, & exercise them in nothing but according to the will of thy Superiour" (240). Although this call dovetails with monastic obedience, Saint Catherine finds "that she could not, because her hart was not in her power" (241). This inability to obey, a virtue for which Catherine was well known, suggests the rectitude of her Franciscan leanings and the corresponding fallibility of the superior's anti-Franciscanism. Such tension with superiors over the spiritual direction of the convent likely held special significance for the Gravelines Poor Clares, who were experiencing a similar discord over Franciscan jurisdiction. Indeed, when the conflict boiled over into open warfare in the 1620s,

[49] Mary Martin McLaughlin, "Creating and Recreating Communities of Women: The Case of Corpus Domini, Ferrara, 1406–1452," in *Sisters and Workers in the Middle Ages*, ed. Judith M. Bennett et al. (Chicago: University of Chicago Press, 1989), 261–88.

Abbess Tyldesley was a primary figure of opposition to the Franciscans supposedly in charge of the house. The final results of Saint Catherine's battle would perhaps have been read as authorization of the pro-Franciscan minority, which included Evelinge. Saint Catherine refuses to leave the convent, "with an assured hope that at the last it would be inclosed, and be agayne one day reduced to the Rule and Institute of S. Clare" (252), and the eventual imposition of Poor Clare rule on the convent legitimates her resistance. In addition to justifying a return to Franciscan origins, Saint Catherine authorizes limited opposition to superiors' wishes and so provides a model for those pro-Franciscan nuns at Gravelines who welcomed the spiritual jurisdiction of the friars as a return to the spirit of Saint Clare. In doing so, *The Admirable Life* suggests that the cloistered warfare over Franciscan spirituality was only part of a larger battle to reclaim English Catholicism, subtly urging the Poor Clares to take up Franciscan sentiment and disseminate it beyond their cloister.

The complex publication history of *The Admirable Life* reveals that Evelinge's translation also assisted Sancta Clara's larger effort to use the Gravelines convent to authorize Franciscan spirituality. The 1621 edition of *The Admirable Life* (*STC* 5350.7) was bound with a translation of the *Rule* of Saint Clare taken from William Cape's *Chronicle*. The 1622 edition (*STC* 5350) was a two-part volume, consisting of the 1621 edition plus a second volume with additional selections from Cape's *Chronicle*: the lives of Saint Clare, Saint Agnes of Bohemia, and Saint Agnes of Assisi, Clare's biological sister. These pairings of Evelinge's text with works edited by Sancta Clara suggest her shared interest in Sancta Clara's agenda of returning to the origins of Franciscanism. Because her translation of Paleotti was published with the *Rule* of Saint Clare, readers could infer the English Poor Clares' commitment to Franciscan spirituality. The accompanying *Rule* translated by Cape certainly presents Clare as an obedient daughter of Saint Francis: "And as in the beginning of her Conversion, she with her Sisters, vowed Obedience unto the most holy Father S. Francis: so in like sort doth she vow to observe the same Obedience inviolably unto all his successours. And the other Sisters are alwayes bound to obey the Succesours of the Holy Father S. Francis."[50] This message was only heightened by the 1622 edition's inclusion of texts detailing the lives of early female Franciscan saints. Saint Clare's biography underscored the link between the submission to Franciscans advocated by the *Rule* and the exemplary poverty of Saint Clare herself. Saint Agnes of Assisi was the first adherent of Clare's new order and helped spread the Poor Clares by establishing convents throughout Italy. As Cape's translation noted, Agnes also "planted … the observance and profession of Evangelicall poverty."[51] Saint Agnes of Bohemia was yet another contemporary of Clare, who established a monastery in Prague, where she "rigorously observ[ed]

50 William Cape, trans., *The Rule of the Holy Virgin S. Clare* (Saint-Omer, 1621) in *Elizabeth Evelinge III*, 8.

51 William Cape, trans., *The Life of the Glorious Virgin S. Clare*, by Marcos da Silva (Saint-Omer, 1622), 178.

the intention of the holy Father Saint Francis, & Saint Clare, in the vow of poverty, which is yet to this day in the same manner observed in the sayd Monastery."[52] Thanks to the context provided by these paratexts, we can assert that Evelinge's translation probably assisted the friars in hastening the restoration of the English Province; meanwhile, the pro-Franciscan nature of these accompanying texts heightened the text's ability to bolster the case of those nuns who supported Franciscan jurisdiction at Gravelines.

Evelinge's 1622 translation of Saint Colette's *Declarations and Ordinances* complemented her previous work by continuing to bolster Franciscan ideals. A natural corollary to the *Rule* of Saint Clare published with her previous translation, *Declarations* demonstrated Evelinge's continued interest in reviving the origins of Franciscan spirituality. The *Rule* of Saint Clare had called for the nuns of her order to embrace strict poverty (i.e., no ownership of property), a limitation that set the Poor Clares apart from other female monastic communities. However, this *Rule* applied only to Saint Clare's original convent at San Damiano.[53] As later Poor Clare communities were founded, popes allowed the new establishments to own shared property. Viewing communal ownership as a violation of the spirit of Saint Clare's *Rule*, Saint Colette (1381–1447) led a reformation of the order that reinstated strict poverty.[54] Saint Catherine of Bologna herself had been a vocal advocate of the Colettine reformation, and *The Admirable Life* describes her as "another S. Clare" for her vigorous devotion (116). Questions as to whether the Poor Clares should follow this stricture remained pressing during the early modern period. The Gravelines convent had been founded on the basis of communal ownership, but the *Gravelines Chronicle* records that Abbess Gough feared the Jesuit directors at Gravelines would require the convent to "take rents."[55] Gough's concerns indicate her own preference for the Colettine *Rule*, which expressly dictates that the nuns refuse "inheritances or rents."[56] Gough even authored a petition addressed to English Catholics asking for alms that would allow the convent "to observe their Rule in the strictest manner, which [meant] being to live on alms."[57] Because Gough's anxiety was well known at Gravelines, the printing of Evelinge's *Declarations* (which included the Colettine *Rule*) may have been construed within the community as a justification of the friars' spiritual rule and therefore probably intervened in rising friction over Jesuit spirituality at the convent.

---

52 Ibid., 210.

53 Jos Blom and Frans Blom, introductory note to *Elizabeth Evelinge II* (see n. 5), x–xiv.

54 Ibid., xii.

55 *Gravelines Chronicle*, 30. Walker usefully discusses the role of poverty at Gravelines and beyond in *Gender and Politics*, 84–6.

56 Elizabeth Evelinge, trans., *The Declarations and Ordinances Made Upon the Rule of our Holy Mother S. Clare* (Saint-Omer, 1622) in *Elizabeth Evelinge II*, 90. All further references to this text will be given parenthetically.

57 *Gravelines Chronicle*, 34.

This translation may have been intended to quell debate among the English Poor Clares by substantiating the spiritual authority of the friars. The Colettine *Rule* unequivocally states that the friars bear responsibility for the guidance of the Poor Clares: "the care and governement of them [Poor Clares] hath bin wholy, and in every respect committed unto the Generall and Provinciall-Ministers of the Friar Minors" (126). This control is justified by the subordinate position of Saint Clare in respect to Saint Francis, as she was his first female adherent. An accompanying endorsement of Colettine reformation makes this very point:

> the said devout Daughters present & to come [should] receave the said Statutes with great devotion ... knowing for certaine that by the observance of them (through the merits of the most glorious Father S. Francis, the founder of their holy Rule, and of the most worthy Virgin S. Clare, the first Plante of that most fruitfull field (to wit of the holy Religion) & most plentifully abounding in vertues) they shall obtaine the plentifull reward of eternall life. (6)

With its emphasis on the primacy of Saint Francis, "founder of their holy Rule," this text could be read as a legitimization of the authority of the Franciscans. The metaphor of Saint Clare as Francis's "first Plante" further suggests that the order of the Poor Clares itself is subject to the friars, the origin of Franciscanism. Most importantly, this passage could have been interpreted as providing spiritual justification for those sisters who followed the friars, since only by adhering to the statutes of the order can the sisters "obtaine the plentifull reward of eternall life." This text also includes a similar exhortation by Benignus à Genua, current General Minister of the Franciscans. Genua urges the Poor Clares to "keep before their eyes the holy Ghospell, the Rule which they have promised to God, the holy and laudable customes, the memorable examples of Saints of their Order, in particular of their founders" (145). In its privileging of Saint Francis as the true founder of the Poor Clares, Evelinge's translation helped enhance support for the friars within the community and subtly encouraged the convent to accommodate itself to its new place within the English Franciscan hierarchy.

Evelinge's translation of *The Declarations* was also an official expression of Franciscanism that heightened the order's respectability among English Catholics. By publishing her work anonymously, Evelinge was able to become the official voice of English Franciscanism, and in doing so, she gained agency as an endorser of the spiritual validity of her order. Genua had reauthorized Colette's composition on January 22, 1622, the same year that Evelinge published her work, suggesting that Franciscan authorities were involved in her translation (140). Indeed, Evelinge's translation was published before the Latin source text became public, suggesting that she may have had access to an early official copy.[58] As Evelinge either worked from this Latin text or a French rendition, her work was directly connected to Genua's official attempts to burnish the Franciscan order.[59] Since

[58] Blom and Blom, introductory note, xiv.

[59] Ibid., xiii–xiv.

Evelinge's translation addresses an English Catholic audience, her composition also supported the efforts of English Franciscans to bolster their spiritual reputation among their compatriots. While her work may have been anonymous, Luke Wadding's attribution of the translation to Evelinge suggests that the English Franciscan community—and perhaps their contacts—were well aware of her authorship. Among those in the know, Evelinge's profound humility probably only heightened the authority of her translation as a symbol of English Franciscanism.

The text itself testifies to the power of Franciscan spirituality through several texts added by Genua. A section on "The Perfections of the Rule" elaborates on the moral excellence of the Poor Clares, who embody obedience, poverty, chastity, humility, simplicity, and charity (153–7). Furthermore, "Prayse of the Rule" quotes Saint Francis on the spiritual efficacy of the Franciscan Rule: "It was the booke of life: the fruit of wisdom: the marrow of the Ghospell: the hope of health: the path of salvation: the ladder by which one ascendeth to heaven: the key of Paradise: and the pledge of Eternall Peace" (158). For those English Catholics concerned about their spiritual health, these promises of "salvation," "Paradise," and "Eternall Peace" may have been highly compelling reasons to join or provide financial support for the friars, Poor Clares, and Third Order. At the very least, Saint Francis' praise suggests that Franciscans have access to a special religious knowledge that guarantees them the "key of Paradise." Genua also appends texts documenting special privileges which Francis received, particularly a wide array of plenary indulgences for acts such as receiving the Eucharist on all feast days (162–3). As plenary indulgences removed all need for Purgatory for a specific sin, members of this order could reap great spiritual benefits in the hereafter for performing Catholic acts of devotion that might be almost impossible in England's hostile atmosphere. Despite her anonymity, Evelinge's work therefore advertises the merits of Franciscanism to promote her order among all English Catholics. Both of Evelinge's early translations seek to redress tension within the house while supporting Franciscan spirituality within England. In fact, these two aims were one and the same, as a unified convent would only heighten the spiritual legitimacy of the friars and help to restore the English Franciscan Province. This restoration had an even higher goal, the reclamation of England as a Catholic nation, making Evelinge's intervention in monastic warfare a skirmish within the larger battle faced by all English Catholics.

Elizabeth Evelinge contributed substantially to contemporary efforts to restore English Franciscanism and to reclaim England as a Catholic nation. Evelinge's *The Admirable Life* probably even influenced the scholarly piety of the Cambrai Benedictines, since Baker included it in a list of books "most helping toward Contemplation."[60] Yet Evelinge's self-effacing modesty, though consonant with the

---

[60] Baker recommends "The Lives of St Clare and St Cath[erine] of Bologna in one tome." Augustine Baker, *A Catalogue of Such English Books as Are in This House Most Helping Toward Contemplation.* Beinecke Rare Book and Manuscript Library, MS Osborn b. 268, p. 254. The 1622 edition of Evelinge's *The Admirable Life* was the only publication

humility of her order, has allowed her work to be overlooked. Focusing on those Catholic women who were in obvious places of power, critics have concentrated on women associated with the English court, such as Henrietta Maria and Elizabeth Cary. Cary has proved particularly attractive, perhaps because her religious and literary works subverted patriarchal paradigms. Besides flagrantly converting to Catholicism and separating from her husband, Cary composed original works that appear to bear out the rebelliousness of her religious defiance: *The Tragedy of Mariam* and *The History of the Life, Reign, and Death of Edward II*. Although Cary's translation of Jacques Davy Du Perron was equally, if not more, subversive than her original works, only now have scholars begun to discuss this work.[61] The only early modern nun to receive comparable attention is Mary Ward, another potent symbol of female rebellion.[62] Ward's attempt to establish a female version of Jesuitism, the IBVM, was quashed by male contemporaries who found the uncloistered nature of this new order unsuitable for women. Cary and Ward both dared to raise identifiably female voices that challenged the constraints of their times. A writer like Evelinge, who assumed a quasi-anonymous voice rooted in the cloister, may pale in comparison with these defiant women. However, closer scrutiny of Evelinge's translations reveals that women could be highly subversive even when taking up an anonymous voice. The Gravelines cloister was a political battlefield, full of public significance for the future of the larger English Catholic community, and Evelinge challenged her monastic superiors by crafting a literary voice that took up Sancta Clara's cause. The relevance of her voice was ensured by its apparent privacy, which signaled Evelinge's undeniable spiritual authenticity. The early works translated by Evelinge are therefore not just important for their ability to shed light on the role of learning at English convents beyond the Cambrai Benedictines, but also for their capacity to transform our understanding of how women reshaped the conventions of verbal chastity expected by their contemporaries. For Evelinge, anonymity and misattribution were not just coy means of evading the "stigma of print" or limitations on women's public speech, but rather expressions of a profound humility that legitimated the resurgence of English Franciscanism.

---

to package both lives together. Baker also lists the work in "A Catalogue of some printed bookes that I have in this house," suggesting he owned it himself. Ibid., 250.

[61] Karen L. Nelson, "'To Informe Thee Aright': Translating Du Perron for English Religious Debates," in *The Literary Career and Legacy of Elizabeth Cary, 1613–1680*, ed. Heather Wolfe (New York: Palgrave Macmillan, 2007), 147–63.

[62] Margaret Mary Littlehales, *Mary Ward: Pilgrim and Mystic, 1585–1645* (Tunbridge Wells, Kent: Burns & Oates, 1998).

Chapter 5
Lady Anne Clifford and the Uses of Christian Warfare

Julie Crawford

Despite John Donne's purported claim that she "knew well how to discourse of all things, from Predestination to Slea-silk,"[1] Lady Anne Clifford is not known for her religiosity. Yet religious texts, as they did for most early modern book collectors, made up a large part of her library, and she mentions reading them and, as I will argue in this essay, making strategic use of them throughout her diaries. Anne Clifford seems to have been in practice a "Prayer Book Protestant."[2] Her conventional will attests to her wish "to dye a true childe of the Church of England and a professor of the true orthodox faith and religion established and maintained in that church in which myselfe was borne, bred and educated by my blessed mother," and her secretary recounts that she was a by-the-Book Protestant in her household practice.[3] Yet, as I argue here, Clifford's often public and performative use of religious texts was concerned with her battle to inherit the Clifford family property—a battle that pitted her against her husband and many influential members of the court, including the king himself—and thus also attests to a particular kind of religious and political alignment.[4] My point here is not to

[1] Edward Rainbowe, *A Sermon Preached at the Funeral of the Right Honorable Anne Countess of Pembroke, Dorset and Montgomery* .... (London, 1677), 39.

[2] The term is Judith Maltby's, see *Prayer Book and People in Elizabethan and Early Stuart England* (Cambridge: Cambridge University Press, 1998).

[3] The will is cited in George C. Williamson, *Lady Anne Clifford, Countess of Dorset, Pembroke and Montgomery, 1590–1676: Her Life, Letters, and Work* (Kendal: Titus Wilson and Son, 1923), 465. The discussion of her religious practice is from George Sedgwick, "A Summary or Memorial of My Own Life, Written by Me, December 10, 1682," in *The History and Antiquities of the Counties of Westmorland and Cumberland*, ed. Joseph Nicholson and Richard Burn. 2 vols. (London, 1777) 1: 302: "the psalms of David appointed for the day she constantly read, and had three or four chapters read to her by some of her women daily. She and her family received the sacrament at least four times in the year; and if she removed to some other of her houses, then also with a sermon. She had in the worst of times the liturgy of the church of England duly in her own private chapel." See also Rainbowe's discussion of her faithfulness to the Church of England during the Civil War. *A Sermon*, 57–60.

[4] Briefly, against entail, Clifford's father left the Clifford family lands in the north of England to his brother. She and her mother fought for them as Clifford's rightful inheritance for years, and in the negotiations she was pressed, by her husband but also by the king himself, to give up her claims for a cash settlement. For the details of the case, see

deny that Clifford was interested in religion or concerned about her own salvation, but rather to suggest the extent to which she used her religious reading for other ends.[5] In considering Clifford's use of religious books as part of her dynastic and political negotiations, I illustrate the ways in which textual conversations, particularly those associated with religious and political factions and movements, could be unmoored from personal belief and associated instead with positions of resistance. Clifford's reading suggests that religious texts could be used for a range of what we might call parareligious uses, particularly as they pertained to negotiations of political power.

In the period in which Clifford was writing and reading, most religious texts, including sermons and interpretations of scripture, had polemical purposes. Religious texts were associated with the battle over faith, both between and among confessions, and with the battle for the collective and individual soul. And reading of all kinds, as Anthony Grafton, Lisa Jardine, and William Sherman have shown, was frequently undertaken in the service of specific ends, such as providing political advice, or preparing for disputation.[6] People read, as Sherman puts it, "to direct themselves in courses of action."[7] I want to argue here that Anne Clifford deploys her reading of religious texts not only in the service of her own politicized strategy of resistance and possession, but also as a means of publicly signaling

---

Mary Chan and Nancy E. Wright, "Marriage, Identity, and the Pursuit of Property in Seventeenth-Century England: The Cases of Anne Clifford and Elizabeth Wiseman," in *Women, Property, and the Letters of the Law in Early Modern England*, ed. Nancy E. Wright, Margaret W. Ferguson, and A.R. Buck (Toronto: University of Toronto Press, 2004), 162–82; Katherine O. Acheson, introduction to Anne Clifford, *The Memoir of 1603 and The Diary of 1616–1619*, ed. Katherine O. Acheson (Peterborough, ON: Broadview Press, 2007), 9–34; and Chapter 3 in Richard T. Spence, *Lady Anne Clifford: Countess of Pembroke, Dorset and Montgomery (1590–1676)* (Stroud: Sutton Publishing, 1997).

5 Some of Clifford's religious reading was immediately religiously purposeful. After she spent most of Good Friday 1617 "in hearing Kate Buxton read the Bible and a book of Preparation to the Sacrament" she received communion on Easter Sunday. Anne Clifford, *The Memoir of 1603 and The Diary of 1616–1619*, ed. Acheson (see n. 4), 129. All subsequent references to the diary will be from this edition and will be cited parenthetically in the text. Yet even here Clifford positions both reading and sacrament in a fraught context: after she and her Lord received communion from Mr. Ran, she writes, they "had a great falling out." Her final note in the entry, "all this time I wore my white satin gown and my white waistcoat" (131), is, like her "worthy" sacramental preparation, a public sign of her righteousness in the face of oppression.

6 See Lisa Jardine and Anthony Grafton, "'Studied for Action': How Gabriel Harvey Read His Livy," *Past and Present* 129 (1990): 30–78, and Lisa Jardine and William H. Sherman, "Pragmatic Readers: Knowledge Transactions and Scholarly Services in Late Elizabethan England," in *Religion, Culture, and Society in Early Modern Britain: Essays in Honour of Patrick Collinson*, ed. Anthony Fletcher and Peter Roberts (Cambridge: Cambridge University Press, 1994), 102–24.

7 William H. Sherman, *John Dee: The Politics of Reading and Writing in the English Renaissance* (Amherst: University of Massachusetts Press, 1995), 65.

her agenda to those around her, including those who would read her diary.[8] Her reading, like her actions, was grounded less in private or selfish concerns than in a providentially righteous sense of her land rights (as we will see, "Exodus" features prominently in her reading), and in a textually informed, divinely understood resistance to the coercion of those she frequently called her "enemies."[9]

Above all, Clifford's use of religious texts illuminates the extent to which she saw Christian providentialism as the vindicating logic of her battle for her land, and, implicitly, for her political rights. When a preacher came to talk with her on January 30, 1617, for example, Clifford records that he "told me that now they began to think at London that I had done well in not referring this business [about the land dispute] to the King and that everybody said God had a hand in it" (117). While her reading of religious texts is thus a form of holding hands with God, it is also a record of opposition to the king and alignment with a set of reading and interpretive practices associated simultaneously with aristocratic privilege and godly resistance. It was, in short, a political practice.

In reading religious texts, Clifford was thus not merely passing her time in the "typical" (and somehow apolitical) pursuits of an English gentlewoman, nor was she advertising her Christian or wifely submission.[10] Intensely dialogic and

8 On the diary as genre rather than private expression, see Aaron Kunin, "From the Desk of Anne Clifford," *English Literary History* 71, no. 3 (2004): 587–608. On Clifford's diary as a public, testatory document, see Susan Wiseman, "Knowing Her Place: Anne Clifford and the Politics of Retreat," in *Textures of Renaissance Knowledge*, ed. Philippa Berry and Margaret Tudeau-Clayton (Manchester, UK: Manchester University Press, 2003), 199–221, and Acheson: "the diary survives because of the legal conflicts that Clifford wanted to document for the future uses of her family members and herself" (26). Nancy E. Wright's work on Clifford's account books also suggests that the diaries were meant as public records, "Accounting for a Life: The Household Accounts of Lady Anne Clifford," in *Early Modern Autobiography: Theories, Genres, Practices*, ed. Ronald Bedford, Lloyd Davis, and Philippa Kelly (Ann Arbor: University of Michigan Press, 2006), 245. There is no surviving original version of the diary, either in Clifford's hand or that of one of her secretaries. See Acheson, introduction, 36–38.

9 See, for example, 14 February 1617. Anne Clifford, *The Diaries of Lady Anne Clifford*, ed. D.J.H. Clifford (Phoenix Mill, UK: Sutton Publishing, 1990), 119.

10 For the claim that "women's reading ever re-inscribed them within domestic circumstances and spaces," see the introduction to *Reading, Society and Politics in Early Modern England*, ed. Kevin Sharpe and Steven N. Zwicker (Cambridge: Cambridge University Press, 2003), 13. Assertions about the "leisure" (i.e., non-political nature) of women's reading are frequently made without any evidentiary support. In an important essay on an early woman book collector, Paul Morgan assumes that Frances Wolfreston had books because "she enjoyed relaxing with them." See "Frances Wolfreston and 'Hor Bouks': A Seventeenth Century Woman Book-Collector," *The Library*, 6th Ser., 11 (1989): 210. David Cressy describes gentlewomen readers as "privileged women whose literacy was a social ornament," *Literacy and the Social Order: Reading and Writing in Tudor and Stuart England* (Cambridge: Cambridge University Press, 1980), 128. For a critique of such generalizations about women's reading, see Sasha Roberts, "Shakespeare 'Creepes

contentious, Clifford's frequent co-reading with her minister was neither private and personal, nor a sign of subordination.[11] Rather, she was gleaning precepts for action, sharpening her skills through adversarial engagement with her texts, and using her reading to announce and buttress her position as an embattled but resolute landowner. Scholars are now starting to look at the marginal annotations that mark the pages of Clifford's books,[12] and it's no coincidence that these comments were often political in nature, signaling, among other things, her criticism of and resistance to the government and policies of James I.[13] The reading Clifford records in her diary serves a similar set of purposes, providing providentialist reassurance through narratives of resolution, resistance, and eschatological vindication.

The title of this essay is taken from John Downham's *The Christian Warfare* (1604), a text aimed, in its own words, "to arm the Christian against the temptations of 'our spiritual enemies,'"[14] and one of the texts featured in the first panel of the "Great Picture," an 18-by-9-foot triptych portrait scholars have rightly seen as Clifford's *summa*: a record of her history as a literate Christian woman

---

into the Womens Closets about Bedtime': Women Reading in a Room of their Own," in *Renaissance Configurations: Voices/Bodies/Spaces, 1580–1690*, ed. Gordon McMullan (New York: St. Martin's Press, 1998), 30–63.

[11] I make this point at greater length in "Reconsidering Early Modern Women's Reading, or How Margaret Hoby Read Her De Mornay," *Huntington Library Quarterly* 73, no. 2 (2010): 193–223.

[12] See, for example, Stephen Orgel, "Marginal Maternity: Reading Lady Anne Clifford's *A Mirror for Magistrates*," in *Printing and Parenting in Early Modern England*, ed. Douglas A. Brooks (Aldershot: Ashgate, 2005), 267–89. Orgel discusses an annotation Clifford made to a 1610 copy of the *Mirror for Magistrates* in the 1670s, and suggests that her annotation "celebrates her heroic ancestry, chronicles her days, and serves as the receptacle of her memory" (285). Williamson writes about Clifford's copy of St. Francis de Sales's *Introduction to a Devout Life* (1648) in *Clifford*, 527; and H.R. Woudhuysen comments on the marginalia in Clifford's copy of the 1605 folio of Sidney's works in *Sir Philip Sidney and the Circulation of Manuscripts, 1558–1640* (Oxford: Clarendon Press, 1996), 274.

[13] Wiseman draws attention to Clifford's marginalia in the Kendal Record Office copy of James Anthony Weldon, *The Court and Character of King James* (London, 1650/1). Beside an unflattering description of the king, Clifford wrote "a right description of King James." Wiseman, "Knowing Her Place," 217, n. 61. See also the notes in Clifford's copy of John Barclay's *Barclay His Argenis, Or, The Loves of Poliarchos and Argenis* (1625), a topical romance set against the backdrop of early modern European politics. As Heidi Brayman Hackel notes, Clifford "seems to have been drawn to insights about troubles and Fortune, bidding sayings about Fortune to be underlined and endorsing in her own hand as 'Most true' … 'Many of us are sicke of Kings diseases in our private fortune: wee are Kings to our Suppliants; and againe, hee is a King to us, who hath that in his power for which wee begge.'" *Reading Material in Early Modern England: Print, Gender, and Literacy* (Cambridge: Cambridge University Press, 2005), 238.

[14] The quotation is from P.S. Seaver, 'Downham, John (1571–1652)', *ODNB* (see Chapter 1, n. 14) (accessed March 2008).

vindicated in her long-fought-for status as a great landholder.[15] While Clifford does not discuss reading *The Christian Warfare* in her 1616–19 diary, she does mention reading a wide range of other religious texts, placing them in dialogue or juxtaposition with the marital and courtly battles in which she was engaged.[16]

---

15 On the portrait, see Graham Parry, "The Great Picture of Lady Anne Clifford," in *Art and Patronage in the Caroline Court: Essays in Honour of Sir Oliver Millar*, ed. David Howarth (Cambridge: Cambridge University Press, 1993), 202–19, and Chapter 10 in Spence, *Clifford*. An inscription in the central section states that the work was commissioned by Lady Anne Clifford in 1646. Parry, "Great Picture," 202. The first panel represents a teenage Clifford, the middle, her parents Margaret and George Clifford, Countess and Earl of Cumberland with their two sons (and Anne *in utero*), and the last, a middle-aged Clifford, after her inheritance of the family properties. Most critics attribute the painting to Jan van Belcamp. The following list of the books featured in the Great Picture is from Williamson, *Clifford*, 340–45. See also Spence's list, *Clifford*, 190–91, and Parry's discussion of the featured books, *passim*. The central panel features three books in folio: the Bible, Seneca's works (Thomas Lodge's 1614 translation) and a manuscript book of a medical character. In the left panel, featuring Clifford as a girl, are Camden's *Britannia*, Ortelius's "Map of the World," Cornelius Agrippa's *Vanity of Science*, *Don Quixote*, three volumes of the *French Academy* by Peter de La Primaudaye, Hoby's translation of Castiglione's *Courtier*, Godfrey of Boloigne, *The Variety of Things* by Loys de Roy, *The Chronicle of England in Prose* by Samuel Daniel (her tutor), Montaigne's *Essays*, Gerard's *Herbal*, Sidney's *Arcadia*, Spenser's *Works*, Ovid's *Metamorphoses*, the Bible, Augustine's *City of God*, Eusebius's *History of the Church*, the works of Dr. J. Hall, *The Manual of Epictetus*, *The Philosophical Comforts* of Boethius, the works in verse of Samuel Daniel, Downham's *Christian Warfare*, the works of Du Bartas, and the works of Chaucer. In the right picture, featuring Clifford as heiress and dowager, she rests her hand on two books on a table: Charron's *Book of Wisdom*, translated out of French into English, and the Holy Bible. Above her head are two disordered shelves of books on which appear George Strode's "Booke of Death" (*Anatomy of Morality*), Plutarch's *Lives* and *Morals*, "An apology for the Power and Providence of God" by Hakewill, Gurcherdine's [Guicciardini] French History, the works of Sir Fulke Greville, Sir Henry Wotton's *Booke of Architecture*, George Sandy's verse translation of the Psalms, Philip de Comines in English, Henry More's *A Map of Mortality*, Ben Jonson's *Works*, Donne's *Poems*, Cuffe's *Ages of Man's Life*, George Herbert's *The Temple*, John Barclay's *Argenis*, *The Meditations* of Antoninus (Causabon's translation, 1635), the *Meditations* of William Austin, Donne's *Sermons*, John King's *Sermons* and Marcellinus's *Roman Historie* translated into English by Philemon Holland.

16 The books and papers Clifford mentions reading in the 1616–19 diary are the following: A "prayer book" (19 April 1616, 77); "a great part of the History of the Netherlands" (with Mr. Dumbell, 31 October 1616, 59); Montaigne's *Essays* (read by Rivers and Marsh, 09 November 1616, 99; by Rivers 28 January 1617, 117); "Mr Sandys his Book [...] about the Government of the Turks" (read to her, 9 January 1617, 109–111); Spenser's *The Faerie Queene* (read by Moll Neville, 28 January 1617, 117); the Bible (read to by Mr. Ran, 24, 26, 27 February 1617, 121); "the Chronicles [her family books]" (by herself, February 1617, 121; 29 December 1619, 189); Exodus (with Mr. Ran, 8 March 1617, 123); Leviticus (with Mr. Ran, 13 March, 1617, 123); "Old Testament" and Deuteronomy (with Mr. Ran, 27 March, 1617, 125); "the Bible & a book of the Preparation to the Sacrament [William Bradshaw, *A preparation to the receiving of the sacrament*, 5th ed. (1615)]"

Anne Clifford's diary, I want to suggest, can be read as the record of a strategic form of Christian warfare, an account in which Clifford and divine providence resolutely fight the forces that would crush her. Thus rather than seeing the fact that she owned and read texts by radical Protestants as well as by Church of England conformists as confusing, I see it as instructive. Even when they lost, as was the case with George Hakewill and Henry Cuffe, whose books are featured in the "Great Picture," puritans and controversialists were *combatants*.[17] The presence of their work in her self-presentation suggests that, at least to some extent, Clifford used their strategies and positions to formulate and enact her own.

I have argued elsewhere that Clifford works hard to present herself—in direct contrast to her profligate and sycophantic courtier husband—as a certain type of country aristocrat: learned, country-house dwelling, godly.[18] This representation was intimately related not only to her land claims, but to a larger political agenda of resistance to an absolutist monarch, an attempt to reground political authority not only in the land but in the families who owned it. Her consistent pursuit of, and then identification with, the titles "Baroness Clifford, Westmorland and Vescy, Lady of the Honor of Skipton in Craven and High Sheriffess of Westmoreland," which she eventually obtained in 1643, was thus more than mere vainglory. Mary Ellen Lamb has argued that Clifford's uses of (primarily literary) authors gave

---

(18 April 1617, Good Friday, 129); Chaucer and Sandys's "Turkish History" (26 April 1617, 131); Sidney's *Arcadia* (by Moll Neville, 12 and 13 August 1617, 145); "my Lady's great trunk of papers [...] full of writings of Craven and Westmorland and other affairs with certain letters of her friends and many papers of Philosophy" (read to "pass the time," marginal note next to entries for January 1619, 156); Augustine's *City of God* (by Wat Conniston, 10 February 1619, 159; marginal note that they finished 10 March 1619, 162); "the Kings book upon the Lords Prayer which was dedicated to my Lord of Buckingham" (by Conniston, margin 13 February 1619, 158); "my Ladies book in the praise of Solitary Life" (17 March 1619, 163); "compared the two books of the Cliffords that Mr Knisden [an antiquary employed by Margaret in the research undertaken to support their legal claims] sent me down" (18 March, 1619, 163); "made an end of reading the bible over which was my Lady my mother's" (begun 1st of February, finished 20 March 1619, 163); "Mr Sarragolls booke of the Supplication of Saints" (read by Wat Conniston, 24 March 1619, 163); Ovid's *Metamorphoses* (read by her cousin Mary, week of 6th June, 1619, 179); "Parsons resolution & Burneys resolution" (read by cousin Mary, margin of entry for 30 June 1619, 180); "I paid Mr Give 10 pieces upon his return from Jerusalem who told me much news from Rome, Naples and other Places" (11 September 1619, 182); "sea papers upon my father's voyages" (read by Sir Francis Slingsby, 24 November 1619, 187); "Leicesters Commonwealth" (2 December 1619, 187); and "the book of Josephus" (by Wat Conniston, 14 December 1619, 189).

[17] See P.E. McCullough, "Hakewill, George (1578–1649)," *ODNB*. On Cuffe's fall via the Earl of Essex, see Paul E.J. Hammer, "Cuffe, Henry (1562/3–1601)," *ODNB*. While his status as a combatant was primarily political, Hammer points out that Cuffe was described as a 'purytan' by one of his enemies in 1601. Downham was also something of a controversialist; see Seaver, "Downham, John," *ODNB*.

[18] "The Case of Lady Anne Clifford; Or, Did Women Have a Mixed Monarchy?" *PMLA* 121.5 (October 2006): 1682–89.

her an ancestral, vertical set of authorities in which to ground her land claims, and Susan Wiseman has brilliantly highlighted the extent to which the primarily antiquarian and chorographical books she displays in her portrait suggest her creation of a "principality" in Westmoreland.[19] I want to argue that her relationship with the scriptural and religious texts I discuss in this essay was *active*—they were living texts, rather than merely part of an authoritative, grounding past—and that a key part of this was their association with specific positions of resistance and resolution. If, as William Sherman argues, libraries were "of the utmost importance in the government of an empire," they were equally important in the government, and acquisition, of a dynasty.[20]

The Promised Land and the City of God

In her diary, Clifford frequently associates her reading of religious texts with her land case. On April 19, 1616, after telling her husband Richard Sackville, Earl of Dorset, that she "would not stand to this Award of the Judges what misery soever it brought me to," she writes that "[a]bout this time I used to rise early in the morning and go to the standing in the garden and taking my prayer book with me and beseech God to be merciful towards me and to help me in this as He hath always done" (77). In this account, her prayer book functions simultaneously as spiritual support and public sign, testifying to her Christian patience and resilience in the face of oppression.[21] Clifford's reading of the Old Testament functions in a similarly pointed way. On March 8, 1617, Clifford writes that she "made an end of Exodus with Mr Ran," and a few days later reports finishing Leviticus (123). In the Book of Common Prayer, neither Exodus nor Leviticus is the suggested text for March.[22] Her reading, then, as Peter Stallybrass suggests was true of most biblical reading in the period, is best characterized as "random access for specific purposes": a choice to read particular books because of their application to one's own situation.[23] Indeed, in the margin next to the entry for Leviticus, Clifford notes

---

19 Mary Ellen Lamb, "The Agency of the Split Subject: Lady Anne Clifford and the Uses of Reading," *English Literary Renaissance* 22, no. 3 (1992): 347–68, and Wiseman, "Knowing her Place."

20 Sherman, *John Dee*, 78.

21 Indeed carrying one's prayer book around as a sign of one's righteousness was something of a commonplace. In *The Merchant of Venice*, the playboy Gratiano promises Bassanio that when he goes on a wooing mission to Belmont he will "wear prayer books in [his] pocket," *The Merchant of Venice*, ed. Leah S. Marcus (Norton, 2006), 2.2.175.

22 *The Book of Common Prayer, 1559: The Elizabethan Prayer Book*, ed. John E. Booty (Charlottesville: Published for the Folger Shakespeare Library by the University Press of Virginia, 1976), 38.

23 Peter Stallybrass, "Books and Scrolls: Navigating the Bible," in *Books and Readers in Early Modern England: Material Studies*, ed. Jennifer Andersen and Elizabeth Sauer (Philadelphia: University of Pennsylvania Press, 2002), 46.

that the next day her uncle and cousin came to Dorset House to see her husband "where he and they signed and sealed the writings and made a final conclusion of my business and did what they could to cut me off from my right." She, on the other hand, "referred [her] cause to God" (122), identifying a providentialist, promised-land faith wholly in keeping with the specific content of her bible reading.

The most interesting diary entry on the Old Testament reading, however, occurs on March 27. After she records (once again) fighting with her husband, Clifford writes that later on the same day "my Lord found me reading with Mr Ran and told me that it would hinder his study very much so as I must leave off reading the Old Testament until I can get somebody to read it with me" (125). While Clifford explicitly ignores his advice—"This day I made an end of reading Deuteronomy" is her next note—it is the contradiction I find interesting: she clearly *was* reading with someone—Mr. Ran, her minister—and it thus seems that Dorset was objecting less to the reading of scripture *per se* than to the particular *type* of reading his wife was doing.[24] The fact that she repeatedly associates her intently sequential Old Testament reading—the progression from the chosen people's dispossession to their attainment of the promised land—with her own land dispute suggests that Dorset might well have done so too, and thus that he recognized her reading as part of their ongoing battle.[25] The day after Clifford records finishing Deuteronomy she writes of hoping that things may be "the better hereafter for me and my child knowing that God often brings things to pass by contrary means" (127), a paraphrase of Deuteronomy 23:5.

Indeed it is not, I think, coincidental that in 1676, long after these events, Clifford remembers the land case "which spit out a great deal of trouble to us" in light of the promises of Deuteronomy 23:5 "the Lord thy God would not hearken unto Balaam but the Lord thy God turned the curse into a blessing unto thee, because the Lord thy God loved thee."[26] Indeed in a life marked by scriptural

---

24 Williamson suggests that he wanted her to find someone "who perhaps had a quieter voice than Mr. Ran," and he surmises that "Mr Ran" might be the Rev. Edward Randes who was the rector of Hartfield, a Sackville living, in 1622. *Clifford*, 114, 111, n. 48.

25 Clifford expresses consistent interest in the Holy Land, reading Sandys's "Government of the Turks," the highlight of which is the journey to the Holy Land (111, n. 13), and, on one intriguing occasion in February 1617, paying seven pounds for information about Jerusalem (119), and on another, in September 1619, paying one "Mr Give 10 pieces upon his return from Jerusalem who told me much news from Rome, Naples, and other places" (182).

26 "I remembered how this day was 60 years [since] I and my blessed Mother in Brougham Castle in Westmorland, where wee then lay, give in our answer in writing that we would not stand to the Award the then four chief Judges meant to make concerning the lands of mine Inheritance, which did spit out a great deal of trouble to us, yet God turned it for the best." Cited in Sharon Cadman Seelig, *Autobiography and Gender in Early Modern Literature: Reading Women's Lives, 1600–1680* (Cambridge: Cambridge University Press, 2006), 71, and Williamson, *Clifford*, 280.

tags from the Hebrew Bible,[27] Deuteronomy 23:5 seems to have been one of her favorites. It is referenced in the caption of the first panel in the "Great Picture" in a discussion of the meeting between Clifford and James I "wherin God gave hir grace to deny that King to yeld or consent to that award, which was the means that preserved the Lands of hir Inheritance to hir, and disposeing by the mercifull providence of Allmighty God"; when she records a fight with her husband over the land case; and when she writes of being delivered from her enemies during her widowhood, "for without the merciful power of God, it had bene impossible for mee to have escaped them."[28] The fact that she associates this book, chapter and verse, so consistently with the land case, suggests that her husband knew the specific purpose behind her "random access" of the books of the Old Testament most clearly associated with promised land.

The polemical use of the Old Testament idea of the promised land was not, of course, peculiar to Clifford. The providence that Clifford so explicitly relied on was a guiding belief system for many early modern people, and it was frequently based on a typological similitude between ancient Israel and England.[29] Clifford seems to have picked up on the frequently promulgated idea of a "Heavenly Contract" between God and the English nation as the new Israel for her own political purposes.[30] The concept of the heavenly contract relied simultaneously on the immutability of the Lord's "eternal and unchangeable" Deuteronomic decree, and the necessity of "perpetual, purposeful action, with direct and dynamic government of the terrestrial realm," a combination exemplified in each of Clifford's resolute accounts of her land battle.[31]

---

[27] Each of the castles she restored after finally taking possession of her property, to take a notable example, was given a plaque bearing a quotation from Isaiah 58:12. See *Diaries*, D.J.H. Clifford, 101.

[28] The first citation is from Williamson, *Clifford*, 496; the second is from Williamson, 270, "I remembered how this day was 52 years, in the withdrawing Room Chamber at Knowle House in Kent as we satt at dinner, had my first Lord and I a great falling out, when but the day before I came from London, from being Godmother to his Brother's youngest son. Deut. C. 23, v. 5: Nevertheless the Lord thy God would not hearken unto Balaam but the Lord thy God turned the curse into a Blessing, because the Lord thy God loveth thee." The last is from Clifford's account of the year 1652; see *Diaries*, D.J.H. Clifford, 114.

[29] Patrick Collinson, *The Birthpangs of Protestant England: Religious and Cultural Change in the Sixteenth and Seventeenth Centuries* (New York: St. Martin's Press, 1988), 7. See also Christopher Hill, *The English Bible and the Seventeenth-Century Revolution* (New York: Penguin, 1993), especially Chapter 11; Patrick Collinson, "Biblical Rhetoric: The English Nation and National Sentiment in the Prophetic Mode," in *Religion and Culture in Renaissance England*, ed. Claire McEachern and Debora Shuger (Cambridge: Cambridge University Press, 1997); 15–45; and Alexandra Walsham, *Providence in Early Modern England* (Oxford: Oxford University Press, 1999), Chapter 6.

[30] Hill, *English Bible*, 265. See also David Zaret, *The Heavenly Contract: Ideology and Organization in Pre-Revolutionary Puritanism* (Chicago: Chicago University Press, 1985).

[31] Walsham, *Providence*, 9, 10.

The concept of England as an elect Nation, moreover, did not necessarily apply to the entirety of the English nation.[32] The distinction between the nation of Israel and the chosen people *within* Israel was likely key to Clifford's own providentialist convictions. If preachers used the idea of a godly minority for what Collinson calls "immediate pastoral advantage," Clifford used it for immediate pastoral advantage of another kind: accruing the divine status as chosen and elect to herself, and thus, by extension, applying the logic of the promised land to her own much-sought-after land.[33] If the idea of the promised land was used to legitimate the colonization of Virginia and Ireland, it makes perfect sense that it could be used as the vindicating logic for a land claim within England itself.[34]

The idea of a chosen or godly minority as the rightful inheritors of the promised land was also central to Clifford's understanding. The Geneva Bible glossed Deuteronomic promises as specific to the godly: "a precious people unto himself, above all the people that are upon the earth" (Deut. 14:2). Their self-identification as the chosen or elect may help to explain Clifford's interest in puritan writers. The idea of election allowed those identified as a minority to feel a sense of superiority,[35] and Clifford consistently assumed a minoritized position in relation to the court, the church, the law, and her husband's familial and political connections. Indeed, as Christopher Hill and Patrick Collinson suggest, the idea of the English as God's people was—or could be—a way of resisting the king; in the Old Testament paradigm, neither the nation nor God himself was ever on good terms with the institution of monarchy for very long.[36] Clifford's excision of her promised land from the jurisdiction of the king, in fact, counters James's much-promulgated theory of the divine right of kings with one of the divine right of aristocrats, dependent, not coincidentally, on the logic and argumentative labors of a godly minority. The fact that the labors of this godly minority were often supported by her family is less a coincidence for Clifford than a history devoutly to be claimed.[37]

After her minister, Clifford's most frequent co-reader was her attendant Wat Conniston, who read her a wide range of works in early 1619, including "the Kings book upon the Lords Prayer which was dedicated to my Lord of Buckingham,"

---

32 Collinson, *Birthpangs*, 20.

33 Ibid., 21.

34 Hill, *English Bible*, 269. In 1616 John Rolphe, Secretary to the Virginia Company, attributed to Sir Thomas Dale the view that the English were "'a peculiar people marked and chosen by the finger of God' to possess North America." Ibid., 270.

35 Collinson, "Biblical Rhetoric," 27.

36 Ibid., 26. Collinson relies heavily on Hill, "The Protestant Nation," in *Collected Essays of Christopher Hill, Volume Two: Religion and Politics in 17th Century England* (Amherst: University of Massachusetts Press, 1986).

37 Clifford's mother and her aunt, Anne Dudley, Countess of Warwick (1548/9–1604), were prominent courtiers under Elizabeth and zealous puritans. Both women are featured in the Great Picture and are discussed further below.

"Mr Saragoll's book of the Supplication of Saints which my Lord gave me," and Augustine's *City of God* (159, 158, 163).[38] In her entries on her reading with Wat Conniston, Clifford refers frequently to another Conniston. The same day that "Wat Conniston began to read St. Austin" to her, Clifford tells us, she "received a Letter from M. Davys with another enclosed in it of Ralph Conniston, whereby I perceived things went in Westmorland as I would have them" (159). Ralph Conniston had been a servant in her mother's employ and was now an executor of her will and working on Clifford's behalf in the north.[39] Similarly, after she mentions Wat Conniston reading her "Leicester's Common Wealth" and beginning the "Book of Josephus" (not only an account of the oppression of God's chosen people, but the source for Elizabeth Cary's antityrannical and protofeminist play *The Tragedy of Mariam*, published a few years earlier), Clifford writes that she signed a "Letter of Attorney for Ralph Conniston to receive those debts which were due to my Lady [her mother] of the tenants" (187, 189).[40] "[T]his day," she continues, "Ralph Conniston went away towards his journey into the north. After supper my Lord and I had a great falling out, he saying that if ever my Land came to me, I should assure it as he would have me" (189). Clifford makes it clear the reading she does with Wat Conniston is contextually associated with the Clifford properties in which the Conniston family was involved, both historically and in the present, on her behalf. *The City of God*, like the Old Testament, thus figures prominently in her reading during a period of the land battle concerned with her legal rights to the northern properties and with her husband's attempts to control the terms of those rights.

The 1610 edition of the *City of God*, dedicated to William Herbert, Earl of Pembroke (Mary Sidney Herbert's son, Anne Clifford's relative on her mother's side, and the chief puritan factor in James's court), was a godly text. Not only did *De Civitate Dei* offer an unimpeachable argument for the distinction between the City of God and the earthly and corrupt City of Man—an endlessly deployable justification for religious and political resistance—but it had more recent polemical purchase in the form of political advice. In his sixteenth-century edition of Augustine's *City of God*, Juan Luis Vives draws an analogy between the church father and the king of England: he argues that both Augustine and Henry VIII

38 These three books are: James I, *A Meditation upon the Lords Prayer* (1619), Thomas Sorocold, *Supplication of saints. A booke of prayers: divided into three parts ... Wherein are three most excellent prayers made by the late famous Queene Elizabeth* (1612, 1616, 1619) and St. Augustine, *Of the citie of God with the learned comments of Io. Lod. Vives. Englished by I.H.* [John Healey] (1610).

39 "Raiphe Coniston" was a servant of Margaret Clifford's and one of the executors of her will. Williamson, *Clifford*, 458. Acheson also notes that Wat Conniston is listed in the Knole catalogue as an attendant to Anne Clifford (89, n. 61). See also Williamson for letters and details about Ralph Conniston serving as Clifford's agent (148–50).

40 The purpose of the pro-Catholic anti-puritan authors of *Leicester's Commonwealth* "had been to defame Robert Dudley Earl of Leicester, Queen Elizabeth's favourite and the leader of the Puritan cause in his private as well as his public life." Spence, *Clifford*, 71.

endeavored to defend the "better Rome" against Babylon.[41] Yet Augustine did not believe that the City of God could be found on earth or that one could fruitfully think of the monarch as analogous to God on earth or even as a means of reaching God. Augustine thus rejected on principle any adulation of the state or the ruler. Many critics of monarchical power therefore cited *The City of God* to distinguish between the eternal lord and a temporal one, and *The City of God*, somewhat surprisingly for a "Catholic" book, became a favored text of the puritans.

As Mark Vessey has shown, a number of the agents involved in the production of Healey's 1610 edition were also involved in the Virginia Company.[42] Extant neo-Imperial readings of *The City of God* in a time of colonial expansion—not unlike those of the Old Testament and the "promised land"—lead him to ask whether *The City of God* "should be added to the list of works drawn up by John Parker under the title of Books to Build An Empire?"[43] Given Clifford's intent reading of this enormous book with Wat Conniston—they finish it in less than a month—it seems likely that its lessons in (resistant) empire building and in attending to the ruling ethos of the City of God rather than that of Man (and King) were ones that Clifford applied, much like her reading of the Old Testament, directly to her own situation. Contemporary godly uses of *The City of God* were clearly analogous to contemporary godly uses of Old Testament narratives of the chosen people and promised land: both sought to excise the middlemen that stood between Christians and their God; both believed in an ultimately vindicating eschatological frame; and both insisted—and this, I believe, is key for Clifford—that no Christian had single citizenship in either the promised land or the City of God. The Christian, in other words, had civic obligations as well, and for Clifford, these were being effected with the help of the Connistons who, not coincidentally, were reading *The City of God* as they were drawing up the very terms of Anne Clifford's civic existence.

Resolution

In a diary entry for June 1619, Anne Clifford notes ruefully that "my Lord received the last payment of my portion" from the cousin who had inherited the land that she believed was rightfully hers (179). In a marginal note added later, Clifford points out that "about this time my cousin Mary made an end of reading Parson's resolution and Burneys resolution all over to me" (180). These texts were staples of religious reading: Robert Persons's Catholic text and Edmund Bunny's Protestantizing of

---

41 Åke Bergvall, *Augustinian Perspectives in the Renaissance* (Uppsala: Uppsala University Press, 2001), 170.

42 Mark Vessey, "*The Citie of God* (1610) and the London Virginia Company," in *History, Apocalypse, and the Secular Imagination: New Essays on Augustine's City of God*, ed. Mark Vessey, Karla Pollmann, and Allan D. Fitzgerald (Charlottesville, VA: Philosophy Documentation Center, 1999), 257–81.

43 Ibid., 273.

it symbolized the tensions as well as the affinities between the two religions.[44] Clifford explicitly identifies the texts as "resolution[s]" and clearly associates reading them with her land case. As the most recent editor of the text discusses, the distinguishing characteristic of *The First Booke of the Christian Exercise Appertayning to Resolution* "is its rhetorical disposition." "In concentrating the reader's mind on a single, crucial choice," he continues, "Persons adopted the form of a deliberative oration—a speech designed to persuade the audience to a certain course of action."[45] The Catholic Persons, moreover, intended the book to reinforce the missionary campaign against compromise. In his correspondence he consistently linked resolution with recusancy, and he later explained that the *Resolution* was meant "to encourage Catholics to patience and firm resolve to bear the present persecution" at the hands of their enemies.[46] The Protestant Bunny, in turn, determined both to claim those recusants for the Protestant faith and to steer the Protestant reader away from acts of penance to "painful labour in his vocation."[47] Both writers, in other words, saw their works as training manuals in the confessionally appropriate arts of perseverance and resolution.

Resolution, as the term's various definitions attest, refers not only to the solving of a doubt or the settlement of a dispute, but, more broadly, to confidence and conviction. The two *OED* definitions that seem most relevant to my discussion of Clifford's particular investments in the *Resolution* are "firmness or steadiness of purpose; unyielding temper," and "A formal decision, determination, or expression of opinion, on the part of a deliberative assembly or other meeting." If Clifford's divinely mandated sense of purpose is everywhere present in her diary, she also seems to have read her texts as a means of formalizing and expressing that determination. While her co-readings may not have been official deliberative assemblies or meetings, they nonetheless served the purpose of buttressing her resolution to keep fighting for her property rights with firmness and steadiness of purpose.

Indeed both the concept of resolution and the term itself were central to Margaret and Anne Clifford's presentation of their battle. In 1615, Margaret Clifford wrote to her daughter encouraging her to "keep your resolutions with silence and what

---

44 The Jesuit Robert Persons published *The First Booke of the Christian Exercise, Appertayning to Resolution* in 1582; it was popularly known as *The Christian Directory*. The text received its Protestant refashioning by Edmund Bunny in 1584, and 18 editions of Bunny's *A Booke of Christian Exercise, appertaining to Resolution, by R.P. Perused and accompanied now with a Treatise tending to Pacification* appeared by 1589. See Victor Houliston, introduction to *Robert Persons SJ: The Christian Directory (1582): The First Booke of the Christian Exercise, Appertayning to Resolution*, ed. Victor Houliston (Leiden: Brill, 1998), and Brad S. Gregory, "The 'True and Zealouse Service of God': Robert Parsons, Edmund Bunny, and *The First Booke of the Christian Exercise*," *Journal of Ecclesiastical History* 45.2 (1994): 238–68.

45 Houliston, *Robert Persons*, xxxviii.

46 Ibid., xix.

47 Ibid., xxiv.

gentle persuasion you can, but alter not from your own wise course."[48] On January 18, 1617, Clifford herself wrote in her diary that although her husband sometimes "used fair means and persuasions, and sometimes foul means," she was nonetheless "resolved before so as nothing would move" her (111). Clifford's language is in fact similar to that of Bunny's *Resolution.* Bunny's encouragement of the reader's "painful labour in his vocation" includes chapters on "Difficulty or hardness, which seemeth to be in virtuous life" and "Persecution, affliction, and tribulation." "An Advertisement to the Reader" ends with a plea to let us "be myndfull to praye for our persecutors: who finallie will prove to be our best freendes: being in deed the hammers which beate and polish us, for making us fytt stones, for the building of Gods new Jerusalem in heaven," a providential language in which Clifford was, as we have seen, intently invested.[49] Later, in May 1617, she writes that although she sees "how much my Lord is offended with me and that my enemies have the upper hand of me," she is "resolved to take all patiently casting all [her] care upon God" (135).[50] Indeed Bishop Rainbowe picked up on this as the defining characteristic of her life when he praised Clifford in her funeral sermon for her "constancy, wisdom, and resolution."[51] Resolution, in other words, was a kind of family heraldry, a key word for Clifford determination and resistance. It is also, not coincidentally, a key term of political opposition. Clifford's co-reading of the Persons/Bunny *Resolutions* was training in spiritual, rhetorical, and political resolution. While in the immediate context it was geared towards her lineal property rights, it was also a part of a larger political strategy of perseverance and opposition grounded *in* such property rights.[52] If Clifford was eventually able to become, as one observer put it,

[48] Cited in Barbara Kiefer Lewalski, *Writing Women in Jacobean England* (Cambridge, MA: Harvard University Press, 1993), 135.

[49] Edmund Bunny, *A Booke of Christian Exercise* .... (London, 1584), 4. Clifford wrote that her mother died "Christianly and willingly, often repeating a little before her death, that she desired to be dissolved and to be ... in the Heavenly Jerusalem." Williamson, *Clifford*, 95.

[50] Clifford also uses the term in describing a July 1617 visit from Lady Wotton, post hunt, in which "she stayed not above an hour in regard she saw I was so resolutely determined not to part with Westmoreland" (141). The tenor, moreover, of many of her entries, reflect this divinely mandated resolution. On April 5, 1617, she writes that "sometimes I had fair words from [Dorset] and sometimes foul but I took all patiently and did strive to give him as much content and assurance of my love as I could possibly yet I always told him that I would never part with Westmorland upon any condition whatsoever" (127).

[51] Cited in Lewalski, *Writing Women*, 134. She was, he writes, "absolute Mistris of her *Self*, her *Resolutions*, *Actions*, and *Time.*" Rainbowe, *A Sermon*, 53. Earlier, Rainbowe writes that she was "very constant to all her determinations ... She used, as she said, to chew the Chud, ruminating of the next days business in her night wakings. When she had once weighted the Circumstances, and resolved; she did not like to have any after considerations, or be moved by them" (45).

[52] As Spence points out, the battle between Clifford and her husband was seen not only as a battle of wills, but as a political battle. When Samuel Daniel wrote to Countess

"as absolute in [her home] borough as any are in any other," when she inherited her estates in the 1640s, it was through a resolute resistance to the absolutist tendencies of the monarch and based in the ownership of vast properties.[53]

"[M]y Lady my mother's" Books and the Practices of Christian Neo-Stoicism

The person with whom Clifford most frequently associated specific texts was her mother, Margaret Clifford, Countess of Cumberland, her greatest champion in the land case. On subsequent days in March 1619, in the midst of battles with her husband over "releasing her thirds" (relinquishing her rights to the land and providing him with cash), Clifford "made an end of my Lady's book in the praise of a Solitary Life" (a text dedicated to her mother), "compared the 2 [manuscript] books of the Cliffords that [her antiquarian] Mr Knisden sent me down," and "made an end of reading the bible over which was my Lady my mother's" (163).[54] All of these texts were, in a range of senses, her mother's, and Clifford clearly sees both the history of these texts and her possession of them as vindicating evidence for her rightful inheritance of the Clifford properties.

Her mother's Bible is, in fact, featured in the central portrait of the "Great Picture," in a triad of books that includes a manuscript of alchemical writings and Seneca's *Works* (see Fig. 5.1). Indeed it is difficult to imagine a better emblem for the hopes of the Christian Stoicism–driven godly activism of the 1580s and 1590s to which Margaret Clifford and her sisters—all of whom are represented in the "Great Picture"—devoted so much energy. Yet there is also a fourth book in the picture. In her left hand, which is posed above her belly,

Margaret saying that Dorset with "Resolution & Wilfullness" intended to take the portion and sacrifice Anne's inheritance as the judges' award allowed," he counseled that Anne should "endure the Storms that may come from an angry husband with Patience & sufferance." Spence, *Clifford*, 65. As Spence puts it, "there is in Daniel's intervention a whiff of oppositionism, from a faction embracing the Countess, her daughter and friends and their queen's circle" (65). The language of Stoicism, as we'll see shortly, was often the language of resistance to arbitrary monarchical privilege.

53 After Clifford had finally inherited the Clifford property and took control of appointing MPs for her region, a local agent warned an interloper about that resolve: "Unless you can be able to fix my Lady for you, which I fear will be hard to do, you'll have a cold appearance of the electors of Appleby, since I am informed they dare not go any way but that which is chalked them out by my Lady, she is (I believe) as absolute in that borough as any are in any other." Cited in Williamson, *Clifford*, 296. As another letter puts it "To move the Countess in anything that is averse to her own resolutions (as Sir Philip Musgrave can tell you) would not only be labour in vain, but even a prejudice to those should press it to her," and still another, "if my Lady continues still her resolutions for some of her own relations, it's probable she will prevail in what she's resolved upon." Ibid., 299.

54 Her mother's Bible was clearly of the greatest importance to Clifford. The household accounts for 1675 record her payment "for new binding an old bible that was my Mother's Margaret Countesse of Cumberland's." Cited in Wright, "Accounting for a Life," 242.

the Countess of Cumberland holds a small book of Psalms. The inscription in the portrait revealing Anne Clifford's presence *in utero* in this panel highlights the providentialism of Anne Clifford's place in the dynastic storyline.[55] I would add, moreover, that Margaret Clifford's hands-on presentation of the Psalms cites another powerful woman, aligned, like Margaret Clifford and her sisters, with the Protestant activism of the late Elizabethan era. The famous Simon de Passe portrait of Mary Sidney Herbert (Fig. 5.2) also features "Davids *Psalmes*," whose translation and circulation was associated with the cause of international Protestantism and its criticism of monarchical stonewalling.[56]

Indeed when Mary Sidney Herbert advised the Queen in the dedicatory poem that was to be sent to her with the Psalms to "doo what men may sing," she was encouraging both a more active commitment to the Protestant cause in France and the Low Countries, and the rights of the singers—here the Sidney faction—to provide advice to princes.[57] Much like the historical books of the Old Testament, in other words, the Psalms became anthems for the elect and a form of defense against their oppressors.

It thus should not come as much of a surprise that Anne Clifford makes use of the Psalms in her writings in much the same way as she does of the first books of the Old Testament. (This is true despite, or in addition to, the fact that her secretary claimed she always read them out "on the appointed day.")[58] Suzanne Trill and Sharon Cadman Seelig have highlighted the extent to which Clifford aligned her own genealogy and experience with that of the Israelites in the Psalms, appropriating the discourse of the Psalms so that it "truly applied unto [her self]."[59] The passages in the Psalms to which Clifford most frequently refers celebrate

---

55 See Hackel, *Reading Material*, 225 and n. 102. Anne Clifford in fact tells a story related to her mother's pregnancy that involves her inheritance. Margaret Clifford "was the rather induced to believe [that Anne would inherit the lands] by reason of a strange kind of divine dream or vision, that appeared to her in a fearfull manner in Barden Tower in Craven, when she was great with child … which told her she should be delivered a little after of a daughter which should be the only child to her parents and live to inherit the antient lands of her father's ancestors; which after proved to be true." Cited in Eve Rachel Sanders, *Gender and Literacy on Stage in Early Modern England* (Cambridge: Cambridge University Press, 1998), 195.

56 On the Sidney psalms, see Margaret P. Hannay, "'Princes you as men must dy': Genevan Advice to Monarchs in the *Psalmes* of Mary Sidney," *English Literary Renaissance* 19.1 (1989): 22–41.

57 See the "Dedicatory Poem in the Tixall Manuscript of the Psalmes," in *Collected Works*, Hannay, Kinnamon, and Brennan, 1:102–4. The citation is from the last line of the poem, line 96.

58 Sedgwick, "A Summary," 302.

59 Suzanne Trill, "'Speaking to God in his Phrase and Word': Women's Use of the Psalms in Early Modern England," in *The Nature of Religious Language: A Colloquium*, ed. Stanley E. Porter (London: Sheffield Academic Press, 1996), 277–8. See also Seelig, *Autobiography*.

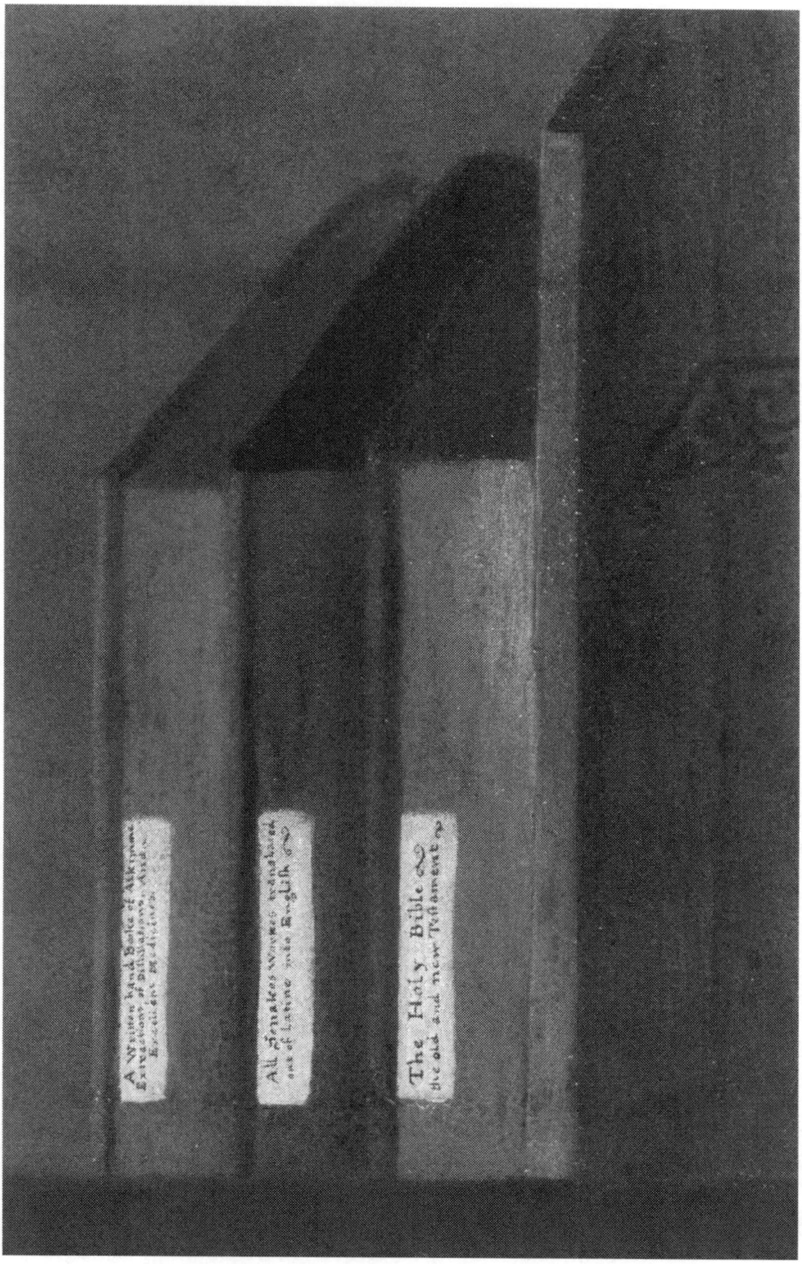

Fig. 5.1 Detail from "The Great Picture," attributed to Jan van Belcamp. Reproduced by courtesy of Abbot Hall Art Gallery, Kendal, Cumbria. © Lakeland Arts Trust.

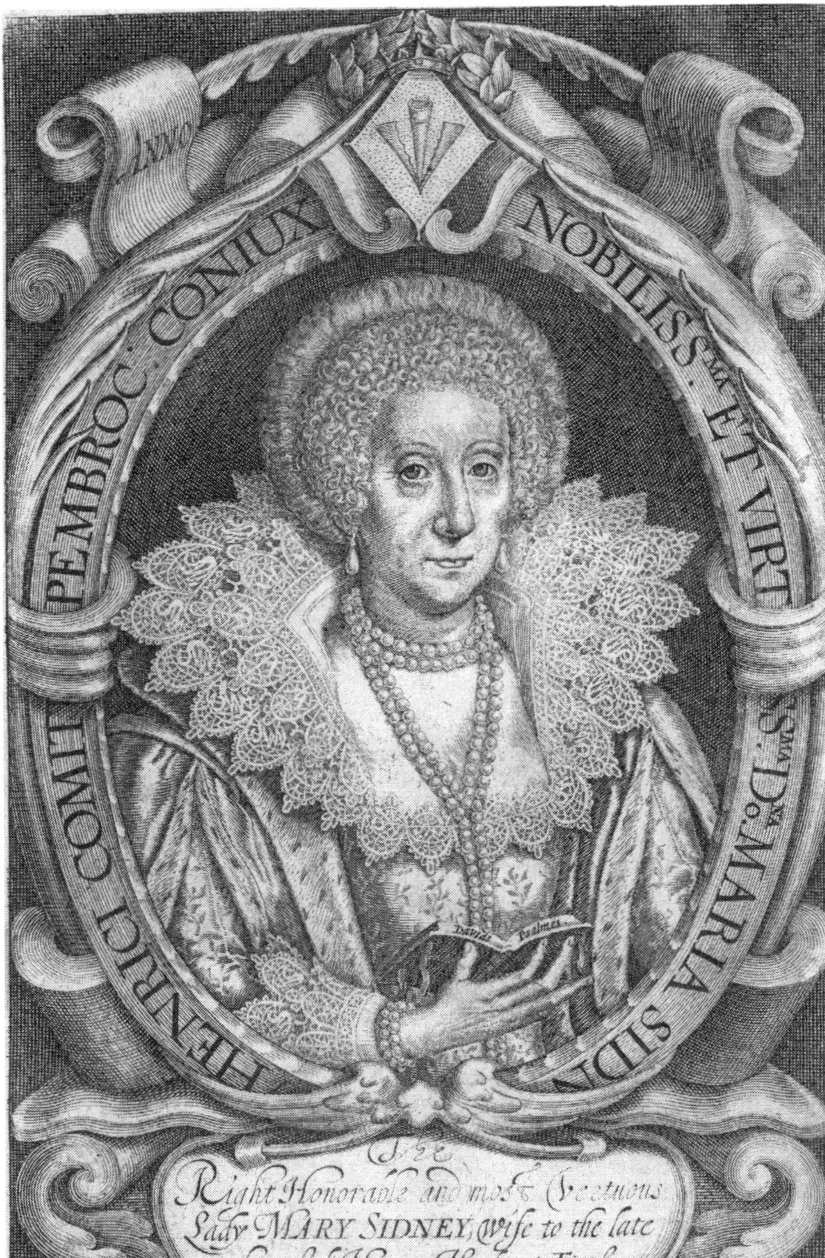

Fig. 5.2 Simon de Passe, Portrait of Mary Sidney Herbert, Countess of Pembroke. Reproduced by permission of the National Portrait Gallery, London.

deliverance from a time of travail ("images of the Israelites wandering in the wilderness or enduring the Babylonian captivity"), and stress God's love for the "righteous" for whom he will provide just reward; passages, in other words, which strike Clifford as applicable to her own situation.[60]

The Psalm verse Clifford uses most frequently in later discussions, particularly when writing about her desire that her own children (and their children) should inherit the property that she fought so hard to attain, is Psalm 16.6: "The Lot is fallen unto mee in a pleasant place. I have a fair Heritage."[61] In fact, Clifford explicitly asks her heirs to apply this verse to themselves, and follows it with the following lines: "And I may truly say that here: From many Noble Progenitors I hold / Transmitted Lands, Castles and Honours, which they sway'd of old."[62] Like Deuteronomy 25:3, in other words, the Psalms speak directly to Clifford's attainment of a promise. In full circle, it is her mother who most helped her attain this promise and thus it is her mother with whom Clifford most frequently associates her readings of the Psalms. In particular, she singles out her mother's role in bringing the divine favor promised in Psalm 41 into Clifford's own life: "All which Benefitts have been bestowen upon mee for the heavenly goodness of my Deare Mother, whose fervent prayers were offered upp with greater zeale to Almighty God for mee and mine, and had such return of Blessings followed them, as that though I mett with some bitter and Wicked Enemies and many greate oppositions in this world, yet were my Deliverance so greate, as would not befall to any who were not visibly susteyned by a Divine favour from above. / Ps. 41."[63] As Trill points out, Clifford's reference to Psalm 41, defined by Théodore de Bèze as a Psalm of praise and a source of comfort for those beset by traitors, not only serves to justify her position and praise God for her deliverance, but also associates her Psalm reading with the traditions of godly resistance—here that of the French Huguenots—with which women like her mother had associated themselves.

The other book that Clifford most clearly identifies with her mother, "my Lady's book in the praise of a Solitary Life" (163) was, despite its rather misleading title, no text of privatized feminine piety.[64] It was compiled for Margaret Clifford by her kinsman—and fellow political player—Sir John Harington from a range of

---

60 Seelig, *Autobiography*, 61.

61 *Diaries*, D.J.H. Clifford, 102. See also Trill, "Speaking," 277.

62 These lines are cited from Clifford's account of the year 1651. *Diaries*, D.J.H. Clifford, 112.

63 Ibid. See also Trill, "Speaking," 279–80.

64 Appendix II in Spence is "A Catalogue of the Books in the Closset in the Passage Room next the Pantry in Skipton Castle 28th August 1739." It includes the following item: "The Praise of Private Life, a folio Manuscript." Spence, *Clifford*, 257. This text is included in *The Letters and Epigrams of Sir John Harington Together with The Prayse of Private Life*, ed. Norman McClure (Philadelphia: University of Pennsylvania Press, 1930). Samuel Daniel presented it to Margaret Clifford. Spence, *Clifford*, 45. Based on Petrarch's *De Vita Solitaria*, the manuscript includes citations from Horace, Virgil, Cicero, and Seneca.

Petrarchan, Senecan and neo-Stoic texts, the cornerstones of a political discourse which James himself recognized as resistant to the extension of arbitrary monarchical power and thus as a vehicle of dissent.[65] Wiseman has argued that Clifford's careful presentation of her mother and aunts in the triptych "highlights kinship connected with the Elizabethan court" and resistant to that of the Stuarts.[66] She also argues that Clifford's display of books asserts her ambitions, making the link between virtue and stoic self-discipline and the "architecturally and chorographically articulated claim to a kind of private Princehood."[67] I have already pointed to the suggestiveness of the inclusion of Henry Cuffe on these shelves, a man known, most notoriously, for his role in Essex's rebellion and his particularly virulent form of "study[ing] for action." But I would also draw attention to the key texts of Roman history included on the shelves, not least Plutarch's *Lives* and *Morals* in French, and to the factional entrenchments of the other authors: Greville, for example, was her aunt's godson and a key advocate of the Sidney cause; and Guicciardini and de Commines, continental source texts for thinking outside of absolutist models of rule, were standard reading of the Sidney faction.[68] In addition to highlighting the fact that women, like men, "studied for action"—indeed, at one point Clifford thanks her secretary for his collection of "sayings out of Antoninus and Seneca,"[69] both of which are also featured on her bookshelf in the "Great Picture"—Anne Clifford's active reading list blazons her alignment with a cause. This is true even as she uses it—and its key religious texts—less for the pursuit of a religious cause *per se* than for its collateral concern with limiting, and providing the grounds of resistance to, monarchical power.

It is thus illustrative that Clifford's own pose in the final portrait mimics that of her mother in the central portrait (see Fig. 5.3). Clifford's hand lies upon

---

65 J.H.M. Salmon, "Stoicism and Roman Example: Seneca and Tacitus in Jacobean England," *Journal of the History of Ideas* 50, no. 2 (1989): 199–225. On Harington, see Spence, *Clifford*, 71.

66 Wiseman, "Knowing Her Place," 212–13. Her mother, Margaret Russell, was the daughter of the puritan second Earl of Bedford, and her aunt, under whom she had her chief breeding, was the puritan courtier Anne Russell Dudley, Countess of Warwick (herself known for her extensive and often coercive reading). See Lewalski, *Writing Women*, 137. Wiseman argues that Clifford's use of political language even in the early diary "offers strong evidence that Clifford sees herself and invites her reader to see her, in the highly politicized contexts of the law and the contrast between the Elizabethan and Jacobean courts." *Conspiracy and Virtue: Women, Writing, and Politics in Seventeenth Century England* (Oxford: Oxford University Press, 2006), 83. Seelig makes this point as well, drawing attention to the following comment: "we all saw a great change between the fashion of the Court as it is now and that in the Queen's time, for we were all lousy by sitting in the chamber of Sir Thomas Erskine." Cited in Seelig, *Autobiography*, 37.

67 Wiseman, "Knowing Her Place," 213–14.

68 Both are quoted in the Sidney Commonplace books held in the Kent Archives Office, Maidstone, De L'Isle and Dudley Papers, U1475, Z1.

69 Williamson, *Clifford*, 218.

The Holy Bible and Pierre Charron's *Books of Wisdom*,[70] identifying these texts as her key weapons and emblems in the same way as the Psalms served her mother.[71] *De la Sagesse* (On Wisdom) (1601) focuses upon the image of the Stoic ethical ideal, the wise man or sage (sophos), and the task of progressing towards that ideal. It is not merely a treatise on ethics but primarily a guide to the life of wisdom, following the form of Epictetus's *Enchiridion*. Charron focuses upon self-knowledge, self-examination, behavior, and the traditional virtues of prudence, justice, fortitude, and temperance. Charron's book was translated out of French into English by Samson Lennard, an antiquary who worked in the service of William Camden (whose *Britannia*, as Wiseman points out, provided some of the grounding for Anne Clifford's claims to the Clifford property) and was, at least by his own account, with Sir Philip Sidney at Zutphen.[72] Lennard's translation of Charron, much like his translation of De Mornay, was part of the tradition of Protestant criticism associated first with Sidney, then Essex and, before his death in 1612, with Prince Henry. When Lennard writes to the prince in his translation of De Mornay's Huguenot text that he hoped to "live to march over the Alpes, and to trayle a pike before the walls of Rome" behind the prince's standard, he was using the language of militant Protestantism for which Henry, until his death in 1612, had been the new standard bearer.[73] The book on which Anne Clifford rests her hand was, in fact dedicated to none other than Prince Henry himself, and served, in a newly skeptical way, the neo-Stoic cause. Among other things, neostoicism helped English aristocrats to imagine bringing England and Europe into alignment with the unfolding of a providential plan in which the aristocracy was more powerful and autonomous than sixteenth-century consolidations of monarchical power allowed.[74] Clifford's choice of a key neo-Stoic text and the Holy Bible as her personal emblems thus simultaneously indicates her continuation of her family traditions and the grounds of her own political claims and ambitions.

---

[70] Charron's text was popular in its day and appeared in thirty-six editions by 1672. It is a compendium of existing material, drawing upon a variety of ancient and modern authors, and Charron openly acknowledges his debt to Neostoicism, including Lipsius. For a recent discussion of Charron's work (including *La Sagesse*), see Richard H. Popkin, *The History of Scepticism: From Savonarola to Bayle* (Oxford: Oxford University Press, 2003), 57–61.

[71] The Great Picture features three standard Senecan works: Boethius (1556), Epictetus (1567), and Antoninus (1577), as well as Seneca's *Works* and the modern French neostoicism of Charron.

[72] In a dedication to William, Earl of Pembroke, Lennard invoked the memory of his service with Sidney at Zutphen. See Sampson Lennard, trans. *Luthers fore-runners: or, A cloud of witnesses, deposing for the Protestant faith*, by J.P. Perrin (London, 1624). See also Sampson Lennard, trans. *The Mysterie of iniquitie: that is to say, the history of the Papacie*, by Philippe Du-Plessis-Mornay (London, 1612). See Jan Broadway, 'Lennard, Sampson (d. 1633)', *ODNB* (accessed March 2008). Wiseman, "Knowing her Place," 214.

[73] Lennard, *Mysterie of iniquitie*, iiiv.

[74] Joel Davis, "Multiple Arcadias and the Literary Quarrel between Fulke Greville and the Countess of Pembroke," *Studies in Philology* 101, no. 4 (2004): 407.

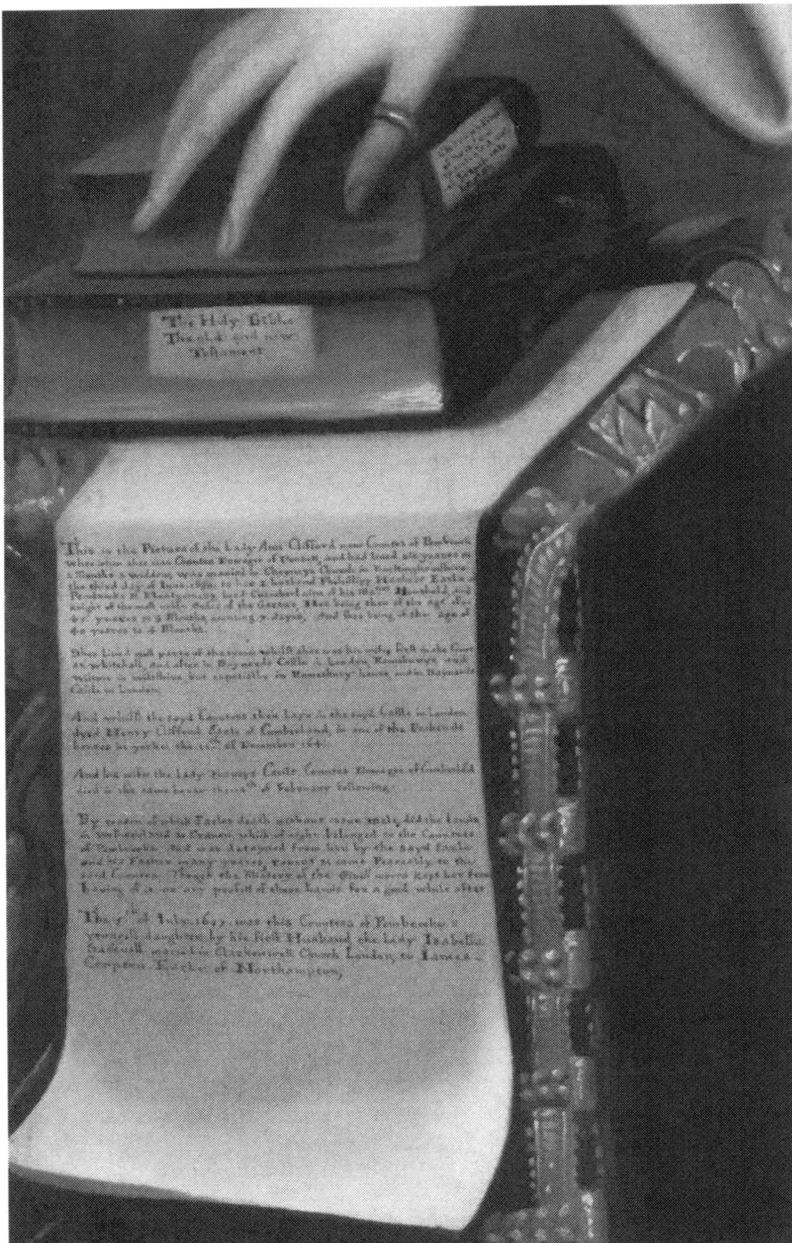

Fig. 5.3 Detail from "The Great Picture," attributed to Jan van Belcamp. Reproduced by courtesy of Abbot Hall Art Gallery, Kendal, Cumbria. © Lakeland Arts Trust.

Her own regional "absolutism," we will recall, was not just a form of dynastic entrenchment, but also a form of baronial opposition to monarchical control and centralization.

Deeply invested in a providentialist narrative of election, spiritual and behavioural resolution, and Christian neo-Stoicism, Anne Clifford read her religious books in intimate dialogue with—indeed as a key part of—her pursuit of land and position. Rather than simply refuge or ornament, Clifford's reading testified to a set of alliances forged in no small part by her own family, and signalled her commitment to and reliance on those alliances. Geared towards establishing and enacting the rights of a great landowner—a status, as this account makes clear, that was always political—Anne Clifford's reading illustrates the great variety of uses early modern readers had for their "religious" books.

PART 2:
Reading Intertextual Prose Genres

Chapter 6
Prospecting for Common Ground in Devotion: Queen Katherine Parr's Personal Prayer Book

Janel Mueller

The Text in Context

British Library Harley MS 2342 has been known as "Lady Jane Grey's Prayer Book" because of its demonstrable associations with her. When she was beheaded for usurping Queen Mary's right to the throne in 1553, she took it with her to the scaffold and there entrusted it to the keeping of Sir John Bridges, lieutenant of the Tower of London. Inside the compact prayer book, across the bottoms of four pages, is a brief exchange of messages of comfort in the handwritings of Guildford Dudley and Jane Grey, husband and wife, awaiting their deaths in separate cells, and a message to Bridges in Jane's handwriting, referring to his having instructed her "to write in so worthy a book."[1] The implicit drama is not difficult to piece together. The compassionate Bridges evidently helped Jane and Guildford convey their farewells to Jane's father, the Duke of Suffolk, before the executions of all three by carrying the prayer book with its messages from the one to the other, allaying any possible suspicions with his show of piety. At this juncture, the prayer book unquestionably belonged to Jane.

Its earlier history, however, lies entirely with Queen Katherine Parr. I have identified the handwriting on all 143 vellum leaves of Harley 2342 as hers. I believe that Katherine gave Jane this tiny prayer book in early September 1548 when Katherine lay dying of puerperal fever after giving birth to her only child, a daughter, Mary, on September 2. Jane was residing in the household, her presence due to the intrigues of Katherine's husband, Lord Thomas Seymour, who aimed at arranging a marriage between Jane and his nephew, the boy king Edward VI. Jane was the chief mourner at Katherine's funeral, held in the chapel of the manor house at Sudeley in Westmorland, where Katherine had gone for her confinement.

---

[1] See the anonymous contemporary account, *The Chronicle of Queen Jane, and of Two Years of Queen Mary*, ed. John Gough Nichols, Publications of the Camden Society no. 48 (London, 1849), 55–6, for a transcription of these messages, which occupy the bottoms of fols. 78r–80r. Here and hereafter, I modernize spelling in quotations from Harley 2342 and other texts.

I believe that Katherine retained possession of Harley 2342 until close to her end, for her otherwise controlled and distinct handwriting becomes wobbly, oversized, and faint on the last five leaves, and ornamentation of any kind ceases.

Unusually for this age, "Queen Katherine's Personal Prayer Book" offers access to the spirituality of one strongly motivated, highly placed, and deeply studied woman in the swirling climate of religious and political contestation and transition that was England's in the mid- to late 1540s. I specify the mid- to late 1540s as the likely period in which this text was compiled because all of Parr's other known literary activity dates to and after her queenship as Henry VIII's sixth wife. Her literary activity seems to be the direct product of the incentives and opportunities that came with her queenship. Her handwriting in her prayer book, moreover, closely resembles that of her letters from 1544 to 1548. Beyond this evidence, the versicles and prayers inscribed on the prayer book's miniature leaves (measuring 3 x 4 inches) are ornamented with gold-retraced capital letters on red-and-blue fields, and with red-and-blue rectangles, some with vine-like gold tracery, inserted in blank spaces at line ends. This is exactly the decorative program used by Parr in her incomplete autograph manuscript of *Prayers or Meditations* (the Kendal Town manuscript), reportedly made as a gift for a Mistress Tuke, an attendant at the Henrician court, presumably in or after 1545.[2]

As her own creation, Harley 2342 should be known as "Queen Katherine Parr's Personal Prayer Book." I stipulate "personal" because Parr seems not to have intended its contents for publication, as she so clearly did intend with her *Psalms or Prayers taken out of the Holy Scriptures* (1544), her *Prayers or Meditations* (1545), and her *Lamentation of a Sinner* (1547).[3] Harley 2342, however, is as deserving of circulation and critical attention as are the three published works.[4] Parr's personal prayer book is as characteristic of her textual procedures and interests as is the other instance in which we know her to have excerpted, recast, and rearranged a prior source—her production of *Prayers or Meditations* out of the materials of Book 3 of Thomas à Kempis's *De imitatione Christi* in the English translation made by Richard Whitford, published under the title *The Following of Christ*.[5] I have argued that Parr's sensitive and systematic interventions in Whitford's text result in a radically refashioned devotional work that makes personal access to Christ available to any reader, without the gender and status

2 The undated Kendal Town autograph manuscript is the principal copy text for *Prayers or Meditations* in my forthcoming edition, *Katherine Parr: Complete Works and Correspondence* (Chicago: University of Chicago Press, 2011).

3 For discussion of the respective circumstances of publication of these three works, see Susan E. James, *Kateryn Parr: The Making of a Queen* (Aldershot: Ashgate, 1999), 200–207; 214–19; 234–49.

4 "Queen Katherine's Personal Prayer Book" is the fourth and final prose work in my edition (n. 2 above). My introduction to the text there is substantially similar to the discussion in the present chapter.

5 The identification of Whitford as Parr's source was made by C. Fenno Hoffman Jr., "Catherine Parr as a Woman of Letters," *Huntington Library Quarterly* 53 (1959): 349–67.

markings of Whitford's (and à Kempis's) original, and on this basis I have staked a claim for Parr as an author, not merely an adapter, in *Prayers or Meditations*.[6]

A similar but more intricate line of argument can be advanced regarding Parr's personal prayer book. Generically, this compilation conforms to the widely popular type of prayer book for lay devotion known as the Book of Hours—or, in English nomenclature, the Primer. English Primers variously manifested a traditional or a reformist orientation in scores of separate editions from many publishers. The orientation would emerge through the choice of language (Latin, Latin and English, English only); through the inclusion or exclusion of prayers to the Virgin Mary and the saints, prayers for the souls of the departed, formulaic prescriptions of penance that remitted time in purgatory; and through the emphases shaping their instructional materials, whether geared, in a traditionalist fashion, more to the priestly office and the sacramental system or, in a reformist fashion, more to individual accountability and the exemplary precedents of Biblical heroes and heroines. Yet, whatever its orientation overall, every Primer would display an introspective, reverential turning away from the world and an attendant placing of primary focus on Christ as the sole Saviour of sinful humankind.[7] This inward turn and this Christocentricity constituted a notable common denominator in the devotionalism of a contestatory age. On the evidence of Parr's personal prayer book, she recognized this common denominator and applied herself to exploring its possibilities.

The prayer book's generic interest is twofold. There is, first, the question of which sources (overwhelmingly, Primers and Psalters) figured in its compilation; secondly, there is the question of what Parr achieved in fashioning a book of devotion from the multiple sources that she excerpted, arranged, and combined into a new, personalized whole. In broader terms, the historically specific, pathbreaking trajectory of Katherine Parr's literary activity, as the first woman in England to publish work of her own in English under her own name, reveals how her intense piety generated and directed this activity, while her status as queen of England empowered her to range across a spectrum of roles as patron, translator, adapter, and author that found public expression and recognition in print. The notable exception, her personal prayer book, could take on certain functions that a secret diary might serve in our own day. Parr could assemble a set of contents that expressed her own priorities and preferences in devotional utterance, without

---

6 Janel Mueller, "Devotion as Difference: Intertextuality in Queen Katherine Parr's *Prayers or Meditations* (1545)," *Huntington Library Quarterly* 53 (1990): 171–97.

7 Two classic studies of sixteenth-century English Primers remain indispensable introductions to the subject: Helen C. White, *The Tudor Books of Private Devotion* (Madison: University of Wisconsin Press, 1951); and Charles C. Butterworth, *The English Primers (1529–1545): Their Publication and Connection with the English Bible and the Reformation in England* (Philadelphia: University of Pennsylvania Press, 1953). The pioneering treatment of the subject, consisting mostly of an enumerative bibliography (now superseded by the *STC*) is Edgar Hoskins, *Horae Beatae Mariae Virginis or Sarum and York Primers with Kindred Books and Primers of the Reformed and Roman Use* (London: Longman, Green, & Co., 1901).

being constrained by institutional or confessional norms, and she could give free rein to the tonalities and vocabulary that resonated most compellingly with her. At certain points, indicated in discussion below, a complementary relation emerges between Parr's personal prayer book and her published prose.

In contrast to the narrow time frame of 1544–48 postulated for its composition, Parr's personal prayer book employs source materials (of which I have identified more than ninety percent) ranging in date from 1530 to 1540; there is no evidence of more recent material. Conspicuous time lags between the date of a published source and the date when Parr utilized it are characteristic of her other works also. John Fisher's *Psalmi seu Precationes*, first published c. 1525, is the text she translates in *Psalms or Prayers* (1544); and Whitford's *Following of Christ*, published c. 1531, is the text she redacts in *Prayers or Meditations* (1545). I can offer no strong reason—only, perhaps, a penchant for retrospection in devotion—to account for the time lags in the case of these two works. I think, however, that there is an explanation of considerable interest to be offered in the case of Parr's personal prayer book.

I will be arguing that Parr undertook, by means of these earlier sources and a compilation destined not to be published, to position herself reflectively with regard to the widening divide but, even more, the extent of common ground in Catholic and Reformed strains of lay devotion. For such an undertaking, she required publications in English that made pertinent developments traceable. The Primers and Psalters of the 1530s and her other sources from this decade did just that, enabling her project of exploration and integration. To be sure, any such incentive to explore alternative modes of Christian devotion could not be neutral from the 1530s onward in England, for conservative Catholics—notably Cuthbert Tunstall, Bishop of London, and his designated vernacular polemicist, Lord Chancellor Thomas More, as well as John Stokesley, Tunstall's successor—sharply decried as heresy all reformist allegations of abuses and proposals for change, especially the proposal to grant worshippers access to the Bible and to devotional materials in English rather than Latin. Moreover, after authorizing the publication and circulation of the Great Bible in English in 1538–39, Henry VIII largely returned the laity of his realm to their status quo ante by curtailing reading of the Bible in English with the dubiously titled "Act for the Advancement of True Religion" (1543).[8] In inquiring for herself into the spirituality of the old religion and the new in her day while including lavish recourse to Scripture in English, Parr exhibits her receptivity to the advent of the English Reformation as she sustains the Christ-centered, inward turn of traditional and reformist modes of lay devotion.

8 This Act permitted only licensed clergy to read publicly from the Bible. Nobles and gentry could read it aloud only within their own households; merchants, noblewomen, and gentlemen could read it only privately. The entire rest of the population was banned from reading the English Bible at all, although the King could choose to suspend this clause if he wished. *Statutes of the Realm* (34 & 35 Henry VIII, c. 1) (London: Proprietors of The Law Journal Reports, 1866–1901), 895–6.

Prospecting for Common Ground: The Range of Source Materials

Parr's personal prayer book begins in a conventional fashion with a summary narrative (source unidentified) focused on the passion and crucifixion of Jesus as the culmination of His life and ministry, and the demonstration that He is the Saviour of humankind. This type of narrative, usually in the form of a far lengthier "harmony" or parallel rehearsal of the events leading to the crucifixion as recorded in the four evangelists, is one among several standard beginnings for the text proper in a Primer, whether Catholic or Lutheran, in Latin or in English. The passion narratives in Primers, however, remain just that: accounts of Jesus's last days, doings, and sayings lifted verbatim from the gospels, whatever the language. No sooner is Parr's very brief narrative launched, however, than it breaks with Primer convention by modulating into a fluid mixture of self-examination, prayer, and non-narrative quotation of Scripture, as this excerpt will illustrate:

> … being so cruelly consumed, He offered Himself a sacrifice to God His Father for us all. Who am I, then, that I should [consider] and suffer with an unpatient mind if any trouble do chance unto me, if I suffer any incommodity, if any persecution of envious persons cumber me, specially seeing no evil can be done unto me which my sins hath not deserved? Therefore I will not suffer grievously that thing which is bestowed righteously, but I shall pray my Lord God to grant me patience in all things. And, in that patience, purging and forgiveness of mine ungraciousness, that He, which vouchsafed to make me partaker of His pains, may also make me partaker of His glory, according to the Apostle's saying, "As ye be fellows of His passions, so shall ye be of His comfort."[9]

Once this modulation occurs, the conventionality of Parr's personal prayer book gives way to its more distinctive course. All of its subsequent contents sustain and intensify the turns of self-examination and redirection that Parr conducts through prayer and nonnarrative Scriptural citation, predominantly verses from the Psalms. While English Primers serve her repeatedly as sources of prayers and Scriptural citations, her appropriations carry no trace of the Primers' prominent internal structure. This might take the traditional form of the canonical hours of the day appointed for prayers and devotions in the medieval Church, followed by the services for the souls of the dead. Or this structure might take a newer form: adaptations of praying and devotion to an everyday routine of arising, going about one's activities, encountering temptation, giving praise for a blessing received, and retiring to rest. In the absence of either of these standard coordinates for devotion pegged to a daily round (however conceived and specified), a profound

[9] British Library, Harley MS 2342 ("Queen Katherine Parr's Personal Prayer Book"), fols. 3v–4v. All subsequent parenthetical references are to this text. Square brackets enclose my conjectural restoration of an illegible word. The freely handled quotation is from St. Paul in 2 Corinthians 1:5.

sense of interiority, of charged and abounding subjectivity, emerges from Parr's stark sequencing of prayers and extensive runs of Psalmic verses.

My incentive for arguing that "Queen Katherine's Personal Prayer Book" is her proving ground for alternative modes and common expressions of Christian devotion in her day arose in the gradual process of identifying her sources.[10] Parr's opening sequence is headed by three English prayers from Thomas More's Tower meditations, written while he was awaiting execution for treason in July 1535 after refusing to swear the Oath of Supremacy declaring Henry VIII (rather than the pope) the supreme head of the Church of England. More's three prayers include a lengthy, impassioned one beginning "O holy Trinity—the Father, the Son, the Holy Ghost—three equal, coeternal Persons and one God almighty, have mercy upon me, vile, abject, abominable, sinful wretch," followed by the short text of "A prayer for our enemies," beginning "Almighty God, have mercy on me, and all them that bear me evil will and would me harm," and then by the yet shorter prayer of self-resignation into God's hands, beginning "Lord, give me patience in tribulation, grace in everything, to conform my will to Thine" (fols. 9r–16r).

Parr enacts her respect and empathy in mostly verbatim transcriptions of More's prayers, but she is not uncritical. She consistently renders his Latin quotations of Scripture into English, and she makes two key excisions, signaled in italics below. One is the reference to purgatory in More's "not for the avoiding of the calamities of this wretched world, *nor so much for the avoiding of the pains of purgatory*, nor of the pains of hell neither." The other is Parr's curt substitution of the single pronoun "Thee" in place of More's fervent salutation to Christ's Real Presence in the consecrated Host of the Mass: "*Thine holy sacraments, and specially ... the presence of Thy very blessed Body, sweet Saviour Christ, in the holy Sacrament of the Altar: ... duly to thank Thee for Thy gracious visitation therewith, and at that high memorial, with tender compassion, to remember and consider Thy most bitter passion.*"[11]

Immediately following the three prayers by More, Parr transcribes, virtually verbatim, two prayers by Nicholas Shaxton from the verso of the title page of the earliest complete Bible in English, Miles Coverdale's *Biblia. The Bible: that is,*

[10] On the ambiguities and ambivalences that characterized religious policy and its implementation in the final decade of Henry VIII's reign (1539–47), see Alec Ryrie, *The Gospel and Henry VIII: Evangelicals in the Early English Reformation* (Cambridge: Cambridge University Press, 2003), esp. chaps. 1, 2, 4.

[11] More's texts are printed in *Treatise on the Passion, Treatise on the Blessed Body, Instructions and Prayers*, ed. Garry E. Haupt, vol. 13 of *The Yale Edition of the Complete Works of St. Thomas More* (New Haven: Yale University Press, 1976), 228–31. How Parr gained access to these prayers of More's is unknown, but there is pertinent evidence that they circulated informally. I have found transcriptions of More's Tower prayers in the Bodleian Library manuscript, Laud Misc. 1, fols. 52r–59r, which is the prayer book of Lady Jane Wriothesley, one of Queen Katherine's ladies of the chamber, and wife of Sir Thomas Wriothesley, Lord Chancellor in the 1540s. The Wriothesleys were active Catholics; Sir Thomas joined with Bishop Stephen Gardiner in attempting to discredit Queen Katherine with King Henry in 1546.

the Holy Scripture, faithfully translated (1535), which completes the translation left unfinished by William Tyndale when he suffered death at the stake for his prohibited labors in Englishing Scripture. The two prayers from the Coverdale Bible title page are "O Lord God almighty, which long ago saidst by the mouth of James, Thine apostle," a petition for efficacy in prayer and for godly wisdom, and a briefer petition, "Lead me, O Lord, in Thy way, and let me walk in Thy truth" (fols. 16r–17v). In inscribing these prayers in her "Personal Prayer Book," Parr omits the identifying rubric that prefaces the first of the pair in the Coverdale Bible: "*Because that when thou goest to study in Holy Scripture, thou shouldst do it with reverence, therefore for thy instruction and loving admonition thereto, the reverend Father in God, Nicholas [Shaxton], Bishop of Salisbury, hath prescribed thee the prayer following, taken out of the same*."[12] Shaxton, a sympathizer with the Reformation, was appointed by Henry VIII to the see of Salisbury in 1535, but he resigned it on refusing to subscribe to the religiously conservative Six Articles (1539). Queen Katherine gives Shaxton a voice in her prayer book as an advocate of vernacular Scripture and Scripture-based prayer who, in the first instance, had been judged worthy by Coverdale, an associate of Luther's and a self-exile in Germany, to supply two prayers as epigraphs on the title page of the first English Bible. This Bible, significantly, had appeared without Henry VIII's authorization.

Thesis and antithesis—More's prayers followed by Shaxton's—but the item that follows is less synthesis than common ground. Parr follows Shaxton's prayers with an English version of a prayer that is a staple item in Primers of the period, whether Roman or Reformed. It is known by its opening phrase in Latin, "*Conditor celi et terre*" (O Maker of heaven and earth). The traditional instruction for the use of this prayer is as the first of the suffrages (petitionary prayers) under the rubric "*Oratio ad imaginem corporis Christi*" (Prayer to the image of the Body of Christ), directing the user to prepare for confession by praying to a crucifix.[13] True to her habitual practice in her prayer book, Parr omits the rubric and thus excises the reference to praying to a crucifix, but she also, for no obvious reason, excises the ascriptive opening clauses of this prayer: "*O Maker of heaven and earth, King of Kings and Lord of Lords, which of nothing didst make me to Thy image and likeness, and didst redeem me with Thine own blood: whom …*." Parr instead begins her text after the *whom*, with "I, a sinner, am not worthy to name, or call upon, nor think on in my heart" (fols. 18r–21r). The effect upon this prayer, a prolonged confession of sin and unworthiness and a plea for God's mercy and

[12] Miles Coverdale, trans., *Biblia. The Bible: that is: the holy Scripture, faythfully translated in to Englyshe* (Southwark, 1535; *STC* 2063.3), unnumbered, first folio sheet. Shaxton and Coverdale had noteworthy subsequent histories. Shaxton realigned as a traditionalist after prosecution in 1546, recanting his reformist beliefs. Coverdale returned from exile in Germany in 1548, encouraged by the vigorous embrace of reformism in Edward VI's reign. Katherine Parr, now Lord Thomas Seymour's wife, appointed Coverdale as one of her chaplains. He officiated at her funeral service in September 1548.

[13] White, *Tudor Books of Private Devotion*, 74.

forgiveness, is to intensify its humility and self-abasement by eliminating its opening salutation to a mighty and glorious Lord Christ.

Parr's source for "*Conditor celi et terre*" is the version in *A Primer in English, with Divers Prayers* (1535), issued by Thomas Godfray, an English Lutheran printer and publisher based in London.[14] Little else is known about him except that he derived his text from the first Primer in English, *Ortulus anime the Garden of the Soul* (1530), a translation from Latin by George Joye, another English Lutheran working in exile in Germany. Godfray was also an associate of the outspokenly Lutheran William Marshall, who was publishing Primers of his own in London in the same period.[15] As will be evident in due course, at one point or another Parr's personal prayer book utilizes all of these English Lutheran sources (and more), beginning with Godfray's Primer. Parr hews closely to the sense of Godfray's version of "*Conditor celi*" with its profuse allusions to Biblical sinners, but she continually refines and tightens its phrasing. She smoothes out many small points of awkwardness in the style (this awkwardness stems from Joye, and is one of the chronic features of his prose).[16] Parr also heightens the emotional and moral cogency of this traditional prayer with a free hand, as this example will illustrate. One of Godfray's catalogues of sins runs headlong into anacoluthon: "*in tasting, in touching, in thinking, in sleeping, in working, and in all ways in which I, a frail man and most wretched sinner, might sin: my default, my most grievous default.*" Parr recasts this catalogue in surer-footed syntax while also significantly eliminating Godfray's gender-specific locution and universalizing the potential frame of reference: "in tasting, in feeling, in speaking, in thinking, in working, and in all manner ways wherein I, an unstable and frail creature, might offend my Maker by any fault or trespass" (fol. 19v).

After honing her compositional skills on Godfray's uneven prose, Parr proceeds to the most literarily interesting and ambitious undertaking in all of her personal prayer book. This is her elaboration on a sequence of sentence prayers from *A Spiritual Consolation, Written by John Fisher, Bishop of Rochester, to His Sister Elizabeth*, the other famous Tower meditation from the other eminent English Catholic who refused to swear the Oath of Supremacy and died as a traitor in 1535.[17] This sequence of sentence prayers, one for each day of the week but not assigned to a particular day, concludes Fisher's reflections on "The Ways to Perfect

---

14 *A primer in Englysshe, with dyuers prayers* (London: Thomas Godfray, 1535?; *STC* 15988a), Ciii v–Ciiii v.

15 Butterworth, *English Primers*, 73–8.

16 Ibid., 41–3.

17 As with More's Tower prayers, there is the question of how Parr obtained Fisher's last writings, which were first published thirty years after his death as *A spirituall consolation, written by John Fyssher* (London, 1578?; *STC* 10899). Here the question of access finds a likely answer in the person of George Day, Fisher's former student and chaplain, who was appointed Parr's almoner (chaplain for alms) when she became queen in 1543. As Katherine's spiritual adviser, Day evidently encouraged her to translate Fisher's *Psalmi seu Precationes* as her *Psalms or Prayers*, for the orders for multiple finely bound presentation copies of both works were billed to him in May 1544. See James, *Kateryn Parr*, 200–207.

Religion." Again characteristically dispensing with a heading, Parr launches into the text of the comprehensive single prayer that she crafts by hinging her serial expressions of devotion to Jesus on Fisher's seven brief sentences.[18]

Fisher's sentence prayers become, for Parr, sweeping gestures of invitation to engage with the prime subject of late medieval Catholic and early Reformed—especially Lutheran—devotion: the sufferings and self-sacrifice of Jesus on the cross, dying to save humankind in obedience to God the Father's will. The affinity in Fisher's and Parr's temperaments shows elsewhere in their work in the prominent yet divergent treatment that they give to "the book of the crucifix," the legibility of salvation in the passion of Christ.[19] Here, in her personal prayer book, Parr demonstrates the heights of lyrical responsiveness to which she is moved, taking up the lead of Fisher's Christocentric intensity, to meditate on the crucified Jesus. Her successive effusions are anchored fore and aft by Fisher's sentences (italicized in the following quotation). Even so, Parr does not stickle at revising his wording with a reformist turn that denies human nature any role in the divine work of redemption, as seen in her substitution of "continual" for Fisher's "natural" in the first clause below:

> *O sweet Jesu, give me* continual *remembrance of Thy passion.* O most benign Jesu, mine whole health and wealth, I confess me, and lowly submit myself unto Thy great mercy and goodness; for I have little remembered Thee, and less I have thanked Thee for Thy great kindness showed unto me and all mankind. Whereas Thou wert rich, for our sakes Thou becamest full poor; Thou tookest great labor to ease us, Thou sufferest many pains to relieve us. Where we were bound, Thou madest us free. We were condemned by justice of the painful prison of hell, and Thou by Thy mercies madest us inheritors to the joyful kingdom of heaven. Thou wert unkindly betrayed. Thou wert traitorously taken, and cruelly bound with hard ropes. Thou wert mocked and scorned and spitted upon. Thou wert beaten and bobbed, and crowned with sharp thorns. Thou wert drawn and stretched and through-pierced into Thy heart. Thy sinews and veins were broken, and Thy skin and flesh was torn. Thy hands and feet nailed to the cross, Thou sheddest all Thy blood, and yielded up Thy ghost. All this and much more Thou diddest and sufferest for sinful man's sake. Moist my dry heart, blessed Jesu, with Thy sweet drops of Thy grace, and *give me* continual *remembrance of* this *Thy* painful *passion. O sweet Jesu, possess my heart, and keep it only to Thee.* (fols. 24v–25v)

While the shared sense of the centrality of Christ's passion to faith and devotion forges connections across the confessional gap between traditionalists and reformers, there are, nonetheless, differences to be found. Aspects of Parr's reformist orientation in this prayer include her careful situating of Christ's death on

---

[18] *The English Works of John Fisher*, ed. John E.B. Mayor, EETS, extr. ser., 27 (London: N. Trübner, 1876), 1:387.

[19] See Janel Mueller, "Complications of Intertextuality: John Fisher, Katherine Parr, and 'The Book of the Crucifix,'" in *Representing Women in Renaissance England*, ed. Claude J. Summers and Ted-Larry Pebworth (Columbia: University of Missouri Press, 1997), 24–41.

the cross within a continuum of actions and initiatives that scripturally certify His role as Saviour; her reiterated, slightly heightened closing petition for "continual remembrance of this Thy painful passion" rather than for participation in the sacramental reenactment of it that is the Catholic Mass; and her restrained use of affective metaphor ("Moist my dry heart").

The emotional intensity of Parr's prayer does not approach the extremes of graphic detail or of physical union with the Saviour imagined in St. Bridget's "Fifteen Oes," a set of lyrical ejaculations on the names of Jesus that is regularly included in traditionalist Primers of the period. One of the briefer ejaculations, originally composed in Latin, runs as follows in English: "O blessed Jesu, deepness of endless mercy, I beseech Thee for the deepness of Thy wounds that went through Thy tender flesh, Thy bowels, and The marr[ow] of Thy bones, that it shall please Thee to draw me out of sin, and hide me ever after in the holes of Thy wounds, from the face of Thy wrath, unt[il] time, Lord, that Thy dreadful doom be passed. Amen. Pater noster. Ave Maria."[20] Parr's tonality and sensibility are closer to the prayers interspersed in Miles Coverdale's *Fruitfull Lessons upon the Passion*. The dynamic of Coverdale's prayer on the passion proceeds, like Parr's, from a dual contemplation of Christ's actions and their benefits to humankind, although here without Parr's serial specificity (conspicuous, however, in Coverdale's preceding prayers on the agony in the Garden, the flagellation, the crowning with thorns, etc.). His prayer, also like Parr's, does not end in imagined physical union but contents itself with tender proximity to the Saviour, invoking His continuing love and its elevating inward effects in time-sanctioned imagery of flying "unto Thee under the protection of Thy holy cross" and being drawn "up on high, O Lord Jesu, from all worldly things."[21]

Prayers of the Bible and of the Passion: Traditional Materials and Lutheran Inflections

The next set of entries in Parr's prayer book confirms that Scripture and the emotions stirred by reading and reflecting on it are fundamental components of her own devotion. The set consists of prayers by prominent men and women of the Bible, each of these introduced by an identifying rubric, including "The prayer of Queen Esther for help against her enemies" (Esther 13); "The prayer of Sarah, the daughter of Raguel, when she was slandered" (Tobias 3); "The prayer of Judith for the victory of Holofernes" (Judith 9); "The prayer of Jesus, the son of Sirach"

20 "The Fifteen Oes in English," in *Hore beatissime virginis Marie ad legitimum Sarisburiensis Ecclesis ritum* (Paris: François Regnault, 1536; *STC* 15987), fol. clixr. Square brackets enclose emendations of typographical errors.

21 Miles Coverdale, *Fruitfull lessons upon the passion, buriall, resurrection, ascension, and of the sending of the holy Ghost* (London, 1593; *STC* 5891), R1r–v. Regarding the comparative lateness of this English edition, the *STC* notes that Thomas Tanner's *Bibliotheca Britannico-Hibernica* (London, 1748), 203, mentions printings of the *Fruitfull Lessons* at Marburg in 1540 and 1547—dates contemporaneous with Parr's literary activity.

(Ecclesiasticus 51); "The prayer of the three children that were delivered from the hot, burning fire" (apocryphal addition to Daniel 3 in the Vulgate); and "The prayer of Manasses, sixth king of Judah" (1 Paralipomenon 36) (fols. 27v–37v). Several observations regarding this set of prayers are germane to the matter of the old religion and the new in Parr's day.

All of these prayers derive from books of the Apocrypha or additions from it to canonical books of the Old Testament, with the one ostensible exception of the prayer of Sarah, daughter of Raguel (fols. 28v–29r).[22] The "Bible" in question here is common ground—the canon of the Latin Vulgate—used by vernacular translators with Lutheran affiliations as their source for the versions of these prayers that Parr handles in varying ways. Her very closely reproduced source for the prayers of Jesus, the son of Sirach, and of the three children in the fiery furnace is Coverdale's 1535 Bible; beyond the near verbatim correspondences of the two texts, the case for this particular source is strengthened by the location of the two prayers on successive folio pages. Common ground remains conspicuous, moreover, with regard to the prayers of Jesus, the son of Sirach, and of Manasses, sixth king of Judah. Not only do these two prayers regularly figure among the suffrages in the Hours of the Blessed Virgin Mary in Latin Primers according to Salisbury use,[23] but they are also staples of the several English Lutheran compilations titled "Prayers of the Bible" that derive, with their sometimes convergent, sometimes discrepant renderings, from the Latin original, *Precationes Biblicae* (1531), assembled out of the Vulgate by Otto Brunfels, one of Luther's associates. The English Lutheran compilations that contain these two prayers (and various others) include Robert Redman's *Prayers of the Bible* (1535?); Coverdale's *Psalter and Certain Other Devout Prayers Taken Out of the Bible* (after 1535); Richard Grafton's *Prayers of Holy Fathers, Patriarchs, Prophets* (1544?); and Richard Taverner's *An Epitome of the Psalms ... With Divers Other Prayers* (1539).[24] What makes these compilations of prayers by men and women of the Bible "Lutheran" is the acted-upon commitment to reproducing and highlighting extracts of Scripture in English, before the authorization to do so was granted by Henry VIII in 1538–39. Otherwise, the extracted prayers engage with none of the differences in belief and practice that were opening a rift in this period between traditionalists and reformers.

Parr handles the first overtly Scriptural material in her personal prayer book with confidence and freedom. It is a noteworthy aspect of her embrace of the spiritual equality of all souls before God that she gives equal billing to prayers

---

[22] Parr's source seems to be Regnault's *Hore beatissime virginis Marie* (see n. 20), Mi v, a traditionalist Latin Primer from which she translates selected portions. A Lutheran source may yet be identified.

[23] See, e.g., *STC* 15984, 15985, and 15987.

[24] For full titles of these compilations and other bibliographical information, see the *STC* entries for Redman (*STC* 20200.3), Coverdale (*STC* 2379), Grafton (*STC* 20200), and Taverner (*STC* 2748).

by men and women—three of each. She likewise maintains her premium on devotional expression that can be lifted above and beyond its circumstantial setting and promptings—her presumptive motive earlier for not identifying More's, Shaxton's, and Fisher's prayers. Now Parr excises from Queen Esther's prayer a lengthy deploring of the Persians' idolatry and oppression of the Jews, which God has allowed because of the Jews' sins. The residue that Parr retains potently distills Esther's predicament into a yearning appeal to God, to help the Jews and to help her in particular: "Think upon us, O Lord, and show Thyself in the time of our distress and of our trouble. Strength me, O Thou, King of Gods and Lord of all power; deliver us with Thy hand, and help me, desolate woman, which have no defense nor helper, but only Thee. Lord, Thou knowest all things. Thou knowest and wotest my necessity" (fols. 27v–28r).[25] Likewise, Judith's prayer is stripped of almost all contextual reference to her daring and ultimately successful plot to behead the enemy giant, Holofernes; there is a single allusion to "this device." What Parr wanted of Judith's words in her personal prayer book were precisely and only these: "O Thou, God of the heavens, Thou, Maker of the waters and Lord of all creatures, hear me, poor woman, calling upon Thee, and putting my trust in Thy mercy. Remember Thy covenant, O Lord, and minister words in my mouth, and stablish this device in my heart. Thou art God, and there is none other but Thou. Amen" (fols. 29r–v).[26]

Parr's prominent endorsement of vernacular Scripturalism in the six prayers of identified men and women is followed in her prayer book by a sequence of prayers taken alternately from traditionalist and reformist Primers. Her traditionalist Primer yields Latin texts which she translates and redacts. Parr's reformist source is William Marshall's *A Goodly Primer in English* (1535), which contains an "Instruction how we ought to pray." The proper use of prayer, modeled for us by Christ's example in "Our Father which art in heaven," reduces to three essential points: "to know thyself a sinner; of whom to take remedy; and how thou shalt obtain it, truly, by prayer."[27] The alternations of the ensuing sequence, from traditionalist to reformist prayers and back again, foster the sense that Parr

[25] Parr's source is Grafton's edition of *Prayers of Holy Fathers*, fols. 22v–23v, and, ultimately, Coverdale's translation of the book of Esther.

[26] Parr's source is Grafton's edition of *Prayers of Holy Fathers*, fol. 21r–v, and, ultimately, Coverdale's translation of the book of Judith. Among the prayers of male figures, Parr excises references to the Persians' idolatry and to animal sacrifices in "The prayer of the three children," (fols. 32v–35v), but otherwise leaves intact the body of the text, from Coverdale's translation of Ecclesiasticus 51. The lengthy prayers of Jesus, son of Sirach, and Manasses, King of Judah, remain altogether intact.

[27] *A goodly prymer in englyshe, newly corrected and printed, with certeyne godly meditations and prayers added to the same* (London: J. Byddell for W. Marshall, 1535; *STC* 15988), Bi v–Biv v. Marshall's material on the Lord's Prayer derives, in turn, from Luther's *Kurze Form der Zehen Gebote, des Glaubens und des Vater Unsers (Short Form of the Ten Commandments, the Creed, and the Our Father*) (1520); see Butterworth, *English Primers*, 280, 285.

is prospecting for common ground through collocation and comparison of the texts she chooses, both in style and in substance. The net effect of her alternating sequence is a remarkable demonstration of the extent to which adherents of the old religion and the new could pray together in the same words.

A reflexive turn—a prayer about the nature of prayer—characterizes the initial item in this sequence, taken all but verbatim from the last prayer of the ninth canonical hour, just before Evensong, in Marshall's *Goodly Primer*: "Our merciful Father, which in teaching us to pray by Thy Son, Christ, hast commanded us to call Thee Father, and to believe that we are Thy well-beloved children; which stirrest up none of Thine to pray, but to the intent Thou wouldest hear them ..." (fols. 38r–v).[28] Identifying rubrics for the individual prayers are, again, mainly lacking in this alternating sequence. Now follow three markedly traditionalist prayers: the first (source unidentified) a petition to be enabled to cooperate with divine grace in the sacrament of penance and in works of mercy: "Grant me, O Lord my God: in my heart, repentance; in my spirit, contrition; in my eyes, a fountain of tears; out of my hands, liberality of alms" (fol. 39r). The second of this trio of traditionalist prayers is Parr's translation of "*De sanctissima trinitate*" [To the most holy Trinity], which immediately follows the section "*In elevatione corporis Christi*" [At the elevation of the Body of Christ] in a 1534 Latin Primer commissioned for sale by a London bookseller, John Groute. A large woodcut image of the Trinity precedes this Latin prayer in Groote's edition. Parr effectively sustains the incantatory energies of its repeated petitions to the Persons of the Godhead, together and severally:

> O the true and unfeigned Trinity, the great and incomparable goodness, the everlasting and sweet cleanness, and the inseparate majesty of the Father, the Son, and the Holy Ghost, have mercy on me. O good Father, and meek Son, O Holy Ghost, O light that cannot be put out; O Thee, only Father of heaven, have mercy on me. Thee, good Lord do I call upon; to Thee I do make my intercession and prayer. (fols. 42v–43r)[29]

The third of these traditionalist prayers follows in close proximity to "*De sanctissima trinitate*" in Groote's Primer. With this prayer Parr selects for translation and inclusion in her prayer book a Latin text that could indisputably find a place in a Lutheran primer. She thereby signals and stakes common ground. This prayer is another serial petition for mercy that proceeds on the strength of Biblical examples of deliverance—"Daniel from the lake of the lions ... the three children, Shadrach, Mesach, Abednego, from the hot, burning fire ... Thy beloved disciple Peter, being in great jeopardy of drowning"—to invocate a "merciful God" to "save and deliver me from all tribulation and enemies ...

28 See *A goodly prymer* (Marshall), Hiv v–Ii r.

29 See *Thys prymer of salysbury use* (Paris: Y. Bonhomme, widow of T. Kerner, at the expenses of J. Groute, 1534; *STC* 15985), fol. lxxxviii r–v.

For I am ignorant … to whom I should flee, or seek for help or comfort, but only to Thee, which art my Maker and Redeemer" (fols. 44v–45r).[30]

From this rapprochement on devotional common ground Parr next proceeds to transcribe, closely for the most part, but sometimes selectively, the devotional commentary on the sixth petition, "And lead us not into temptation," and on the seventh, "But deliver us from evil," in "The Prayer of Our Lord" section in Marshall's *Goodly Primer*. The expansions of the phrasing of both clauses in this reformist source emit their own incantatory energy, which evokes the momentum of a vernacular litany: "Keep us that we fall not into the sin of hate and envy, what occasion soever be given to us. Keep us that we doubt not in the faith, neither fall in desperation now, nor in the point of death." "Keep us from hunger and dearth. Keep us from war and manslaughter. Keep us from Thy most grievous strokes: the pestilence, French pox, falling sickness, and such other diseases. Keep us from all evils and perils of the body" (fols. 47v, 49r).[31] Such an evocation of a litany in the vernacular may have been premature, or only just on the way to realization, as Parr copied these clauses into her personal prayer book. Not until mid-1545 would Henry VIII grant Thomas Cranmer, Archbishop of Canterbury, permission to compile a litany in English for public worship. It is possible that these litany-like prayer book selections of Queen Katherine's, made in private, proceeded in tandem with the official promulgation of the Litany in the Church of England.

Whether influenced by the authorization of Cranmer's English Litany or not, this section of Parr's prayer book documents a sustained attraction to prayers that are structured by runs of parallel, sometimes slightly varied phrasing, with responsions that likewise take parallel form. After Marshall's elaboration of two clauses of the Lord's Prayer, the unusual appearance of a rubric signals Parr's reversion to the passion of Christ, the central object and subject of Primer devotion: "Here followeth a devout prayer to Christ, the second Person in Trinity, our only Redeemer, God and man." This gracefully styled prayer, the longest in her personal prayer book, proceeds through serial affirmations, ordered associatively rather than chronologically, of belief in the truth of the Gospel narrative of the final events in Christ's life. The recurring form of the affirmations displays felicitous minor variations:

> Lord Jesus Christ, King of mercy and of pity, I believe and knowledge that Thou sufferest in Thy blessed feet, to be nailed grievously on the cross for our sins and offenses …
> Also, Lord Jesus, King of glory, I believe and knowledge that when Thou wert yet hanging on the cross, Thou Lord, openest Thy most holy mouth, and prayed for Thine enemies ….

---

30 See *Thys prymer of salysbury use*, fols. lxxxviii v–lxxxix r. Another closely similar prayer (source unidentified) that proceeds by instancing Biblical figures whom God delivered occurs later in this section of Parr's book (fols. 59v–62v).

31 *A goodly prymer* (Marshall), Ciii r–Ciiii r.

The litany-like structure of the enclosing prayer is rounded out by the responsion to each of the affirmations of belief, also in a recurring form—that of a plea for mercy and forgiveness that recasts the cruelty and injustice done to Christ in His passion as effects of the first-person speaker's own sins:

> I pray Thee, Lord Jesus, ... for the painful wounds that Thou, Lord, sufferest there in Thy feet, that Thou, Lord, forgive me clean all my sin that I have done, in going, in working, idleness, and vanities ...
> I pray Thee, Lord Jesus, ... for the merciful words that proceeded out of Thy holy mouth, forgive me utterly all the sins, the which I have done in my vile speaking, and give me grace that, all the days of my life, I speak no leasings, backbitings, nor harm of any person .... (fols. 51r–54v)

Parr's source for this passion prayer is the compilation titled "Here followeth devout meditations and prayers with contemplations called The Paradise of the Soul" and appended to John Gough's composite Primer—English, with parallel Latin text in the margins—published in 1536.[32] By the late 1520s, Gough was active as a translator, redactor, and compiler of works by such early adherents of the Reformation as John Frith in England and Patrick Hamilton in Scotland. Although recurrently questioned by the ecclesiastical authorities in London, Gough, another English Lutheran, managed to sustain his publishing ventures and, in particular, to circulate his curiously inclusive, composite Primer, with its ample supply of pre-Reformation as well as Reformation materials.[33] Parr very closely reproduces Gough's translation of this prayer to Christ making only one substantive alteration in its lengthy text. In what is now a recognizable reformist move, she deletes a clause following the opening reference to Christ's "painful death," here quoted in italics: "*which body is daily offered in the sacrament of the altar, where ....*"

Yet the overall proceeding and tonality of this section are anything but partisan or adversarial. The original of Gough's English "Paradise of the Soul" is a pre-Reformation Latin compilation, of which the earliest printing is thought to be an *Orationale Paradisus Anime Nuncupatum* (A Manual of Prayers Named the Paradise of the Soul) published at Basel in 1498.[34] What Parr indelibly registers in copying this lengthy passion prayer is the nearly complete compatibility of her own devotion with this traditionalist expression of devotion to the crucified, redeeming Christ, as well as her gravitation to this particular Catholic prayer, plucked out of the matrix of a Lutheran Primer for inclusion in her own compilation. Reaching its midpoint, Parr's personal prayer book documents the significant extent of common

[32] *The prymer of Salysbery use, bothe in Englyshe and in Laten* ([Antwerp: Widow of C. Ruremond for] J. Gough, 1536; *STC* 15992), fols. clxviii v–clxxi r. In Gough, the text of this prayer is prefaced by a half-length woodcut of Jesus, crowned with thorns and dripping blood from His lacerations.

[33] Butterworth, *English Primers*, 120–28.

[34] Ibid., 62 n.

ground for prayer in the old religion and the new, particularly when its substance is given utterance in litany-like responsions for participatory worship by a lay Christian such as herself.

From Personal to Communal: Assemblages of Biblical Verses and Collects

The midpoint of Parr's prayer book is also recognizable, in hindsight, as a pivot that sections her compilation into two halves. The discrete prayers that have been the subject of preceding discussion comprise the first half; the second half preponderantly consists of large assemblages of Biblical verses, mostly from the Psalms, in English translations from various Lutheran sources. Parr's impetus simply to copy a preexisting assemblage into her prayer book was probably aroused by a staple item in many Primers, both traditionalist and reformist: the 189 versicles of what had come to be known as "Saint Jerome's devotion out of David's Psalter." Parr includes 130 of these versicles, in a sequence broken just once, and she again uses as her closely followed source Gough's English–Latin Primer (fols. 77v–96r).[35] Revered as the translator of the Latin Vulgate as well as the self-revising retranslator of the Psalms after he had learned Hebrew, St. Jerome could be considered the patron saint—certainly, an illustrious predecessor—of Parr's intense and rigorous immersion in the text of Scripture, especially the Psalter.

Another lengthy stretch of copied-out material is the Lord's Prayer followed by an assortment of 172 verses from the Old Testament, Apocrypha, and New Testament, for which Parr's source, again closely followed, is another compilation issued by Thomas Godfray, *The Fountain or Well of Life* (c. 1534) (fols. 109v–136v).[36] A shorter run of Biblical material is comprised of Psalms 86, 13, 18:1–6, and 54, copied almost verbatim from Coverdale's English translation of Johan van den Campen's Latin paraphrase of the Hebrew Psalms (fols. 97v–105r).[37] Parr's interest not only in Coverdale's textual labors but also in those of van den Campen, lecturer in Hebrew in the University of Louvain, demonstrates her inexhaustible appetite for multiple renderings of the language of Scripture and the deepened understanding and appreciation that these multiple renderings could offer.

There are, additionally, repercussions of Parr's public literary activity in the latter half of her personal prayer book. Her own initial venture had been to translate into English, as *Psalms or Prayers,* the 15 lyric compositions that John

35 She reproduces *The prymer of Salysbery use* (Gough), fols. cxxvi r–.cxxxvii v.

36 Reproducing *The Fountayne or well of lyfe out of whiche doth springe most swete consolations ... Translated out of latyn into Englysshe* (London: Thomas Godfray, 1534?; *STC* 11211), sigs. Cii v–Dv v. If not Godfray himself, the compiler and translator of this series of verses is unknown.

37 Parr reproduces the specified Psalms from Miles Coverdale, trans., *A Paraphrasis upon all the Psalmes of David, made by Johannes Campensis* (London, 1539; *STC* 2372.6), itself a translation of *Psalmorum omnium: iuxta Hebraicam veritatem paraphrastica interpretatio authore Joanne Campensi* (1534; *STC* 23540).

Fisher had produced by selecting and recombining excerpts from the Vulgate Psalter into new wholes, which he himself styled his Latin "Psalms" (Psalmi). Among the materials that Parr copied into her prayer book, "St. Jerome's Devotion out of David's Psalter" and Godfray's rangy assemblage in *Fountain or Well of Life* were produced by the same process of selection and recombination. So were her *Prayers or Meditations*, in which Parr authored a new text by transformatively redacting a portion of à Kempis in Whitford's translation.

Now, in her personal prayer book, Parr again applies this process, choosing and arranging excerpts from George Joye's *The Psalter of David in English* (1530) to create a new sequence of 83 versicles (fols. 62r–73r).[38] Joye's subtitle announces that his English text is "purely and faithfully translated after the text of Feline." Aretius Felinus was a pseudonym used by the Strassburg reformer, Martin Bucer, the most prominent figure of the 1530s and 1540s, in attempts to maintain peace and amity between Swiss and German Protestants, and between Protestants and Catholics. Parr's uniquely energized responsiveness to Bucer's Psalter in Joye's rendering, which she quarries to create Psalms of her own in her personal prayer book, is as suggestive of affinities in outlook and spirit as was her earlier responsiveness to Fisher in the prayer she composed on Christ's passion.[39] The difference, however, in her authorial responses to Fisher and to Bucer is her complete immersion in the phrases and tonalities of the Psalter in the latter case. Parr's piety attains a Scriptural abundance that approaches repletion in the latter half of her prayer book. On scores of its tiny pages she gives broad devotional implementation to a central Lutheran tenet: "*sola scriptura*" (Scripture alone).

It would, however, be misleading to convey the impression that prayers like those in the first half of Parr's personal prayer book are simply replaced by lengthy sequences of lyric and meditative portions of Scripture in the prayer book's latter half. Individual prayers do make their appearance, although in quite modest proportions. What is striking about them is their clear character as a group: these are texts clearly marked in form and content as prayers originating in public worship, here taken over into a private context. So-called "collects" comprise the largest category of Parr's prayers in the latter half of her prayer book. These are prayers generally in the form of a single capacious sentence, whose origins trace to Latin "*collectio*" (a summation offered by an officiating minister to draw together the various inward responses of the people to the biddings enjoined on them in the liturgy) or to Latin "*collecta*," short for "*oratio ad collectam*" (a prayer said over the gathered people,

[38] Parr selectively utilizes George Joye, *The psalter of David in Englishe purely and faithfully translated aftir the texte of Feline* (Argentine: F. Foxe [i.e., Antwerp: Martin de Keyser,] 1530; *STC* 2370).

[39] To discuss Parr's redacting of Bucer's Psalter in Joye's rendering would require an essay in itself, and will occasion no further comment here. Some preparatory assistance with such a study is offered in my edited text of "Queen Katherine's Personal Prayerbook," which supplies Psalm and verse references for her individual excerpts.

and hence one that speaks for them all as a group). Either etymology conveys the vital associations of the collect with collective or congregational utterance in worship, the difference being a more subjective emphasis in the "*collectio*," and a slightly more institutional one in the "*collecta*."[40]

The source of Parr's first three collects—"A prayer to the Father," "A prayer to the Holy Ghost," and "A prayer to the Trinity"—is a sequence in the service of Matins which reads identically in Marshall's *A Primer in English*, and its revision, *A goodly Primer*; a fourth collect, "A prayer to Jesus Christ," concludes the introductory passion narrative in Joye's *Ortulus anime* (fols. 106r–109v).[41] The subjects of these prayers are familiar as recurrences from the first half of the prayer book, but the sonority, composure, and collective expression of collect form register as novelties in the treatment of these subjects. Here is Parr's transcription of Marshall's "A prayer to the Father":

> O God almighty, our merciful Father, which hast so exceedingly loved us, Thy chosen children, that Thou wouldest vouchsafe to give us Thy only and well-beloved Son, Jesus Christ, our Saviour, to suffer death for our sins, so that all that thus believe in Him might not perish, but have life everlasting: we beseech Thee, for Thy abundant mercy and for that inestimable love which Thou barest to Thy Son, Christ, our Saviour, give us, of Thy grace and power, Thy favor into our hearts, that we may believe, feel, and know perfectly, that Thou only art our God, our Father, and to us an almighty helper, deliverer, and a Saviour from sin, from all the devilish power of hell, of this world, and from death: and that by Thy Son, our Lord, Jesus Christ. Amen.

Parr's notable introduction of collects into her personal prayer book expands the sense of common ground identified and attained that was evoked by the litany-like petitions of the later prayers in the prayer book's first half. Now, in the latter half, she broadens the frame of self-reference from first-person singular to first-person plural, and ushers into corresponding prominence a number of shared Christian concerns. In Marshall's collect, some of these concerns are given a reformist bent, including the petition for God's grace (equated in Lutheran fashion with God's "favor") and the premium placed on personalized faith (faith *in* God and Christ as agents of redemption) rather than objective faith (faith *that* God can hear prayer, *that* Christ is the Son of God), a distinction emphatically pointed by the tripled verb conjunction, "believe, feel, and know perfectly." The echo of John 3:15—"that all that thus believe in Him shall not perish, but have life everlasting"—enhances the sense of inclusiveness elicited by the form and substance of this type of collective prayer.

---

40 On collect form, see Janel Mueller, *The Native Tongue and the Word: Developments in English Prose Style, 1380–1580* (Chicago: University of Chicago Press, 1984), 227.

41 Parr is closely following *A prymer in Englyshe with certeyn prayers [and] godly meditations, very necessary for all people that understonde not the Latyne tongue* (London: J. Byddell for W. Marshall, 1534; *STC* 15986), Mvii r–v, or *Goodly Primer* (Marshall), Gii r–v, and George Joye, *Ortulus anime the garden of the soule* (Argentine: F. Foxe [Antwerp: M. de Keyser], 1530–31) (*STC* 13828.4), Gviii r–v.

That Parr gravitates towards prayers more focused on the Church than on the individual in the latter half of her prayer book is further confirmed by her selection and inclusion of the majestic prayer–hymn to the God of all creation, "*Te Deum laudamus*," under the title "The song of Austin [Augustine] and Ambrose," which is also its title in her source, Marshall's *Goodly Primer*; and her inclusion of the introit, the first part of the traditional "proper" of Matins, beginning with the first verse of Psalm 51, "O Lord, open Thou our lips, and our mouths shall show forth Thy praise," and ending with the doxology, "Glory be to the Father, to the Son, and to the Holy Ghost," for which Marshall (or Gough, who reads identically) is again her source (fols. 74v–76v; 136v–137r).[42] This devotional turn towards collective concerns of Christians, conceived as the body of Christ in the Church, reconceptualizes the body of Christ as conceived in the earlier passion prayers of Parr's prayer book. Equally, this devotional turn towards collective Christian concerns finds counterparts both in her universalizing evocation of the relations of Christ and the soul in her *Prayers or Meditations* and in her vision of the godly potential of England as an aggregate of persons of all estates that concludes her *Lamentation of a Sinner*.

Return of the Personal: The Final Entries

If Parr's personal prayer book had ended with the text that she embellished with retraced gold capitals and vine-like tracery on rectangular fields of deep red and deep blue, then the foregoing account of the dynamic of this work would be complete at this point. The prayer book would stand as Parr's proving ground, the site of her intense and sustained personal engagement with devotional crosscurrents and continuities in the early phases of the English Reformation. But the text of the prayer book does not end with its embellished portion; it continues across five leaves on which Parr's handwriting loosens and eventually trails off altogether. These stark final leaves seemingly inscribe the poignant record of her soul's struggles in the late stages of her only known pregnancy and the onset of the fever that caused her death at the age of 36. The five leaves contain five prayers—"A prayer in trouble," "For the lightening of the Holy Ghost," "In adversity and grievous distress," "For strength of mind to bear the cross," and "A prayer of the faithful in adversity"—with the text of the last one left incomplete. Parr's source for these final prayers is another work by an English Lutheran, Richard Taverner's *Epitome of the Psalms* (1539), which she follows fairly closely but does not transcribe verbatim.

With Parr's appropriation of Taverner's Psalm paraphrases, first-person singular locutions resume, and with them the profound interiority of the prayers in the first half of her prayer book. While registering heights and depths, the subjectivity expressed in these last prayers selected from Taverner is repeatedly steadied by a sense of equipoise, recognized as God's gift. To illustrate, the prayer adapting

[42] Closely reproducing *Goodly Primer* (Marshall), F ir–F iir, Ei r.

Psalm 60, "For strength of mind to bear the cross," pleads "Stop my wounds, for I am all too plagued and beaten. Yet, Lord, this notwithstanding, I abide patiently, ... continually waiting for relief at Thy hand." The speaker then proceeds to identify—using some Lutheran keywords, "favor," "promise"—the wellspring of inward patience: "I have received a token of Thy favor and grace. I mean Thy word of promise concerning Christ, who for me was offered upon the cross, for a ransom, a sacrifice, and satisfaction for my sins. Wherefore, ... be Thou my stay in perils, for all human stays are but vain" (fols. 140r–141v).[43] Likewise, the speaker of "A prayer in trouble" acknowledges a God-granted balance that steadies the soul in its vicissitudes. Uniquely in this group of prayers, this one adapts collect form to personal expression before appending a petitionary cry at its close:

> Lord, hear my petition, and have compassion upon me; turn my sorrow into joy: strip me once of this grievance, and so clothe me with joy, to the end my tongue may blaze Thy name, and give praises unto Thee without stop. Ah, Lord my God, deliver me out of these straits, and to Thee I will sing praises everlastingly. Amen. (fols. 137r–v)[44]

Parr's faltering transcriptions from Taverner's epitomes of selected Psalms draw the massively eclectic compilation of materials in her prayer book to a circular close. The work's movement encompasses a historically specific circuit of devotional common ground for Christians at the advent of the English Reformation. Such a deliberately created assemblage as Parr's, moreover, was a harbinger of developments to come in English devotion. While the authorization of Cranmer's Book of Common Prayer in 1549 for public worship in the Church of England was the single most decisive factor in the decline of Primers, they were replaced by a gamut of publications that approached devotion as personal exercise and cultivation, as Parr had done.[45] Her prayer book's prevailing tendencies in tracing devotional common ground for Christians would prove a no less predictive development. As traces of her own choices and direction, its combining of traditionalist and reformist sources subjected to many minute restylings sets the syncretic stamp of the English Reformation on the remarkable register of spiritual process and progression that is "Queen Katherine's Personal Prayer Book."

---

[43] Following Richard Taverner, trans., *An Epitome of the Psalmes, or briefe meditacions upon the same, with diuerse other moste christian prayers* (London, 1539; *STC* 2748), Giiiir–v. Taverner's original is a Latin work by Wolfgang Capito, an associate of Luther and then of Bucer.

[44] This transcribes the last three sentences only of Psalm 30 in Taverner, *Epitome*, Diii r.

[45] Butterworth, *English Primers*, 274–5, emphasizes the "end of an era" with the advent of the Book of Common Prayer. White, *Tudor Books of Private Devotion*, chaps. 9–12, acknowledges the decline in "official Primers" but argues persuasively for the diffusion of the type into such genres as "Scripture for private devotion," "guides to the devout life," "general prayerbooks," and "adaptation of traditional materials" in the later course of the sixteenth century.

Chapter 7
"Halff a Scrypture Woman": Heteroglossia and Female Authorial Agency in Prayers by Lady Elizabeth Tyrwhit, Anne Lock, and Anne Wheathill

Susan M. Felch

Among the anecdotes recounted about Elizabeth Tyrwhit—a lady of the Privy Chamber in Katherine Parr's court, briefly governess to the Princess Elizabeth in 1549, and composer of an early Protestant prayer book—none is more telling than this: After Henry VIII's death, Tyrwhit and her husband, a cousin by marriage to the dowager queen, continued in the service of Parr and her new husband, Thomas Seymour.[1] During the course of an evening's conversation, Seymour remarked to Robert Tyrwhit, "Master Tyrwhyt I ame talkynge with my Lady your Wyffe in Devynnyte," to which Sir Robert replied that although Elizabeth "was not seyne in Devynnete," that is, she had not received university training in theology, she *was* "halff a Scrypture Woman," by which he likely meant that her speech was formed by and liberally strewn with biblical quotations.[2] This description—"halff a Scrypture Woman"—might well be applied not only to Tyrwhit's conversation and to the prayer book she subsequently compiled, but also to the many biblically based prayers written by women throughout the sixteenth and early seventeenth centuries. These authors included royal women such as Katherine Parr, Jane Grey Dudley, and Queen Elizabeth herself as well as Lady Frances Aburgavenny, Anne Askew, Elizabeth Grymeston, Anne Gawdy Jenkinson, Anne Lock, Dorcas Martin, Lady Grace Mildmay, Elizabeth Melville, Anne Wheathill, and many others.

That Tudor Protestants should have reverted to the Bible in their speech is not surprising given the Reformation commitment to *sola scriptura*. But the specific uses to which scripture was put, especially in Protestant prayers, has not received

---

1 Sir Robert Tyrwhit's aunt Agnes (Anne) Tyrwhit, married Thomas, third Baron Borough; Edward Borough, their son, was the first husband of Katherine Parr. See A.R. Maddison, ed., *Lincolnshire Pedigrees*, The Publications of the Harleian Society, vol. 52 (London, 1904), 3:1019.

2 Samuel Haynes, *A Collection of State Papers Relating to Affairs… Left by William Cecill Lord Burghley* (London, 1740), 1:104. For a discussion of the Tyrwhits' biography and Elizabeth Tyrwhit's prayer book, see Susan M. Felch, introduction to *Elizabeth Tyrwhit's 'Morning and Evening Prayers,'* ed. Susan M. Felch (Aldershot: Ashgate, 2008).

much critical attention. Furthermore, what *is* surprising, upon close examination, is the relative paucity of unmediated biblical citation in these Protestant prayers, particularly given the extensive recitation of biblical material that characterized prayers prior to the Reformation. In fact, there is much more directly cited scripture in the prayer books composed before the Reformation than in prayer books composed by Protestants after 1517. On the other hand, the mediated use of scripture increases dramatically in the Protestant prayer books, and this mediated usage—prayers that are made "halff" of scripture and half of the author's own words—opens a window not only onto the practices of prayer in the sixteenth century, but also onto the question of women's authorial agency.

This essay, which focuses on private prayers and prayer books, interrogates the assumption that the use of scripture and scriptural language in prayers composed by early modern women may best be theorized in terms of a ventriloquism that occludes agency. In this critical scenario, women are allowed to speak only insofar as they utilize or ventriloquize words borrowed from the Bible and other religious materials, and these authorized words, in turn, restrict and contain the scandalous spectacle of women speaking. Thus, the contributors to the seminal volume *Silent But for the Word* argue that the Reformation restricted women "so that they could [not] speak or write their own ideas," and insist that religious writing deprived women "of any original voice."[3] As Gary Waller notes in the concluding chapter, "A very condition of their ability to write is their acceptance of constraints which deny them authentic speech."[4] Similarly, the language of derivation and conventionality obscures the rhetorical complexity of sixteenth-century prayer genres, as when Elaine Beilin notes that Anne Wheathill's prayers are derived from Scripture or Patrick Cullen states that they are "constructed as borrowings" or Betty Travitsky characterizes them as "conventional."[5] In contrast, a careful examination of the structure of scripturally inflected prayer genres, such as the psalm collage and psalm paraphrase, enables us to see the compositional skills on display in women's prayers and to overcome reductive readings that view them as unoriginal and derivative. Mikhail Bakhtin's conception of heteroglossia,

---

[3] Margaret P. Hannay, introduction, and Mary Ellen Lamb, "The Cooke Sisters: Attitudes toward Learned Women in the Renaissance" in Hannay, *Silent But for the Word*, 7, 125.

[4] Gary F. Waller, "Struggling into Discourse: The Emergence of Renaissance Women's Writing," in Hannay, *Silent But for the Word*, 246.

[5] Elaine V. Beilin, *Redeeming Eve: Women Writers of the English Renaissance* (Princeton: Princeton University Press, 1987), 53; Patrick Cullen, introduction to *Anne Wheathill*, EME, Series I, pt. 1, vol. 9, selected and introduced by Patrick Cullen (Aldershot: Scolar Press, 1996), xi; Betty S. Travitsky, "The Possibilities of Prose," in *Women and Literature in Britain, 1500–1700*, ed. Helen Wilcox (Cambridge: Cambridge University Press, 1996), 243. Beilin does note that "scripturalism" provided women both knowledge and expressive language (55) and Cullen acknowledges that Wheathill "mastered the cadence of the best English religious prose of her age" (xi); neither, however, foregrounds her creativity.

applied to the composed prayers and prayer books of early modern women, also provides a way to understand these prayers as dense and participative speech acts that engender authorial agency and "originality" not despite, but because they borrow half their words from the scriptures.

Lady Elizabeth Tyrwhit and the Construction of Psalm Collage

Scripture texts themselves, primarily from the book of Psalms, have characterized Christian prayers from the earliest period of the church.[6] Immediately prior to the Reformation, laypersons commonly used Latin manuscript Books of Hours or printed primers for their daily prayers. These Books of Hours and primers were simplified versions of the monastic hours of prayer (also known as the Divine Offices), which organized prayer into eight services—Matins, Lauds, Prime, Terce, Sext, Nones, Vespers, and Compline—to be said at regular three-hour intervals throughout the day and night.[7] Each "office" ordinarily consisted of liturgical formulae, hymns, composed prayers, and psalms, all of which were to be recited individually or by members of the household together. One such primer will serve as an exemplar of this traditional prayer book and its inclusion of scriptural texts.

John Gouge's Latin and English primer, printed in 1536—the year the former queen Katherine of Aragon died, the current queen Anne Boleyn was beheaded, and the Bible translator William Tyndale was burned at the stake—followed the traditional Books of Hours format, although it highlighted an English translation of the Hours, relegating the original Latin to the margins. The hour of Terce, usually recited around 9:00 in the morning, illustrates the typical prayer service.[8] It begins with a short introit composed of conventional liturgical formulae:

6 For a history of liturgical prayer, see Robert Taft, *The Liturgy of the Hours in East and West: The Origins of the Divine Office and its Meaning for Today*, 2nd rev. ed. (Collegeville, MN: The Liturgical Press, 1993).

7 A useful introduction to the Books of Hours may be found in Roger S. Wieck, *Time Sanctified: The Book of Hours in Medieval Art and Life* (New York: George Braziller,1988). For sixteenth-century printed prayer books, see William Maskell, *Monumenta Ritualia Ecclesiae Anglicanae*, vol. 2 (London: William Pickering, 1846); Edgar Hoskins, *Horae Beatae Mariae Virginis, or, Sarum and York Primers with Kindred Books and Primers of the Reformed Roman Use* (London: Longmans, Green, and Co., 1901); Helen C. White, *The Tudor Books of Private Devotion* (Madison: University of Wisconsin Press, 1951); Charles C. Butterworth, *The English Primers (1529–1545): Their Publication and Connection with the English Bible and the Reformation in England* (Philadelphia: University of Pennsylvania Press, 1953); and Felch, introduction, 19–32. By the fifteenth century, compressing the hours of prayer into fewer segments, in order to accommodate the layperson's schedule, was common; see Susan M. Felch, "The Development of the English Prayer Book," in *Worship in Medieval and Early Modern Europe: Change and Continuity in Religious Practice*, ed. Karin Maag and John D. Witvliet (Notre Dame: University of Notre Dame Press, 2004), 132–61.

8 *The prymer of Salysbery use, bothe in Englyshe and in Laten* ([Antwerp], 1536; *STC* 15992), H4v–H7r.

"O God bende thy self to my helpe. Lorde haste thou to helpe me. Glory be to the father to the son \ and to the holy ghoste. As it was in the begynnyng \ as it is nowe and ever shalbe. So be it." The service continues with the hymn *Veni Creator*, "Cum holy ghost \ O creatour eternall In our mindis \ to make visitation," and then prints Psalm 119 in the Vulgate numbering (120 in the Hebrew and Protestant numbering), followed by Psalms 120 and 121. The Gloria Patri, a short meditation and response on Christ's virgin birth, and a prayer for "contynuall helth of body and soule" complete the canonical hour of prayer. Three of the five octavo leaves that comprise Gouge's Terce are intact biblical psalms.

In contrast, there is not a single straightforward citation of an entire biblical psalm in all of Elizabeth Tyrwhit's prayer book and few in any of the Protestant prayer books that preceded or followed hers.[9] Tyrwhit's prayer book, probably composed in the early 1550s, is organized into two main parts, Morning and Evening Prayers, each of which is prefaced by confessional and preparatory prayers; it concludes with a set of "godlie sentences" or moral maxims.[10] Tyrwhit employs both prose and poetry throughout the prayer book. In addition to original prayers, she draws on numerous sources including the medieval Hours of the Cross, traditional liturgical materials, Lutheran hymns, previously composed meditations and prayers, and, of course, the Bible to create a encyclopedic, "ecumenical" prayer book. Yet the only intact biblical citations she includes are short, prose doctrinal passages, such as "Whosoever shall call upon the name of the Lord shall be saved" (Acts 2:21), that are titled "anthems."[11] What replaces the traditional citation of complete biblical psalms in the work of this "halff a Scrypture woman" are strategies of mediated composition that exemplify and employ a heightened sense of authorial agency.

The strategy closest to citation that Tyrwhit uses is the psalm collage, in which a variety of scripture texts are joined to create a continuous narrative.[12] A humanist genre, the psalm collage was popularized by the so-called King's Psalms, thought

9 Some one hundred distinct titles of private prayer books, many in multiple editions, were published by 1600, suggesting the popularity of household prayers as well as raising questions about their critical neglect; see Andrew Maunsell, *The first part of the catalogue of English printed bookes* (London, 1595; *STC* 17669), G6r–H2r.

10 Elizabeth Tyrwhit's *Morning and Evening Prayers* was printed in an abbreviated form in 1574 and again in its original format in Thomas Bentley, *The monument of matrones conteining seven severall lamps of virginitie* (London, 1582). For a discussion of the relationship of the two printed editions, see Felch, introduction, 58–64.

11 *Elizabeth Tyrwhit's 'Morning and Evening Prayers,'* Felch, 88. All subsequent parenthetical references will be from this edition.

12 The popular medieval St. Jerome's Psalter was also a compilation of verses drawn from various psalms, but rather than juxtaposing citations to form a narrative, it gathered them into a *florilegium*, an abridged anthology that could be recited by those who were sick, traveling, at war, or otherwise unable to recite full-length psalms or the psalter as a whole; see Paul J. Griffiths, *Religious Reading: The Place of Reading in the Practice of Religion* (New York: Oxford University Press, 1999), 98–104.

to have been composed in Latin by Bishop John Fisher but most likely seen into print and possibly translated by Katherine Parr.[13] Tyrwhit includes one of Fisher's "psalms" in her prayer book (45–6; 78–80; 109–10), but also employs the genre in her own first "psalm" for Evening Prayer (46; 90–92; 113–16). A beautiful prayer some 80 lines in length, this opening psalm draws on numerous biblical images taken from various passages to invoke God's mercy and protection. Near the conclusion of this complicated collage, Tyrwhit weaves together Trinitarian and liturgical formulae along with verses from the "Canticle of the Three Children" (Daniel 3:52–88) and Psalms 100, 103, 107, and 150, all of which enjoin creation to "praise the Lord."[14] It is worth citing this section of Tyrwhit's psalm collage at length in order to demonstrate both its narrative coherence and its complex compositional method. Although the prayer reads easily as a single evocation of praise, the source citations in square brackets show the author skipping nimbly from text to text:

> [Canticle:] Blessed art thou O Lord God of our fathers, for thou art praise and honour-worthie, and to be magnified for ever. Blessed be the glorie of thy holie name, for it is worthie to be praised, and above all to be magnified for ever. Blessed art thou, [Trinitarian formula:] O Father, O Sonne, and O holie Ghost, [Canticle:] for thou art worthie to be praised, and above all to be magnified for ever. Blessed be thou in the firmament of heaven, for thou art praise-worthie for ever. [Psalm 107:1:] O give thanks unto the Lord all his creatures, for he is kind-harted and mercifull: yea his mercie endureth for ever. [Psalm 103:22:] Oh speake good of the Lord all ye works of his in all places of his dominion: [Psalm 150:6:] and let everie thing that hath breath praise the Lord, and give him thanks: [Psalm 107:1:] for his mercie endureth for ever. [Psalm 107: 8, 15, 21, 31:] O that all men would therefore praise the Lord for his goodnesse, and declare the wonders that he doth for the children of men! [Psalm 103:2:] Praise thou the Lord O my soule, and forget not all his benefits, [Psalm 103:1:] yea and all that is within me praise his holie name, [Psalm 100:5:] for his loving mercie and for his truth, which endureth for ever, [Liturgical formula:] and worlds without end, Amen." (91–92)

Although these words sound—and are—unimpeachably scriptural (and may lure the unsuspecting critic into a fruitless search for their source in single, biblical psalm), they are in fact an original, creative composition. The ability to stitch together diverse texts into a congruent whole argues both a high degree of familiarity with the scriptural text and a keen compositional eye, suggesting one manner in which a woman might earn the sobriquet "halff a scrypture woman."

---

[13] *Psalmi seu precationes ex variis scripturae locis collectae* (London, 1544; *STC* 2994); *Psalmes or prayers taken out of holye scripture* (London, 1544; *STC* 3001.7). Susan E. James makes a case for Katherine Parr as the translator of these psalms. *Kateryn Parr: The Making of a Queen* (Aldershot: Ashgate, 1999), 201–10. Cecilia A. Hatt, however, does not believe these prayers are the work of Fisher. Cecilia A. Hatt, ed. *English Works of John Fisher, Bishop of Rochester: Sermons and Other Writings, 1520–1535* (Oxford: Oxford University Press, 2002), 429.

[14] Unless specified, Psalm numberings follow the Hebrew and Protestant tradition.

In Tyrwhit's case, her eye extended beyond the fabric of biblical collage to the literary genre of paraphrase. The main body of the psalm collage from Evening Prayer described above utilizes selections from Psalms 77 and 89–91 as found in the paraphrases of Wolfgang Capito, translated by Richard Taverner, as well as Tyrwhit's own authorial insertions (46). In one section, for instance, Tyrwhit begins with an allusion to Psalm 91, turns to the paraphrase of Psalm 89, and then moves to Psalm 90, stitching these paraphrases together with her own commentary:

> [Tyrwhit:] In full trust whereof O Lord I come unto thee, beseeching thee to [Psalm 91 paraphrase:] hide my life with Christ within thee, and under the shadowes of thy wings to defend me, [Psalm 89 paraphrase, changed from first person plural to first person singular with modified vocabulary, syntax, and order of phrases:] that thy grace and covenant may be with me evermore.
>
> Turne not thy mercie from me, [Tyrwhit:] O Lord, nor [Psalm 89:] bring me downe to destruction [Tyrwhit:] as I have deserved: but [Psalm 89:] shew thy [Tyrwhit:] grace [Psalm 89:] and favour unto me, [Tyrwhit:] that I may live, and (being [Psalm 89:] exalted through thy righteousnesse) [Tyrwhit:] praise thy name most joifullie.
>
> [Psalm 89 paraphrase modified:] Remember my corrupt nature [Tyrwhit:] O Lord, how short my life is, [Psalm 89 paraphrase, modified:] and that thou madest not man for nothing. No man can deliver himselfe from death: no man can save his owne soule from hell: thou onelie [Tyrwhit:] O Lord [Psalm 89:] must do it, namelie, to such as beleeve in thee.
>
> [Psalm 90 paraphrase, modified vocabulary, syntax, and order of phrases:] This life passeth as doth a dreame, or grasse in the field, which to daie is greene, and to morrow drie. If thou be displeased, then we be lost: if thou chafe, then we shrinke for feare, for through sinnes we be dead unto thee; with whome a thousand yeares be but as one daie, yea as the least minute of an houre. (90; see also 113–14)

In this section of the psalm collage, Tyrwhit not only amplifies the sense of assurance and blessing God's grace conveys, for instance by inserting the clauses "that I may live … and praise thy name most joifullie," but she also anticipates the turn to the images of dream and grass in Psalm 90 with her inserted phrase "how short my life is." Both amplification and anticipation illustrate the compositional skill she employs in her scriptural prayers.

The Construction of Humanist Paraphrase

As can be seen from these examples from Tyrwhit's prayer book, psalm collage encoded authorial agency within the seamless texture of biblical citations, often making it visible only upon close examination or audible only to a highly trained ear. Tyrwhit and many of the women who followed her, however, also employed another scripturally grounded genre—the Biblical paraphrase, a genre that highlighted authorial agency by expanding a single biblical text into didactic, theological, or even political speech.

A paraphrase might be as simple as Tyrwhit's elaboration on the traditional opening of Matins from Psalm 51:15: "O Lord open thou my lips, that my mouth may *speake and* shew foorth *that which is to* thy *glorie and* praise. *And shut my mouth from speaking of anie thing, whereby I should offend thy divine majestie, or be hurtfull to my neighbor*" (76, italics indicate Tyrwhit's additions). Here, within a short compass, Tyrwhit's allusion to the great commandment, "love God and your neighbor as yourself" signals a shift from a contemplative to an ethically active modality. But biblical paraphrase in the sixteenth century tended toward larger proportions and was itself linked ineluctably to Erasmus, who published his first Latin paraphrase of the Epistle to the Romans in 1517 and concluded the New Testament paraphrases with the Acts of the Apostles in 1524. It was thus a broadly humanist, rather than narrowly Protestant, genre. Erasmus had planned to write a formal commentary on Romans, but found himself instead producing a paraphrase whose main purpose was to clarify the tangled language of Paul and make his writings accessible to the layperson—to "make Paul speak … in the Roman tongue but more intelligibly."[15] While Erasmus was primarily concerned to reach the educated elite of the Continent and England for whom Latin was a second vernacular, the Latin paraphrases became widely popular not only with princes and prelates, but with ordinary citizens as well, so much so that Erasmus himself noted that "they are thumbed everywhere, even by laymen."[16] For example, Richard Pace wrote to Erasmus in 1519:

> I have read your paraphrase on the two Epistles to the Corinthians with the greatest care and wish to say that from this labour of yours I have gained so much that at long last (for such a thing never happened to me before) I dare affirm that up to a point (not to rate my own wits too highly) I understand both what St Paul says and what he means.… As it is, your paraphrase has made all so clear to me that I shall bid farewell to all the commentaries by modern interpreters of the Apostle, seeing how in so many places they have merely spread darkness over an author who had enough obscurity and to spare of his own already.[17]

This attractive "vernacular" Latin, easily accessible to educated men and women in England, appealed to Tudor reformers as a replacement for the medieval glosses, and they seized upon the genre itself as a suitable accompaniment to the

[15] *The Correspondence of Erasmus*, trans. R.A.B. Mynors and D.F.S. Thomson, annotated by Peter G. Bietenholz, vol. 5 of *Collected Works of Erasmus* (Toronto: University of Toronto Press, 1979), 196.

[16] *The Correspondence of Erasmus*, trans. R.A.B. Mynors; annotated by Peter G. Bietenholz, vol. 8 of *Collected Works of Erasmus* (Toronto: University of Toronto Press, 1988), 331.

[17] *The Correspondence of Erasmus*, trans. R.A.B. Mynors and D.F.S. Thomson; annotated by Peter G. Bietenholz, vol. 6 of *Collected Works of Erasmus* (Toronto: University of Toronto Press, 1982), 293.

newly translated English Bible. Even before Nicholas Udall, under the direction of Katherine Parr, organized the translation of Erasmus's New Testament paraphrases into English in the late 1540s, the paraphrase genre, in both prose and verse form, was being utilized for didactic, theological, and political purposes.

Leonard Cox's 1534 translation of Erasmus's paraphrase on the book of Titus, for instance, was rushed into print after Henry VIII's marriage to Anne Boleyn in order to teach the English people "howe moche and howe straytly we be bounde to obey next God our kyng and soverayne lorde."[18] In light of the momentous changes that had recently overtaken England, Cox understood the importance of shoring up the king's authority through appeal to scripture. But the scriptures themselves needed to be interpreted—to be mediated—and so Cox noted that he had added "the paraphrase of Erasmus which shall make all thing playne."[19] "Playne" here echoed Pace's encomium that Erasmus had "made all so clear" without acknowledging, as Pace had, that the biblical text itself was obscure. By drawing attention to its transparency and accessibility, however, Cox situated paraphrase as the antithesis to scholastic—and now by extension Roman Catholic—commentary. At the same time, Cox pressed his own paraphrase of Ezekiel 34 into political service, reconstructing the title "Defender of the Faith," which Pope Leo X had bestowed on Henry VIII in 1521 for opposing the importation of Lutheran books into England, into a Protestant badge of merit and representing the king not simply as a "moste redoubted soverayne" but more pertinently as the head shepherd of God's sheep.[20]

The challenge that faced writers, such as Cox, was to keep the genre of paraphrase from becoming *paraphronesis*, a caricature of the original text.[21] The goal, said Erasmus, was to "say things differently without saying different things."[22] Yet paraphrase was much more than translation, let alone replication; it aimed to "say things differently" even as it claimed to remain loyal to the original text. Paraphrase, as was soon recognized, was thus more nearly a species of commentary than translation, a "speaking alongside the original." Indeed, Erasmus, in a letter to Thomas More, noted that his paraphrase "truly deserves the name," referring to the Greek word *para* which means "alongside," because it was a continuous narrative of the biblical text rather than a segmented exegesis in commentary form.[23] Elsewhere, Erasmus described the paraphrases as "a kind of commentary," although he also distinguished the genre from the larger,

---

18 Leonard Cox, trans. *The paraphrase of Erasm[us] Roterdame upon [the] epistle of sai[n]t Paule unto his discyple Titus lately tra[n]slated into englysshe and fyrste a goodly prologue* (London, 1534; *STC* 10503), B1r. Cox was a schoolmaster at Reading and friend of the early reformer and later martyr John Firth.

19 Ibid., B2r.

20 Ibid., A6v.

21 *The Correspondence of Erasmus*, 5:196.

22 Ibid.

23 Ibid., 217.

more traditional commentaries.[24] Commentary is also how Coverdale defined the genre in his 1539 translation of the Campensis' *Paraphrase of the Psalms*: it is "a plain declaracion, exposicion or glose,"[25] he says, although Erasmus himself thought the Psalms, as poetry, unamenable to paraphrase. As commentary, however, paraphrases looked both inward into the text and outward toward the reader, combining exposition and application in one fluid narrative, as Cox had demonstrated in his preface. Indeed, as Udall noted a decade later in his preface to the English Paraphrases, they constituted "in a fewe leaves a wholle librarie of good doctrine, bothe for the private edifiyng of everie one particularly, and also for the enstruccion and teaching of eche other in common."[26]

Such breadth accorded well with Erasmus's suggestion in *De Copia* that paraphrase be considered an exercise in amplification.[27] The New Testament Paraphrases, then, combined Erasmus's interests in the exposition of Scripture and the development of literary studies. As he noted with pleasure, "Literary studies flourish and go forward, to the impotent fury of the theologians."[28] For Erasmus, the paraphrases were meant to entice readers, particularly those unskilled in theology, to return to the scriptures by making them plain and simple. Yet the way to plain and simple lay not in a spare and literal translation of the biblical text, but in its imaginative elaboration, an elaboration that highlighted authorial purpose and agency. As Erasmus noted in the preface to the Paraphrase of St. John: "it is the paraphrast's business to set forth at greater length what has been expressed concisely."[29] This "setting forth at greater length" called on all the rhetorical and literary resources the paraphrast, whether male or female, could muster and provided, if not an antidote, at least a counterbalance to the more restrictive requirements of Bible translation and literal commentaries.

For example, Calvin, commenting on Luke 10, objected to paraphrastic embellishments of the Good Samaritan parable. He particularly disliked the "allegory" in which the Samaritan is made out "to be Christ, because He is our protector: they say that wine mixed with oil was poured into the wound because

24 *The Correspondence of Erasmus*, trans. R.A.B. Mynors, annotated by James M. Estes, vol. 9 of *Collected Works of Erasmus* (Toronto: University of Toronto Press, 1989), 243.

25 Miles Coverdale, trans. *A paraphrasis upon all the Psalmes of David, made by Johannes Campensis* (London, 1539; *STC* 2372.6), A2r.

26 Nicholas Udall, "To the Jentel christian reader" in Erasmus, *The first tome or volume of the Paraphrase of Erasmus upon the Newe Testamente* (London, 1548; *STC* 2854.3), A1r.

27 *Literary and Educational Writings*, ed. Craig R. Thompson, vol. 24 of *Collected Works of Erasmus* (Toronto: University of Toronto Press, 1978), 303.

28 *The Correspondence of Erasmus*, trans. R.A.B. Mynors and Alexander Dalzell, annotated by James M. Estes, vol. 10 of *Collected Works of Erasmus* (Toronto: University of Toronto Press, 1992), 302.

29 *Paraphrase on John*, trans. and annotated by Jane E. Phillips, vol. 46 of *Collected Works of Erasmus* (Toronto: University of Toronto Press, 1991), 3. By the early seventeeth century, paraphrase was simply defined as "exposition of any thing by many words." Robert Cawdrey, *The First English Dictionary 1604: Robert Cawdrey's A Table Alphabetical*, ed. John Simpson (Oxford: Bodleian Library, 2007), 120.

Christ heals us with repentance and the promise of grace.... Anyone may see that these speculations have been cooked up by meddlers, quite divorced from the mind of Christ."[30] By contrast, Erasmus's paraphrase, while avoiding the more fanciful speculations, sidled between allegory and exegesis in creating a literary narrative:

> All the universal progenie of mankynde beeyng through the malice of Satan spoiled out of the clothyng of innocencie, sore wounded with al kynde of vice, cast asyde, destitute of healpe, half dead, and even at the next doore to desperacion, Jesus cumming down from heaven, vouchesalved to visite and see theim, ... And this Samaritane Jesus too, hath his hostes and inneholders.... And by these inneholders are to bee understanded the Apostles, and their successours, by whom even at this daie he dooeth cure and helpe mankynde, and gathereth the same from the violence of theves into the hostrie of the churche, where the woundes of synne are healed.[31]

The paraphrast's literary voice, as Robert Sider notes, thus added rhetorical "precision and colour" to scenes and portraits;[32] extended the range of the biblical text by drawing on allusions to other parts of scripture; and made explicit theological statements.

One important supplement to the English translations of Erasmus's paraphrases was Richard Taverner's 1539 translation of Wolfgang Capito's prose psalm paraphrases.[33] Insofar as writers followed Erasmus's injunction against paraphrasing the Psalms, they were unable creatively to engage and modify the primary biblical source for prayers. The popular Taverner-Capito Psalter, however (excerpts from which can be found in several Protestant prayer books including that of Elizabeth Tyrwhit), reshaped devotional practice by compactly combining prayer, doctrine, and pedagogical allusions to other biblical passages, thus mediating the psalms rather than presenting them for recitation as in earlier Books of Hours and printed primers.[34] So, for instance, the paraphrase of Psalm 23:2, which in the Great Bible translation reads "he shall feed me in a green pasture and lead me forth beside the waters of comfort," becomes in the Taverner-Capito paraphrase "let me lye in the fedynge groundes of thy plenteous worde, nygh unto the pleasaunt ryvers of thy

30 John Calvin, *A Harmony of the Gospels: Matthew, Mark and Luke*, ed. David W. Torrance and Thomas F. Torrance, trans. A.W. Morrison, vol. 3 of *Calvin's New Testament Commentaries* (Grand Rapids, MI: W.B. Eerdmans, 1972), 39.

31 Erasmus, *First tome or volume*, O5r.

32 *Paraphrase on the Acts of the Apostles*, ed. John J. Bateman, trans. and annotated by Robert D. Sider, vol. 50 of *Collected Works of Erasmus* (Toronto: University of Toronto Press, 1995), xiv.

33 Richard Taverner, trans. *An epitome of the Psalmes, or briefe meditacions upon the same, with diverse other moste christian prayers* (London, 1539; *STC* 2748); translation of Wolfgang Capito, *Precationes Christinae ad imitationem psalmorum copositae* (Strasbourg: Rihel, 1536). Taverner was a protégé of Thomas Cromwell.

34 Among other consequences, mediated scripture in prayer promoted literacy since newly composed paraphrases required reading rather than recitation of unvaried texts.

holy spirite, that I maye be refreshed, and bowe to thy correccion and providence."[35] The paraphrase emphasizes both the Reformation doctrine of *sola scriptura* and the necessity of the Spirit to awaken spiritual life, and it does so by reimagining the simple biblical text to make it more "plain." Similarly, the paraphrase of verse 4 highlights *sola scriptura* where the shepherd's simple "staff" becomes "the staffe of thy worde," and "the table [prepared] before me in the presence of them that trouble me" in verse 5 is glossed to mean "the bourde of thy worde [spread] before me."[36] Although such authorial intrusions are coded within the genre of paraphrase as "plain exposition," they require a high degree of theological and literary acuity. Indeed, paraphrase as a rhetorical trope demands the skill and imagination we associate with "original and authentic" poetic voices, and it is anachronistic to deny authorial agency to women and men who wrote paraphrases simply because the materials they paraphrased are authorized religious texts.

Thus, paraphrase provided a genre for sixteenth-century writers that allowed scripture to be married to an expansive literary and didactic framework. When carried over into the psalms, such paraphrases produced a prayer genre that was catechetical, devotional, and literarily complex. Broadly speaking, paraphrase helped to validate for intensely devout Protestants the ongoing creation of literary works. Within the bounds of religious writing, paraphrase provided an opportunity for imaginative writing, and it did so by recourse to highly developed rhetorical and literary skills.

M.M. Bakhtin and the Uses of Heteroglossia

The recognition of psalm collage and psalm paraphrase as respected and complex sixteenth-century literary genres prompts us to question contemporary critical perspectives that view scripturally mediated prayers as unoriginal, inauthentic, and derivative. Such perspectives subscribe (often unconsciously) to modernist views of originality as *sui generis* and implicitly favor "secular" over "religious" genres, since the latter are seen as constrained by doctrine and other forms of religious authority while the former are construed as "free" and unconstrained. In contrast, M.M. Bakhtin's notion of heteroglossia offers a robust, multidimensional, and nonindividualistic account of linguistic creativity that better fits both the production and the function of women's written prayers, not least because binary distinctions of all sorts, including the division between secular and religious, are not privileged within his paradigm. Heteroglossia—literally, "many tongues"—describes for Bakhtin the actual social conditions of any viable culture, which is necessarily framed, shaped, and populated by varieties of speech: the inflections of an older generation, the slang of friends, terminology from different academic disciplines, the accents of various ethnic groups, liturgical language, the contractual terms of an apartment lease, and so forth. As Bakhtin notes,

35 Taverner, *An epitome*, C3v.

36 Ibid., C4r.

> [A]t any given moment of its historical existence, language is heteroglot from top to bottom: it represents the co-existence of socio-ideological contradictions between the present and the past, between differing epochs of the past, between different socio-ideological groups in the present, between tendencies, schools, circles and so forth, all given a bodily form.... Therefore languages do not *exclude* each other, but rather intersect with each other in many different ways.[37]

In fact, it is not languages abstractly considered that intersect with each other, but rather languages as "they encounter one another and co-exist in the consciousness of real people" (292).[38] Real people live quite naturally, and necessarily, within this maelstrom of heteroglossia.

Thus Bakhtin begins with the premise that "in the everyday speech of any person living in society, no less than half (on the average) of all the words uttered by him will be someone else's words," a hyperbolic statement that nevertheless points to an important insight (339). Unlike Ferdinand de Saussure and his successors, who bracketed the messy complications of actual speech (*parole*) in order to concentrate on the structural simplicity of language (*langue*), Bakhtin refuses to release speech or writing either from its embeddedness in social contexts or from its communicative functions.[39] Language is never one's own; it is never neutral but instead is always "shot through with intentions and accents.... [I]t is populated—overpopulated—with the intentions of others" (293–4). Furthermore, language is directed both toward objects and toward others. It is embedded in prepositions: it speaks *about* the world *to* other people. As Bakhtin says in a pointed critique of Saussure, "*To study the word as such, ignoring the impulse that reaches out beyond it, is just as senseless as to study psychological experience outside the context of that real life toward which it was directed and by which it is determined* .... [L]anguage is heteroglot from top to bottom" (292; 291, emphasis by the author).[40]

---

[37] M.M. Bakhtin, "Discourse in the Novel" in *The Dialogic Imagination: Four Essays*, ed. Michael Holquist, trans. Caryl Emerson and Michael Holquist (Austin: University of Texas Press, 1981), 291. All subsequent parenthetical references will be from this text.

[38] For Bakhtin, novelists are best poised to utilize to greatest effect the potential of heteroglossia.

[39] See, for instance, his comment on word and world in "Forms of Time and Chronotope in the Novel" in Holquist, *The Dialogic Imagination*, 254: "However forcefully the real and the represented world resist fusion, however immutable the presence of that categorical boundary line between them, they are nevertheless indissolubly tied up with each other and find themselves in continual mutual interaction; uninterrupted exchange goes on between them, similar to the uninterrupted exchange of matter between living organisms and the environment that surrounds them.... The work and the world represented in it enter the real world and enrich it, and the real world enters the work and its world as part of the process of its creation, as well as part of its subsequent life, in a continual renewing of the work through the creative perception of listeners and readers."

[40] Only in Eden, notes Bakhtin, did humans experience unmediated language, a "yet verbally unqualified world" (279).

One consequence of such heteroglossia is that authorial agency is judged not by its distance or independence from sources, but rather by the use an author makes of the multiple voices which inevitably surround her. All writers—indeed all speakers—must appropriate the words of other people, pushing through the "social heteroglossia," that "Tower-of-Babel mixing of languages that goes on around any object" (278). Because language is inevitably both social and heteroglot, there can be no conscious or unconscious privileging of originality. As Bakhtin notes, "the word does not exist in a neutral and impersonal language (it is not, after all, out of a dictionary that the speaker gets his words!), but rather it exists in other people's mouths, in other people's contexts, serving other people's intentions: it is from there that one must take the word, and make it one's own" (294).

Artistic competence then, and indeed maturity both of self and of voice, is defined by Bakhtin as the "process of selectively assimilating the words of others" (341). The key question for authorial agency and authenticity, therefore, shifts from originality to selective assimilation. Here Bakhtin's distinction between authoritative and internally persuasive discourse is helpful. Because language is heteroglot and formed from the words of others, both authoritative and internally persuasive discourse begin with words and ideas that originate outside ourselves; they come from tradition, from our immediate family, from all the formal and informal languages in the larger cultures that surround us. Authoritative discourse, however, "demands our unconditional allegiance" (343). It is a binding word that can be either recited or rejected, but cannot be assimilated or appropriated. Authoritative discourse is composed of words that come *at* us, and Bakhtin identifies it as "the word of a father, of adults and of teachers" (342). In contrast, internally persuasive discourse consists of words that come *to* us. As we take these words into our own mouths, as we frame them, speak them, and modify them, they are "affirmed through assimilation," and are "tightly interwoven" with our own words (345). Through the work of internally persuasive discourse, we are imbued with authorial agency. The words that once belonged to someone else awaken new words and new thoughts in us and create the capacity for further ideas that remain unfinished and full of possibility. Bakhtin puts it this way:

> [T]he internally persuasive word is half-ours and half-someone else's. Its creativity and productiveness consist precisely in the fact that such a word awakens new and independent words, that it organizes masses of our words from within, and does not remain in an isolated and static condition. It is not so much *interpreted* by us as it is further, that is, freely, *developed*, applied to new material, new conditions; it enters into interanimating relationships with new contexts.... When such an influence is deep and productive, there is no external imitation, no simple act of reproduction, but rather a further creative development of another's (more precisely, half-other) discourse in a new context and under new conditions. (345–7, emphasis mine)

The phrases "half-ours and half-someone else's" and "half-other" inevitably recall the description of Elizabeth Tyrwhit as "halff a Scrypture woman."

Within a Bakhtinian framework, such a description, far from being dismissive or even derivative, recognizes and honors the agency that is implied in such an "interanimating" relationship.

Within this Bakhtinian framework, it is not difficult to see that simple recitation of scripture, as in the Books of Hours and some early printed primers, may, although it need not necessarily, be coded as authoritative discourse. Psalm collages, however, and even more particularly paraphrased psalms are clearly examples of internally persuasive discourse in which an author's own creativity, imagination, and literary skill are called forth and displayed. Indeed, one of the arguments used by Reformation authors against mere recitation of prayers—even when that recitation consisted of biblical texts—was that such recitation, "the labour of pronouncyng holy wordes and praiers," may, and frequently does, go astray if "the herte and mynde wandreeth from God."[41] Exposition, paraphrase, and newly composed prayers were needed to keep heart and tongue, mind and lips fully engaged.

Anne Lock, Anne Wheathill, and the Uses of Psalm Paraphrase

Certainly Anne Lock seems to have been aware of the possibilities afforded by paraphrase to engender and perform internally persuasive discourse. Lock's prose dedicatory epistles to her 1560 translation of John Calvin and her 1590 translation of Jean Taffin as well as her poems that conclude each of those volumes make ample use of biblical images, themes, and paraphrase. For example, in the 1560 preface to Calvin's sermons on Hezekiah, Lock follows Erasmus's view of paraphrase (rather than Calvin's) in her elaborate exposition of the Good Samaritan parable that compares Hezekiah with the beaten traveler lying in distress along the road to Jericho. For Lock, the Good Samaritan then becomes "the heavenly Physician" who anoints the king "with the merciful Samaritans oyle" and strengthens "his stomack with the holsome conserve of Gods eternall decree," ultimately setting "hym on foote with assured faith of Gods mercy, and staieng his yet unstedy pace and foltring legges with the swete promyses of Gods almyghtye goodnes."[42] At the same time, Lock does not merely replicate Erasmus's paraphrase, but rather pursues her own theological and literary agenda, emphasizing the sovereign work of God in the individual believer (rather than the work of the church) and linking the Samaritan's "oyle" to the lamp oil possessed by the wise virgins as well as to the medicinal oil of the scorpion, which heals the scorpion's own sting. Scorpion oil, in turn is exegetically tied to the story of the brass serpent that, in Hezekiah's

41 *[Devo]ut meditacions, [psal]mes and praiers [to] bee used aswell in the morning as eaventyde gathered out of the holy scriptures and other godly wryters* (London: Edward Whitchurche, 1548; *STC* 2998.5). Whitchurche repeats, in lament mode, Cranmer's defense of vernacular prayer in the Litany.

42 *The Collected Works of Anne Vaughan Lock*, ed. Susan M. Felch (Tempe: Arizona Center for Medieval and Renaissance Studies, 1999), 8.

day, became an idolatrous snare to the people of Israel but that, recuperated by New Testament typology, became an emblem of the crucified Christ. In the space of just a few pages, Lock thus creates a tightly woven narrative—a sermon in fact—that deploys densely allusive literary and medicinal images, all connected to oil, while ranging scripturally from the Deuteronomic texts of wilderness wandering, to the salvation offered by Christ, to the eschaton.[43]

When Lock turned to the genre of prayer, she retained her hold on paraphrase, entitling her 1560 sonnet sequence on Psalm 51 "A Meditation of A Penitent Sinner: Written in Maner of a Paraphrase."[44] As Cox had done with Ezekiel 34, didactically extending the paraphrase to embrace Henry VIII as the "head shepherd," so Lock utilizes the paraphrase genre to create her own didactic and narrative frame, that of a penitent sinner hauled to the very gates of hell by her own conscience and Despair's accusation, yet summoning just enough breath to call for mercy and plead repentance. To draw on the categories that Sider identifies, Lock uses paraphrase to add rhetorical "precision and colour," by crafting a speaker who is at once particular and universal, a recognizable anguished penitent whose unenumerated sins could be those of Everywoman or Everyman. She also extends the range of Psalm 51 by drawing on allusions to other biblical texts: for instance, in Prefatory Sonnet 5 she invokes the resonant image of the Syro-Phoenician woman who begs Jesus to give her the "crumbs" from the master's table (Matthew 15:21–8; Mark 7:24–30); and in Psalm Sonnet 10, she cites the "dredfull threates and thonders of the law" from Exodus 19:16 and 20:18 as well as the phrase "pearce myne ears" from Psalm 40:6.[45] Finally, she makes explicit theological—and political—statements, issuing a call at the conclusion of the sonnet sequence for rebuilding the walls of Jerusalem, an exhortation consonant with the hopes of the returning Marian exiles who desired to find in their new Queen Elizabeth a Nehemiah worthy of the name. Lock's references to the dangers of undermining fraud and "mighty violence," her evocation of the church that stands "in despite of tyrannie," and her confidence that "Jerusalem" will once again prove to be "[a] safe abode for them that honor thee," are transparent references to the reign of Mary Tudor and the patently unsafe environment she had created for Protestants.[46] Like Erasmus's and Cox's texts, Lock's prayer–poem thus paraphrases the "plain" scriptures through imaginative elaboration and a complex layering of voices that foreground her own interests and agency.

Less well known than Anne Lock is Anne Wheathill, of whose biography we know almost nothing. In 1584, she published a single book of 49 prose prayers, *A handfull of holesome (though homelie) hearbs, gathered out of the goodlie garden of Gods most holie word; for the common benefit and comfortable exercise of all such as are devoutlie disposed.* Its title page further dedicates the book to all

43 For a more detailed examination of these linked images, see ibid., xlvii–xlviii.

44 Ibid., 62–71.

45 Ibid., 63, 67.

46 Ibid., 71.

"religious" readers, the dedicatory letter specifying further those who love "true religion."[47] Such "true religion," after the 1572 St. Bartholomew's Day massacre in Paris, had become a code word for the English reformers, indicating their adherence to correct doctrine and practice and their alignment with Protestants on the continent.[48] Published within months of John Whitgift's consecration as Archbishop of Canterbury, Wheathill's prayers, which are arranged by both number and title, are shot through with a sense of present and impending persecution and the need to distinguish the present suffering endured by God's elect from the ultimate judgment he will visit upon the ungodly. She regularly contrasts the fleeting pleasures of earth with both the current chastisement of God's "flock" and the perfect "beatitude" they will enjoy in the future, seeing both chastisement and blessing as marks of God's love.[49] Wheathill's printer, Henry Denham, had also published Thomas Bentley's *The Monument of Matrones* in 1582, and in that compilation Bentley had praised women who "for the common benefit of their countrie, have not ceased … to spend their time, their wits, their substance, and also their bodies, in the studies of noble and approoved sciences, and in compiling and translating of sundrie most christian and godlie bookes."[50] It may well be that in the aftermath of Whitgift's accession, Wheathill, who picks up the language of "common benefit" on her title page, felt called to "bestowe the pretious treasure of time" and her own "talent" on a community that was feeling increasingly beleaguered and therefore in need of prayers (A2r).

What is certainly true is that Anne Wheathill's prayers display her ability as "halff a scrypture woman" to write complex and sophisticated scripturally mediated prayers. A single extended example and briefer comments on several other prayers will provide a model for reading women's scriptural prayers and understanding

---

[47] Anne Wheathill, *A handfull of holesome (though homelie) hearbs, gathered out of the goodlie garden of Gods most holie word; for the common benefit and comfortable exercise of all such as are devoutlie disposed* (London, 1584; *STC* 25329), A2r. All subsequent parenthetical references are from this text.

[48] See, for instance, John Field's dedicatory preface to Elizabeth Tyrwhit in which he commends her for her "forwardnes, fidelity and sinceritie in the religion of Christ Jesus." John Field, preface to *An excellent treatise of Christian righteousness* (London, 1577; *STC* 15512), A2r–A3v, and Anne Lock's use of "religion" in her 1590 poem on "The necessitie and benefite of affliction." See *Collected Works*, Felch, 188–9 and Micheline White, "Renaissance Englishwomen and Religious Translations: The Case of Anne Lock's *Of the Markes of the Children of God* (1590)," *English Literary Renaissance* 29 (1999): 375–400.

[49] Little analysis has been done on the content of Wheathill's prayers. Colin and Jo Atkinson have argued for an elaborate hexaemeral pattern with each week of seven prayers ending in a Sabbath, the whole concluding with a Sabbath week. See Colin B. Atkinson and Jo B. Atkinson, "Numerical patterning in Anne Wheathill's *A Handfull of Holesome (Though Homelie) Hearbs* (1584)," *Texas Studies in Literature and Language* 40 (1998): 1–25; and "Anne Wheathill's *A Handfull of Holesome (though Homelie) Hearbs* (1584): The First English Gentlewoman's Prayer Book," *Sixteenth Century Journal* 27 (1996): 659–72.

[50] Bentley, *Monument of matrones*, B1r.

their authorial agency. The major portion of Prayer 36, the second of two prayers of "thankesgiving unto God for the redemption of the world, wherein is shewed from what graces he fell, and how he was restored" is a paraphrase of Psalm 23. The paraphrase is framed by a brief doctrinal discourse on creation, fall, and redemption (at the beginning) and citations of Psalm 127 and 2 Corinthians 5 (at the end). The prayer as a whole, including the paraphrase of Psalm 23, becomes a sermon on human frailty, the benefits of baptism, the perils of this world, the joy of heaven, and the grace through Jesus Christ by which Christians are saved, and it incorporates passages from Ezekiel, Psalm 127, the gospel of John, the Pauline epistles, and the book of Hebrews (J10r–K1v). Placing Wheathill's prayer alongside the Great Bible translation that she would have known from the Book of Common Prayer, the Geneva Bible that she likely read on a regular basis, and the Taverner-Capito Psalter that she may have known from other sixteenth-century prayer books, allows us to see more clearly her authorial hand at work.[51]

The opening statement in the Great Bible translation, "The Lord is my shepherd; therefore can I lack nothing," paraphrased simply by Taverner-Capito as "Lorde, my shepeherde, fede me thy poore caytyfe shepe, than shal I lacke nothynge," is expanded by Wheathill into the following:

> And not being contented with this kindnesse, thou also Lord, considering our weake and fraile nature, readie to sinne, dooest with thy grace, guide us and governe us, as the sheepheard dooth his shéepe, suffering us not to want anie thing, defending thy poore flocke from the ravening woolves, that would else devoure us. (J10r–v)

Not only does Wheathill develop the biblical notion of "poore caytyfe shepe" toward which Taverner-Capito had nodded, explicitly noting the weak, frail, sinful selves who are dependent upon grace, but she also elides the sheep of Psalm 23 with the sheep of Ezekiel 34 and John 10, sheep who are dependent upon good shepherds as well as the Good Shepherd to defend them from ravening wolves.[52]

The next clause, "He shall feed me in a green pasture," paraphrased by Taverner-Capito as "let me lye in the fedynge groundes of thy plenteous worde," is expanded in Wheathill to read

> Thy blessed sonne hath put us to féed in the pleasant, gréene, and beautifull pasture of his holie church, making us to rest in the unitie thereof, by a livelie faith

[51] Even if she did not know the Taverner-Capito Psalter, it serves as a useful benchmark of earlier paraphrases.

[52] The predators in Ezekiel 34 are wild beasts; in John 10 and other New Testament texts such as Acts 20:29 they are specified as wolves. The Genevan text of Matthew 7:15 uses the phrase "ravening wolves," a designation picked up twice in the ubiquitous Calvinist-inflected household prayers appended to the Sternhold and Hopkins Psalter. *The whole booke of Psalmes collected into Englysh metre by T. Sternhold, J. Hopkins, & others* (London, 1562; *STC* 2430), 395–410. In each instance, "ravening wolves" refer to religious leaders or "hypocrites" who oppose the true people of God.

> and hope in him. Which church is verie plentifull, abounding with all spirituall meate of the word of God, which nourisheth and giveth life to the soule, as bread and other food féedes the bodie. With this food thou diddest féed the prophet Ezechiel, when thou diddest cause him to eate a booke, wherewith his bowels were filled, and it séemed in his mouth swéeter than honie. (J10v–J11r)

Here Wheathill employs the typology common to contemporary sermons to read the psalm both messianically and ecclesiastically: Christ himself, the blessed son, is the Good Shepherd who brings his people into the church where they are nourished through sound teaching. Such typology has a sermonic edge both because it depends upon Christian exegesis of Old Testament texts and because it forwards a didactic application—the food that the church should offer is the "spirituall meate of the word of God" and that meat only. References to New Testament texts undergird Wheathill's exegesis—she refers to the lively hope of 1 Peter 1:3 and makes an analogy between manna and spiritual meat that is suggested in the narrative of the temptation of Christ and is made explicit in 1 Corinthians 10. But in the final sentence, she deliberately reverts to the book of Ezekiel and its potent story in the third chapter of the prophet physically eating God's "booke," thus making her application, with its emphasis on scripture, more forceful.

The "waters of comfort" next mentioned in the biblical text and glossed by Taverner-Capito as "the pleasaunt ryvers of thy holy spirite" are by Wheathill converted specifically into the "running water of godlie doctrine" and "a water of spirituall washing by baptisme" (J11r), which she elaborates with reference to the river that pours from the temple in the prophecy of Ezekiel 41:1:

> This water saw the prophet Ezechiel long ago, gushing foorth of the right side of the temple, and grew to a great river, that no man could wade over; to which water whosoever we come, was made whole. Even so, in the water of our baptisme, we were borne againe, in the water of godlie doctrine we are nourished, and without these we are but dead in sinne and wickednesse, and at the end shall go to everlasting death: but these waters are to us a well springing up unto everlasting life. (J11v)

With this last clause, Wheathill situates the prophecy of Ezekiel within the context of the Gospel of John where Jesus, both to the Samaritan woman and later within the temple precincts, claims to be the source of water that springs up to eternal life (John 4:14; 7:38). The emphasis on spiritual washing and godly doctrine again forefronts the scriptural focus of Wheathill's prayers.

As the psalm turns to "paths of righteousness," Wheathill returns to her opening theme, human frailty, and takes the opportunity to move her typology from the messianic to the prototypical Christian:

> And if at anie time by our frailtie we fall into sinne; yet is thy mercifull sonne readie to receive us to his grace, and quicken our soules; if we be sorowfull and penitent. By which grace he maketh us also to knowe how to love him, and not to estéeme the pleasures of this world, but to have our eies onelie fixed upon him.

> So that with thine apostle Paule, we account all things but losse, that we may winne Christ, and be found in him, not having our owne righteousnesse, but that which springeth of the faith which is in Jesus Christ. (J11v–J12r)

Here Wheathill invokes the exemplum of St. Paul as a type of the faithful Christian, a move she makes frequently throughout her prayer book, drawing on numerous biblical figures. Characteristically, she closely follows the text of Philippians 3:8–9 in its account of spiritual loss and gain, but substitutes the word "springeth" in the final clause to echo the earlier language of waters that are a well "springing up unto everlasting life." The springing water and springing righteousness neatly illustrate Wheathill's compositional eye and literary ear.

Later in the paraphrase, Wheathill develops the psalm's "rod and staff" into emblems of correction, drawing from Hebrews 12:6: "his rod of discipline and correction dooth chasten us, when we swarve at anie time out of the right waie: by which we judge that he dooth love us; whosoever he be that he loveth, him he dooth chasten." And at the close of the psalm she draws both on Psalm 127:1 and 2 Corinthians 5:1 to elucidate the meaning of "house of the Lord" for the Christian believer:

> Thou Lord must helpe our house, or else we labour in vaine, thou must be our beginning and end, and then we be sure to dwell in the house of the Lord for ever. For we know surelie, that if our earthlie mansion, wherein we now dwell, were dissolved we have a building ordeined of God, an habitation not made with hands, but eternallie in heaven, where is perpetuall joie and beatitude, world without end, Amen. (K1r–v)

The eschatological richness with which Wheathill embroiders the simple evocation of "house of the Lord" provides a fitting conclusion to her meditation on Psalm 23.

Wheathill embeds another psalm paraphrase in Prayer 28, "Another praier unto the sonne, wherein the miseries of this our mortall life are remembred," this time utilizing the famous prayer of Moses in Psalm 90 (G11r–H3r). She ranges freely across the psalm, glossing some verses at length and ignoring others, while incorporating biblical allusions as well as liturgical formulae ("God of God, light of light," "Of earth we came, in the earth we travell, of earth we live, and into earth we must returne againe"). In her prayer, the "refuge" of the first verse of Psalm 90 is typologically understood as Christ's passion, a common exegetical move, but the prayer itself is less messianic than exemplary. For instance, her paraphrase of Psalm 90:4 incorporates the "ages of man" trope: "For the life of man is to be likened unto a night watchman, that when his houre is past, taketh his rest. Thus fareth it by the life of man, who first passeth awaie his childhood, next in youth, the third in manhood, the fourth in age, which vanisheth awaie like smoke that passeth awaie out of the chimneie" (G12v–H1r). The overall effect of the prayer, as exemplified by the ages of man trope, is to heighten the contrast between youth and age (a frequent topic in her prayer book) and to reflect more intensely on the rapid passage of life.

It is difficult to conceive of these paraphrases, which deserve to be examined in full detail, as anything other than creative compositions or, to use Bakhtin's terminology, as internally persuasive discourses. Rather than being contained within an authoritative structure or restricted from developing an individual voice, Wheathill employs an array of biblical figures, moves freely among texts, comments on theologically divisive issues (such as the meaning of baptism), and draws, in the best fashion of reformed preachers, on the *analogia scriptura* to develop what can only be called sermonic narratives.[53] Such sermonic gestures can also be observed in the ways Wheathill semantically appropriates the biblical text. Addressing the Holy Spirit, for instance, Wheathill does not only use familiar terms such as comforter and guide, but also, drawing on Hebrew images of God writing the law with his finger, prays, "O thou finger of God, touch my heart, and unlose the same from all worldlie vanitie" (H4r). In Prayer 10 she picks up the rhetoric of biblical proverbs when she writes, "Thou shalt deliver us in sixe troubles, and in the seaventh there shall none evill come unto us" (C11v–C12r). The parallelism of Hebrew poetry, when confronted with the need to find a synonym for a number, usually supplies the next in the series: "These six things doth the LORD hate: yea, seven are an abomination unto him" (Proverbs 6:16). Similarly, rather than simply stating that "the Lord will deliver us from troubles," Wheathill appropriates the language and cadence of biblical poetry so closely that the reader is tempted to hear it as a direct quotation. Such integral reworkings of the biblical text not only give Wheathill's prayers a distinctive and graceful voice but also witness the extent to which she had absorbed the language and cadence of biblical English—the extent to which it had become an internally persuasive and therefore creative discourse.

In sum, from the 1550s through the 1580s and beyond, Protestant women actively contributed to the project of theological clarification through the prayers they wrote and the prayer books they published. Their employment of mediated strategies, in particular the psalm collage and the psalm paraphrase, pushed the practice of prayer from the authoritative discourse of recitation to the internally persuasive discourse of creative composition. This mediated sculpting of scripture both enabled and required biblical literacy, a compositional eye, rhetorical awareness, an exegetical and sermonic mode of discourse, and literary skill—all of which argue for a heightened sense of authorial authenticity and agency.

[53] Beilin also notes that Wheathill "assume[s] the role of preacher." Beilin, *Redeeming Eve*, 55.

Chapter 8
Authority, Scripture, and Typography in Lady Grace Mildmay's Manuscript Meditations

Kate Narveson

At her death in 1620, Lady Grace Mildmay, a Northamptonshire gentlewoman and daughter-in-law of Sir Walter Mildmay, left her daughter a 900-page manuscript of devotional meditations written in her own neat italic hand.[1] The manuscript, a large, bound quarto, opens with an autobiographical memoir, and the meditations that follow address theological topics—mortality, sin, repentance, grace, the Lord's Supper, marriage, God's attributes, and so forth. They are not arranged in any particular order, and Mildmay regularly revisits topics she has considered earlier. Her theology is essentially Calvinist, reflecting the commitment to godliness learned in the household of her puritan father-in-law, Sir Walter Mildmay.[2] The manuscript is laid out as a fair copy with wide, ruled margins, running heads, catchwords, marginal scripture citations often connected by tie-letters to the text, and chapter numbers and (occasionally) titles. Mildmay, though, continued to revise this carefully prepared manuscript, deleting words or inserting new phrasings or additions in a tiny secretary hand above the main text. The following passage is typical:

> The Sunne, the Moone, & the Starres, with the
> whole firmament shall fayle: & the whole earth shall
> be ~~consumed~~ melted with fyre./

---

[1] Northamptonshire Record Office, Lady Grace Mildmay's Meditations. Mildmay numbered the autobiographical section with which she opens with page numbers followed by a superscript "o" and then started the numbering over again with the meditations. I will cite the manuscript parenthetically in the text, and will follow Mildmay's method of distinguishing page numbers in the autobiography from those in the meditations. I am grateful to Luther College and to the Folger Shakespeare Library for grants that supported this research.

[2] Linda Pollock, *With Faith and Physic: The Life of a Tudor Gentlewoman, Lady Grace Mildmay, 1552–1620* (New York: St. Martin's Press, 1995), and Retha Warnicke, "Lady Mildmay's Journal: A Study in Autobiography and Meditation in Reformation England," *Sixteenth Century Journal* 20 (1989): 55–68, discuss Mildmay's religious views. For a discussion of her memoir, see Randall Martin, "The Autobiography of Grace, Lady Mildmay," *Renaissance and Reformation /Renaissance et Réforme* 18 (1994): 33–81.

> But the word, oath, & promises of God, unto
> Abraham, Isaac, Jacob, & David shall stand for ever,
> for the stability & strength of all his redeemed people.
> Wherefore let us hold fast thereby, ~~in~~ laying up
> the word of God in our harts & meditating therein. (514)

The themes and sentiments here are conventional—earthly transience, the word given to patriarchs, and the strength that the redeemed find in meditation on that word. Yet the passage reveals that Mildmay was not only a product of godly culture but also a producer of her own narrative within it. The phrasing is scriptural in style, using the rhythms and images of prophetic discourse and of Mary's response to the Annunciation, yet it is Mildmay's own language, and she speaks authoritatively in the first-person plural. Further, the passage locates her in various positions, alongside patriarchs, alongside readers of Scripture, with the redeemed, within a transient cosmos, and finally in relation to the lasting Word held in her heart. In her words we see the confidence of voice, method, and style made possible by Scripture reading.

Although the nature of Mildmay's authorial confidence is complex, her mediations have received little attention, perhaps because it would be simple to conclude that they reveal only how thoroughly a woman could internalize dogma that corrals her actions and denigrates her sex. One could adduce plentiful evidence of Mildmay's profound sense of sin and masochistic embrace of the chastisements of a patriarchal God and could dismiss the meditations as, finally, lacking much interest. Her "authentic" voice, the argument might run, is subsumed under a patriarchal religious narrative. It is symptomatic of our modern preference for women's writing that was outside the norm that more attention has been given to Mildmay's medical manuscripts than to her much larger body of religious writing. But we should not too quickly dismiss the main work of this woman simply because its contents seem to indicate a cooptation by masculine discourse. As Danielle Clarke has argued, it is "naïve in the extreme" to assume that when women write in a male-dominated discourse it "can necessarily be attributed to the pressures bequeathed by a monolithic patriarchalism" since that presumes that a "real" female voice "always proceeds from the body" rather than reflecting "a motivated choice."[3] This presumption, Clarke points out, discounts

---

[3] Danielle Clarke, introduction to *'This Double Voice': Gendered Writing in Early Modern England*, ed. Danielle Clarke and Elizabeth Clarke (Houndmills, Basingstoke: Macmillan Press, 2000), 6. See also Rosalind Smith, "'In a Mirrour Clere': Protestantism and Politics in Anne Lok's *Miserere mei Deus*," in Clarke and Clarke, *'This Double Voice,'* 41–60. Citing theorists such as Elizabeth Grosz, Smith warns against "homogenizing" women in terms of their relationship to patriarchy, rather than examining them "in terms of their specific position in a complex intersection of cultural discourses," and she demonstrates the value of a "contingent and local" reading of the way that gender intersects with politics in defining "the patronage circles and subject positions open to a particular middle class woman" (49–52).

the nature of all voices as constructions, all writing as rhetorical. Mildmay's meditations, written in her own hand and for her daughter, offer rare evidence of a woman's rhetorical self-presentation free of the complications created by the mediation of male scribes, editors, or printers.

Further, while "meditations" are a genre that gave considerable scope to writers, they have received little attention from scholars, except insofar as they suggest the methods that lie behind the devotional poetry of figures such as John Donne and Richard Crashaw.[4] The scriptural meditations that appeared in collections of meditations and prayers can seem formulaic and conventional, yet this sort of writing did allow an independence of self-construction that deserves notice. Believers were taught to apply doctrine to their particular circumstances, and this imperative meant that even while adopting the "common rhetoric of spiritual discourse" that homogenized English Calvinist writing, writers such as Mildmay did two things that allowed a confident sense of authority:[5] they examined their own experiences, and they selected the specific scriptural and doctrinal frameworks by which they interpreted those experiences. Scripture provided an abundant source of stories, characters, moral dicta, and figurative language. Though far from the high literary culture Ben Jonson imagined when he theorized the potential for fresh expression in the imitation of classical literature, a writer like Mildmay nonetheless practiced a kind of Jonsonian imitation in that she drew from her own literary culture "not, as a creature, that swallows, what it takes in, crude, raw, or indigested," but as one "that feeds with an appetite, and hath a stomach to concoct, divide, and turn all into nourishment," converting "the substance, or riches, of [Scripture], to his own use."[6] In this analysis of Mildmay's self-presentation, I will attend to a range of intersecting forces that contribute to the remarkable confidence of her rhetoric, and will assess how factors such as the physical layout of her manuscript, her comments about reading Scripture, her compositional practices, and her sense of her relationship to the divine shed light on her claims for her work's authoritative status.

---

4 The seminal study in this vein is Louis Martz, *The Poetry of Meditation: A Study of English Religious Literature of the Seventeenth Century* (New Haven: Yale University Press, 1962).

5 The phrase is from Paul Seaver, *Wallington's World: A Puritan Artisan in Seventeenth-Century London* (Stanford: Stanford University Press, 1985), 16. Lisa Gordis's study of lay writing in colonial New England, though, contends that "the practices of this interpretive community tended toward fluidity, rather than toward determination," because the Puritan laity "were expected to engage in active reading not only of the biblical text, but of the sermons in which their ministers 'opened' that text as well." See Gordis, *Opening Scripture: Bible Reading and Interpretive Authority in Puritan New England* (Chicago: University of Chicago Press, 2003), 99.

6 Ben Jonson, "Timber: or Discoveries," in *The Complete Poems*, ed. George Parfitt (New York: Penguin Books, 1988), 448.

Mildmay's Manuscript and the Humanist *Mise En Page*

Recent work on the history of the book has made us aware of the many ways in which women engaged early modern manuscript culture: women participated in literary circles that created miscellanies, they kept journals, they wrote religious verse, and they created presentation copies. Scholars have demonstrated that few women produced manuscripts that were strictly private, and that there was great variety in the ways manuscripts were prepared for their anticipated audiences, so that women's manuscripts range from notebook jottings to carefully prepared "scribal publications."[7] In Mildmay's case, the use of extensive marginal citations, tie-letters to the text, and running heads add up to something like the "humanist" page layout used in learned texts, with headings and printed marginal notes (Fig. 8.1).[8] This layout is quite unusual, though, for a devotional manuscript. Lay people occasionally left manuscript books of devotion formatted in imitation of printed books with features such as ruled margins, ornate capitals, or tables of contents, but none that I have seen share Mildmay's use of extensive marginal citations or running heads. Manuscript miscellanies also often included meditations, prayers, or sermon notes, but these are almost always copied as plain blocks of text, without any formatting or paratextual elements beyond the occasional reference to Scripture jotted at the side.[9] One of Mildmay's contemporaries, Elizabeth Hastings, Countess of Huntington, left four fair copies of a collection of devotional material and, like Mildmay's manuscript, these were created for family members. Yet Hastings's manuscript is quite simple, copying out a range of texts without systematic or elaborate formatting.[10] What does the care Mildmay lavished on her manuscript's *mise en page* tell us about her conception of her writing, and in particular what does it reveal about her sense of her text's authority?

It might appear that Mildmay's format indicates that she accorded her work the considerable authority of learned humanist texts and that her manuscript is a form of scribal publication. However, even though it is as carefully laid out as

---

[7] See, for example, the essays in Victoria E. Burke and Jonathan Gibson, eds., *Early Modern Women's Manuscript Writing: Selected Papers from the Trinity/Trent Colloquium* (Aldershot: Ashgate, 2004).

[8] For the humanist page, see Anthony Grafton, "The Humanist as Reader," in *A History of Reading in the West*, ed. Guglielmo Cavallo and Roger Chartier, trans. Lydia G. Cochrane (Amherst: University of Massachusetts Press, 1999), 204; Elizabeth Eisenstein, *The Printing Revolution in Early Modern Europe* (Cambridge: Cambridge University Press, 1993), 63–72; David R. Carlson, *English Humanist Books: Writers and Patrons, Manuscript and Print, 1475–1525* (Toronto: University of Toronto Press, 1993), 31.

[9] Examples of manuscript fair copies of devotional collections include Folger MS V.a.482; BL MS Stowe 30; BL Add. MS 10397; BL MS Stowe 983; Lambeth MS 1159; Bodleian MS Rawl. C.473, MS Rawl. C.583, MS Rawl. C.765; Society of Antiquaries Library MS/295. Rougher manuscript collections of prayer and devotion include BL MS Carte.265; BL MS Egerton 607; Bodleian Add. MS. B.58; and Northamptonshire Record Office MS FH 246.

[10] Huntington Library MS HM 15369.

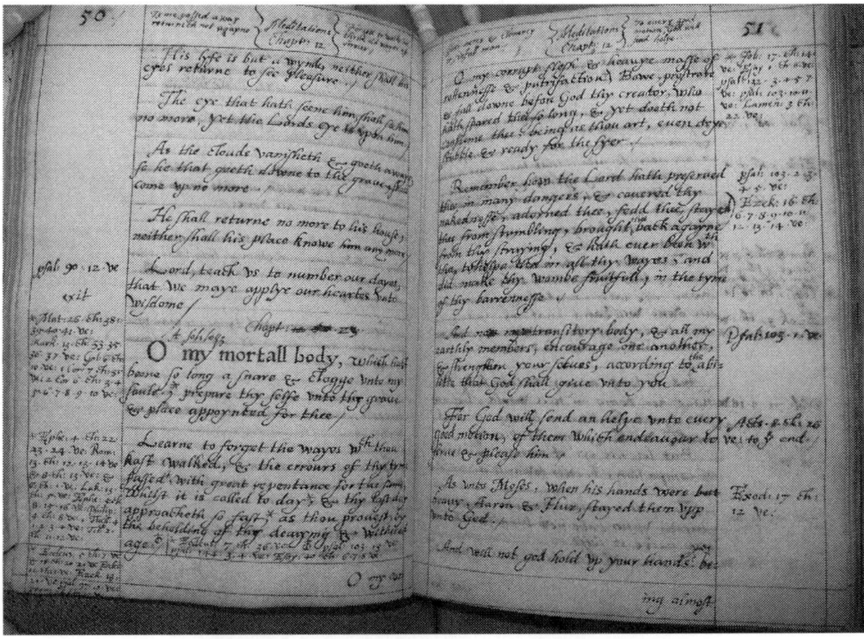

Fig. 8.1 Lady Grace Mildmay's Meditations, 50–51. Reproduced by permission of the Northamptonshire Record Office.

many presentation copies, scribal publication, with its implicit claims to authority, seems not to have been her intent. The manuscript was clearly a working book that saw daily use in her devotional practice, as she regularly inserted corrections and additions. She did see the manuscript as useful to others besides herself, but only within her extended family; she bequeathed it to her daughter, prefaced it with advice to her grandson, and seems at one point to have intended to make several copies.[11] The possibility that she was imitating learned texts is also unlikely because in the rare places where she comments on her writing, she explicitly disclaims learning or method, and her work itself makes no effort to employ the rhetorical structures that characterize the prose style and method of learned texts. The development of ideas within the meditations is quite random, and the arrangement of the meditations in the manuscript is equally arbitrary, following neither common orders of theological loci, liturgy, nor church calendar. She was also not imitating published prayer books since the lack of an ordering

[11] In her dedicatory epistle to her daughter Mary she writes that she gives her book "unto each of them," inserting "my daughter and her children" above the line. This line, though, is crossed out and she has written instead that she gives "the booke of my meditations, written" (5). Also, at one point she notes at the head of the page that the following meditation on the sacraments is "set with the lyke in the 301 page of the new booke, and 558 page in this booke" (29°).

principle is in contrast with collections of private prayers which generally were rooted in liturgy (morning and evening prayer, or a weekly order of prayer) or were occasional collections that began with morning and evening prayers and then were arranged topically—prayers before meals, in time of sickness, before travel, etc. In Mildmay's collection, the ordering of topics appears random: a meditation on the wickedness of these latter times is followed by a meditation on the way that the Lord sends godly motions. In short, the page layout is that of printed books, in particular the humanist page, but the compositional principles are not.

Mildmay was aware that her book lacked a system, but it is not clear that she regarded this as a flaw. She certainly accepted her culture's belief that less was to be expected of women than men intellectually: in the memoir that prefaces her meditations, for instance, the superlative compliment that she pays her governess is that she "could apprehend, and contrive any matter whatsoever propounded unto her … as well as most men could have done" (9°), and she warns her daughter to read her meditations "not looking for Eloquence, exact Method, or learning, which could not proceed from me, who have not been raised up in universitie learning" (31°). Yet Mildmay also hints that she did not see her plainer style as an impediment. Early in her manuscript, she makes an apparently self-deprecating comment with regard to an unfinished project of abstracting John Foxe's *Actes and Monuments*, saying that she leaves it to others "to perform it in a better manner then myne abilitie could afford" (20). Yet it is not clear whether the comment reflects assumptions about her limitations as a woman, since she first offers an explanation, "I could not proceed therein bycause my sight did sodeynely goe from mee," which she emends to "I was interrupted in proceeding therein" (20), indicating that she discontinued the project because of practical exigencies, not because she lacked ability. Further, she follows the comment about leaving the work to those who can perform it better with a self-satisfied "yet I trust God will accept of his owne giftes according to the measure thereof" and with the pointed hope that God will bless their effort "who are moved with an humble and faithfull heart thereunto. / But assuredly God will not assiste an arrogant spirit in these divine Labours" (20). Using standard doctrinal tenets—that God accepts of efforts according to the talents God has given, that none has reason for pride in service to God—Mildmay is able to find good grounds for confidence that a lack of sophisticated schooling need not hinder a child of God. But if she is not claiming humanist learning as the basis of, or even necessary to, her authority, on what ground does she, then, base her devotional authority, and why did she design her page as she did?

Mildmay herself would point to Scripture as that which authorizes what she writes. As she declares, readers of her meditations will find "every poynt of doctrine confirmed and approoved by the Scriptures" (5). This desire to signal her dependence on God's Word helps to explain her distinctive page format. In setting up her page, she seems to be imitating the devotional works of Thomas Rogers, who translated Thomas à Kempis's *Imitation of Christ* and a number of pseudo-Augustinian meditations in the 1580s and who helped to establish a new print layout for the devotional page.[12] (Figure 8.2). The usual *mise en page* for printed collections of prayers and meditations was a page with a decorative border, a format derived originally from medieval books of hours and continued during the transition to print.[13] This format was modified in many manuscript prayer books, which retained decorative elements such as elaborate capitals, red-ruled margins, and scrolls or flourishes along the edges or bottoms of the page.[14] In either case, such a page leaves no room for marginal notation. But Rogers explicitly sought to Protestantize these medieval works by noting Scripture references in the margin. He explains in the introduction to *A Pretious Booke of Heavenlie Meditations*, for instance, that seeing the work to savor

> of Gods holie word; and to be as holie for phrase, as for matter holie…: me thought were the places of Scripture annexed in the margine, it would be a quick spur … unto the true Christians zealouslie to read this ancient and godlie Father, when they should see al his sentences in a maner to be nothing but verie Scripture.[15]

Rogers thus adapted the format of the humanist page for his purposes, and Mildmay, who likely owned Rogers's translation of à Kempis, seems to have followed suit.[16] Her use of the humanist format, then, rather than signaling a learned intertextuality, is intended to signal that she defers in every point to the authority of Scripture.

Mildmay's Meditations and Early Modern Scripturalism

Mildmay's commitment to showing that every statement is anchored in Scripture is witnessed by the care she took to refer to scriptural sources in the margins and to devise symbols to connect her text to scriptural references clearly. She experimented with elaborate systems to signal typographically the relationship between margin and text. At some points she used a set of symbols—trefoil, ◊, ♀, and many others—to connect references in the margin to the text, and at

---

[12] The pseudo-Augustinian works are *A Pretious Booke of Heavenlie Meditations*; *A Right Christian Treatise, Entituled S. Augustines Praiers*; and *S. Augustines manuel Conteining special, and piked meditations*, all first printed in 1581.

[13] Eamon Duffy, *Marking the Hours: English People and their Prayers 1240–1570* (New Haven: Yale University Press, 2006), chs. 8–10.

[14] For instance, Folger MS V.a.482; BL Stowe 30; and BL Add. MS. 10397.

[15] Thomas Rogers, trans. *A Pretious Booke of Heavenlie Meditations, called a Private Talke of the Soule with God* (London, 1597), A6v–A7r.

[16] Mildmay includes à Kempis among the four books her mother gave her. If the books were given at her marriage in 1567, she would have received the translation by E.H. Seene, published that year. However, Mildmay continued to buy updated editions of books such as Foxe's *Actes and Monuments*, and by far the more popular translation of à Kempis was that by Rogers, first published in 1580 and seeing at least eighteen editions by 1640. It seems likely that Mildmay would have acquired this standard edition.

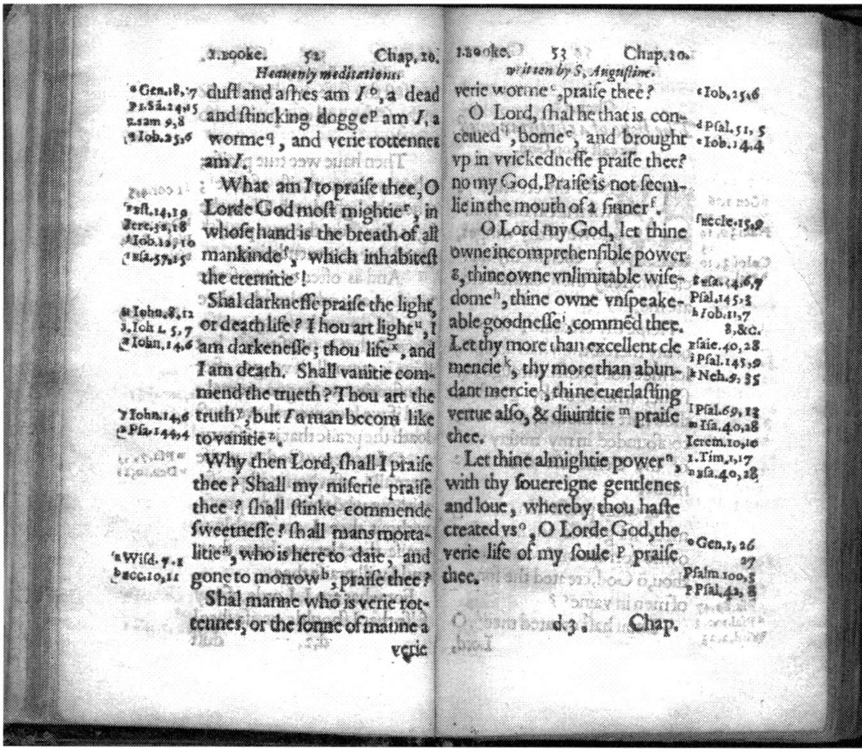
1. booke. 52 Chap. 10.
Heauenly meditations.
dust and ashes am I, a dead and stincking dogge am I, a worme, and verie rottennes am I.
What am I to praise thee, O Lorde God most mightie, in whose hand is the breath of all mankinde, which inhabitest the eternitie!
Shal darknesse praise the light, or death life? Thou art light, I am darkenesse; thou life, and I am death. Shall vanitie commend the trueth? Thou art the truth, but I a man becom like to vanitie.
Why then Lord, shall I praise thee? Shall my miserie praise thee? shall stinke commende sweetnesse? shall mans mortalitie, who is here to daie, and gone to morow, praise thee?
Shal manne who is verie rottennes, or the sonne of manne a verie

1. booke. 53 Chap. 10.
written by S. Augustine.
verie worme, praise thee?
O Lord, shal he that is conceiued, borne, and brought vp in wickednesse praise thee? no my God. Praise is not seemlie in the mouth of a sinner.
O Lord my God, let thine owne incomprehensible power, thine owne vnlimitable wisedome, thine owne vnspeakeable goodnesse, commend thee. Let thy more than excellent clemencie, thy more than abundant mercie, thine euerlasting vertue also, & diuinitie praise thee.
Let thine almightie power, with thy soueraigne gentlenes and loue, whereby thou haste created vs, O Lorde God, the verie life of my soule praise thee.
Chap.

Fig. 8.2 A Page from Thomas Rogers's translation of ***A Pretious Booke of Heavenlie Meditations*** (London, 1597), 52–3. Reproduced by courtesy of the Rare Book & Manuscript Library, University of Illinois at Urbana-Champaign.

other times she used alphabetical tie-notes, the method used in the Geneva Bible. Mildmay explicitly comments in several places on the reading practices that inform this aspect of her manuscript. For example, she claims in her memoir that her knowledge of Scripture was based on methodical daily reading: "every daye as my leisure would give me leave, and the grace of God permitt and drawe me," she would "read a chapter in the bookes of Moses, another in one of the prophetes one chapter in the Gospells, and another in the Epistles to the end of the revelation, and the whole psalmes appoynted for the daye" (45°). Mildmay held Bible reading to be a believer's most fundamental activity, and in the very first words of her memoir, she advises her readers to "beginn with the scriptures to read with all diligence continually every daye in some measure untill we have gone thorough the whole booke of God … and then beginn agayne and so over and over without weariness" (1°). This intensive reading produced a familiarity with Scripture that allows Mildmay to cross-reference texts from the Old and New Testaments independently of the concordance published with her Geneva Bible.

Further, because many topics recur throughout Scripture, Mildmay notes that "I have quoted [related verses] in the margins of the booke for proofe and our further [directing] and instruction" (20°).

An examination of the meditations themselves reveals that she drew on this knowledge of Scripture in a number of ways. One frequent means is to incorporate verses from Scripture into a prayer or meditation. Early in the manuscript, Mildmay signals such direct quotation by placing one asterisk next to her transcription of the verse, and another in the margin next to the scriptural reference. Other times, she simply copies out extended passages, noting the reference in the margin at the outset. In some cases, she adjusts the syntax of the verse to fit her context, as when she uses Isaiah 1:18, which is in the declarative mode, and turns it into the subjunctive (175). The prayer in which she uses this verse also includes Micah 7:18–20 (the opening), Psalm 51:126; Psalm 141:2–3; and Psalm 19:14, and thus is an example of the collage prayers that appear regularly in manuscript miscellanies and printed prayer books.[17] Mildmay also composes whole meditations by means of Scripture collage, often using longer passages, as when she concludes one meditation with Romans 7:14–25, and then opens the next meditation with Colossians 1:18–20, Colossians 2:13–14, and Hebrews 10:19–25, all texts related to Christ's regenerative work and the renewal of Christian fellowship. As she declares at another point in her memoir, "the less of my own additions in our meditations, the better" (16°).

But Scripture collages make up only a small part of Mildmay's manuscript. In other cases, she composes meditations in her own words, and the marginal citations refer to scriptural passages on related topics. For instance, in one meditation Mildmay writes "I minister thy mercyes but as the servant and disciple of my Lorde, as I have learned of him, and as he hath commaunded me." For this sentence she cites Luke 10:30–37, which is the story of the good Samaritan. The story might not seem to fit Mildmay's theme, since at first blush it is not about someone following Christ's commandment but about an outsider showing mercy. However, the parable concludes with Christ asking his interrogator "which nowe of these three, thinkest thou, was neighbour unto him that fell among the theeves? And he sayde, he that shewed mercie on him. Then sayde Jesus unto him, Goe, and do thou likewise" (Luke 10:36–7; Geneva). Mildmay seems to have had that final injunction in mind. She makes a similar connection to a parable seen in light of its concluding application in her next line: "It is the holy name of our lord Jesus Christ that is the lyfe of all that liveth, and the health and salvation of all that is preserved." She cites Acts 3:1–17, the story of Peter and John healing a cripple. Again the story seems only marginally relevant until we get to the final line, when

---

[17] Susan Felch notes that collage prayers reflect Protestant emphases by "compactly combining prayer, doctrine, and pedagogical allusions to other scriptural passages, all within the authoritative voice of Scripture." Susan M. Felch, introduction to *Elizabeth Tyrwhit's 'Morning and Evening Prayers,'* ed. Susan M. Felch (Aldershot: Ashgate, 2008), 42. See also the essay by Susan Felch in this collection.

the apostles tell the crowd "his Name hath made this man sound, whome yee see, and knowe, through faith in his Name" (Acts 3:16; Geneva). Mildmay, then, remembered not only the stories related in the parables but also the "sententia" with which each concluded, and she applies those scriptural cases of mercy and healing encouraged by Christ in a way that places her own work in the same context. Her procedure, here, is not so much a matter of proof-texting as it is of a typological mentality that sees events in Scripture and in her own life as part of the same interpretive field.

This typological cast of mind equally shapes the way that Mildmay justifies sharing her meditations with others. Randall Martin has characterized these meditations as completely private in nature, with little sense on Mildmay's part of herself as an author, since she does not adopt "presentational strategies which might be used to carry along an imagined audience."[18] And yet the introductory matter indicates that Mildmay does have a clear sense that her meditations may be profitably read by others. She insists that "I have not sett them downe for ostentation or vanitie, as God himselfe is witnesse but with the zeale of my hart. / Knowing that there is nothing hath happened unto me in the course of my lyfe, either in prosperitie or adversitie in any kynde whatsoever, but the lyke maye fall out to some other, wherein my comforts and remedies may be approved unto them as they have been unto mee" (30–31°). Just as there is no historical distance between the experiences recorded in Scripture and Mildmay's experiences, so the experiences of the godly "fall out" alike, and the thoughts that Jesus has "brought into" Mildmay's mind may comfort others (5°). This assumption was standard in devotional writing of the time as writers stated in prefatory letters that they had published their meditations with the hope that they would be helpful to readers in like circumstances.[19] Thus while Martin holds that Mildmay later came to see her meditations as "counsels," I would argue that she conceives of her thoughts not as abstract instructions but as *experiences*. They are to be dwelt on and internalized, "approved" in the sense of "put to the proof" or "tested by experience," because they will speak to the reader's own case. It is telling that she calls them "remedies." Not just "counsels," they are analogous to the medical remedies that she recorded with similar care, meant to minister healing to others.

Mildmay's meditations also present us with a further quality that is a product of her engagement with Scripture, her prose style. Mildmay's use of language is indelibly marked by Scripture, a quality that can best be seen if we look closely at one extended section. Chapter 228 offers a meditation on mortality, the vanity of the flesh, and the need to subsume our wills completely in God's will. It opens with a comment about Mildmay's personal condition as an aging woman:

---

[18] Martin, "Autobiography," 34.

[19] See, among numerous examples, Thomas Lant, *Daily Exercises of a Christian* (London, 1623); William Leighton, *The Teares or Lamentations of a Sorrowfull Soule* (London, 1613); G.R., *Divine Meditations and Contemplations* (London, 1641); and Henry Tozer, *Directions for a godly life* (Oxford, 1628).

"The countenance of my face is changed from youth to age, and my old and earthy body tendeth unto the grave" (695). The sentence sounds like a verse from Scripture, but, in fact, is not. Rather, it testifies to how thoroughly Mildmay has internalized a scriptural idiom. There are frequent uses of the phrase "goes down to the grave" in the Old Testament (e.g., Job 21:13, "They spend their days in wealth, and in a moment go down to the grave"), and Mildmay's articulation of the sentiment employs a characteristically Hebraic parallelism. Further, the sentiment is a version of the "vanity of life" topos from Ecclesiastes, a book which Mildmay glosses repeatedly in the margins of this meditation. We could say, then, that although this sentence is not a direct quotation from Scripture, its form and content are overdetermined by Mildmay's total immersion in Scripture.[20]

The sentence initiates what for Mildmay is an unusually sustained meditation that draws together a range of biblical passages, including both brief echoes ("neither is any able to divide me from my saviour Jesus Christ" or "let us walk as children of the light") and extended quotations; she incorporates, for instance, all of 1 Corinthians 1:26–31, and Luke 18:10–14. Mildmay not only builds her meditation using phrases from Scripture, but she also uses a scripturalist style for the passages that are her own composition. She responds to the statement of her mortality thus:

> Now then, what hath myne eye gathered of all that I have seene? or myne eare of all that I have heard? or my tongue of all that it hath uttered? Or my tast of all that I have tasted? Or what have I gathered of all my feeling that I have felt, but vanytie and repentance for all? What hath beene the worke and labour of my hands? And whether hath my feete caryed me in all my wayes? And what is my reward for all my travayles and endeavours of my whole life? But eternall condemnation and judgement? (695)

The parallelisms, doublets, and series of rhetorical questions are stylistic techniques drawn from the Pauline epistles and from Ecclesiastes, and the passage employs the recursive conjunction that Janel Mueller has identified as a hallmark of sixteenth-century scripturalist style.[21] Mildmay's scripturalism, in short, goes well beyond subject matter; she speaks in "Scripture phrase."

And Mildmay uses this idiom to develop her own thoughts. Another meditation on death illustrates how Mildmay pursues her own agenda even when rooting her ideas in Scripture. She writes:

---

[20] For a similar example of how immersion in family Bible reading could color a person's language, see the account that David Hall gives of Samuel Goodrich, who "realized that he could not write without invoking in some manner the key motifs and narrative style of the Bible. His imagination was founded on a language he had learned almost unconsciously." *Cultures of Print: Essays in the History of the Book* (Amherst: University of Massachusetts Press, 1996), 56–7.

[21] Janel Mueller, *The Native Tongue and the Word: Developments in English Prose Style 1380–1580* (Chicago: University of Chicago Press, 1984), 181–201.

> Every daye of this lyfe passed, present, and to come, forsaketh us from our youth unto age. Wee waxe old, and wither, and from our age in the grave we consume and turne to our dust and wee become as though we had never been. And all that knewe us, shall never knowe us more, all our thoughtes perish and our yeares are spent, and come to an end even as a tale that is told. Yet though we appeare as nothing in the sight of the world, and in the world be cleane forgotten, we are registered in the booke of lyfe in perpetuall memory before our God for ever. (40)

Mildmay sounds a number of familiar notes in the passage: we wither and return to dust, we come to an end "even as a tale that is told," and yet we are registered in the book of life. These notes echo the verses that she cites in the margins: Ps. 39:5; Ps. 90:9–11; Ps. 102:11; Isaiah 40:6–8; James 1:10–11; Ps. 22:6; Ps. 31:12; John 15:19; and Ps. 139:15–16. Yet in drawing on these verses, Mildmay ignores the images or ideas in those verses that do not contribute to her agenda, so that, for instance, when the image of the grass that withers appears in the context of the Lord's wrath, she ignores that context because her focus is not on sin and judgment. She touches on the grass only lightly, to figure the transience of the flesh. Similarly, there are images in the verses she cites that fail to register, such as the images of the broken vessel from Psalm 31:12 ("I am forgotten, as a dead man out of mind: I am like a broken vessel") and the worm in Psalm 22:6 ("But I am a worm, and not a man; a shame of men, and the contempt of the people"). Mildmay ignores these images because her interest is in a different issue, the idea that she is "as nothing in the sight of the world." She also chooses to ignore the rich image of our fashioning in secret in the womb (Ps. 139:15–16) because her point is that "we are registered in the book of life in perpetuity," and what matters for her purposes is that the Psalm speaks of all things being written before they were made. Thus, because Mildmay has her own point to explore, her passage is not limited by the dominant language and imagery in the biblical verses she cites. Her imagination lingers on the idea that we shall be "as though we had never been," that the very memory of us shall vanish. The idea that "our yeares are spent, and come to an end even as a tale that is told," sounds like a phrase from the Bible both in syntax and sentiment, but it is a re-rendering for her purposes of Psalm 90:9. For all of Mildmay's care that Scripture ratify and confirm all of the thoughts that she records, they are nonetheless her thoughts.

As these examples indicate, Mildmay's associations are wide-ranging throughout even the minor books of the Bible. They closely fit the particular focus of her thoughts, and in that way go beyond the standard groupings familiarized by the liturgy. Further, in separate meditations on the same topic, such as the meditations on death discussed above, Mildmay will refer to different clusters of Scripture for each meditation, as if she has a mental repertoire of relevant texts to draw on. William Sherman finds that it was frequent for a reader to note "the precise reference for an unidentified scriptural passage" in the margins of printed sermons, indicating "how thoroughly familiar many lay readers had become with the Bible."[22] Evidently, Mildmay had that kind of thorough familiarity. In her commitment to intensive reading, Scripture collation, and a typological understanding of the connection between biblical narrative and personal experience, Mildmay's use of Scripture matches the central practices of early modern lay readers, demonstrating not only a mastery of Scripture but of the compositional techniques Scripture reading inspired.

Mildmay's Words and God's Writing

Mildmay's command of Scripture is so thorough that it invites us to suppose that she derived her textual authority and confidence from her mastery of the note-taking techniques for Bible reading that were recommended in devotional guides or from her skillful navigation of the complex paratextual elements in printed bibles that may have directed lay reading.[23] But Mildmay's intertextual references are not tied either to the concordance that was commonly bound with the Geneva Bible or to its marginal cross-references. Guides to reading Scripture give directions on how to construct a scriptural commonplace book, and it is tempting to think that Mildmay might have been working from her own such book, for she does use terminology associated with commonplacing.[24] For example, in her address to her grandson, Mildmay Fane, she advises him to "meditate, and gather the hony of whatsoever you read, or heare spoken," and envisions his heart as a commonplace book; he is to do this "that your hart may be the treasury of all vertue" (72^{v}).[25] The most suggestive evidence of commonplacing is found in the occasional manuscript leaves that collect Scripture verses under headings. For example, in the prefatory address to her daughter, Mildmay tipped a page of verses in between folios four and five that address proper relations between different categories of people: children

22 William H. Sherman, "'The Book thus put in every vulgar hand': Impressions of Readers in Early English Printed Bibles," in *The Bible as Book: The First Printed Editions*, ed. Paul Saenger and Kimberly Van Kampen (London: The British Library, 1999), 129.

23 Peter Stallybrass, "Books and Scrolls: Navigating the Bible," in *Books and Readers in Early Modern England: Material Studies*, ed. Jennifer Andersen and Elizabeth Sauer (Philadelphia: University of Pennsylvania Press, 2002), 72–4.

24 See Patrick Collinson, Arnold Hunt, and Alexandra Walsham, "Religious Publishing in England 1557–1640," in *The Cambridge History of the Book in Britain*, ed. John Barnard, D.F. McKenzie, and Maureen Bell (Cambridge: Cambridge University Press, 2002), 60. Examples of Bible commonplace books include Folger MS V.b.261–2; Northamptonshire Record Office MS FH 260; Devon Record Office Z19/55/2, two of which seem to have been created by ministers. A devotional treatise created by the commonplacing method is BL MS Stowe 983.

25 For metaphors of beehives and treasuries applied to commonplacing, see Ann Moss, *Printed Commonplace-Books and the Structuring of Renaissance Thought* (Oxford: Clarendon Press, 1996), x.

and parents, masters and servants, etc. These instances demonstrate a habit of mind that sees scripture as a source of "places"—pieces of useful guidance, directions, examples—to be collected, and they indicate the note-taking habits that would have been preparatory to the production of individual meditations. Mildmay, like Lady Margaret Hoby, may have first used erasable writing tables or notebooks before copying her meditations into the manuscript that we have, and at one point she uses the image of a "payre of writing tables" (70).[26]

However, while this physical evidence of Mildmay's familiarity with the techniques of lay Biblical commonplacing provides the modern reader with a way of accounting for her meditations, she explicitly locates her authority very differently. Her use of the metaphor of the writing tables is most striking because it reveals that she saw Scripture less as a physical text than as a forceful Word that configured her inward self and allowed her to speak with authority. In context, the metaphor of the "writing tables" is an image of inward identity that inscription permanently transforms. The metaphor appears in a prayer as Mildmay adapts the Old Testament image in which God writes on the heart and asks: "let my heart be in thy blessed hands, as a payre of writing tables. Wherein it maye please thee to wryte, imprint, and grave deepely, thy lawes, commandements, ordinances, covenants, threatenings, and promises. Whereby all our senses, reason, and judgement, body, and members, may be dyrected a right course in every action. Amen" (70).[27] This image is complex. Mildmay begins with the image of God writing on her own heart, open before him like a pair of writing tables, a likely reference to a hinged tablet, often ivory with a precious frame, on which a valued text would be inscribed.[28] Such tables might be given as gifts; they also evoke the two tables of the Ten Commandments, the law engraved on stone. In the superimposition of the figure of writing on tables onto the figure of the heart, God's laws and promises are corporeally inscribed, as if those laws can thereby govern all her movements, volitional and physical. God's writing, for Mildmay, is powerfully performative. As she declares in her introduction, "So soone as the Lord had spoken the worde, all things were created that were made, and even so soone as our faith laith hold on Christ and is confirmed in that worde, we are renewed and made new creatures unto God" (17^{v}). But as we see in the slippage

[26] For Hoby's note-taking, see Joanna Moody, ed. *The Private Life of an Elizabethan Lady: The Diary of Lady Margaret Hoby, 1599–1605* (Phoenix Mill: Sutton Publishing, 1998), xl.

[27] For an overview of the Old Testament references to God's writing on the heart, see Robert A. Erickson, *The Language of the Heart, 1600–1750* (Philadelphia: University of Pennsylvania Press, 1997).

[28] See Peter Stallybrass, Roger Chartier, John Mowery, and Heather Wolfe, "Hamlet's Tables and the Technologies of Writing in Renaissance England," *Shakespeare Quarterly* 55 (2004), 379–419. As late as the nineteenth-century, women used such ornamental tablets. In *Great Expectations*, Miss Havisham records her gift of money to Herbert Pocket on "a yellow set of ivory tablets, mounted in tarnished gold." Charles Dickens, *Great Expectations* (Boston: Houghton Mifflin Co., 1962), 357.

in pronoun number from "my" to "our," the idea of what God writes, his laws and commandments, shifts Mildmay to a sense of the relation of divine law to all believers—laws direct all "our" faculties. Mildmay herself, then, accounts for her practice not as the product of a range of reading and note-taking skills but as the result of this kind of inscription by God, or, to switch to another metaphor that she used for the transforming effect of Scripture, the result of a humble and thorough "seasoning" of her heart and thoughts through immersion in God's Word. This seasoning flavors all that she writes, so that the Gospel becomes the linguistic element in which she thinks. There is a delicate balance here between her will and God's direction. From our perspective, she uses her medium with an independence of mind; but for Mildmay, the use of marginal references is a painstaking attempt to demonstrate the dependence of all she writes on God's Word and God's writing.

But while it is true that her prose is heavily dependent on Scripture, the question of authority is more complicated than Mildmay's deferential gestures might suggest, and not simply because she is able to use Scripture phrase to develop her own ideas. There is a further, less conventional way in which Mildmay conceives of her work's authority that allows her to vest in her own meditations a profound, spiritually irreproachable significance as God's Word. The locution Mildmay uses regularly is that her meditations "come into [her] mind," a phrase that is key to her sense of their significance as witnesses to God's love. They are a mode of communion, and they are the result of God's initiative. Their function as communion is evident in her repeated reference to the meditations as a "Jacob's ladder" that leads her to God and a "Jacob's pillar" that testify to her relationship with God (see 5°, 4). Her sense that God initiates this communion appears in her description of occasions when she tried to meditate and "found myself empty and void at that very instant of any one thought or disposition to pray or meditate … Yet notwithstanding before I went from that place, the Lord did minister such plenty of divine matter unto my mind as I was not able to comprehend" (4). Indeed, she explains that she found herself enjoying such an abundance of godly thoughts that she "was not able to comprehend and express; so that I was constrayned to leave off for that tyme, being afrayde to proceede or presume too farre" (4). Mildmay represents communion as God's ministration of thoughts, as an experience of "divine matter" flooding her mind.

Mildmay's claim that God sent her these thoughts may seem to be a standard authorization trope, claiming for her words divine legitimacy. The claim, though, is quite presumptuous within the terms of mainstream Protestant devotion. Manuals of meditation teach the believer to expect the Holy Spirit's participation in softening the heart and warming the affections, but they do not teach that the believer's thoughts are given by God. As Daniel Featley notes, true devotion must be "felt before it can be spoken of, and it must be kindled in the heart by the Spirit."[29] I would argue that Mildmay is able to represent her meditations as

[29] Daniel Featley, *Ancilla Pietatis: Or, the Hand-Maid to Private Devotion* (London, 1626), B2r.

coming from God without heretically claiming direct divine inspiration because of the particular way in which she develops the authorization trope. She figures herself as a woman pledged to Christ as a lover and claims that the meditations that so abundantly "come into her mind" testify that God is in turn pledged to her. They are "true testimonyes unto my soule and conscience of the love and gratious presence of God which never forsooke me in all my dayes Whereby I am encouraged stedfastly to believe that he will be the same god unto me for ever" (5°). The emphasis here is on the meditations as witnesses of steadfast love and presence, not as new revelation. Their function as witnesses is a recurring theme, as in a later prayer: "let them be for ever unto me, as pledges, and testimonyes of thy favour, and of thy love" (70), and in a statement that appears 500 pages later: "All these my meditations which the holye spirit of the Lord hath gathered and brought into my remembrance, are testimonyes unto my conscience of his gratious presence. And when I presente them unto him, in the sincere devotion of my mynde, my soule receiveth unspeakable consolation which is also a testimony unto my Conscience of his presence and his gratious favoure and love" (513). Because they witness to God's love, they are inexpressibly sweet, "the consolation of my soule, the joye of my hart and the stabilitie of my mynde" (30°).[30] The focus on the affective nature of the meditations and of the communion they represent shifts the emphasis from the claim that God gave the thoughts to the experience of them.

In this self-representation, Mildmay resembles women discussed by Elizabeth Clarke who use "disabling tropes" such as spiritual emptiness filled by God not simply as men do, to claim "strength through weakness" and stress their writing's divine inspiration, but also "as a stage in the transcending shift to spiritualised tropes of femininity" whereby female submission to a divine husband grants a kind of authority and freedom from human constraints.[31] But where the women Clarke studies figure God as husband, their poems as offspring, and their godly "motions" as the movements of the child in the womb, Mildmay characterizes her meditations as love tokens. God is a spiritualized lover who bestows meditations as favors or pledges that are tokens of his presence, and when "offered up," those meditations give consolation that also witnesses God's presence. And yet if God's presence is known through these tokens, they are in effect signs of an absent lover, substitutes for presence. Further, insofar as they are products of Mildmay's pen

[30] See also: "All these my meditations and prayers so far as they are approved by the word of God, I must acknowledge hath proceeded from God himselfe by the motions of his holy spirit as a perfect token of his love, grace and favour towards me" (686). Mildmay calls her meditations the "onely stabilitie of my mynde" again (45°), and credits them with giving her the strength to endure the afflictions and financial uncertainties that troubled her middle age. Randall Martin's transcription of her memoir contains information about those uncertainties; see Randall Martin, ed. *Women Writers in Renaissance England* (London: Longman, 1997), 209–10.

[31] Elizabeth Clarke, "Ejaculation or Virgin Birth? The Gendering of the Religious Lyric in the Interregnum," in Clarke and Clarke, *'This Double Voice,'* 223.

they are deeply flawed, "changling and corrupted prayers," and that Mildmay is not condemned for them is another "token of the love, grace, favour, and mercy of God towards me" (686). In this sense, the meditations witness a gendered sense that security and fulfillment depend on a male other. And yet, significantly, it is Mildmay who has created the tokens that stand for the other. Clarke finds the offspring trope, in which poems are the products of union with a divine husband, a valuable one for women because it links female sexuality and holiness.[32] Mildmay's trope of dependence on the mementos of a divine but absent lover could seem less fortunate, but before we conclude that it bespeaks a disempowerment, it is important to recognize that by means of this trope, she has defined her own writing as texts that are not only divinely authored but that take priority above all other things. She has linked the products of her pen and holiness.

To do so, Mildmay engages in a curious and telling construal of agency. If we were to judge only by her descriptions of the meditations as testimonies of God's presence, we might assume that they were independent of her reading. But in fact Mildmay's ability to represent her meditations as God's pledges depends on her conviction that their claims are witnessed in every point by Scripture, and that therefore they must be the work of the Spirit. They are so far reassuring and comfortable "as they are approved by the word of God, and as I doe approove them in myne owne conscience by the same word" (30°). As modern readers, of course, we are likely to observe that the meditations are witnessed by Scripture because they are the product of so thorough an immersion in Scripture that when Mildmay writes every phrase is either directly from the Bible or shaped by its idiom. It is true that Mildmay saw reading as immersion: we read, she declares, "to the end that our hart, soule, spirits, and whole inner man, maye first be seasoned within and receive the true stampe and impression thereof" (1°). The point of reading is transformation. Referring to gospel reading, Mildmay insists that "it cannot be but that the same must frame and change us from evill to good, and from corruption to incorruption" (483). Given such sustained immersion in a text, Mildmay's sense that God put her meditations into her mind indicates that all of the scriptural language that suffused her consciousness came to seem to her like God's word, given to her. From our perspective, intensive reading of Scripture led to its internalization and cultivated scriptural patterns of thought and expression, so that Mildmay naturally writes in "Scripture phrase." Yet for Mildmay, whether she is quoting Scripture directly or recording the "thoughts that came into [her] mind," it is Scripture as God's voice that speaks, and this belief is a powerful warrant for the authority of her writing. Her hope that others will profit from her meditations rests on that same ground. Others may read them and "may make good use of them, especially seeing they shall fynde every poynt of doctrine confirmed and approoved by the Scriptures" (5°). The reader will indeed find every point confirmed both because Mildmay has noted biblical verses in the margins, imitating Thomas Rogers's adaptation of the humanist page, and because to her, Scripture in fact grounds her every utterance.

---

[32] Ibid.

What is striking, then, is that while we might focus on the concrete reading and writing techniques that made her command of Scripture possible, for Mildmay, it is the transformative power of Scripture to create a new inward identity that serves as the basis for her self-confidence. And yet in the attempt to subordinate her voice to God's Word, she paradoxically created a manuscript page that bears the typographical insignia of authority, and she found a way to appropriate for her words not just a divine warrant but a divine origin.

Chapter 9
Lady Margaret Beaufort's Translations as Mirrors of Practical Piety

Brenda M. Hosington

Over the past few decades, translation has come to be thought of as a process rich in cultural and social complexities, an act of creativity in its own right. This is largely due to changes that have taken place in the field of translation studies inspired in part by Benjamin, Foucault, and Derrida, all of whom have invited us to think of translating as a means of ensuring the life of a work, discovering its multiple and ever-evolving meanings, and transferring it from one sociocultural context to another. Also influential have been theorists such as Lefevere and Venuti, who have taught us to see translations as ideological constructs, rewritings emanating from new contexts, influenced by factors such as gender, patronage, and even the marketplace, and by manipulations dictated by the translator's beliefs, place in time and space, purpose, and audience.[1] Furthermore, practice upholds theory in seeing translation as an active, and indeed creative, process involving interpretation and re-creation. Translators actually take far more opportunity to intervene and appropriate the text than detractors of translation imagine. Their work entails making choices: selecting a source text, determining which methods and strategies to adopt in transferring it, and deciding how to deal with its lexical, syntactical, and stylistic features. Finally, as the male- and female-authored paratexts of the early modern period reveal, translators believed that their work was useful and saw the translation of religious, classical, or Continental works for the less educated as a service to state, church, and population. As Micheline White states,

---

[1] Walter Benjamin, "The Task of the Translator," trans. Steven Randell, *Traduction, Terminologie, Rédaction* 10, no. 2 (1997): 151–65; Michel Foucault, "What is an Author?" in *Language, Counter-Memory, Practice*, trans. Donald F. Bouchard and Sherry Simon (Ithaca, NY: Cornell University Press, 1977), 113–38; Jacques Derrida, "Les Tours de Babel," trans. Joseph F. Graham, in *Difference and Translation*, ed. Joseph F. Graham (Ithaca, NY: Cornell University Press, 1985), 165–207, and "Living On/Borderlines," trans. James Hulbert, in Harold Bloom et al., *Deconstruction and Criticism* (New York: Seabury Press, 1979), 75–176, and "Roundtable on Translation," in *The Ear of the Other: Otobiography, Transference, Translation*, ed. Christie V. McDonald, trans. Peggy Kamuf (New York: Schocken Books, 1985), 91–161; Lawrence Venuti, *The Translator's Invisibility* (London: Routledge, 1995); André Lefevere, *Translation, Rewriting, and the Manipulation of Literary Fame* (London: Routledge, 1992).

"translators of both sexes saw themselves as powerful cultural agents."[2] In the case of religious works, in particular, they also saw themselves as possible instruments of reform and even savers of souls, and their translations played a crucial role in pre-Reformation, Reformation, and Counter-Reformation England. Women contributed by making available a variety of foreign texts: devotional, theological, polemical, and meditational works, prayers, sermons, and saints' lives.[3]

When evaluating Renaissance translators and their works, several factors must be taken into account. Understanding the historical context is essential, for neither original texts nor translations exist in a vacuum; they constitute an integral part of a whole sociocultural web of activity at a given time. Personal contexts, too, can be significant such as other works written or translated by the translator, or in the case of religious or political translations, his or her beliefs or affiliations. His or her relationship with a patron, dedicatee, or printer can also be revealing, although this has to be viewed with caution. As in any period, audience appropriateness must also be considered in comparing an original and its translation. Finally, evaluation of translations can take different forms but close, textual examination constitutes a very fruitful approach. Microcosmic analysis should, in fact, be a prerequisite to macrocosmic claims about a whole work. Avoiding the pitfalls of overgeneralization and impressionism, microcosmic analysis reveals patterns within translations that shed light on the translator's strategies and are essential for providing evidence for specific claims, especially if ideologically or gender-based. While it is impossible to analyze a whole work within the confines of an article, one can focus on one particular theme or aspect of the translation. Such is the approach that I have taken in discussing two translations produced by Lady Margaret Beaufort.

Like many of the translations penned by Renaissance women, Lady Margaret's English renderings of Book IV of the *De imitatione Christi* and the whole of the *Speculum aureum animae peccatricis* have never been discussed in detail. Among her contemporaries, John Fisher, her protégé and spiritual advisor, refers to them only as translations of "dyuers bokes" in French without mentioning them by

---

2 Micheline White, "Renaissance Englishwomen and Religious Translations: The Case of Anne Lock's *Of the Markes of the Children of God* (1590)," *English Literary Renaissance* 29 (1999): 375–400.

3 The so-called overwhelming importance of women's religious translations as compared with secular has however been exaggerated, as Micheline White demonstrated for the sixteenth century ("Renaissance Englishwomen"). The claim nevertheless persists. My ongoing research for the longer period of 1500–1660 confirms White's findings. In "Translation and Women Translators," in *The Encyclopedia of Women in the Renaissance: Italy, France, and England*, ed. Diana Robin, Anne R. Larsen, and Carole Levin (Santa Barbara, CA: ABC–Clio Press, 2007), 370–71, I said that of the 54 translations I had consulted, 32, or 58.1 percent, were religious. Today, those figures have changed slightly but still demonstrate that religious translating does not dominate the field: of 62 translations, 40, or 60.4 percent, are religious. As for the 31 women translators I have identified, only 17, or 54.8 percent, translate exclusively religious texts, while three (Elizabeth I, Mary Sidney, and Elizabeth Cary) translate both religious and secular works.

name in his long and detailed sermon on the occasion of Lady Margaret's death in 1509. Lord Morley, another protégé living in her household, makes no mention of her erudition at all.[4] Thomas Baker, prefacing his 1708 edition of Fisher's sermon, praises her love of learning, manifested in founding colleges and professorships, but says nothing of her translations. George Ballard and Horace Walpole mention them, but without comment.[5] Nineteenth-century biographers are no more prolix, although Charles Cooper provides a bibliographical description of the *Mirroure of golde*, challenges Lady Margaret's description of her first translation as the fourth book of the *Imitation of Christ*, and mistakenly ascribes the 1531 translation from the Latin to the printer Thomas Godfray.[6] Edmund Lodge mentions her two translations and love of learning, saying "she stepped widely, it is true, out of the usual sphere of her sex, to encourage literature by her example and her bounty," which, he says with an audible sigh of relief, did not interfere with her son's governance of the realm.[7] Two twentieth-century works praise Lady Margaret for her contribution to the New Learning, yet the first mentions her *Imytacion* only in passing, and the second ignores both translations.[8] Most recently, Michael Jones and Malcolm Underwood discuss at length her association with the universities and early printers, yet say only that her *Imytacion* "is a landmark in the history of the book in England" and completely ignore the *Mirroure of golde*.[9] Nor has Lady Margaret as translator been better served by specialists of Renaissance women writers, except for Patricia Demers.[10] Perhaps she is felt somehow to belong to the medieval world rather than the sixteenth century, although she was clearly a patron of humanism, founding two Cambridge colleges and several Oxbridge professorships intended to promote the New Learning; patronizing John Fisher,

---

[4] John Fisher, *Mornynge remembraunce*, in *English Works of John Fisher* (see Ch. 7, n. 18), 1: 291; Henry Parker Lord Morley, BL, Add. MS 12060, f. 21^r.

[5] Thomas Baker, preface to *The Funeral Sermon of Margaret, Countess of Richmond and Derby* (London, 1708); George Ballard, *Memoirs of Several Ladies of Great Britain, who have been Celebrated for their Writings or Skill in the Learned Languages, Arts and Sciences* (Oxford, 1752), 14–16; Horace Walpole, *A Catalogue of the Royal and Noble Authors of England, with Lists of their Works* (Edinburgh, 1796), 288.

[6] Charles Henry Cooper, *Memoir of Margaret Countess of Richmond and Derby*, ed. John E.B. Mayor (Cambridge: Cambridge University Press, 1874), 95, 108–10.

[7] Edmund Lodge, *Portraits of Illustrious Personages of Great Britain* (London, 1821–34), vol. 1 (entered under Lancaster, Margaret of).

[8] Margaret Emma Tabor, *Four Margarets* (New York: Macmillan, 1929), 22; Anthony Martienssen, *Queen Catherine Parr* (London: Secker & Warburg, 1973), 3–4.

[9] Michael K. Jones and Malcolm G. Underwood, *The King's Mother: Lady Margaret Beaufort, Countess of Richmond and Derby* (Cambridge: Cambridge University Press, 1992), 84, 197–201.

[10] Patricia Demers, the only critic to have discussed the actual translations, offers some perceptive comments. However, for the *Imytacion* she uses a Latin source text as a point of comparison, while for the *Speculum* she mentions none. *Women's Writing in English: Early Modern England* (Toronto: University of Toronto Press, 2005), 65–9.

whose humanist credentials are beyond reproach; and generously supporting England's first printers. Perhaps the fact that she made her translations, not from the original Latin source texts, but from less "prestigious" and largely inaccessible French metatexts has been the cause of their neglect. Even the anonymous English translator of the whole work complained in his 1531 preface that her translation of the *De imitatione Christi* "somtyme [did] vary in wordes" for it could not "follow the latyn so nyghe ne soo dyrectely as yf it had ben translatyd out of latyn."[11]

Such neglect is, however, completely unjustified because Lady Margaret's two translations represent an extraordinary accomplishment. They were the first translations into English of both Book IV of the *De imitatione Christi* and the *Speculum*. Her rendering of the former, one of the world's greatest and most widely read Christian devotional manuals, remained unrivalled for twenty-eight years, and even then the same translator who had criticized her use of a French metatext was at pains to explain that he had kept its "substaunce" and "effecte"; indeed, a comparison of his and her translations of Book IV reveals that he must have worked with hers beside him. Not until the mid-twentieth century had it ever been translated by any other woman.[12] The present study will bring new light to bear on Lady Margaret's methods and goals and this should lead to a greater appreciation of her achievement as Renaissance England's first female translator.

Context: Translation, Devotion, and Practical Piety

One author sees the history of Catholic devotion in early modern Europe as inseparably linked to the circulation of translated devotional texts.[13] Monastic library catalogues throughout Western Europe bear eloquent witness to such a view. Carlos Eire examines the significance of translated fifteenth-century devotional texts of the sort produced by Margaret Beaufort for both the clergy,

---

[11] *A boke newely translated out of Laten in to Englysshe, called the folowynge of Cryste. (Here after folowyth the fourthe boke of the folowynge of Cryste)* (London: Robert Wyer, 1531; *STC* 23961), Aiv. Richard Whitford for a long time was believed—and still is by some—to be the translator, but this was challenged by Glanmore Williams, "Two Neglected Welsh Clerics: Richard Whitford and Richard Gwent," *The Transactions of the Honorable Society of Cymmrodorion* 1 (1961): 30–32. His authorship remains moot according to Victoria Lawrence, "Richard Whitford and Translation" in *The Medieval Translator 4*, ed. Roger Ellis and Ruth Evans (Binghamton, NY: MRTS, 1994), 136–52.

[12] *The Imitation of Christ by Thomas à Kempis*, trans. Betty I. Knott (London: Collins, 1963). Katherine Parr reworked passages from Book III of the 1531 English translation in her 1545 *Prayers and Meditations*. See C. Fenno Hoffman Jr., "Catherine Parr as a Woman of Letters," *Huntington Library Quarterly* 23, no. 4 (1959): 349–67; Janel Mueller, "Devotion as Difference: Intertextuality in Queen Katherine Parr's *Prayers or Meditations* (1545)," *Huntington Library Quarterly* 53 (1990): 171–97; and Susan E. James, *Kateryn Parr: The Making of a Queen* (Aldershot: Ashgate, 1999), 213–16.

[13] Friedrich Rennhofer, *Bücherkunde des katholischen Lebens: Bibliographisches Lexikon der religiösen Literatur der Gegenwart* (Vienna: Hollinek,1961), v.

for whom vernacular texts were translated into Latin, and the laity, for whom the reverse occurred. He describes the dissemination of mystical texts via translations, particularly those produced by German Carthusians, as crucial to the spiritual renewal that swept through Germany, the Low Countries, and Spain, although this translation movement was dominated by religious elites. Interestingly, his example of such cultural control is the early modern Spanish translations of the *De imitatione Christi*, which he calls one of the most significant works of the devotional movement. All, need we add, were produced by male clerics.[14]

The dissemination in England of devotional texts in both original versions and translations was also largely attributable to the clergy, especially the Carthusians, from the fourteenth century on. They were instrumental in importing texts from Low Countries authors, among whom was Thomas à Kempis, the presumed author of the *De imitatione Christi*, and they translated other Continental devotional writings too.[15] However, few works associated with the *devotio moderna*, a fourteenth-century religious movement started by a Dutch Carthusian and continued by his disciples who founded the Brethren of the Common Life, appear to have made their way into English Charterhouses, although this cannot be confirmed because their library catalogues are not extant.[16] Even the most famous, the *De imitatione Christi*, seems to have been less popular than contemporary English writings, although Lovatt has argued that its first English translation is very possibly of Carthusian origin. Two of the four manuscripts were written in Sheen Charterhouse, one at the request of Elizabeth Gibbs, the Abbess of the only Bridgettine house in England.[17]

Like the Carthusians, the Bridgettines placed great importance on the written word and encouraged their members to translate. Their house, Syon Abbey, was founded as a twin establishment for men and women, with each part having a rich, modern, and extremely varied library collection containing many works of devotion including the *De imitatione Christi* and *Speculum aureum animae peccatricis*.[18]

---

[14] Carlos Eire, "Early Modern Catholic Piety in Translation," in *Cultural Translation in Early Modern Europe*, ed. Peter Burke and R. Po-Chia Hsia (Cambridge: University of Cambridge Press, 2007), 83–100.

[15] Michael G. Sargent, "Ruysbroeck in England. *The Chastising of God's Children* and Related Works," in *Historia et spiritualitas Cartusiensis*, ed. Jan de Grauwe (Destelbergen, Belgium: Drukkerij De Windroos, 1983), 303–13, and "The Transmission by the English Carthusians of Some Late Medieval Spiritual Writings," *Journal of Ecclesiastical History* 27, no. 3 (1976): 225–40.

[16] Hogg claims the *devotio moderna* made very little impact on English Carthusians on account of their religious conservatism. James Hogg, "The English Charterhouses and the *Devotio Moderna*," in *Historia et spiritualitas Cartusiensis*, Grauwe, 257–68.

[17] Roger Lovatt, "The *Imitation of Christ* in Late Medieval England," *Transactions of the Royal Historical Society*, 5th ser., 18 (1968): 97–121.

[18] Unlike the library records of the English Charterhouses, the catalogue of the Brothers' library at Syon Abbey is extant; sadly, the Sisters' is not. See Mary Bateson, ed. *Catalogue of the Library of Syon Monastery, Isleworth* (Cambridge: University of Cambridge Press, 1898).

A good number of the Syon printed books were translations, or retranslations updating the English and demonstrating a concern for style.[19] The importance of reading for the nuns has been amply demonstrated by Ann Hutchison, who marshals many pieces of evidence, perhaps the most important being a section on the "deuout redyng of holy Bokes" in *The Myrroure of oure Lady*, a fifteenth-century English translation of their Latin service.[20]

David Bell has been able to identify the nuns' ownership of thirty-eight works in manuscript and eleven printed books. Six constitute complete translations and seven contain one translation each: all are devotional works. He attributes ownership of another twelve books to either the Sisters or Brothers at Syon, one a translation, another containing two translations, a third containing three.[21] Among them is an English rendering of the *Fifteen Oes* attributed to St Bridget, a text that Lady Margaret and her daughter-in-law, Queen Elizabeth, commissioned Caxton to print in 1491. The importance of translation in this context cannot be overestimated.

My reasons for writing in some detail of the works associated with these religious houses are twofold. Like all translations, Lady Margaret's must be read in the light of similar works being produced and circulated at the same time; second, her link with them was very personal. Going beyond well documented biographical facts, Susan Powell draws a parallel between her attitude toward spirituality and learning and that of the Carthusians and Bridgettines. All, she claims, favored similar means of putting piety and scholarship into practice.[22] Lady Margaret commissioned and financed Carthusian- or Bridgettine-connected books printed by Caxton, Wynkyn de Worde, and Pynson, while the Brothers provided de Worde and Pynson with religious texts they wanted printed. She also bought devotional books, many by Carthusian authors, through both English and Continental agents. Moreover, the famous wealth of Syon Library was reflected in her own personal collection of books.[23] Lastly, the Carthusians' and Bridgettines' interest in translation was reflected in her own activities.

---

19 J.T. Rhodes, "Syon Abbey and its Religious Publications in the Sixteenth Century," *Journal of Ecclesiastical History* 44, no. 1 (1993): 11–25.

20 Ann M. Hutchison, "Devotional Reading in the Monastery and in the Late Medieval Household," in *De Cella in Seculum: Religious and Secular Life and Devotion in Late Medieval England*, ed. Michael G. Sargent (Cambridge: D.S. Brewer, 1989), 215–27.

21 David N. Bell, *What Nuns Read: Books and Libraries in Medieval English Nunneries* (Kalamazoo, MI: Cistercian Publications, 1995). Bell's study of 144 English convents reveals 118 works written or intended for nuns; 41, or just under one-third, are translations, while many contain Latin texts of services with English rubrics and collections of bilingual prayers.

22 Susan Powell, "Syon Abbey and the Mother of King Henry VII: The Relationship of Lady Margaret Beaufort with the English Birgittines," *Birgittiana* 19 (2005): 211–24.

23 For a detailed discussion of Lady Margaret's own library and her dealings in books, see Susan Powell, "Lady Margaret Beaufort and her Books," *The Library*, 6th ser., 20, no. 3 (1998): 197–240.

Lady Margaret dovetailed her frequentation of religious institutions with her own personal adaptation of the monks' and sisters' forms of devotion and taste for intellectual pursuits. However, this made her no contemplative recluse or joyless bluestocking, for she also shared their belief that these should be put to practical use. Lord Morley tells her granddaughter, Mary Tudor, of her delight in merry tales, which she heard before passing to stories of virtue and godliness.[24] He emphasizes her liberality, popularity, and managerial competence, but also her piety, evident in her daily prayers before the Sacrament and in her room, and her alms-giving and care of the sick—her putting of piety into practical mode.[25]

Another portrait of her practical piety is provided by Fisher's memorial sermon, in a detailed comparison between Lady Margaret and Martha, the active rather than contemplative sister of the Gospel story, which stresses their shared bodily discipline and spiritual godliness. Notably, he never mentions Mary, despite the fact that medieval religious writers like Thomas à Kempis and St. Bridget, both important in Lady Margaret's life and entourage, insisted that the Christian should be a blend of both sisters.[26] Fisher nevertheless also emphasizes Lady Margaret's "wysedome ferre passynge the comyn rate" of her gender, a familiar topos in male praise of women, her good memory, ready wit, and her ability to study the many "ryght derk" English and French books in her possession. He also tells us that "for her exercyse & for the prouffyte of other she dyde translate dyuers maters of deuocyon out of Frensshe into Englysshe."[27] The comment commands our attention. The topos of the woman translator working only for her own "exercise," not intending to put her work into print, was part of a long tradition of modest and self-deprecating female *and* male authorial prefaces.[28] Fisher, however, adds the important phrase, "for the prouffyte of other." Here, then, is clearly articulated her belief that translation was useful and could serve as a means to blend piety and practicality. It places her in the tradition of her grandmother, Margaret, Duchess of Clarence, who practiced piety and patronage, purchasing books for the libraries at the Mount Grace Charterhouse and Syon Abbey, and supporting translators like Symon Wynter at Syon.[29]

---

[24] Parker, BL, Add. MS 12060, f. 21^r.

[25] Ibid., f. 23.

[26] Fisher, *Mornynge remembraunce*, 288. For a discussion of Mary and Martha in the Middle Ages, particularly with regard to writers associated with the *devotio moderna*, see Giles Constable, *Three Studies in Medieval Religious and Social Thought* (Cambridge: Cambridge University Press, 1995), 44–144.

[27] Fisher, *Mornynge remembraunce*, 291–2.

[28] The topos often included a reference to well-intentioned but interfering friends who submitted the translation to print without the translator's permission. This variation became so popular that Elizabeth Cary felt the need to reject it in the preface to her 1630 *Reply of the most illustrious Cardinall of Perron.*

[29] See George R. Keiser, "Patronage and Piety in Fifteenth-Century England: Margaret, Duchess of Clarence, Symon Wynter and Beinecke MS 317," *Yale University Library Gazette* 60 (1985): 32–46.

Lady Margaret's extreme piety explains her choice of texts to translate and publish. According to Fisher, she attended devotions, matins, and daily masses before breakfast, worshipped at the various altars in her chapel, heard evensong, and engaged in psalm reading, not perhaps such an unusual regimen for a woman of her rank with strong religious sentiments. However, a few details raise the level of her devotion above the ordinary: the prickly hair shirts and girdles that pierced her skin, the back pain caused by her continual kneeling, and the floods of tears at confession, often made every third day, and upon receiving the Eucharist, which she did a dozen times a year.[30] Such excessive emotion and frequent confession and communion were unusual for the laity. However, Book IV of *De imitatione Christi* stresses the importance of both, while the *Speculum* speaks at length on Christians' unworthiness to receive the sacraments on account of their corruption and vileness.

Lady Margaret's Translations and their Sources

De imitatione Christi, confusingly attributed to both Jean Gerson, the Paris theologian, and Thomas à Kempis, a member of the Brethren of the Common Life, went through an amazing twenty-six editions in the twenty-five years following the *editio princeps* of 1471. Printed translations into Italian, German, and French appeared before 1500. Two different anonymous French translations were published in 1484 and 1493. The first printed English version was commissioned some time in 1502 or 1503 by Lady Margaret, who, no doubt through her Cambridge connections, chose as her translator William Atkynson, Fellow of Pembroke Hall and Jesus College, before becoming prebendary of Southwell. He translated Books I–III from a Latin source text. She then translated Book IV from a French version, adding it to his translation and commissioning Richard Pynson to print the whole work.[31]

The first French translation of 1484, *Le liure tressalutaire de la ymitacion Jhesu Christ et mesprisement de ce monde*, published by Henri Mayer in Toulouse, was believed by the EETS editor of Lady Margaret's translation to be her source text and the very few who have commented on the translation have followed suit.[32] However, after collating the two translations, I am convinced she used the later 1493 French version, *Le livre tressalutaire de limitation de nostre seigneur jesucrist*, published in Paris by Lambert. It proved far more popular and was reissued, unchanged, by Lambert and another Parisian printer, Jean Treperel, in 1494. Apart from the fact that her phrasing is much closer to the Lambert than to

30 Fisher, *Mornynge remembraunce*, 294–5.

31 In her *ODNB* entry on Atkinson, Corinne R. Berg mistakenly states that both his and Lady Margaret's translations were from French and attributes the first edition to Wynkyn de Worde, an error in the *STC* but corrected in the *ESTC*. Corinne R. Berg, "Atkinson, William," in *ODNB* (accessed December 23, 2009).

32 *The Earliest English Translation of the First Three Books of the De Imitatione Christi*, ed. John K. Ingram. EETS, extra ser., 63 (London: Kegan Paul, 1893), xxvii.

the Mayer translation, two other factors are persuasive. The Mayer version breaks down the first chapter into two separate chapters, each with a title, whereas the Lambert one, following the Latin source, does not; neither does Lady Margaret's. Secondly, her translation sometimes uncannily resembles the language and style of the Latin original, which I found puzzling until I consulted the Lambert translation. Given her virtual ignorance of the language, attested by Fisher,[33] and the likelihood that had a Latin edition with Book IV existed in England Atkynson would surely have translated it himself, the case for the Lambert source text becomes very persuasive. It is indeed far more Latinate in style and language than the Mayer version and placed alongside the English translation strikingly and vibrantly reveals Lady Margaret's debt to its translator. Its Book IV, unchanged, was also included with a 1447 manuscript translation of Books I–III in a work entitled *De linterioire conuersacion*, published in 1493 by Jehan le Bourgeois in Rouen. Perhaps Lady Margaret used this particular edition, which would have given her access to the whole work in one volume. Rouen printers had connections with Syon and she herself dealt with one in particular, Inghelbert de la Haghe, who also kept a bookstore in London.[34]

The Syon library catalogue describes the *De imitatio Christi*, of which it had four manuscript copies, as "solitariis et contemplativis utilis," useful for those of a solitary and contemplative nature.[35] Indeed, Lovatt claims that its circulation in late medieval England was restricted to a small, conservative, intellectual group, consisting of Carthusian monks, Bridgettine brethren and "a small activist group of learned secular clergy," and that the aim of the first, mid-fifteenth-century English translation was not to make the text more accessible to potential readers. Moreover, the value of the work in England seems to have been its teachings on monastic vocation rather than its links with the *devotio moderna*, which emphasized "inner devotion" and pursued the goal of bringing the knowledge of God and means of spiritual renewal to both cleric and layperson, both scholar and peasant.[36] Yet Lady Margaret must have viewed the work in no elitist or narrowly monastic way, discovering in its pages the ideal of imitating Christ's humanity and the means of attaining it. By withdrawing into an inner spiritual life, but only after struggling with sin, conquering the flesh, and examining one's conscience, could one join

---

33 Fisher, *Mornynge remembraunce*, 292.

34 Inghelbert de la Haghe published a Hereford Breviary for Lady Margaret in 1505, with her coat of arms on the title page, and dedicated it to her. W.H. Frere and E.G. Langton, eds. *The Hereford Breviary Edited from the Rouen Edition of 1505 with Collation of Manuscripts*, 3 vols (London, 1904), vol. 1. De la Haghe also bought books for her on the Continent at a later date. See also Powell, "Lady Margaret and her Books," 226–7.

35 Bateson, *Catalogue of the Library of Syon Monastery*, 127.

36 Lovatt gives other reasons for believing the work was not very popular in England: only 20 of the surviving 800 manuscript versions originated there; it was not, like other imported devotional works, used for English compilations; and there is no evidence that other religious houses owned copies. Lovatt blames not the nature of the work itself, but the "isolationism and devotional torpor of these orders." Lovatt, "The *Imitation of Christ*," 113–16.

with Christ through the sacrament of the Eucharist. She must also have believed the work's significance went beyond the confines of Latin-literate monks since she bought many copies of her translation for her household and had many sent to Syon, where some nuns knew little or no Latin. This was consistent with her commissioning of Atkynson's translation of Books I–III. It omitted much material pertaining to monastic life, suggesting that it was probably intended primarily for lay readers whose reading was entirely or mostly confined to English.

As suggested above, Lady Margaret must have found Book IV of particular interest on account of its emphasis on the right way to partake of the Eucharist, for she was particularly devoted to praying before the sacrament at her various altars. She was also possibly influenced by the Carthusians, Bridgettines, and Fisher, all committed to Eucharistic devotion. Her gender might well have played its part too, for as Caroline Bynum notes, several factors demonstrate a gender-oriented level of reverence for the sacrament throughout the Middle Ages.[37] Whatever her personal reason for finding Book IV particularly attractive, she most certainly believed the whole work should be made available in English and in 1503 commissioned Richard Pynson to print it. He entitled it *A ful devout gostely treatyse of y[e] imytacio[n] and folowynge y[e] blessed lyfe of our savyour cryste* and gave Book IV its own title-page [*STC* 23954]. The volume's popularity is well attested: Pynson reissued it only one year later in 1504 [*STC* 23955] and produced a second edition in 1517 and a variant in 1518 [*STC* 23957, 23958]; de Worde also published an edition of Books I–III (Pt. I) in 1518, with Book IV (Pt. II) following in 1519 [*STC* 23956] and brought out a new edition of Pt. I in 1528 [*STC* 23960].

Perhaps encouraged by the success of her first printed translation, Lady Margaret turned her attention to Englishing another devotional work, the *Speculum aureum animae peccatricis*, nowadays attributed to either Jacobus de Gruytroede or Jacobus de Clusa, both Carthusians, rather than to Denys the Carthusian, although the work was printed in Denys's *Opera omnia* as late as 1913.[38] The *Speculum* was one of a group of late fifteenth-century "mirrors" amplifying the *contemptus mundi* theme of earlier works but also representing a new type of spiritual exercise aimed at adapting monastic ascetism to lay audiences.[39] The third part of a Carthusian manual, *Speculum humanae salvationis*, *Speculum aureum* showed how one's self-knowledge as a humble sinner is mirrored as a route to salvation. Inspired by the *De imitatione Christi*, but less stylized, the *Speculum* may be described as a compilation of quotations from the Bible, Church Fathers, and various saints.

---

37 Caroline Walker Bynum, *Holy Feast and Holy Fast: The Religious Significance of Food to Medieval Women* (Berkeley: University of California Press, 1987), 73–112.

38 See Eugen Gerard Hoekstra, "Jacques de Gruytrode" in *Dictionnaire de spiritualité ascétique et mystique* (Paris: Beauchesne, 1932), vol. 8: cols. 36–8.

39 See Hasenohr for a detailed description of these late medieval "mirrors" and their relation to the popular *ars moriendi* works. Geneviève Hasenohr, "La Littérature Religieuse," in *Grundriss der Romanischen Literaturen des Mittelalters/La littérature française aux XIVe et XVe siècles*, ed. Daniel Poirion (Heidelburg: Carl Winter, 1988), 1: 277–81.

However, unlike the *De imitatione Christi*, also a compilation of similar sources, it contains virtually no reflection on the quotations and much less contemplation. Its focus on human sinfulness, the brevity of life, and the necessity of making a good death through repentance is resolutely practical, with one chapter of instructions for each day of the week.

The *Speculum* was not as popular and influential as *De imitatione Christi*. It nevertheless went through twelve Latin printed editions between 1476 and 1503 and was included in another work, *Opusculum, quod speculum aureum anime peccatrice inscribitur felicite a quodam cartusiense*, published three times in Paris, in 1480, 1485, and 1503. Like the *De imitatione Christi*, it was twice translated into French. The earlier manuscript version dates from 1451 and was included with two other "mirrors" by the same translator, Jean Miélot, in a volume entitled *Miroir d'humilité*. This was not Lady Margaret's source text. The second translation, *Le mirouer dor de lame pecheresse tres utile et profitable*, was anonymous and printed in 1484 by Robin Foucquet and Jehan Cras at Bréhant-Loudéac, in Brittany. It went through three more editions before 1500, in all of which the text was followed by a ballad, with two adding the refrain "C'est le miereir de lame pecheresse." Neither ballad nor refrain is in Lady Margaret's translation, which suggests her source was the 1484 edition, although she might simply have chosen to omit them.[40]

For the publication of her translation, Lady Margaret again commissioned Richard Pynson, who printed it in 1506 under the title *The mirroure of golde for the synfull soule. Translated out of laten in to frensshe, and nowe of late in to Englisshe Margaret countesse of Richemond & derby* [*STC* 6894.5]. It was printed by J. Skot for Wynkyn de Worde in a new edition [*STC* 6895] and variant [*STC* 6896] in 1522, with another new edition and second issue appearing in 1526 [*STC* 6897.5; 6897.5]. The French translator prefaces the author's Prologue with the remark that his work, effected in Paris, was "seen and corrected at length of many darkis doctours, and maisters in diuinite." To this is added, most probably by Pynson, "Nowe of late translated oute of frenche in to Englisshe by the right excellent princesse Margaret moder to souerain lorde kinge Henry the vii. and Countesse of Richemond & derby."[41]

Lady Margaret's interest in the *Speculum* no doubt lay in its emphasis on sin and the vileness of the human condition, both curable by penitence and humility, but especially by imitating Christ's example, a belief also central to the *De imitatione Christi*. In his Prologue, the original author gave two reasons for "compiling the present treatise," which are closely translated in the French. The first is to rescue

[40] For descriptions of these translations, see M. Pellechet, ed. *Catalogue général des incunables des bibliothèques publiques de France* (Paris: 1909; repr. Nendeln, Liechenstein: Kraus-Thompson, 1970), nos. 4326–9.

[41] Lady Margaret Beaufort, trans. *The mirroure of golde for the synfull soule* (London: Richard Pynson, 1506), Aii. All quotations in English are from this text. All quotations from the French translation are taken from *Le mirouer dor de lame pecheresse tres utile et profitable* (Bréhant-Loudéac: Foucquet-Cras, 1484).

the suffering soul from the wiles of the devil and, helped by "authoritees" and the Holy Spirit, redirect the sheep to its "vray Pasteur" (ai). Lady Margaret must have misread this as "vert Pasture," despite the masculine form of the adjective, since she translates it as "grene paster," perhaps influenced by Psalm 23:2. The notion is nevertheless the same, of the soul returning to its rightful abode (Aii). The second reason is to make the soul recognize the peril it is in, confess its error, make penance through inner contemplation, and attain eternal life. Lady Margaret makes only one change: "peril" becomes "sin," which weakens the sense of the imminence of the danger threatening the unrepentant soul but emphasizes human sinfulness. She made similar changes throughout both her translations.

Translation Strategies

As mentioned above, John Fisher stressed that part of Lady Margaret's desire in translating was "for the prouffyte of other." She wanted to provide those less educated than herself with foreign devotional works in order to make them more aware of both their own sin and Christ's promise of salvation if they repented and emulated him. Unfortunately, neither of her translations is accompanied by any paratextual materials explaining her goals or methods, but certain principles are implicit: if her translations were to be useful, they must be easily understood; and if they were to be fruitful, they must impress upon readers the nature of their sinfulness in order to prepare them for confession and penitence. At the same time they must strike a personal note, so that readers might identify with the thoughts being expressed. Lady Margaret, as I shall demonstrate, adopted specific translating strategies to achieve her aims. These include textual explication, inclusion and personalization, intensification, and the retention of certain stylistic features.

Explication in Lady Margaret's translations takes the form of glossing, a universal feature of medieval translation. Here, however, it is not used for explaining difficult words, creating neologisms, or paraphrasing. Rather, it mostly serves to clarify meaning. Since the *De imitatione Christi* is being translated for a lay readership rather than a monastic one, and the *Speculum* for an "unlettered" one, they must contain no ambiguities. Two chapter headings (vi and viii) from the former will demonstrate her technique, although there are many more examples in both works (the italics throughout are mine):

> Une interrogation *dexercice deuant la communion.* (miiii^{v})[42]
> A inwarde remembraunce *and exercyse that a man ought to haue afore the receyuynge of the body of our lorde iesu cryst.* (bii)

[42] All quotations from the French are from the Bodleian Library copy of *Le livre tressalutaire de limitation de nostre seigneur jesucrist* (Paris: Lambert, 1494). All quotations from Beaufort's English translation are from *A full devout [and] gostely treatyse of the Imytacion and Folowynge the Blessed Lyfe of oure Moste Mercyfull Savyoure Criste* (London: Richard Pynson, 1504; *STC* 23955).

By turning the French impersonal, nominal construction into a full subordinate clause and using the noun *man* (which in Middle English could, even with an article, denote a person irrespective of gender) and auxiliary verb *ought*, Lady Margaret emphasizes and makes explicit the importance to each individual Christian preparing to take communion of simple self-interrogation, but also of "exercise." By adding this to the text, she makes it clear that the communicant must make a conscious effort to reflect. The choice of "inwarde remembraunce" to translate "interrogation" also emphasizes the fact that this is a private, informal, and intensely personal act. She also makes explicit the French word "communion," rather than simply using its English direct equivalent, by using *étoffement*, or amplification of meaning for the purpose of clarity: "the receyuynge of the body of our lorde iesu cryst." The second chapter heading reveals a similar strategy.

> De l'oblacion de iesucrist en la croix et de *sa* propre resignacion. (miii)
> Of the oblacion of Jesu cryst in the crosse: *of the propre resignacion that man shulde make of hym selfe*. (bii)

The French possessive adjective "sa" is rather ambiguous; it could stand in grammatical relationship to Christ, who demonstrated resignation, or to the sinner, who in the text is asked to do so. Lady Margaret, however, risks no ambiguity, using a subordinate clause introduced by the relative "that" followed by an indefinite pronoun, *man*, and the modal *should*, adding, for absolute clarity, a genitive, "of hym selfe."

One other traditional form of glossing, providing an explanation or a reference for an allusion or a quotation that the reader might not understand, is used in both texts and is also useful for a less educated or lay readership. In the *Mirroure*, for example, Lady Margaret expands the French "Et pour tant se saint pierre fut mort au peche *de la tierce negation*" (bii^{v}) to "for & saint peter had dyed in synne *when he the thirde tyme denyed our lord*" (Biii). Further on, she expands a reference to St. Gregory's "omelie du riche" (g^{v}): "In an omelie of the riche man *that settel all his felicite and pleasure in eatynge and drinkynge and inordinate apparell*" (Iviii^{v}). Sometimes her added chapter and verse biblical references are accurate, but at other times not, as illustrated in a passage towards the end of the *Mirroure* containing two references to the Apocalypse (gvii) which she identifies precisely but incorrectly (Jiv).

In the majority of cases, the glossing manages simultaneously to elucidate, personalize, and make the text inclusive. In fact, this blending of effects is a notable feature of Lady Margaret's translations, particularly as regards the *Imytacion*. It is achieved in several ways: by changing the syntax, replacing impersonal constructions with subordinate clauses; by adding the noun *man* or adding a variety of personal pronouns, especially the second-person singular, "thee," and first-person plural, "we"; and by replacing impersonal French pronouns like *plusieurs* (many or several) and *beaucoup* (many) with personal ones. Thus, the impersonal "excedant *tout entendement*" becomes "aboue the *understandynge of man*"; "Et ayme sur toutes choses *que cuer peut desirer*" is rendered as

"Desyred aboue all desyres *of mannys herte*." Far more effective, however, is her use of the personal pronouns *me, us, we, the,* and the possessive pronoun *my* to make meaning clear and at the same time reinforce the sentiment that the narrator is relating an intensely personal experience, one he or she is willing to share with the reader in their mutual quest for salvation.

Lady Margaret makes many of the French chapter headings more personal and inclusive. For example, that of Chapter XVII, "De lardent amour et grande affection de recepuoir iesucrist" (cii), is rendered as "Of the brennynge loue and great affeccion *that we shuld haue to receyue* our sauyour cryst iesu" (ciii^{v}). The French infinitive construction "de recepuoir" becomes personalized by the pronominal English one. A similar shift renders the impersonal pronominal construction in Chapter XV's heading, "Comment on acquiert la grace de deuocion en humilite et renonciacion de soymesmes" (ci) to the more personal and more emphatic "How mekly *thou oughtest* to beseche the grace of deuocion and to renounce *thy selfe*" (cii). This is achieved in three ways: by changing the French impersonal pronouns "on" and "soymesmes" to personal ones, "thou" and "thy selfe," which address the reader directly; by changing the finite verb "acquiert" to the modal "ought"; and by mistranslating "acquiert" to mean, not "acquires", but "beseeches." Thus she creates a mood of greater intimacy and immediacy.

These strategies to elucidate, personalize, and make the text more inclusive are also used throughout the body of the text, as the following examples will demonstrate. Lady Margaret's continuing habit of translating "on" as "we" or "thee" constitutes a choice on her part, for it can also be rendered in English by "one," "they" or the passive voice; these, however, would have the contrary effect of distancing the narrator from the reader. Another frequently used strategy is to add the first-person plural pronouns "we," "us," and "our" to a statement, even if not needed grammatically, or to an impersonal phrase: "Tu as donne"/"thou hast gyuen *us*"; "louanges te sont deues"/"louynges be due unto the of *us*"; "Ce fait a douloir"/"*we ought to haue* sorowe." In this way she draws the reader into the text, at one with the narrator and, in a wider context, with the communion of sinners who, by Christ's grace, will be saved. Even more noteworthy in this respect is her frequent addition of the first-person singular object and possessive pronouns "me" and "my," which engage her actively in the text: "pain de vie" becomes "bread of *my* life, "tu conuyes *le pouure*" is "thou lysteth … *me, that am so poor*." Sometimes the effort to increase the text's immediacy results in more radical changes: "Et a entendre & comprendre telles choses *n'y a personne ydoine*" becomes "For there is *no man founde able of hym selfe* to conceyue."

In the *Speculum*, four of the seven chapter headings demonstrate how Lady Margaret personalizes her French source in order to make it inclusive and intensifies sentiments and thoughts by using doublets.[43] Chapter V, for example,

[43] In the Table of Contents of *The mirrour of golde* "on" is translated as "they" although in the same chapter headings within the text, Margaret uses "we." Probably Pynson was responsible for the Table, which would explain the change.

has the heading "Comment lon doibt despriser le monde" (diii). In "Howe *we* ought to *dispise and hate* the world" (dviii), she personalizes the French indefinite pronoun "on" and makes the single verb "despriser" into the doublet "dispise and hate." Many similar examples of personalization and inclusion occur in this work but in fewer numbers than in the *De imitatione Christi*, no doubt because the text, being essentially a compilation and far less reflective, does not lend itself as easily to such strategies.

Both the *De imitatione Christi* and *Speculum* were intended to teach Christians, exiles on earth, about the depravity of human nature and exhort them to seek redemption through meditating on Christ and his presence in the Eucharist. In Book IV of the former, the narrator describes himself as he prepares to take communion, a wretched sinner weighed down with vice. The picture is resolutely negative. However, Lady Margaret makes it more so by employing intensification strategies. Given their number and variety, this cannot be accidental. No fewer than five different techniques serve to achieve this end. The first is to use stronger adjectives to describe the state of the sinner: "miserable" becomes "cursed"; "inutile" is replaced by "vnworthy"; "si *froidement* et en si *tiede* deuocion," by "so *rudely* and so *cold* deuocion" (*rudely* here meaning extremely coldly). The second is to add intensifying adverbs like *very, so, much* to the text: "negligent et tiede" becomes "*very* necligent and cool"; "un pecheur" becomes "*such* a sinner." The use of *but* as an adverb meaning "merely" or "only" constitutes a third frequent strategy, for example, "Ie suis recuilli" becomes "I am *but* loosely gathered together," while "terre et cendres suis" becomes "I am *but* erthe and ashes." Fourth, additions to the text intensify the sense of sin expressed by the narrator. These can be one or two words in a list: "presse de passions" becomes "*entryked and* oppressed with *many yuel* passions," "pecheur" becomes "*wretched* sinner." They can take the form of doublets which, although a characteristic of both unilingual composition and translation in the Middle Ages and Renaissance, do serve to heighten impact. They can also comprise an extra adjective, phrase, or sentence, but this is infrequent in Lady Margaret's translations, which follow their originals closely, in what Workman believes is the dominant mode of fifteenth-century translating.[44] Nevertheless, and especially in the narrator's self-portraits, they increase the sense of spiritual inadequacy: "I am abashed that," "I am so slow and dull to the fervour of virtue," "So colde in deuocion at the tyme of masse." Finally, Lady Margaret's mistranslations often have the effect of intensification, although whether they are made consciously or not is difficult to determine: "maintenant," becomes *many times*," "les miseres de *tes* passions" becomes "the mysteries of *all* thy passions," "pluseurs" is "very many times."

---

[44] Samuel K. Workman, *Fifteenth Century Translation as an Influence on English Prose* (Princeton: Princeton University Press, 1940), 8. Workman focuses on English translations from Latin and syntactic rather than semantic closeness. For Lady Margaret's translation he uses Ingram's edition and for the French original, the Mayer translation.

These techniques are not used exclusively for increasing the speaker's sense of sin; they sometimes, but far more rarely, serve to increase a positive sense of self. For example, in the *Speculum* the reader is told of the value of knowing oneself, which is "plus louable," "more praisable" in Lady Margaret's words, than knowing all the workings of the natural world. She emphasizes the worthiness of self-knowledge by adding a second adjective, this time in superlative form, "moost auayllable," meaning "most effectual." No such examples, however, are found in the *De imitatione Christi*. There, the impact of the French narrator's portrait of his depravity and his emphasis on human weakness are lessened rather than increased in only three places and all concern a reduction of French doublets to single words. "Creature *puante et* pourrie" is rendered as "a corrupt creature"; "ma vilite *et infamete*" becomes simply "myne vnworthynesse," while "unworthynesse" ranks far lower on the scale of sins than "vilite"; "I am the fylthe" inadequately renders "je suis l'ordure et farge."

Lady Margaret's two translations, with their intensified sense of sin, impart a greater feeling of urgency in exhorting Christians to mend their ways. Like all devotional writers whose purpose was to incite their readers to contemplate sin, do penance, prepare for death, and achieve salvation, she could dispose of an array of rhetorical devices with which to persuade them. Many such texts were written in a patterned style, with short and balanced sentences, similar groups of consecutive clauses, and figures of speech like alliteration, assonance, antithesis, repetition, and rhyme.[45] The *De imitatione Christi* and the *Speculum* both display the stylistic characteristics of the genre, often difficult to render in translation. The French translators of both texts successfully transferred most from the Latin and, indeed, sometimes added their own. It remained for Lady Margaret to accomplish a similar feat and make her translations as persuasive as her source texts.

The following comparison of a short passage taken from the Latin original text of the *De imitatione Christi*, the French Lambert translation, and Lady Margaret's English one will illuminate her adroit handling of rhetorical strategies.[46]

> Accedo eger ad saluatorem/esuriens et sitiens ad fontem vitae/egenus ad regem coeli/seruusad Dominum/ creatura ad creatorem. (ki^{v})
> Ie accede a toy malade a mon sauueur/esurient et sitient a la fonteine de vie/ Pouure au roy du ciel/seruiteur a seigneur/creature au createur. (lvii)

[45] Biggs's article on the Middle English translation of the *De imitatione* has been very helpful in evaluating Lady Margaret's techniques in both her translations. Brendan Biggs, "The Style of the First English Translation of the *Imitatio Christi,*" in *The Medieval Translator/Traduire au Moyen Age*, vol. 5, ed. Roger Ellis and René Tixier (Tournhout, Belgium: Brepols, 1996), 187–211.

[46] Latin quotations are from *De imitatione Christi & de contemptu omnium vanitatum mundi* (Paris: Johannes Higman for E. and G. de Marnef, 1489). For the French and English texts, see n. 42.

> I seke and *come unto* my sauyour/I hungry and thursty *unto* the fountayne of lyfe/poor and nedy unto the kynge of heuen/the seruaunt vnto his lorde/the creature unto his maker. (aiv)

The French, following the Latin exactly, comprises a series of five groups of words placed in apposition to the subject, "Ie" (the Latin "accedo" of course not needing a pronoun). The English sentence is modeled exactly on the same pattern: in apposition to "I" are five groups of words: seke; hungry and thursty; poor and nedy; servaunt; creature. As in the Latin and French, each group contains a preposition of motion; the repetition is for rhetorical effect. Here the English is actually more emphatic than its source text because "unto" is used throughout, as is "ad" in the Latin; the French, for grammatical reasons, requires a switch from "a" to "a la" to "au." Lady Margaret also heightens the effect by repeating "I" at the beginning of the second group of words in apposition. The sentence contains three sets of antitheses in the French (as in the Latin): "poure/roy" ("egenus/Regem"), "seruiteur/seigneur" ("seruus/Dominus"), and "creature/createur" ("creatura/creatorem"). Again, Lady Margaret follows suit. However, for some reason—certainly not linguistic—she ignores the aural and visual wordplay of the third pair, choosing to translate "createur" as "maker." Only once does she use a doublet; the French uses none. Significantly, this occurs in the narrator's self-description: "poor and nedy." As we have argued above, she often uses doublets to intensify the sense of sinfulness. She also demonstrates her sensitivity to the effectiveness of symmetrical syntactical structure. In the French it is achieved by the repetition of the verb–preposition–pronoun *viens a toy* followed by words in apposition in each of the four main clauses; these form a pattern: "saulueur et medecin," "fontaine de vie," "roy du ciel," "creature au createur." Lady Margaret replaces this with another, similarly effective symmetrical structure, a verb–preposition–complement format: "come unto my sauyour" is followed by four more preposition–complement phrases, with, as we said above, an added emphasis achieved through repetition of "unto." Other passages demonstrate her use of figures often found in devotional works, *isolocon* (clauses of similar length) and *parison* (similar syntactical arrangements).

Elsewhere, Lady Margaret shows how sensitive she is to the French translator's other rhetorical effects like alliteration or repetition, particularly when used to reinforce the sense of sin. I have chosen a passage from the *Speculum* to show that this sensitivity is not limited to her translation of *De imitatione Christi*.

> Or considere donc et regarde toy homme mortel & miserable que estoit de toy deuant ta natiuite.... Certainement tu as este de ton commencement chose vile, *puante*, detestable et abominable, conceu en ordure et *pourreture* de chair, en *puanteur* de concupiscence, chaleur & embrasement de *puante* luxure, et qui *pire* est, tu es conceu en souillure & macule de *peche*. (aii^{v})

> Nowe consider & beholde thou mortall & miserable man what was of the before thy natiuitie. ... certainly thou hast been frome thy begynnynge a thynge vile, *stinkynge*, detestable and abominable, conceyued in *filthe*, the rotennes of *flesshe*, & *stinkynge fylthie* concupiscence and in the imbracement of *stinkynge* lechery & that, *worse, is conceyued* in the unclene *spott* of *synne*. (Aiii^v)

The three final lines of the French contain a repetition of the adjective "puante" and its related noun, "puanteur." Lady Margaret also uses a triple repetition but hers is more effective by being confined to one word, "stinkynge." The alliteration of the explosive consonant "p" in six French words finds an equivalent in the equally vehement English alliteration of the fricative "f" in "filthe," "flesshe," and "filthy." Lastly, both French and English texts exhibit an effective use of the sibilant "s" to attract the reader's attention and imitate a disapproving hissing sound, but again Lady Margaret outdoes her source by providing, not seven, but thirteen instances of the consonant, in initial, medial, and final position.

The closeness of the translation and its rhetorical effects makes the omission in the passage that immediately follows all the more surprising. The French describes the blood that nourishes the foetus as "infait et menstrueux" and then repeats what various authorities have said, that merely touching it stops wheat from germinating and trees from bearing fruit, causes grass to die, and dogs to develop rabies (aii^v–aiii). Lady Margaret calls the blood "corrupt & infet" but not "menstrual" and omits all its negative effects; the "authorities," she says, testify simply to its corruption and infection (Aiv). Such long omissions (eight lines) are rare in the translation. One can only assume that Lady Margaret found it distasteful to talk about menstrual blood and unnecessary to repeat clerkly prejudices of the sort found in medieval misogynist texts.

Conclusion

In this essay, I began by arguing that translations must be evaluated in context, not as isolated compositions, that a source text's meanings are multiple and therefore open to interpretation, that translators exercise choices when transferring these meanings, and that translation in the early modern period was perceived as playing a very important role in secular and religious discourse. In the late fifteenth and early sixteenth centuries, in particular, it was used as a practical means to encourage spiritual renewal through piety. How do such claims relate to Lady Margaret's translations?

We find in her an example of a woman who worked in a male dominated context, that of translating monastic devotional texts for a wider audience. What Eire says of the early modern Spanish translations of *De imitatione Christi* holds true for their English counterparts. The first English translation of Books I–III was probably done by a Carthusian or Bridgettine monk and the scribes were both at Sheen; Atkynson was a cleric; the anonymous author of the 1531 complete translation was a brother at Syon; the later English versions of 1567 and 1584 were made by two men, Edward Hake, a lawyer, and Thomas Rogers, an Anglican clergyman. Lady Margaret was not only the first translator of Book IV and the whole of the *Speculum* into English, but also the *only* female translator of the works in Europe throughout the whole medieval and early modern period, commanding a place among monks, priests, and university-trained men.

In terms of leaving a personal stamp on a translation, we have seen how she reworked her source texts, although her translations are, overall, close ones. She intensified the sense of sin, personalized the texts so that they spoke to the reader in a more powerful way, and exploited—and at times surpassed—the French translator's rhetorical effects. Examples of such strategies, when taken singly, are perhaps not highly significant; however, when sufficient in number to form a pattern, they influence the work's perspective. By making the text more inclusive, Lady Margaret drew her readers into the narrative, and thus into the community of believers, progressing from individual to collective. By making it more accessible, she reached out from a monastic to a lay audience. Finally, it is plausible to suggest that Lady Margaret thought of her translations as constituting a valuable contribution to the advancement of religion, and particularly of the pietistic movement; they would turn people away from the vanities of the world to inner contemplation and the pursuit of a more pious life. If so, she would be a worthy forerunner of another English woman translator, Margaret Roper. Her translation of Erasmus's *Precatio dominica*, published some twenty years later, was also, I argue elsewhere, part of a pietistic movement in England that saw a rush of printed works, both original and translated, seeking to spread Erasmian theology to a lay and unlettered community.[47] But, as Lady Margaret's biographers from Fisher to Jones and Underwood assert, her piety was marked by a strong practical streak.[48] These two translations, like her alms-giving, care for the sick, support of the universities, and patronage of printers, are indeed mirrors of her own special blend of practical and spiritual piety, of value to all, both religious and lay.

---

[47] See my article, "Translation in the Service of Politics and Religion: A Family Tradition for Thomas More, Margaret Roper and Mary Clarke Basset," in *Between Scylla and Charybdis: Learned Letter Writers Navigating the Reefs of Religious and Political Controversy in Early Modern Europe*, ed. Jeanine De Landtsheer and Henk Nellen (Leiden: Brill, 2010), 93–108.

[48] Jones and Underwood, *The King's Mother*, 201.

Chapter 10
"Nether bitterly nor brablingly": Lady Anne Cooke Bacon's Translation of Bishop Jewel's *Apologia Ecclesiae Anglicanae*

Patricia Demers

Translation, an act and art of creation, throws into sharp relief vexing questions about the interpretability of language. In early modern England it was also a daring, often perilous enterprise. Although in the twenty-first century we have daily familiarity with political violence fueled by religious controversy, it is worth noting some identifying markers of early modern debates about belief and language. Archbishop of Canterbury Thomas Arundel's Constitutions (1408) had outlawed "vernacular theology" as heresy unless approved by the highest levels of the clergy.[1] Clerical surveillance was a fact of early modern cultural existence, as was the public reinforcement of the risk of transgression. "Official" English reaction to Luther furnishes an instructive example of the theatricality and rhetoric of clerical control, a control usually pronounced in English. The campaign against Luther began with a ceremonial public burning of a selection of his works by Cardinal Wolsey in 1521, followed by a sermon in English by John Fisher, Bishop of Rochester. Fisher had had to translate Luther in order to mount his vernacular offensives against him. Moreover, at a time when there was not an agreed-upon text of the English Bible, the "endless glossing" between Thomas More and William Tyndale illustrates both the real dangers of translation and the fierce battles it could instigate.[2] With the publication in Germany of Tyndale's secret English translation of the New Testament in 1525, the confrontation between him and Henry's Lord Chancellor began in earnest. More's *Dialogue Concerning Heresies* and Tyndale's *Obedience of a Christen Man* and his later *Answere* were textual touchstones in the fray. In reply to More's satire on Tyndale's position that the literal sense was the truly spiritual one, Tyndale volleyed back:

> Master More declareth the meninge of no sentence he describeth the propir signification of no worde ner the difference of the significations of any terme

---

1 Brian Cummings, *The Literary Culture of the Reformation: Grammar and Grace* (Oxford: Oxford University Press, 2002), 188.

2 Ibid., 196.

> but runneth forth confusedly in unknowen wordes and general termes. And where one worde hath many significations he maketh a man some time believe that manye thinges are but one thynge and some time he leadeth from one signification unto another and mocketh a mans wittes.[3]

As sobering codas to these verbal skirmishes we should remember that More was executed for treason in 1535 and Tyndale for heresy the next year.

Religious debate was the pulse of early modern society, throbbing throughout the three centuries of upheaval which "in the course of time transformed the way in which the descendants of Reformation and Counter-Reformation Europeans viewed themselves, their society and their place in the world around them."[4] These tectonic shifts took place in language whose passionate intensity and concepts of obedience and fidelity might seem very remote to the unbelief and indifference of most postmodern readers. But this language of religious controversy—sometimes catapulting across eras and at others firmly sealed in the heat of ancient debates—needs careful consideration if we ever want to understand the outlook of past generations. And translation, proof of the ultimate alchemy of language, is an ideal means of apprehending the amplitude, fineness, and subtleties of early modern religious discourse.

The act of translation invites and requires company. In the first instance, there is a source text, a target language and audience, including critical, skeptical readers, and a translator (or translators) who is/are willing, eager, capable and, occasionally, commissioned. Widening the concentric circles of company is a latter-day readership, our contemporary selves, sometimes encountering an early modern text for the first time, curious to discover a rich, deep, living, complex expressivity and wondering if English any longer has "a faculty of religious language."[5] Do we admit to being moved, or affected, or bemused by the claims of the translators of the King James Bible, who averred: "Translation it is that openeth the window, to let in the light, that breaketh the shell, that we may eat the kernel; that putteth aside the curtain, that we may look into the most Holy place; that removeth the cover of the well, that we may come by the water."[6] Or, we could ask, are we too far removed from "the God-shaped mentality, … intensity of conviction and plangent, heart-gripping godliness"[7] that characterized sixteenth-

3 William Tyndale, *An Answere unto Sir Thomas Mores Dialoge*, ed. Anne M. O'Donnell and Jared Wicks, vol. 3 of *Independent Works of William Tyndale* (Washington: Catholic University of America Press, 2000), 195.

4 Diarmaid MacCulloch, *Reformation: Europe's House Divided 1490–1700* (London: Allen Lane, Penguin Books, 2003), 669.

5 Adam Nicolson, *God's Secretaries: The Making of the King James Bible* (New York: HarperCollins, 2003), 236.

6 "The Translators to the Reader," *The Bible; Authorized King James Version*, with introduction and notes by Robert Carroll and Stephen Prickett (Oxford: Oxford University Press, 1997), lvii.

7 Nicolson, *God's Secretaries*, 239.

and seventeenth-century religious debate? When the text is John Jewel, Bishop of Salisbury's *Apologia Ecclesiae Anglicanae*, the official Elizabethan defense of the Church Settlement, first published in 1562, and translated anonymously that year and by Anne Cooke Bacon two years later, our own preliminary questions might become more inflected and pointed. Can polemics about articles of faith, matters of life and death four and a half centuries ago, hope to engage a contemporary secular audience? Do we greet their passionate words with schooled indifference, bafflement, or cautious interest?

I want to introduce two different sight lines through which to filter our postmodern response to this early modern translation. The first is the published commendation of the original reviewers of Lady Bacon's submission: Matthew Parker, Archbishop of Canterbury, and Bishop Jewel, the author of the Latin text. Parker's prefatory epistle, "To the right honorable learned and vertuous Ladie A.B., M.C. [that is, Matthew of Canterbury] wisheth from God grace, honoure and felicitie," provided his commentary on Lady Bacon's "studious labour of translation,"[8] an exercise doubly vetted and approved, in a tone that was laudatory but not fawning or obsequious:

> You have used your accustomed modestie in submittinge it to judgement, but therin is your prayse doubled, sith it hath passed iudgement without reproche. And whereas bothe the chiefe author of the Latine worke and I, severally perusinge and conferringe youre whole translation, have without alteration allowed of it, I must bothe desire youre Ladiship, and advertise the readers, to thinke that wee have not therein given any thinge to any dissemblinge affection towards you, as beinge contented to winke at faultes to please you, or to make you without cause to please your selfe: for there be sundry respectes to drawe us from so doinge.

Parker catalogued the self-reflecting reasons for their honesty:

> Your own judgement in discerning flatterie, your modestie in mislikinge it, the layenge open of oure opinion to the world, the truth of our friendship towards you, the unwillingnesse of us bothe (in respect of our vocations) to have this publike worke not truely and wel translated, are good causes to perswade, that our allowance is of sincere truth and understanding.

Moreover, he underscored the honour, exemplarity, clarity, and precedent-setting encouragement of Lady Bacon's accomplishment:

---

8 Matthew Parker, "To the right honorable learned and vertuous Ladie A. B.," in Anne Cooke Bacon, trans., *An Apologie or answere in defence of the Churche of Englande, with a briefe and plaine declaration of the true Religion professed and used in the same* by John Jewel (London, 1564; *STC* 14591), np. Bacon's translation is available in *Anne Cooke Bacon*, EME, Series 1, pt. 2, vol. 1, selected and introduced by Valerie Wayne (Aldershot: Ashgate, 2000).

> By which your travail (Madame) you have expressed an acceptable dutye to the glorye of GOD, deserved well of this Churche of Christe, honourablie defended the good fame and estimation of your owne natiue tongue, shewing it so able to contend with a worke originally written in the most praised speache: and besides the honour ye have done to the kinde of women and to the degree of Ladies, ye have done pleasure to the Author of the Latine boke, in delivering him by your cleare translation from the perrils of ambiguous and doubtful constructions: and in makinge his good woorke more publikely beneficiall: wherby ye have raysed vp great comforte to your friendes, and have furnished your owne conscience joyfully with the fruit of your labour, in so occupienge your time: whiche must needes redounde to the encoragemente of noble youth in their good education, and to spend their time and knowledge in godly exercise, havinge delivered them by you so singular a president.

Parker's ultimate accolade, after having received the "boke writen," is to return it "printed: knowing that I have therin done the beste, and in this poynte used a reasonable pollicye: that is, to prevent suche excuses as your modestie woulde have made in staye of publishinge it." Although Alan Stewart reads Parker's letter as a "blatantly disingenuous" preface to a translation exhibiting "the hallmarks of an official, commissioned work,"[9] his letter touches all the central concerns affecting the creation and circulation of early modern women's writing: an approved use of learning, a duty to God and country, a lucid and insightful transfer from a classical language to the vernacular, an example to others of the social responsibilities of education, and, with "modestie" being mentioned three times, an acknowledgment and tacit acceptance of the humility topos.

The second sight line, George Eliot's brief review essay, "Translations and Translators," moves us halfway closer to the present. Although it is doubtful that Eliot read Lady Bacon's *Apologie*, she was likely aware of the text's importance; as well, she was herself an experienced translator from German to English, having translated David Freidrich Strauss's *Life of Jesus*, Ludwig Feuerbach's *Essence of Christianity*, and Baruch Spinoza's *Ethics*. Her *Leader* review (20 October 1855) of a recent translation of Kant and of a selection of German lyrical poetry draws attention to the critical importance of the confident knowledge of languages. She cites the example of the translators of the Septuagint, who "had some understanding of their business to begin with," as an instructive warning "to all young ladies and some middle-aged gentlemen, who consider a very imperfect acquaintance with their own language, and an anticipatory acquaintance with the foreign language, quite a sufficient equipment for the office of translator."[10] She discounts the conventional image of the translator, who "having ventured into deep waters without learning to swim, clings to the dictionary, and commends himself to

[9] Alan Stewart, "The Voices of Anne Cooke, Lady Anne and Lady Bacon," in Clarke and Clarke, *'This Double Voice,'* 93–4.

[10] George Eliot, "Translations and Translators" (*Leader*, VI, 20 October 1855), in *Essays of George Eliot*, ed. Thomas Pinney (London: Routledge and Kegan Paul, 1963), 208.

Providence," in favor of the artist who shows "the patience, the rigid fidelity, and the sense of responsibility in interpreting another man's mind."[11] Her admittedly desultory remarks, which she dismisses as gossiping on the subject, nevertheless spotlight a crucial, but often slighted or taken for granted, proficiency.

With a recognition of both early modern and continuing criteria of judgment, we should turn to a consideration of the specific context of Lady Bacon's work. Because this *Apologie* is actually an attack on a preceding belief system, we could find ourselves oriented in different directions depending on the critical signposts we heed. John E. Booty, Jewel's twentieth-century biographer, sets up a historical context by referring matter-of-factly to royal visitations "erasing the remnants of Romish superstition from the cathedrals and parish churches of England."[12] By contrast, Eamon Duffy, attending to "traditional" religion in England from 1400 to 1580, sifts through "astringent and strident words" and laments the "relentless torrent carrying away the landmarks of a thousand years."[13] Lest we fasten on the symbolic importance of a single work of Reformed Protestantism and its polemical tone, Diarmaid MacCulloch draws attention to a vast range of controversial texts that provided benchmarks of a uniquely English development. He focuses on the "shy but precociously intelligent" fourteen-year-old Richard Hooker, Jewel's protegé at Corpus Christi College, "the Bishop's old college," as the future author of *The Laws of Ecclesiastical Polity*, one of the "chief starting points for England's move away from mainstream European Protestantism."[14]

A caution of a different sort, against inflating claims for the expressivity and independence of early modern women's efforts as translators, emerges from one of the first overviews of the Cooke sisters' work. The translator of Jewel's work is Lady Anne Cooke Bacon (1527/8–1610), the second-born of the five daughters of Sir Anthony Cooke and Lady Anne (Fitzwilliam) Cooke, one of "the wealthiest ten or twelve families in Essex."[15] According to Marjorie McIntosh, in the family seat of Gidea Hall, Romford, a rigid, reform-minded attitude toward religion held as much sway as the learning of Greek and Latin and the importance of family ties in arranging marriages. The Cooke sisters, all eager and exceptionally capable pupils, received "probably a better education" than their four brothers, only two of whom survived to adulthood—with one entering Gray's Inn and the other "devoted to hunting."[16] At the time of her translation of *An Apologie*, Anne Cooke Bacon was the mother of two young boys, Anthony (future diplomat) and Francis (future Lord

---

[11] Ibid., 208, 211.

[12] John E. Booty, introduction to John Jewel, *An Apology of the Church of England*, ed. John E. Booty (Ithaca, NY: Cornell University Press, 1963), ix.

[13] Eamon Duffy, *The Stripping of the Altars: Traditional Religion in England 1400–1580* (New Haven: Yale University Press, 1992), 593.

[14] MacCulloch, *Reformation*, 503–4.

[15] Marjorie Keniston McIntosh, "Sir Anthony Cooke: Tudor Humanist, Educator, and Religious Reformer," *Proceedings of the American Philosophical Society* 119 (1975): 236.

[16] Ibid., 239.

Chancellor), and stepmother to Sir Nicholas Bacon's six children from a previous marriage. Though Lady Bacon was anything but "a mere household drudge,"[17] her work has been characterized as repressed and subordinate. In her commentary Mary Ellen Lamb sees translation not as a vehicle of "self-expression" but rather of "repression," with "exceedingly literal" translations carrying "too much official weight to allow tampering" and thus perverting the "professed goals of a humanistic education [as] applied to women."[18] Expanding this thesis, Louise Schleiner views translation as "a pathway women found into writing through religious activism," although she locates the Cooke sisters in general as "marginalized female participants."[19] Concentrating mainly on Cooke's earlier translation of nineteen sermons from Italian by the firebrand ex-Capuchin reformer Bernardino Ochino, Schleiner delimits the originality of the translation of polemical work, defining it as "the most subordinately paratextual mode of writing."[20]

In light of early modern criteria and contexts, along with the relatively slight range of scholarly caveats, I intend to pursue an examination of Lady Bacon's language, its fidelity to and flavoring of the Latin, and its distinction from the earlier translator's efforts. Without exaggeration it seems to me that her accomplishment in *An Apologie of the Churche of England* far surpasses literal precision and exactitude. The boldness and color of her idiomatic flourishes, the declarative vigor of her text's assertions, and her conceptual ordering of subordinate clauses to underscore sequence, causation and effect, all argue for a secure and convinced grasp of the source text and determination to communicate its pithy content in engaging, zesty, direct English.

Although Bacon espouses a moderate tone and tempered understanding of hatred, mockery and belittlement, there is nothing shy or diffident about her language. Citing the precedent of prophets and martyrs—Isaiah, Jeremiah, Daniel, Amos, Paul, and Christ—she exhorts readers to follow the high ground: "wherefore wee oughte to beare yt the more quyetlye, which have taken uppon us to professe the Gospell of Christ."[21] The directive "to beare yt the more quyetlye" not only abides by the Latin order ("*Quo nos animo aequiore ferre debemus quiqunque professionem Euangeli Iesu Christi suscepimus*"),[22] but it foregrounds

[17] Mary Bradford Whiting, "The Learned and Virtuous Lady Bacon," *The Hibbert Journal* 29 (1931): 272.

[18] Mary Ellen Lamb, "The Cooke Sisters: Attitudes toward Learned Women in the Renaissance," in Hannay, *Silent But for the Word*, 124–5.

[19] Louise Schleiner, *Tudor and Stuart Women Writers* (Bloomington: Indiana University Press, 1994), 33.

[20] Ibid., 51.

[21] Anne Bacon, trans., *An Apologie or answere in defence of the Churche of Englande* (see n. 8), Aiiii. Subsequent quotations will be identified parenthetically.

[22] John Jewel, *Apologia Ecclesiae Anglicanae, authore Ioanne Iuello olim Episcopo Sarisburi* (London: George Bishop, 1606; *STC* 14586), 6. Subsequent quotations will be identified parenthetically. The italics are mine.

quiet endurance much more adroitly than the clumsy 1562 text, where the point is muffled until the end: "So muche the more ought we that have taken the profession of Jesus Christ, to take it in better parte."[23] Animosity over exclusion from the Council of Trent, unless one were prepared to recant ("*nisi si quis forte esset, qui vellet palinodiam canare, & mutare sententiam*" 16–17), is the announced, rankling pretext for this defense: "nother can we yet forget, how Julius the third, above ten yeares past, provided warely by his writt, that none of our sorte shoulde bee suffered to speake in the Councell (except that there were som paradventure y[t] wolde recante and chaunge his opinion). For this cause chieflye we thoughte it good to yelde up an accoumpte of oure faith in writing & truely and openly to make aunswere to those things wherwith wee have ben openly charged" (Bii). Despite the caution from St. Jerome to "deal herein nether bitterly nor brablingly" (Biii), the colloquial force of Bacon's "brablingly," meaning "contentiously, riotously, tumultuously," does more than capture the sense of "*nos tamen nec acerbe aut dicaciter agemus, nec esseremur iracundia*"; although prefaced with a cancelling negative, the righteous indignation of "brablingly" seeps through.

English exclusion from the Council of Trent (1545–63), dedicated to reform in faith and practice along the lines of more ancient discipline, is a major cause of this vehemence, especially evident in Bacon's text completed after the Council's final session. After many delays and in response to repeated calls for reform—from the Council of Constance (1414–18) to Luther's Ninety-Five Theses (1517) and the demands of the Diet of Nuremburg (1523)—the convocation of the Council began in the Cathedral of St. Vigilius in the mountain-surrounded city of Trent in northern Italy. Though aiming to heal the confessional split, the three sessions (1545–48, 1551–52, 1562–63) concentrated on spiritual renewal and reform: "Half of the decrees of Trent were about reform—*de reformatione*."[24] The assembled prelates addressed problems of decay and neglect, which Jewel's *Apologia* would articulate and Bacon's translation would intensify: among them, the poor preparation of members of the lower clergy, nepotism, the holding of several benefices (pluralism) and corresponding absenteeism, the debt of the papacy, and the disrepair of monasteries. The sense of Catholic awakening, at the Council and beyond, involved explicit reiteration of doctrine, long-argued points of contention for Jewel and Bacon—about seven sacraments, the Real Presence in the Eucharist, the co-existence of grace and faith as the necessary condition of justification—along with the publication of such approved texts as Tridentine catechisms, a revised *Index* of forbidden books, and a reformed *Breviary* for daily clerical devotion.

---

[23] Anonymous, trans., *An Apologie or Aunswer in Defence of the Churche of Englande* (London, 1562; *STC* 14590), Aiiii. Subsequent quotations will be identified parenthetically.

[24] John W. O'Malley, *Trent and All That: Renaming Catholicism in the Early Modern Era* (Cambridge, MA: Harvard University Press, 2000), 18.

A deliberate, often ironic mimicking of Tridentine discourse surfaces at many critical points in *An Apologie* within the context of the sixteenth-century English Reform cause. Bacon translates "*sacrificuli*" (33) not, as in the 1562 text, as "sacrificing Preestes" (Ciiii), but as "the cōmen Massing preestes" (Ciiii). On the passage of consecrated bread through the body, which the 1562 text described as "that bread which is sanctified by the word of God goeth into the belly, and is cast into the withdrawing place" (Diii), Bacon treats "*in ventrem abit, & in secessum ejicitur*" (43) with non-prudish directness: "Bread ... goeth into ye belly, and is cast out into the privey" (Dii). In recounting the abuses of the Lord's Supper, she addresses what Reformers considered the displays of liturgy, "*Christi sacramenta ac scenam iam & pompam traduxerunt*" (45), as "a stage play ... to the end that mens eyes should be fedde with nothing els but with mad gazinges and foolishe gaudes" (Diiii), a considerably more forceful denunciation than the 1562 text's "pagent & a solemne pompe" (Diiii). The image of Pope Joan in labour in the streets and playing "the naughtie Packe" (Fii)—a term now obsolete, but used in the sixteenth century according to the OED, for persons of low or worthless character—is an especially vivid rendering of "*in illa sancta sede aliorum libidini exposuisset, postremo in lustranda ciuitate ... palam pareret in publico*" (70), more pungent than the earlier translation's "she had applied herselfe in ye holy seat unto other mens lustes" (Fiiii). The powerful image of greed fed by ambition, gluttony, and excess ("*ambitio, venter, luxus*" [202]) means that clergy concentrate only on themselves. Bacon's treatment of "*hinc illae lachrymae: animus est in patinis*" (202–3), "Hence cometh their whining: their hearte is on their Halfepennye" (Qv), captures the venality of the self-absorbed gaze with a sixteenth-century expression that is much more suggestive than the earlier prosaic "their minde is upon their platters" (Si).

Bacon is acutely aware of the cumulative, accretive power of language. She renders Jewel's definition of heresy precisely as "a forsaking of salvation, a renouncing of God's grace, a departing from the body and spirite of Christe" (Biiii) where he reads "*Est enim haeresis destitutio salutis, abiecto gratiae Dei, discessio a corpore & spiritui Christi*" (18), but she concentrates on the potent repetition of incriminatingly active present participles. When she seeks to uncover heresy in action, often masquerading behind biblical phrases and snippets, she makes Jewel's example of the accusation of Sophocles as an incompetent old man a stinging indictment of his accusers and, by extension, of those who fling about the charge of heresy. Unlike the literal but uncolored exactness of the 1562 text, Bacon's version tells a story, accentuating the indignity of the accusation from his *own* sons, the artist's need to "clear" his reputation, and the overall effect of his recited piece of work. It is worth noting how Bacon's control of subordinate clauses and chronology sets the scene and exposes the irony of the accusation. The stress on the diligence and elegance of Sophocles' verses in one rendition contrasts with the emphasis on the alertness and insight of his tragedy in the other. Here are the two versions:

> Sophocles the poet, when he was accused, beinge an olde man, to the Judges, of his sonnes for a dotarde and a foole, and as one that fondely consumed his goodes, and therefore seemed to have neede of a tutor: for to purge himselfe of this slaunder came into the courte, and after he had reade Oedipus Coloneus, a tragedie, which even in the selfe same time that he was accused in, he had writen wyth great diligence and very elegantly, by and by he asked of the Judges, whether that verse seemed to be the verse of a dotinge man. (Anon., *Apologie*, 1562, Ci)

> Men say that Sophocles, the tragicall poet, when in his oulde days he was by his own sonnes accused before the Judges for a dotinge and sottishe man, as one that fondelye wasted hys own substaunce, and seemed to neede a Governour to see unto him: to thintent he might cleere him selfe of the faulte, he came into the place of Judgemente, and when he had rehearsed before them his Tragedye called Oedipus Coloneus, which he had written at the very time of his accusation, marvelous exactly and conningly, did of him selfe aske the Judges, whether they thought any sottish or doting man could do the like peece of worke. (Bacon, *Apologie*, 1564, Bv)

It is not obvious that the anonymous translator actually got the connection between *Oedipus at Colonus* and the trumped-up charges against Sophocles, or the pertinent connection between sophistical argument and charges of so-called heresy. Oedipus, we remember, was shunned by his own sons and banished from Thebes. This tragic hero's ultimate destiny was to safeguard the city of Athens, not his native Thebes. Bacon's adverbial description of Sophocles's work "written at the very time of his accusation, maruelous exactly and cunningly" conveys her full grasp of familial and civic betrayals in ancient Greece and their parallels with reactions to perceived hypocrisy and violation of trust within the community of Reform-minded faithful in sixteenth-century England.

As adroit as she is in focusing long passages, Bacon is equally skilled at synthesizing with a single phrase or word. For instance, at the close of the introductory section and before the itemized list of the Creed, she adds her own hinging, annunciatory sentence, "This therefore is oure Belieffe" (Bv), before continuing with the translation of "*Credimus ergo unam quandam naturae esse*

& uim diuinam quam appellamus Deum" (24). Her diction skewers as readily as it reveals emotion. When facing a catalogue of Romish "notorious deeds," Bacon translates "*Tædet exemplorum*" (85) as "Wee are cloyed with exaumples" (Giiii), sounding more than a hint of exasperation and expressing less overwhelmed fatigue than the 1562 text's "I am weary of examples" (Hi). The examples of the primitive church, which the *Apologia* cites frequently, furnish another instance of Bacon's vivid down-to-earthness. In contrast to the earlier translation's bland remarks about "a cause abandoned so longe time" with "no worde at all" (Lii), Bacon weighs in with this colourful observation: "Whye lyeth so auncient a cause thus longe in the duste destitute of an advocate? Fyre and sword they have had alwayes at hande. But as for the olde Councels and the fathers, all mum, not a word" (Kiii). She does not shy away from strong statements either, adding her own exclamations to the sense of outrage in the original. "But good God, what manner of felowes be these, which blame us for disagreing?" (Ev) is her inflected rendering of "*Verum, o Deus bone, quinam isti tandem sunt, qui dissensiones in nobis reprehendunt?*" (60), her barely controlled anger conveying a very different attitude from the demureness of the earlier version, "But Lorde, what men, trowe ye, be these that fynde faulte with dissensions amongest us?" (Eiiii). In contrast to the earlier translator's unwillingness to expostulate and exclaim, Bacon echoes the sentiments (and punctuation) of the Latin in exploding, "O holy Scribes and Pharises, which knew not this kind of holines. O what holynes, what a Catholike faith is this: …" (Fv). Her combined skills in sentence construction and emotional expression make her version an emphatic *tour de force*, as the following variations illustrate. In the 1562 text, the contrast between the claims of the ancient church and the liturgies of current adherents emerges in this tepid observation: "They have not, O mercifull God, they have not those thinges, which thei boaste themselves to have, nother antiquitie, nor universalitie, nother the consent of all places, nor of all times" (Mi). Bacon's repetitions drill home the point of hypocrisy: "Thei have not, good Lord, thei have not (I say) those things which they boast they have: they have not y^{t} antiquitie, they have not that universalitie, they have not that consent of all places, nor of all times" (Lii).

Another salient feature of Bacon's writing is its concreteness. She makes the Latin text a visual English reality. One of the most prominent examples involves the catalogue of different practices among orders of friars and monks. The earlier version dutifully records sartorial contrasts—"wherof some of them do appoint their holiness to be in fishe, some in herbes, some in shooes, some in slippers, some in a linen garment, some in a wollen, some go in white, some in blacke, some are shaven broder, some narrower, some are shodde, some are barefoote, some girded, some ungirded" (Fi)—connecting these variants with views of the Eucharist:

> There be some that write that the body of Christ in the sacramēt hath quantitie and bygnesse, on the other side there be some that denye it: that there be some that saye, Christ did consecrate by a certaine power of divinitie, some y^{t} by blessing, some by five specially prescribed wordes. (Fi)

Instead of claiming, like the previous translator, to "passe ouer" differences, Bacon begins her lengthy exposition with the sly confession of wishing to say nothing, before she creates this fully corporeal image of friars and monks eating, wearing garments, and walking about:

> And yet saye I nothing of so many diversities of fryers and monkes, howe some of them put a great holynes in eating of fyshe, and some in eatyng of hearbes: some in wearing of shewes, and some in wearing of sandalles: some in going in a lynnen garment, and some in a wollen: some of them called whit, some blacke: some being shaven broade, and some narowe: some stalking abroade uppon patens, some barefooted: some girte, and some ungerte. (Ev)

Although both translators address the specialty of the five particular words of the consecration of the bread (*hoc est enim corpus meum*), Bacon's rendering is both more explicitly pedagogical, daring to include and explicate the Latin, and syntactically easier to follow:

> Some also of them there be, whiche write ye body of Christ is *quantum in Eucharistia*, that is to say, hath his perfite quantitie in the Sacrament: some other againe saye naye. That there be others of them whiche saye, Christ did consecrate with a certain divine power, some that he did the same with his blessing, some againe that say hee didde it with utteringe five solemne chosē words, and some with rehearsing the same woordes afterwarde againe. (Evi)

"Perfect quantity," "divine power," "solemn chosen words": these lucid descriptions of complex and contested theological mysteries show how capably Bacon grappled with a belief system from which she found herself distanced more and more.

Her reaction to the final session of the recently concluded Council of Trent shadows and informs Bacon's translation, arguably as much or more than English exclusion from the Council affected Bishop Jewel and his first translator. One of the *Apologia*'s strongest statements about the Council concerns the perceived appropriation of divine authority and inerrancy. The first translator asked: "what if they [the Bysshops] should, not colorably or darkely, but evidently and flatly make a decre contrary to the expresse worde of God? Trow ye that whatsoever these men say, that shall be straight waye the gospell? Trow ye this shall be gods army; trow ye Christ will be present there?" (Oii). There is some forceful parallelism, repetition and direct engagement in these questions. Now consider Bacon's version:

> Shortly, what though thei make Decrees expreslye against Gods worde, and that not in huckermucker or covertly but openly & in the face of the worlde: muste it needes yet be Gospell straighte whatsoever these men say? Shall these be Gods holy army? Or will Christe bee at hande amonge them there? Shall the holy ghost flow in their tongues, or can they with truth say, We and the holy Ghoste have thoughte so? (Ni)

She continues by implicating one of the councilors, "*Peter a Soto*,"[25] whom she identifies as "Peter Asotus" (*asotus* meaning "a worthless or debauched character"), as justifying the decree of the ancient council that condemned Jesus Christ to death. In this passage Bacon is meeting the boldness of the Council's public declarations with the vehemence of her own response. Her interrogatives, "must it needs yet," "shall these be," "will Christ be," "shall the Holy ghost flow," and "can they say," not only drum on the implausibility of these positions, but allow for the swelling chorus of negative responses.

In translating from a classical to a modern language, Bacon brings to life sharp rifts and extreme themes in sixteenth-century discourse about belief and loyalty. Today her vivid language illuminates Reformation arguments for the benefit of postmodern readers. She never embroiders, but stresses the urgency of clarification and the need to discriminate between opposing views. Her success as a creative translator suggests to me a parallel with Robert Alter's recent translation of the Psalms. Though Alter is working with poetry and Bacon with prose, what unites them over the centuries is a zeal for conveying the essence of the original in ways that are faithful, fresh, and widely accessible. Mirroring the plainness, rhythms, and parallelism of the original through magnificent English cadences "with slightly antique coloration," Alter's project aims "to represent Psalms in a kind of English verse that is readable as poetry yet sounds something like the Hebrew."[26] He explains:

> emulating its rhythms wherever feasible, reproducing many of the effects of its expressive poetic syntax, seeking equivalents for the combination of homespun directness and archaizing in the original, hewing to the lexical concreteness of the Hebrew, and making more palpable the force of parallelism that is at the heart of biblical poetry.[27]

With adjustments for the formality of Jewel's Latin, but with equal stress on concreteness and directness, it seems to me that Bacon's project shares a similar motive and method.

A cursory glance at the first two translations of Jewel's *Apologia* might suggest that there are only superficial differences between them. A closer comparative analysis, sketched here, reveals the unquestioned superiority of Lady Bacon's work. As her earliest reviewers realized, the achievements of Bacon's language—its rhetorical vigor and steely determination along with its lucid and intuitive grasp of the resonances of English syntax—account for the strength of this translation. In fact, when Thomas Harding, "former Regius professor of Hebrew and warden-

[25] John E. Booty, *John Jewel As Apologist of the Church of England* (London: S.P.C.K., 1963), 109.

[26] Robert Alter, introduction to *The Book of Psalms; A Translation with Commentary* (New York: W.W. Norton, 2007), xxx, xxxi.

[27] Ibid., xxxi.

elect of New College, Oxford,"[28] mounted his *Confutation of the Apologie of the Church of England*, published in Antwerp in 1565, this English Catholic refugee at Louvain quoted Bacon's translation throughout. For dispute or defense her text had quickly become the standard. Ironically, when the next translation of the *Apologia* appeared, by Thomas Cheyne, rector of Lilly in the county of Hertford, in 1720, Cheyne referred to the "well known" character of Bishop Jewel and his justification of "our Separation, by shewing the many absurd Errours and corrupt Practices in the Romish Church," but dismissed "the Old Translations" as "so obscure, by reason of the variableness of our Language, that the English Reader … cannot be much benefited by them."[29] The variableness, fluctuations, moodiness of the language seem to me to be precisely the point. It's not enough, I will conclude, for modern critics to pronounce on the restrictions and controls of the busy work of early modern translation. Rather, we need to read and sift carefully to uncover the daring, the emotional contours, and the passageways to imaginative expressivity embedded in the vernacular theology of such an early modern woman translator as Lady Anne Cooke Bacon.

---

[28] Cummings, *Literary Culture*, 328.

[29] Thomas Cheyne, trans., *Apologia ecclesiae anglicanae; or, the Apology of the Church of England* (London, 1720), v, vii, ix.

Works Cited

Manuscript Sources

Arundel Castle Archives
"The Life of the Right Honourable & Virtuouse Lady, the Lady Anne Late Countesse of Arundell & Surrey"
Receipt Book MS

Beinecke Library, New Haven
MS Osborn b. 268

Bodleian Library, Oxford
MS Laud Misc. 1

British Library, London
Harley MS 2342
Add. MS 12060
Lansdowne 101
Lansdowne 68
Lansdowne 104

Durham Cathedral
Hunter MS 112

Gonville and Caius College, Cambridge
MS 218/233

Hatfield House, Hertfordshire
Salis MS 52.52
Salis MS 140.82
Salis MS 175.92
Salis MS 197.53

Huntington Library, San Marino, California
MS HM 15369

Lambeth Palace, London
Talbot Papers MS 3203

Northamptonshire Record Office, Northampton
Lady Mildmay's Meditations

Monastery of Poor Clares, Much Birch
MS *Aire Register*
MS *Gravelines Chronicle*

The National Archives, London
SP Dom 12/77, no. 11
SP Dom 12/262, no. 53

York Minster, York
Add MS 151

Printed Primary Sources

Anonymous. *A Boke Newely Translated Out of Laten in to Englysshe, Called the Folowynge of Cryste*. London: Robert Wyer, 1531.
———. *The Earliest English Translation of the First Three Books of the De Imitatione Christi*. Edited by John K. Ingram. EETS extr. ser., 63. London: Kegan Paul, 1893.
———. *The Imitation of Christ by Thomas à Kempis*. Translated by Betty I. Knott. London: Collins, 1963.
———. *De imitatione Christi & de contemptu omnium vanitatum mundi*. Paris: Johannes Higman for E. and G. Marnef, 1489.
———. *Le livre tressalutaire de limitation de nostre seigneur jesucrist*. Paris: Lambert, 1494.
———. *Le mirouer dor de lame pecheresse tres utile et profitable*. Bréhant-Loudéac: Foucquet-Cras, 1484.
———. trans. *An Apologie or Aunswer in Defence of the Churche of Englande*. London, 1562.
Bacon, Anne Cooke, trans. *An Apologie Or Answere in Defence of the Churche of Englande, with a Briefe and Plaine Declaration of the True Religion Professed and used in the Same*. London, 1564.
Baker, Augustine. *The Life and Death of Dame Gertrude More*. Edited by Ben Wekking. Salzburg: Institute für Anglistik und Amerikanistik, 2002.
Bakhtin, M.M. "Discourse in the Novel." 259–422 in *The Dialogic Imagination: Four Essays*. Edited by Michael Holquist. Translated by Caryl Emerson and Michael Holquist. Austin: University of Texas Press, 1981.
———. "Forms of Time and Chronotope in the Novel." 84–258 in *The Dialogic Imagination: Four Essays*. Edited by Michael Holquist. Translated by Caryl Emerson and Michael Holquist. Austin: University of Texas Press, 1981.

Beaufort, Lady Margaret, trans. *Book IV* of *A Full Devout [and] Gostely Treatyse of the Imytacion and Folowynge the Blessed Lyfe of Oure Moste Mercyfull Savyoure Criste*. London: Richard Pynson, 1504.

———, trans. *The Mirroure of Golde for the Synfull Soule*. London: Richard Pynson, 1506.

Bentley, Thomas. *The Monument of Matrones Conteining Seven Severall Lamps of Virginitie*. London, 1582.

Bèze, Théodore de. *The Psalmes of David Truely Opened and Explaned by Paraphrasis, According to the Right Sense of Every Psalme*. Translated by Anthony Gilby. London, 1590.

The Book of Common Prayer, 1559: The Elizabethan Prayer Book. Edited by John E. Booty. Charlottesville, VA: Published for the Folger Shakespeare Library by the University Press of Virginia, 1976.

Bunny, Edmund. *A Booke of Christian Exercise, appertaining to Resolution*. London, 1584.

Calvin, John. *Commentary on the Book of Psalms*. Translated by James Anderson. 5 vols. Edinburgh: The Calvin Translation Society, 1845–46.

———. *A Harmony of the Gospels: Matthew, Mark and Luke*. Edited by David W. Torrance and Thomas F. Torrance. Translated by A.W. Morrison. Vol. 3 of *Calvin's New Testament Commentaries*. Grand Rapids, MI: W.B. Eerdmans, 1972.

———. *Institutes of the Christian Religion*. Edited by John T. McNeill. Translated by Ford Lewis Battles. 2 vols. Philadelphia: Westminster Press, 1960.

———. "Sermons upon the Songe that Ezekias made." In *The Collected Works of Anne Vaughan Lock*, edited by Susan M. Felch, 4–71. Tempe: Arizona Center for Medieval and Renaissance Studies, 1999.

Cape, William, trans. *The Life of the Glorious Virgin S. Clare, by Marcos Da Silva*. Saint-Omer, 1622.

———. *The Rule of the Holy Virgin S. Clare*. In *Elizabeth Evelinge III*. EME, Series I, pt. 4, vol. 1, selected and introduced by Claire Walker, 1–80. Aldershot: Ashgate, 2006.

Castiglione, Baldesar. *Book of the Courtier*. Translated by Charles Singleton. New York: Doubleday, 1959.

Cawdrey, Robert. *The First English Dictionary 1604: Robert Cawdrey's A Table Alphabetical*. Edited by John Simpson. Oxford: Bodleian Library, 2007.

Cheyne, Thomas, trans. *Apologia Ecclesiae Anglicanae; Or, the Apology of the Church of England*. London, 1720.

The Chronicle of Queen Jane, and of Two Years of Queen Mary. Edited by John Gough Nichols. London: Publications of the Camden Society no. 48, 1849.

Cicero. *De Officiis*. Edited and translated by Walter Miller. Cambridge, MA: Harvard University Press, 1913.

Clifford, Anne. *The Diaries of Lady Anne Clifford*. Edited by D.J.H. Clifford. Phoenix Mill, UK: Sutton Publishing, 1990.

———. *The Memoir of 1603 and the Diary of 1616–1619*. Edited by Katherine O. Acheson. Peterborough, ON: Broadview Press, 2007.

Coverdale, Miles, trans. *Biblia. the Bible: That is: the Holy Scripture, Faithfully Translated in to Englyshe*. Southwark, 1535.

———. *Fruitfull Lessons, upon the Passion, Buriall, Resurrection, Ascension, and of the Sending of the Holy Ghost*. London, 1593.

———, trans. *A Paraphrasis upon all the Psalmes of David, made by Johannes Campensis*. London, 1539.

Cox, Leonard, trans. *The Paraphrase of Erasm[us] Roterdame upon [the] Epistle of Sai[n]t Paule Unto His Disciple Titus*. London, 1534.

[Devo]Ut Meditacions, [Psal]Mes and Praiers [to] Bee used Aswell in the Morning as Eaventyde Gathered Out of the Holy Scriptures and Other Godly Wryters. London: Edward Whitchurche, 1548.

Dickens, Charles. *Great Expectations*. Boston: Houghton Mifflin Co., 1962.

Eliot, George. "Translations and Translators." In *Essays of George Eliot*, edited by Thomas Pinney, 207–11. London: Routledge and Kegan Paul, 1963.

Erasmus, Desiderius. *The Correspondence of Erasmus*. Translated by R.A.B. Mynors and D.F.S. Thomson. Annotated by P.G. Bietenholz. Vol. 5 of *Collected Works of Erasmus*. Toronto: University of Toronto Press, 1979.

———. *The Correspondence of Erasmus*. Translated by R.A.B. Mynors and D.F.S. Thomson. Annotated by P.G. Bietenholz. Vol. 6 of *Collected Works of Erasmus*. Toronto: University of Toronto Press, 1982.

———. *The Correspondence of Erasmus*. Translated by R.A.B. Mynors. Annotated by Peter G. Bietenholz. Vol. 8 of *Collected Works of Erasmus*. Toronto: University of Toronto Press, 1988.

———. *The Correspondence of Erasmus*. Translated by R.A.B. Mynors. Annotated by James M. Estes. Vol. 9 of *Collected Works of Erasmus*. Toronto: University of Toronto Press, 1989.

———. *The Correspondence of Erasmus*. Translated by R.A.B. Mynors and Alexander Dalzell. Annotated by James M. Estes. Vol. 10 of *Collected Works of Erasmus*. Toronto: University of Toronto Press, 1992.

———. *The First Tome Or Volume of the Paraphrase of Erasmus upon the Newe Testamente*. London, 1548.

———. *Literary and Educational Writings*. Edited by Craig R. Thompson. Vol. 24 of *Collected Works of Erasmus*. Toronto: University of Toronto Press, 1978.

———. *Paraphrase on the Acts of the Apostles*. Edited by John J. Bateman. Translated and annotated by Robert D. Sider. Vol. 50 of *Collected Works of Erasmus*. Toronto: University of Toronto Press, 1995.

———. *Paraphrase on John*. Translated and annotated by Jane E. Phillips. Vol. 46 of *Collected Works of Erasmus*. Toronto: University of Toronto Press, 1991.

Evelinge, Elizabeth, trans. *The Admirable Life of the Holy Virgin S. Catherine of Bologna*, by Dionisio Paleotti. In *Elizabeth Evelinge III*, 81–394. EME, Series I, pt. 4, vol. 1, selected and introduced by Claire Walker. Aldershot: Ashgate, 2006.

———, trans. *The Declarations and Ordinances made upon the Rule of our Holy Mother S. Clare*. In *Elizabeth Evelinge II*, EME, Series I, pt. 3, vol. 5, selected and introduced by Jos Blom and Frans Blom. Aldershot: Ashgate, 2002.

Featley, Daniel. *Ancilla Pietatis: Or, the Hand-Maid to Private Devotion.* London, 1626.

Fenton, Geoffrey, trans. *Actes of Conference in Religion, Holden at Paris, Betweene Two Papist Doctours of Sorbone, and Two Godlie Ministers of the Church.* London, 1571.

———. *A Forme of Christian Policie.* London, 1574.

———, trans. *Monophylo.* London, 1572.

Field, John. "Preface." In *An Excellent Treatise of Christian Righteousness.* London, 1577.

Fisher, John. *Mornynge Remembraunce.* In *The English Works of John Fisher,* edited by John E.B. Mayor. EETS, extr. ser., 27. London: N. Truebner, 1876.

———. *Psalmes Or Prayers Taken Out of Holye Scripture.* London, 1544.

———. *Psalmi Seu Precationes Ex Variis Scripturae Locis Collectae.* London, 1544.

———. *A Spiritual Consolation, Written by John Fisher.* In *The English Works of John Fisher,* edited by John E.B. Mayor. EETS, extr. ser., 27. London: N. Truebner, 1876.

Fitzalan-Howard, Henry Granville, ed. *The Lives of Philip Howard, Earl of Arundel, and of Anne Dacres, His Wife.* London, 1857.

The Fountayne or well of lyfe out of whiche doth springe most swete consolations... Translated out of latyn into Englysshe. London: Thomas Godfray, 1534.

Frere, W.H. and E.G. Langton, eds. *The Hereford Breviary Edited from the Rouen Edition of 1505 with a Collation of Manuscripts.* London, 1904.

Gerard, John. *John Gerard: The Autobiography of an Elizabethan.* Translated by Philip Caraman. London: Longmans, 1951.

A Goodly Prymer in Englyshe, Newly Corrected and Printed, with Certeyne Godly Meditations and Prayers Added to the Same. London: John Byddell for William Marshall, 1535.

Hall, Joseph. *Holy Observations. Lib. 1. also some Fewe of Davids Psalmes Metaphrased.* London, 1607.

Harington, John, Sir. *The Letters and Epigrams of Sir John Harington, Together with the Prayse of Private Life.* Edited by Norman Egbert MacClure. Philadelphia: University of Pennsylvania Press, 1930.

Harmar, John. *Praxis Grammatical.* London, 1623.

Herbert, Mary Sidney. *The Collected Works of Mary Sidney Herbert, Countess of Pembroke.* Edited by Margaret P. Hannay, Noel J. Kinnamon, and Michael G. Brennan. 2 vols. Oxford: Oxford University Press, 1998.

Hore Beatissime Virginis Marie Ad Legitimum Sarisburiensis Ecclesie Ritum. Paris: François Regnault, 1536.

Jewel, John. *Apologia Ecclesiae Anglicanae, Authore Ioanne Iuello Olim Episcopo Sarisburi.* London, 1606.

———. *An Apology of the Church of England.* Edited by John E. Booty. Ithaca, NY: Cornell University Press, 1963.

Jonson, Ben. "Timber: Or Discoveries." In *The Complete Poems,* edited by George Parfitt, 373–458. New York: Penguin Books, 1988.

Joye, George. *Ortulus Anime the Garden of the Soule*. Argentine: [Antwerp], 1530–31.

———, trans. *The Psalter of David in Englishe Purely and Faithfully Translated Aftir the Texte of Feline*. Antwerp, 1530.

Langdale, Alban. *Reasons Why Catholics may Go to Church*. London, 1580.

Lennard, Sampson, trans. *Luthers Fore-Runners: Or, A Cloud of Witnesses Deposing for the Protestant Faith*, by J.P. Perrin. London, 1624.

———, trans. *The Mysterie of Iniquitie: That is to Say the Histoire of the Papacie*, by Philippe Du-Plessis-Mornay. London, 1612.

Lock, Anne Vaughan. *The Collected Works of Anne Vaughan Lock*. Edited by Susan M. Felch. Tempe, AZ: Arizona Center for Medieval and Renaissance Studies, 1999.

———. "Meditation of a Penitent Sinner." In *The Collected Works of Anne Vaughan Lock*, edited by Susan M. Felch, 62–71. Tempe, AZ: Arizona Center for Medieval and Renaissance Studies, 1999.

Lodge, Thomas. "Defence of Poetry." In *Elizabethan Critical Essays*, edited by G. Gregory Smith, 1: 61–86. London: Oxford University Press, 1904.

Luther, Martin. *Commentarie upon the Fiftene Psalmes*. Translated by Henry Bull. London, 1577.

———. *Selected Psalms*. Edited by Jaroslav Pelikan. Vol. 12 of *Luther's Works*. St. Louis: Concordia Publishing House, 1955.

Marprelate, Martin [pseud.]. *The Epistle*. East Molesey, 1588.

Maunsell, Andrew. *The First Part of the Catalogue of English Printed Bookes*. London, 1595.

Moody, Joanna, ed. *The Private Life of an Elizabethan Lady: The Diary of Lady Margaret Hoby, 1599–1605*. Phoenix Mill: Sutton Publishing, 1998.

More, Thomas. *Treatise on the Passion, Treatise on the Blessed Body, Instructions and Prayers*. Edited by Garry E. Haupt. Vol. 13 of *The Yale Edition of the Complete Works of St. Thomas More*. New Haven: Yale University Press, 1976.

Parker, Matthew. "To the Right Honorable Learned and Vertuous Ladie A.B." In *An Apologie Or Answere in Defence of the Churche of Englande, with a Briefe and Plaine Declaration of the True Religion Professed and used in the Same*. Translated by Anne Cooke Bacon. London, 1564.

Perkins, William. *A Salve for a Sicke Man*. London, 1595.

Petti, Anthony, ed. *The Letters and Despatches of Richard Verstegan*. London: Publications of the Catholic Record Society, 1959.

Plato. *Euthyphro*. In *Plato: The Collected Dialogues*, edited by Edith Hamilton and Cairns Huntington, 169–85. Princeton: Princeton University Press, 1961.

Playfere, Thomas. *The Meane in Mourning*. London, 1595.

Praiers of Holy Fathers, Patriarchs, Prophets. London: Richard Grafton, 1544.

A Primer in Englysshe, with Dyuers Prayers. London: Thomas Godfray, 1535.

A Prymer in Englyshe with Certeyn Prayers [and] Godly Meditations, very Necessary for all People that Understonde Not the Latyne Tongue. London: John Byddel for William Marshall, 1534.

The Prymer of Salysbery use, Bothe in Englyshe and in Laten. Antwerp: Widow of C. Ruremond for John Gough, 1536.
Thys Prymer of Salysbury use. Paris: Y. Bonhomme, widow of T. Kerner, at the expenses of J. Groute, 1534.
Puttenham, George. "The Arte of English Poesie." In *Elizabethan Critical Essays*, edited by G. Gregory Smith, 2:1–193. London: Oxford University Press, 1904.
Rainbowe, Edward. *A Sermon Preached at the Funeral of the Right Honorable Anne, Countess of Pembroke, Dorset, and Montgomery*. London, 1677.
Rogers, Thomas, trans. *A Pretious Booke of Heavenlie Meditations, Called A Private Talke of the Soule with God*. London, 1597.
Russell, Elizabeth Cooke Hoby, trans. *A Way of Reconciliation of the Good and Learned Man, Touching the Trueth, Nature, and Substance of the Body and Blood of Christ in the Sacrament*. London, 1605.
———. *The Writings of an English Sappho*, ed. Patricia Phillippy. Toronto: University of Toronto Press, 2011.
Sancta Clara, Franciscus à. "Preface." In *The Chronicle and Institution of the Order of the Seraphicall Father S. Francis*, translated by William Cape, B1–C2. Saint-Omer, 1618.
Shakespeare, William. *The Merchant of Venice*. Edited by Leah S. Marcus. New York: W.W. Norton, 2006.
Sidney, Philip. *An Apology for Poetry: Or, the Defence of Poesy*. Edited by Geoffrey Shepherd and R.W. Maslen. 3rd ed. Manchester: Manchester University Press, 2002.
———. *The Poems of Sir Philip Sidney*. Edited by William A. Ringler Jr. Oxford: Oxford University Press, 1962.
Smith, Richard. *An Elizabethan Recusant House, Comprising the Life of the Lady Magdalen, Viscountess Montague (1538–1608)*. Edited by A.C. Southern. Translated by Cuthbert Furdson. London: Sands & Co., 1954.
Southwell, Robert. *An Epistle of Comfort*. London, 1587.
———. *Two Letters and Short Rules of a Good Life*. Edited by Nancy Pollard Brown. Charlottesville: The University Press of Virginia, 1973.
Sternhold, Thomas and John Hopkins. *The Whole Booke of Psalmes Collected into Englysh Metre by T. Sternhold, J. Hopkins, & Others*. London, 1562.
Taverner, Richard, trans. *An Epitome of the Psalmes, Or Briefe Meditacions upon the Same, with Diverse Other Moste Christian Prayers*. London, 1539.
"The Translators to the Reader." In *The Bible; Authorized King James Version*, introduction and notes by Robert Carroll and Stephen Prickett, liii–lxix. Oxford: Oxford University Press, 1997.
Tyndale, William. *An Answere Unto Sir Thomas Mores Dialoge*. Edited by Anne M. O'Donnell and Jared Wicks. Vol. 3 of *Independent Works of William Tyndale*. Washington, D.C.: Catholic University of America Press, 2000.
Tyrwhit, Elizabeth. *Elizabeth Tyrwhit's 'Morning and Evening Prayers.'* Edited by Susan M. Felch. Aldershot: Ashgate, 2008.

Udall, Nicholas. "To the Jentel Christian Reader." In *The First Tome or Volume of the Paraphrase of Erasmus upon the Newe Testamente*, 6v–A1r. London, 1548.

Wadding, Luke. *Scriptores Ordinis Minorum*. Rome, 1650.

Weston, William. *An Autobiography from the Jesuit Underground, by William Weston*. Translated by Philip Caraman. New York: Farrar, Straus and Cudahy, 1955.

Wheathill, Anne. *A Handful of Holesome (Though Homelie) Hearbs, Gathered Out of the Goodlie Garden of Gods most Holie Word; for the Common Benefit and Comfortable Exercise of all such as are Devoutlie Disposed*. London, 1584.

Wilson, John. "Epistle Dedicatory." In *The Practise of Christian Workes*. Translated by John Wilson, 2–6. London, 1620.

———. "Preface." In *An Epistle or Exhortation of Jesus Christ to the Soule ..., by Johannes Lansperger*, 2–3. Saint-Omer, 1610.

Printed Secondary Sources

Acheson, Katherine O. "Introduction." In Lady Anne Clifford's *The Memoir of 1603 and the Diary of 1616–1619*, edited by Katherine O. Acheson, 9–34. Peterborough, ON: Broadview Press, 2007.

Allison, A.F. "Franciscan Books in English, 1559–1640." *Biographical Studies, 1534–1829* 3, no. 1 (1955): 16–65.

———. "A Question of Jurisdiction: Richard Smith, Bishop of Chalcedon, and the Catholic Laity, 1625–31." *Recusant History* 16 (1982): 111–45.

——— and D.M. Rogers. *The Contemporary Printed Literature of the English Counter-Reformation between 1558 and 1640: An Annotated Catalogue*. 2 vols. Aldershot: Scolar Press, 1994.

Alter, Robert. "Introduction." In *The Book of Psalms; A Translation with Commentary*, translated by Robert Alter, xiii–xxxviii. New York: W.W. Norton, 2007.

Anderson, Gary A. "Sacrifice and Sacrificial Offerings." In *The Anchor Bible Dictionary*, edited by David Noel Freedman, 5:870–86. New York: Doubleday, 1992.

Atkinson, Colin B. and Jo B. Atkinson. "Anne Wheathill's *A Handfull of Holesome (though Homelie) Hearbs* (1584): The First English Gentlewoman's Prayer Book." *Sixteenth Century Journal* 27 (1996): 659–72.

———. "Numerical Patterning in Anne Wheathill's *A Handfull of Holesome (Though Homelie) Hearbs* (1584)." *Texas Studies in Literature and Language* 40, no. 1 (Spring, 1998): 1–25.

Baker, Thomas. "Preface." In *The Funeral Sermon of Margaret Countess of Richmond and Derby, Mother to King Henry VII*, 1–59. London, 1708.

Ballard, George. *Memoirs of Several Ladies of Great Britain, who have been Celebrated for their Writings or Skill in the Learned Languages, Arts and Sciences*. Oxford, 1752.

Barns, Stephen J. "The Cookes of Gidea Hall." *Essex Review* 21 (1912): 1–9.

Bateson, Mary, ed. *Catalogue of the Library of Syon Monastery, Isleworth*. Cambridge: Cambridge University Press, 1898.

Beilin, Elaine V. *Redeeming Eve: Women Writers of the English Renaissance*. Princeton: Princeton University Press, 1987.

Bell, David N. *What Nuns Read: Books and Libraries in Medieval English Nunneries*. Kalamazoo, MI: Cistercian Publications, 1995.

Benjamin, Walter. "The Task of the Translator." Translated by Steven Randell. *Traduction, Terminologie, Rédaction* 10, no. 2 (1997): 151–65.

Bergvall, Åke. *Augustinian Perspectives in the Renaissance*. Uppsala: Uppsala University Press, 2001.

Berry, Edward I. *The Making of Sir Philip Sidney*. Toronto: University of Toronto Press, 1998.

Biggs, Brendan. "The Style of the First English Translation of the *Imitatio Christi*." In *The Medieval Translator/Traduire Au Moyen Age*, vol. 5, edited by Roger Ellis and René Tixier, 187–211. Tournhout, Belgium: Brepols, 1996.

Blom, Jos and Frans Blom. "Introductory Note." In Evelinge, *Elizabeth Evelinge II*, EME, Series I, pt. 3, vol. 5, selected and introduced by Jos Blom and Frans Blom, ix–xvii. Aldershot: Ashgate, 2002.

Booty, John E. "Introduction." In *An Apology of the Church of England*, edited by John E. Booty, ix–xlvii. Ithaca, NY: Cornell University Press, 1963.

———. *John Jewel as Apologist of the Church of England*. London: S.P.C.K., 1963.

Bossy, John. *The English Catholic Community, 1570–1850*. London: Darton Longman and Todd, 1975.

Brennan, Michael G. "'First Rais'de by Thy Blest Hand, and What is Mine / Inspired by Thee': The 'Sidney Psalter' and the Countess of Pembroke's Completion of the Sidneian *Psalms*." *Sidney Newsletter & Journal* 14 (1996): 37–46.

Brown, Nancy Pollard. "Paper Chase: The Dissemination of Catholic Texts in Elizabethan England." *English Manuscript Studies, 1100–1700* 1 (1989): 120–43.

———. "Robert Southwell: The Mission of the Written Word." In *The Reckoned Expense: Edmund Campion and the Early English Jesuits*, edited by Thomas M. McCoog, 193–213. Woodbridge: Boydell Press, 1996.

Burke, Victoria E. and Jonathan Gibson, eds. *Early Modern Women's Manuscript Writing: Selected Papers from the Trinity/Trent Colloquium*. Aldershot: Ashgate, 2004.

Butterworth, Charles C. *The English Primers (1529–1545): Their Publication and Connection with the English Bible and the Reformation in England*. Philadelphia: University of Pennsylvania Press, 1953.

Bynum, Caroline Walker. *Holy Feast and Holy Fast: The Religious Significance of Food to Medieval Women*. Berkeley: University of California Press, 1987.

Carlson, David R. *English Humanist Books: Writers and Patrons, Manuscript and Print, 1475–1525*. Toronto: University of Toronto Press, 1993.

Cavanaugh, William T. "Eucharistic Sacrifice and the Social Imagination in Early Modern Europe." *Journal of Medieval and Early Modern Studies* 31 (2001): 585–606.

Chan, Mary and Nancy E. Wright. "Marriage, Identity, and the Pursuit of Property in Seventeenth-Century England: The Cases of Anne Clifford and Elizabeth Wiseman." In *Women, Property, and the Letters of the Law in Early Modern England*, edited by Nancy E. Wright, Margaret W. Ferguson, and A.R. Buck, 162–82. Toronto: University of Toronto Press, 2004.

Clark, Francis. *Eucharistic Sacrifice and the Reformation*. Oxford: Basil Blackwell, 1967.

Clarke, Danielle. "Introduction." In Clarke and Clarke, '*This Double Voice*,' 1–15.

———. *The Politics of Early Modern Women's Writing*. Harlow, England: Longman, 2001.

——— and Elizabeth Clarke, eds. *'This Double Voice': Gendered Writing in Early Modern England*. Houndmills, Basingstoke: Macmillan Press, 2000.

Clarke, Elizabeth. "Ejaculation Or Virgin Birth? The Gendering of the Religious Lyric in the Interregnum." In Clarke and Clarke, *'This Double Voice,'* 208–29.

Coles, Kimberly Anne. *Religion, Reform, and Women's Writing in Early Modern England*. Cambridge: Cambridge University Press, 2008.

Collinson, Patrick. "Biblical Rhetoric: The English Nation and National Sentiment in the Prophetic Mode." In *Religion and Culture in Renaissance England*, edited by Claire McEachern and Debora K. Shuger, 15–45. Cambridge: Cambridge University Press, 1997.

———. *The Birthpangs of Protestant England: Religious and Cultural Change in the Sixteenth and Seventeenth Centuries*. New York: St. Martin's Press, 1988.

———. *The Elizabethan Puritan Movement*. Berkeley: University of California Press, 1967.

———, Arnold Hunt, and Alexandra Walsham. "Religious Publishing in England 1557–1640." In *The Cambridge History of the Book in Britain*, edited by John Barnard, D.F. McKenzie, and Maureen Bell, 29–66. Cambridge: Cambridge University Press, 2002.

Constable, Giles. *Three Studies in Medieval Religious and Social Thought*. Cambridge: Cambridge University Press, 1995.

Cooper, Charles Henry. *Memoir of Margaret Countess of Richmond and Derby*. Edited by John E.B. Mayor. Cambridge: Cambridge University Press, 1874.

Corthell, Ronald, Frances E. Dolan, Christopher Highley, and Arthur F. Marotti, eds. *Catholic Culture in Early Modern England*. Notre Dame: University of Notre Dame Press, 2007.

Craft, William. *Labyrinth of Desire: Invention and Culture in the Work of Sir Philip Sidney*. Newark: University of Delaware Press, 1994.

Crawford, Julie. "The Case of Lady Anne Clifford; Or, did Women have a Mixed Monarchy?" *PMLA* 121, no. 5 (2006): 1682–9.

———. "Reconsidering Early Modern Women's Reading, or How Margaret Hoby Read Her De Mornay." *Huntington Library Quarterly* 73, no. 2 (2010): 193–223.

Cressy, David. *Literacy and the Social Order: Reading and Writing in Tudor and Stuart England*. Cambridge: Cambridge University Press, 1980.

Cullen, Patrick. "Introduction." In *Anne Wheathill*, EME, Series I, pt. 1, vol. 9, selected and introduced by Patrick Cullen, ix–xii. Aldershot: Scolar Press, 1996.

Cummings, Brian. *The Literary Culture of the Reformation: Grammar and Grace*. Oxford: Oxford University Press, 2002.

Dart, John. *Westmonasterium: Or the History and Antiquities of the Abbey Church of St Peter's Westminster*. London, 1742.

Davidson, Peter and Jane Stevenson. "Elizabeth I's Reception at Bisham (1592): Elite Women as Writers and Devisers." In *The Progresses, Pageants and Entertainments of Queen Elizabeth I*, edited by Jayne Elisabeth Archer, Elizabeth Goldring, and Sarah Knight, 207–26. Oxford: Oxford University Press, 2007.

Davis, Joel. "Multiple Arcadias and the Literary Quarrel between Fulke Greville and the Countess of Pembroke." *Studies in Philology* 101, no. 4 (Fall, 2004): 401–30.

Davis, Natalie Zemon. *The Gift in Sixteenth-Century France*. Madison: University of Wisconsin Press, 2000.

Daybell, James, ed. *Early Modern Women's Letter Writing, 1450–1700*. Houndmills, UK: Palgrave, 2001.

Demers, Patricia. *Women's Writing in English: Early Modern England*. Toronto: University of Toronto Press, 2005.

Derrida, Jacques. "Living On/Borderlines." 75–176 in *Deconstruction and Criticism*. Translated by James Hulbert. New York: Seabury Press, 1979.

———. "Roundtable on Translation." 91–161 in *The Ear of the Other: Otobiography, Transference, Translation: Texts and Discussions with Jacques Derrida*. Edited by Christie V. McDonald. Translated by Peggy Kamuf. New York: Schocken Books, 1985.

———. "Les Tours De Babel." 165–207 in *Difference and Translation*, edited and translated by Joseph F. Graham. Ithaca, NY: Cornell University Press, 1985.

Dockery, John Berchmans. *Christopher Davenport, Friar and Diplomat*. London: Burns & Oates, 1960.

Dolan, Frances E. "Reading, Work, and Catholic Women's Biographies." *English Literary Renaissance* 33, no. 3 (2003): 328–57.

———. *Whores of Babylon: Catholicism, Gender, and Seventeenth-Century Print Culture*. Ithaca: Cornell University Press, 1999.

Donawerth, Jane. "Women's Poetry and the Tudor-Stuart System of Gift Exchange." In *Women, Writing, and the Reproduction of Culture in Tudor and Stuart Britain*, edited by Mary E. Burke, Jane Donawerth, Linda L. Dove, and L. Nelson Karen, 3–18. Syracuse: Syracuse University Press, 2000.

Dowd, Michelle M. and Julie A. Eckerle, eds. *Genre and Women's Life Writing in Early Modern England*. Aldershot: Ashgate, 2007.

Duffy, Eamon. *Marking the Hours: English People and their Prayers 1240–1570*. New Haven: Yale University Press, 2006.

———. *The Stripping of the Altars: Traditional Religion in England, 1400–1580*. New Haven: Yale University Press, 1992.

Eire, Carlos. "Early Modern Catholic Piety in Translation." In *Cultural Translation in Early Modern Europe*, edited by Peter Burke and R. Po-Chia Hsia, 83–100. Cambridge: Cambridge University Press, 2007.

Eisenstein, Elizabeth L. *The Printing Revolution in Early Modern Europe*. Cambridge: Cambridge University Press, 1993.

Elwood, Christopher. *The Body Broken: The Calvinist Doctrine of the Eucharist and the Symbolization of Power in Sixteenth-Century France*. New York: Oxford University Press, 1999.

Erickson, Robert A. *The Language of the Heart, 1600–1750*. Philadelphia: University of Pennsylvania Press, 1997.

Ezell, Margaret J.M. "Re-Visioning the Restoration: Or, how to Stop Obscuring Early Women Writers." In *New Historical Literary Study: Essays on Reproducing Texts, Representing History*, edited by Jeffrey N. Cox and Larry J. Reynolds, 136–50. Princeton: Princeton University Press, 1993.

———. *Writing Women's Literary History*. Baltimore, MD: Johns Hopkins University Press, 1993.

Farber, Elizabeth. "The Letters of Lady Elizabeth Russell (1540–1609)." PhD diss., Columbia University, 1977.

Fehler, Timothy G. *Poor Relief and Protestantism: The Evolution of Social Welfare in Sixteenth-Century Emden*. Aldershot: Ashgate, 1999.

Felch, Susan M. "The Development of the English Prayer Book." In *Worship in Medieval and Early Modern Europe: Change and Continuity in Religious Practice*, edited by Karen Maag and John D. Witvliet, 132–61. Notre Dame: University of Notre Dame Press, 2004.

———. "Introduction." In *Elizabeth Tyrwhit's 'Morning and Evening Prayers'*, edited by Susan M. Felch, 1–66. Aldershot: Ashgate, 2008.

Fisken, Beth Wynne. "'The Art of Sacred Parody' in Mary Sidney's *Psalmes*." *Tulsa Studies in Women's Literature* 8, no. 2 (1989): 223–39.

———. "Mary Sidney's *Psalmes*: Education and Wisdom." In Hannay, *Silent But for the Word*, 166–83.

Foley, Henry. *Records of the English Province of the Society of Jesus*. Vol. 7. London: Burns and Oates, 1883.

Foucault, Michel. "What is an Author?" 113–38 in *Language, Counter-Memory, Practice: Selected Essays and Interviews*. Translated by Donald F. Bouchard and Sherry Simon. Edited and introduced by Donald F. Bouchard. Ithaca, NY: Cornell University Press, 1977.

Fowler, Alistair. *The New Oxford Book of Seventeenth Century Verse*. Oxford: Oxford University Press, 2008.

Freer, Coburn. *Music for a King: George Herbert's Style and the Metrical Psalms*. Baltimore: Johns Hopkins University Press, 1972.

Garrett, Cynthia. "The Rhetoric of Supplication: Prayer Theory in Seventeenth-Century England." *Renaissance Quarterly* 46, no. 2 (1993): 328–57.

Gerrish, B.A. *Grace and Gratitude: The Eucharistic Theology of John Calvin*. Minneapolis: Fortress Press, 1993.

Goldberg, Jonathan. *Desiring Women Writing: English Renaissance Examples.* Stanford: Stanford University Press, 1997.

Goodrich, Jaime. "Early Modern Englishwomen as Translators of Religious and Political Literature, 1500–1641." PhD diss., Boston College, 2008.

Gordis, Lisa M. *Opening Scripture: Bible Reading and Interpretive Authority in Puritan New England.* Chicago: University of Chicago Press, 2003.

Grafton, Anthony. "The Humanist as Reader." In *A History of Reading in the West*, edited by Guglielmo Cavallo and Roger Chartier, 179–212. Translated by Lydia G. Cochrane. Amherst: University of Massachusetts Press, 1999.

Gregory, Brad S. "The 'True and Zealouse Service of God': Robert Parsons, Edmund Bunny, and *The First Booke of the Christian Exercise*." *Journal of Ecclesiastical History* 45, no. 2 (1994): 238–68.

Griffiths, Paul J. *Religious Reading: The Place of Reading in the Practice of Religion.* New York: Oxford University Press, 1999.

Guibert, Joseph De. *The Jesuits: Their Spiritual Doctrine and Practice.* Translated by William J. Young. Chicago: Institute of Jesuit Sources with Loyola, 1964.

Guilday, Peter. *The English Catholic Refugees on the Continent 1558–1795.* New York: Longmans, Green, and Co., 1914.

Hackel, Heidi Brayman. *Reading Material in Early Modern England: Print, Gender, and Literacy.* Cambridge: Cambridge University Press, 2005.

Hall, David D. *Cultures of Print: Essays in the History of the Book.* Amherst: University of Massachusetts Press, 1996.

Hallett, Nicky. *Lives of Spirit: English Carmelite Self-Writing of the Early Modern Period.* Aldershot: Ashgate, 2007.

———. *Witchcraft, Exorcism and the Politics of Possession in a Seventeenth-Century Convent: "How Sister Ursula was Once Bewitched and Sister Margaret Twice."* Aldershot: Ashgate, 2007.

Hamilton, Donna B. *Anthony Munday and the Catholics, 1560–1633.* Aldershot: Ashgate, 2005.

Hamlin, Hannibal. "'The Highest Matter in the Noblest Forme': The Influence of the Sidney Psalms." *Sidney Journal* 23 (2005): 133–57.

———. *Psalm Culture and Early Modern English Literature.* Cambridge: Cambridge University Press, 2004.

Handover, P.M. *The Second Cecil: The Rise to Power, 1563–1604, of Sir Robert Cecil.* London: Eyre & Spottiswoode, 1959.

Hannay, Margaret P. "'Doo What Men May Sing': Mary Sidney and the Tradition of Admonitory Dedication." In Hannay, *Silent But for the Word*, 149–65.

———. "'House-Confinèd Maids': The Presentation of Woman's Role in the *Psalmes* of the Countess of Pembroke." *English Literary Renaissance* 24, no. 1 (Winter, 1994): 44–71.

———. "Introduction." In Hannay, *Silent But for the Word*, 1–14.

———. *Philip's Phoenix: Mary Sidney, Countesse of Pembroke.* New York: Oxford University Press, 1990.

———. "'Princes You as Men must dy': Genevan Advice to Monarchs in the *Psalmes* of Mary Sidney." *English Literary Renaissance* 19, no. 1 (Winter, 1989): 22–41.

———. "'So may I with the *Psalmist* Truly Say': Early Modern Englishwomen's Psalm Discourse." In *Write or be Written: Early Modern Women Poets and Cultural Constraints*, edited by Barbara Smith and Ursula Appelt, 105–34. Aldershot: Ashgate, 2001.

———. "'Unlock My Lipps': The *Miserere Mei Deus* of Anne Vaughan Lok and Mary Sidney Herbert, Countess of Pembroke." In *Privileging Gender in Early Modern England*, edited by Jean R. Brink, 19–36. Kirksville, MO: Sixteenth Century Journal Publishers, 1993.

———. "'When Riches Growes': Class Perspective in Pembroke's *Psalmes*." In *Women, Writing, and the Reproduction of Culture in Tudor and Stuart Britain*, edited by Mary E. Burke, Jane Donawerth, Linda L. Dove and Karen Nelson, 77–97. Syracuse, NY: Syracuse University Press, 2000.

———, ed. *Silent But for the Word: Tudor Women as Patrons, Translators, and Writers of Religious Works*. Kent, OH: Kent State University Press, 1985.

Hasenohr, Geneviève. "La Littérature Religieuse." In *Grundriss Der Romanischen Literaturen Des Mittelalters/La Littérature Française Aux XIVe Et XVe Siècles*, edited by Daniel Poiron, 1:277–81. Heidelburg: Carl Winter, 1988.

Hatt, Cecilia A., ed. *English Works of John Fisher, Bishop of Rochester: Sermons and Other Writings, 1520–1535*. Oxford: Oxford University Press, 2002.

Haynes, Samuel. *A Collection of State Papers Relating to Affairs ... Left by William Cecill Lord Burghley*. London, 1740.

Hill, Christopher. *The English Bible and the Seventeenth-Century Revolution*. New York: Penguin, 1993.

———. "The Protestant Nation." In *The Collected Essays of Christopher Hill* 2:21–36. Amherst: University of Massachusetts Press, 1986.

Hoekstra, Eugen Gerard. "Jacques De Gruytrode." In *Dictionnaire De Spiritualité Ascétique Et Mystique*, 8:36–8. Paris: Beauchesne, 1932.

Hoffman, C. Fenno, Jr. "Catherine Parr as a Woman of Letters." *Huntington Library Quarterly* 23, no. 4 (1959): 349–67.

Hogg, James. "The English Charterhouses and the *Devotio Moderna*." In *Historia et spiritualitas Cartusiensis*, edited by Jan de Grauwe, 257–68. Destelbergen, Belgium: Drukkerij De Windroos, 1983.

Hosington, Brenda M. "Translation and Women Translators." In *Encyclopedia of Women in the Renaissance: Italy, France, and England*, edited by Diana Robin, Anne R. Larsen and Carole Levin, 370–71. Santa Barbara, CA: ABC-Clio Press, 2007.

———. "Translation in the Service of Politics and Religion: A Family Tradition for Thomas More, Margaret Roper and Mary Clarke Basset." In *Between Scylla and Charybdis: Learned Letter Writers Navigating the Reefs of Religious and Political Controversy in Early Modern Europe*, edited by Jeanine De Landtsheer and Henk Nellen, 93–108. Leiden: Brill, 2010.

Hoskins, Edgar. *Horae Beatae Mariae Virginis, Or, Sarum and York Primers: With Kindred Books and Primers of the Reformed Roman Use*. London: Longmans, Green, and Co., 1901.

Houliston, Victor. *Catholic Resistance in Elizabethan England: Robert Persons's Jesuit Polemic, 1580–1610*. Aldershot: Ashgate, 2007.

———. "Introduction." In *Robert Persons S.J.: The Christian Directory (1582): The First Booke of the Christian Exercise, Appertayning to Resolution*, edited by Victor Houliston, xi–lx. Leiden: Brill, 1998.

Howarth, David. *Lord Arundel and His Circle*. New Haven: Yale University Press, 1985.

Hubert, Henri and Marcel Mauss. *Sacrifice: Its Nature and Function*. Translated by W.D. Halls. Chicago: University of Chicago Press, 1964.

Hunnybun, William Martin, ed. "Registers of the English Poor Clares at Gravelines." In *Miscellanea* 9: 25–173. London: Catholic Record Society, 1914.

Hutchison, Ann M. "Devotional Reading in the Monastery and in the Late Medieval Household." In *De Cella in Seculum: Religious and Secular Life and Devotion in Late Medieval England*, edited by Michael G. Sargent, 215–27. Cambridge: D.S. Brewer, 1989.

Jackson, Ken and Arthur F. Marotti. "The Turn to Religion in Early Modern English Studies." *Criticism: A Quarterly for Literature and the Arts* 46 (2004): 167–90.

James, Susan E. *Kateryn Parr: The Making of a Queen*. Aldershot: Ashgate, 1999.

Janton, Pierre. "Prayer in Prose as Literature and the British Reformers of the Sixteenth Century." *Cahiers élisabéthains* 66 (2004): 1–8.

Jardine, Lisa and Anthony Grafton. "'Studied for Action': How Gabriel Harvey Read His Livy." *Past & Present* 129 (1990): 30–78.

——— and William H. Sherman. "Pragmatic Readers: Knowledge Transactions and Scholarly Services in Late Elizabethan England." In *Religion, Culture, and Society in Early Modern Britain: Essays in Honour of Patrick Collinson*, edited by Anthony Fletcher and Peter Roberts, 102–24. Cambridge: Cambridge University Press, 1994.

Jones, Michael K. and Malcolm G. Underwood. *The King's Mother: Lady Margaret Beaufort, Countess of Richmond and Derby*. Cambridge: Cambridge University Press, 1992.

Keiser, George R. "Patronage and Piety in Fifteenth-Century England: Margaret, Duchesse of Clarence, Symon Wynter and Beinecke MS 317." *Yale University Library Gazette* 60 (1985): 32–46.

Kidd, B.J. *The Later Medieval Doctrine of the Eucharistic Sacrifice*. London: The Sidney Press Limited for the Church Historical Society, 1958.

King, John N. "Patronage and Piety: The Influence of Catherine Parr." In Hannay, *Silent But for the Word*, 43–60.

Korsten, Frans. "Introductory Note." In *Elizabeth Evelinge I*, EME, Series 1, pt. 3, vol. 3, selected and introduced by Frans Korsten, ix–xv. Aldershot: Ashgate, 2002.

Kraus, Hans-Joachim. *Theology of the Psalms*. Translated by Keith Crim. Minneapolis: Augsburg Publishing House, 1986.

Krontiris, Tina. *Oppositional Voices: Women as Writers and Translators of Literature in the English Renaissance*. London: Routledge, 1992.

Kunin, Aaron. "From the Desk of Anne Clifford." *English Literary History* 71, no. 3 (2004): 587–608.

Lake, Peter and Michael C. Questier. "Margaret Clitherow, Catholic Nonconformity, Martyrology, and the Politics of Religious Change in Elizabethan England." *Past & Present* 185, no. 1 (2004): 43–90.

Lamb, Mary Ellen. "The Agency of the Split Subject: Lady Anne Clifford and the Uses of Reading." *English Literary Renaissance* 22, no. 3 (1992): 347–68.

———. "The Cooke Sisters: Attitudes Toward Learned Women in the Renaissance." In Hannay, *Silent But for the Word*, 107–25.

Latz, Dorothy L., ed. *The Building of Divine Love, as Translated by Dame Agnes More*. Salzburg: Institut für Anglistik und Amerikanistik, 1992.

———. *"Glow-Worm Light": Writings of 17th Century English Recusant Women from Original Manuscripts*. Salzburg: Institut für Anglistik und Amerikanistik, 1989.

Lawrence, Victoria. "Richard Whitford and Translation." In *The Medieval Translator 4*, edited by Roger Ellis and Ruth Evans, 136–52. Binghamton, NY: MRTS, 1994.

Lefevere, André. *Translation, Rewriting, and the Manipulation of Literary Fame*. London: Routledge, 1992.

Lewalski, Barbara Kiefer. *Writing Women in Jacobean England*. Cambridge, MA: Harvard University Press, 1993.

Littlehales, Margaret Mary. *Mary Ward: Pilgrim and Mystic, 1585–1645*. Turnbridge Wells, Kent: Burns & Oates, 1998.

Llewellyn, Nigel. *Funeral Monuments in Post-Reformation England*. Cambridge: Cambridge University Press, 2000.

Lodge, Edmund. *Portraits of Illustrious Personages of Great Britain*. London, 1821–34.

Longfellow, Erica. *Women and Religious Writing in Early Modern England*. Cambridge: Cambridge University Press, 2004.

Lovatt, Roger. "The *Imitation of Christ* in Late Medieval England." *Transactions of the Royal Historical Society* 5th ser., 18 (1968): 97–121.

McClain, Lisa. *Lest We Be Damned: Practical Innovation and Lived Experience among Catholics in Protestant England, 1559–1642*. New York: Routledge, 2004.

MacCulloch, Diarmaid. *Reformation: Europe's House Divided, 1490–1700*. London: Allen Lane, 2003.

McGrath, Patrick. *Papists and Puritans under Elizabeth I*. London: Blandford Press, 1967.

McIntosh, Marjorie Keniston. "Sir Anthony Cooke: Tudor Humanist, Educator, and Religious Reformer." *Proceedings of the American Philosophical Society* 119 (1975): 233–50.

McLaughlin, Mary Martin. "Creating and Recreating Communities of Women: The Case of Corpus Domini, Ferrara, 1406–1452." In *Sisters and Workers in the Middle Ages*, eds. Judith M. Bennett et al, 261–88. Chicago: University of Chicago Press, 1989.

Maddison, A.R., ed. *Lincolnshire Pedigrees*. London: Publications of the Harleian Society vol. 52, 1904.

Maltby, Judith D. *Prayer Book and People in Elizabethan and Early Stuart England*. Cambridge: Cambridge University Press, 1998.

Marotti, Arthur F. "Alienating Catholics in Early Modern England: Recusant Women, Jesuits and Ideological Fantasies." In *Catholicism and Anti-Catholicism in Early Modern English Texts*, edited by Arthur F. Marotti, 1–34. New York: St. Martin's Press, 1999.

Martienssen, Anthony. *Queen Catherine Parr*. London: Secker & Warburg, 1973.

Martin, Randall. "The Autobiography of Grace, Lady Mildmay." *Renaissance and Reformation/Renaissance et Réforme* 18, no. 1 (1994): 33–81.

———, ed. *Women Writers in Renaissance England*. London: Longman, 1997.

Martz, Louis. *The Poetry of Meditation: A Study in English Religious Literature of the Seventeenth Century*. New Haven: Yale University Press, 1962.

Maskell, William. *Monumenta Ritualia Ecclesiae Anglicanae*. 2 vols. London: William Pickering, 1846.

Mauss, Marcel. *The Gift: The Form and Reason for Exchange in Archaic Societies*. Translated by W.D. Halls. London: Routledge, 2000.

Mayer, Thomas F. "When Maecenas was Broke: Cardinal Pole's 'Spiritual' Patronage." *Sixteenth Century Journal* 27, no. 2 (Summer, 1996): 419–35.

Monta, Susannah Brietz. "Martyrdom in Print in Early Modern England: The Case of Robert Waldegrave." In *More than a Memory: The Discourse of Martyrdom and the Construction of Christian Identity in the History of Christianity*, edited by Johan Leemans, 271–95. Leuven: Peeters, 2005.

Morgan, Paul. "Frances Wolfreston and 'Hor Bouks': A Seventeenth Century Woman Book-Collector." *The Library* 6th Series, 11 (1989): 13–219.

Moss, Ann. *Printed Commonplace-Books and the Structuring of Renaissance Thought*. Oxford: Clarendon Press, 1996.

Mueller, Janel. "Complications of Intertextuality: John Fisher, Katherine Parr, and 'The Book of the Crucifix.'" In *Representing Women in Renaissance England*, edited by Claude J. Summers and Ted-Larry Pebworth, 24–41. Columbia: University of Missouri Press, 1997.

———. "Devotion as Difference: Intertextuality in Queen Katherine Parr's *Prayers or Meditations* (1545)." *Huntington Library Quarterly* 53 (1990): 171–97.

———. *The Native Tongue and the Word: Developments in English Prose Style, 1380–1580*. Chicago: University of Chicago Press, 1984.

Narveson, Kate. "Profession Or Performance?: Religion in Early Modern Literary Study." In *Fault Lines and Controversies in the Study of Seventeenth-Century English Literature*, edited by Claude J. Summers and Ted-Larry Pebworth, 111–29. Columbia: University of Missouri Press, 2002.

Nelson, Karen L. "'To Informe Thee Aright': Translating Du Perron for English Religious Debates." In *The Literary Career and Legacy of Elizabeth Cary, 1613–1680*, edited by Heather Wolfe, 147–63. New York: Palgrave Macmillan, 2007.

Newdigate, C.A. "A New Chapter in the Life of B. Robert Southwell, S.J." *The Month* 157 (1931): 246–54.

Nicolson, Adam. *God's Secretaries: The Making of the King James Bible*. New York: HarperCollins, 2003.

O'Malley, John W. *Trent and All That: Renaming Catholicism in the Early Modern Era*. Cambridge, MA: Harvard University Press, 2000.

Orgel, Stephen. "Marginal Maternity: Reading Lady Anne Clifford's *A Mirror for Magistrates*." In *Printing and Parenting in Early Modern England*, edited by Douglas A. Brooks, 267–89. Aldershot: Ashgate, 2005.

Ostovich, Helen and Elizabeth Sauer, eds. *Reading Early Modern Women: An Anthology of Texts in Manuscript and Print, 1550–1700*. New York: Routledge, 2003.

Parry, Graham. "The Great Picture of Lady Anne Clifford." In *Art and Patronage in the Caroline Courts: Essays in Honour of Sir Oliver Millar*, edited by David Armine Howarth, 202–19. Cambridge: Cambridge University Press, 1993.

———. "Literary Patronage." In *The Cambridge History of Early Modern English Literature*, edited by David Loewenstein and Janel Mueller, 117–40. Cambridge: Cambridge University Press, 2002.

Pearson, A.F. Scott. *Thomas Cartwright and Elizabethan Puritanism, 1535–1603*. Cambridge: Cambridge University Press, 1925.

Pellechet, M., ed. *Catalogue général des incunables des bibliothèques publiques de France*. Repr. Nendeln, Liechtenstein: Kraus-Thomson, 1970.

Pollen, John Hungerford and William MacMahon, eds. *The Ven. Philip Howard, Earl of Arundel, 1557–1595*. London: Catholic Record Society, 1919.

Pollock, Linda A. *With Faith and Physic: The Life of a Tudor Gentlewoman, Lady Grace Mildmay, 1552–1620*. New York: St. Martin's Press, 1995.

Popkin, Richard H. *The History of Scepticism: From Savonarola to Bayle*. Oxford: Oxford University Press, 2003.

Powell, Edgar. *The Registers of Bisham, Co. Berkshire*. London: Parish Register Society, 1898.

Powell, Susan. "Lady Margaret Beaufort and her Books." *The Library* 6th series, 20, no. 3 (1998): 197–240.

———. "Syon Abbey and the Mother of King Henry VII: The Relationship of Lady Margaret Beaufort with the English Birgittines." *Birgittiana* 19 (2005): 211–24.

Prescott, Anne Lake. "King David as 'Right Poet': Sidney and the Psalmist." *English Literary Renaissance* 19 (1989): 131–51.

Pritchard, Arnold. *Catholic Loyalism in Elizabethan England*. Chapel Hill: University of North Carolina Press, 1979.

Questier, Michael C. *Catholicism and Community in Early Modern England: Politics, Aristocratic Patronage and Religion, 1550–1640*. Cambridge: Cambridge University Press, 2006.

———. *Newsletters from the Archpresbyterate of George Birkhead*. Cambridge: Cambridge University Press, 1998.

Quitslund, Beth. "Teaching Us How to Sing?: The Peculiarity of the Sidney Psalter." *Sidney Journal* 23 (2005): 83–110.

Rennhofer, Friedrich. *Bücherkunde Des Katholischen Lebens: Bibliographisches Lexikon Der Religiösen Literatur Der Gegenwart*. Vienna: Hollinek, 1961.

Rhodes, J.T. "Syon Abbey and its Religious Publications in the Sixteenth Century." *Journal of Ecclesiastical History* 44, no. 1 (1993): 11–25.

Richards, Jennifer. "Philip Sidney, Mary Sidney and Protestant Poetics." *Sidney Newsletter & Journal* 14, no. 1 (Summer, 1996): 28–37.

Rienstra, Debra. "The Countess of Pembroke and the Problem of Skill in Devotional Writing." *Sidney Journal* 23 (2005): 37–60.

——— and Noel J. Kinnamon. "Circulating the Sidney-Pembroke Psalter." In *Women's Writing and the Circulation of Ideas: Manuscript Publication in England, 1550–1800*, edited by George L. Justice and Nathan Tinker, 50–72. Cambridge: Cambridge University Press, 2002.

Roberts, Sasha. "Shakespeare 'Creepes into the Womens Closets about Bedtime': Women Reading in a Room of their Own." In *Renaissance Configurations: Voices/Bodies/Spaces, 1580–1690*, edited by Gordon McMullan, 30–62. New York: St. Martin's Press, 1998.

Rowlands, Marie B. "Recusant Women 1560–1640." In *Women in English Society 1500–1800*, edited by Mary Prior, 149–80. London: Meuthen, 1985.

Royal Commission on Historical Manuscripts. *Calendar of the Manuscripts of the Most Honourable the Marquis of Salisbury Preserved at Hatfield House, Hertfordshire*. London: HMSO, 1883–1976.

———. *An Inventory of the Historical Monuments in Essex*. London: HMSO, 1921.

Ryrie, Alec. *The Gospel and Henry VIII: Evangelicals in the Early English Reformation*. Cambridge: Cambridge University Press, 2003.

Salmon, J.H.M. "Stoicism and Roman Example: Seneca and Tacitus in Jacobean England." *Journal of the History of Ideas* 50, no. 2 (Apr, 1989): 199–225.

Sanders, Eve Rachel. *Gender and Literacy on Stage in Early Modern England*. Cambridge: Cambridge University Press, 1998.

Sargent, Michael G. "Ruysbroeck in England: *The Chastising of God's Children* and Related Works." In *Historia et spiritualitas Cartusiensis*, edited by Jan de Grauwe, 303–13. Destelbergen, Belgium: Drukkerij De Windroos, 1983.

———. "The Transmission by the English Carthusians of some Late Medieval Spiritual Writings." *Journal of Ecclesiastical History* 27, no. 3 (1976): 225–40.

Schleiner, Louise. *Tudor and Stuart Women Writers*. Bloomington: Indiana University Press, 1994.

Seaver, Paul S. *Wallington's World: A Puritan Artisan in Seventeenth-Century London*. Stanford: Stanford University Press, 1985.

Sedgwick, George. "A Summary or Memorial of My Own Life, Written by Me, December 10, 1682." In *The History and Antiquities of the Counties of Westmorland and Cumberland*, edited by Joseph Nicholson and Richard Burn. 2 vols. London, 1777.

Seelig, Sharon Cadman. *Autobiography and Gender in Early Modern Literature: Reading Women's Lives, 1600–1680*. Cambridge: Cambridge University Press, 2006.

Shagan, Ethan H., ed. *Catholics and the 'Protestant Nation': Religious Politics and Identity in Early Modern England*. Manchester: Manchester University Press, 2005.

Sharpe, Kevin and Steven N. Zwicker. "Introduction." In *Reading, Society and Politics in Early Modern England*, edited by Kevin Sharpe and Steven N. Zwicker, 1–40. Cambridge: Cambridge University Press, 2003.

Sherlock, Peter. *Monuments and Memory in Early Modern England*. Aldershot: Ashgate, 2008.

Sherman, William H. "'The Book thus put in every vulgar hand': Impressions of Readers in Early English Printed Bibles." In *The Bible as Book: The First Printed Editions*, edited by Paul Saenger and Kimberly Van Kampen, 125–33. London: The British Library, 1999.

———. *John Dee: The Politics of Reading and Writing in the English Renaissance*. Amherst: University of Massachusetts Press, 1995.

Shuger, Debora K. *Habits of Thought in the English Renaissance: Religion, Politics, and the Dominant Culture*. Berkeley: University of California Press, 1990.

Smith, Barbara and Ursula Appelt, eds. *Write or be Written: Early Modern Women Poets and Cultural Constraints*. Aldershot: Ashgate, 2001.

Smith, Rosalind. "'In a Mirrour Clere': Protestantism and Politics in Anne Lok's *Miserere Mei Deus*." In Clarke and Clarke, *'This Double Voice,'* 41–60.

Snook, Edith. *Women, Reading, and the Cultural Politics of Early Modern England*. Aldershot: Ashgate, 2005.

Spence, Richard T. *Lady Anne Clifford: Countess of Pembroke, Dorset and Montgomery (1590–1676)*. Stroud: Sutton Publishing, 1997.

Stallybrass, Peter. "Books and Scrolls: Navigating the Bible." In *Books and Readers in Early Modern England: Material Studies*, edited by Jennifer Andersen and Elizabeth Sauer, 42–78. Philadelphia: University of Pennsylvania Press, 2002.

———, Roger Chartier, John Mowery, and Heather Wolfe. "Hamlet's Tables and the Technologies of Writing in Renaissance England." *Shakespeare Quarterly* 55 (2004): 379–419.

Steck, Francis Borgia. *Franciscans and the Protestant Revolution in England*. Chicago: Franciscan Herald Press, 1920.

Steinberg, Theodore L. "The Sidneys and the Psalms." *Studies in Philology* 92 (1995): 1–17.

Stevenson, Jane. "Women Catholics and Latin Culture." In Corthell, *Catholic Culture in Early Modern England*, 52–72.

Stewart, Alan. "The Voices of Anne Cooke, Lady Anne and Lady Bacon." In Clarke and Clarke, *'This Double Voice,'* 88–102.

Stillman, Robert E. "Deadly Stinging Adders: Sidney's Piety, Philippism, and the *Defence of Poesy*." *Spenser Studies* 16 (2002): 231–69.

Strype, John. *Annals of the Reformation and Establishment of Religion.* London, 1725.

Summit, Jennifer. *Lost Property: The Woman Writer and English Literary History, 1380–1589.* Chicago: University of Chicago Press, 2000.

Tabor, Margaret Emma. *Four Margarets.* New York: Macmillan, 1929.

Taft, Robert. *The Liturgy of the Hours in East and West: The Origins of the Divine Office and its Meaning.* 2nd ed. Collegeville, MN: The Liturgical Press, 1993.

Tanner, Thomas. *Bibliotheca Britannico-Hibernica.* London, 1748.

Targoff, Ramie. *Common Prayer: The Language of Public Devotion in Early Modern England.* Chicago: University of Chicago Press, 2001.

Thaddeus, Father. *The Franciscans in England 1600–1850, being an Authentic Account of the Second English Province of Friars Minors.* London: Art and Book Company, 1898.

Travitsky, Betty S., ed. *The Paradise of Women: Writings by Englishwomen of the Renaissance.* Westport, CT: Greenwood Press, 1981. 2nd ed. New York: Columbia University Press, 1989.

———. "The Possibilities of Prose." In *Women and Literature in Britain, 1500–1700*, edited by Helen Wilcox, 234–66. Cambridge: Cambridge University Press, 1996.

———. *Subordination and Authorship in Early Modern England: The Case of Elizabeth Cavendish Egerton and Her 'Loose Papers.'* Tempe: Arizona Center for Medieval and Renaissance Studies, 1999.

Trill, Suzanne. "Feminism Versus Religion: Towards a Re-Reading of Aemilia Lanyer's *Salve Deus Rex Judaeorum*." *Renaissance and Reformation/ Renaissance et Réforme* 25, no. 4 (2001): 67–80.

———. "Sixteenth-Century Women's Writing: Mary Sidney's *Psalmes* and the 'Femininity' of Translation." In *Writing and the English Renaissance*, edited by William Zunder and Suzanne Trill, 140–58. London: Longman, 1996.

———. "'Speaking to God in His Phrase and Word': Women's use of the Psalms in Early Modern England." In *The Nature of Religious Language: A Colloquium*, edited by Stanley E. Porter, 269–83. London: Sheffield Academic Press, 1996.

———. "Specters and Sisters: Mary Sidney and the 'Perennial Puzzle' of Renaissance Women's Writing." In *Renaissance Configurations: Voices, Bodies, Spaces, 1580–1690*, edited by Gordon McMullan, 191–211. New York: St. Martin's Press, 1998.

Trull, Mary. "Petrarchism and the Gift: The Sacrifice of Praise in Anne Lock's 'A Meditation of a Penitent Sinner.'" *Religion and Literature* 41.3 (2009): 1–25.

Tylor, Edward Burnett. *Primitive Culture.* New York: Henry Holt & Co., 1889.

Valbuena, Olga. "Introduction." In *The History of the Angelical Virgin Glorious S. Clare Translated by Sister Magdalen Augustine*. Renaissance Women Online, Women Writers Project. Brown University. 12 May 2008. <www.wwp.brown.edu/rwoentry.html>.

Venuti, Lawrence. *The Translator's Invisibility*. London: Routledge, 1995.

Vessey, Mark. "*The Citie of God* (1610) and the London Virginia Company." In *History, Apocalypse, and the Secular Imagination: New Essays on Augustine's City of God*, edited by Mark Vessey, Karla Pollmann, and Allan D. Fitzgerald, 257–81. Charlottesville, VA: Philosophy Documentation Center, 1999.

Walker, Claire. *Gender and Politics in Early Modern Europe: English Convents in France and the Low Countries*. Hampshire: Palgrave Macmillan, 2003.

———. "Introductory Note." In Evelinge, *Elizabeth Evelinge III*, EME, Series I, pt. 4, vol. 1, selected and introduced by Claire Walker, ix–xvii. Aldershot: Ashgate, 2006.

Wall, Wendy. *The Imprint of Gender: Authorship and Publication in the English Renaissance*. Ithaca: Cornell University Press, 1993.

Waller, G.F. "A 'Matching of Contraries': Ideological Ambiguity in the Sidney Psalms." *Wascana Review* 9 (1974): 124–33.

———. "'This Matching of Contraries': Calvinism and Courtly Philosophy in the Sidney Psalms." *English Studies* 55 (1974): 22–31.

———. "Struggling into Discourse: The Emergence of Renaissance Women's Writing." In Hannay, *Silent But for the Word*, 238–56.

Walpole, Horace. *A Catalogue of the Royal and Noble Authors of England*. Edinburgh, 1796.

Walsham, Alexandra. *Providence in Early Modern England*. Oxford: Oxford University Press, 1999.

Warnicke, Retha M. "Lady Mildmay's Journal: A Study in Autobiography and Meditation in Reformation England." *Sixteenth Century Journal* 20, no. 1 (1989): 55–68.

White, Christopher. *Anthony Van Dyck: Thomas Howard, the Earl of Arundel*. Malibu: Getty Museum Studies on Art, 1995.

White, Helen C. *The Tudor Books of Private Devotion*. Madison, WI: University of Wisconsin Press, 1951.

White, Micheline. "Recent Studies in Women Writers of Tudor England, 1485–1603 (Mid-1993–Mid-1999)." *English Literary Renaissance* 30, no. 3 (2000): 457–93.

———. "Renaissance Englishwomen and Religious Translations: The Case of Anne Lock's *Of the Markes of the Children of God* (1590)." *English Literary Renaissance* 29, no. 3 (1999): 375–400.

———. "Women Writers and Religious and Literary Circles in the Elizabethan West Country: Anne Dowriche, Anne Lock Prowse, Anne Lock Moyle, Elizabeth Rous, and Ursula Fulford." *Modern Philology* 103.2 (2005): 187–214.

Whiting, Mary Bradford. "The Learned and Virtuous Lady Bacon." *The Hibbert Journal* 29 (1931): 270–83.

Wieck, Roger S. *Time Sanctified: The Book of Hours in Medieval Art and Life.* New York: George Braziller, 1988.

Wilcox, Helen. "'My Soule in Silence'? Devotional Representations of Renaissance Englishwomen." In *Representing Women in Renaissance England*, ed. Claude J. Summers and Ted-Larry Pebworth, 9–23. Columbia: University of Missouri Press, 1997.

Williams, Glanmore. "Two Neglected Welsh Clerics: Richard Whitford and Richard Gwent." *The Transactions of the Honorable Society of Cymmrodorion* 1 (1961): 30–32.

Williamson, George C. *Lady Anne Clifford, Countess of Dorset, Pembroke and Montgomery, 1590–1676: Her Life, Letters, and Work.* Kendal: Titus Wilson and Son, 1923.

Wiseman, Susan. *Conspiracy and Virtue: Women, Writing, and Politics in Seventeenth-Century England.* Oxford: Oxford University Press, 2006.

———. "Knowing Her Place: Anne Clifford and the Politics of Retreat." In *Textures of Renaissance Knowledge*, edited by Philippa Berry and Margaret Tudeau-Clayton, 199–221. Manchester: Manchester University Press, 2003.

Wolfe, Heather, ed. *Elizabeth Cary, Lady Falkland: Life and Letters.* Cambridge: Renaissance Texts from Manuscript, 2001.

———. "Reading Bells and Loose Papers: Reading and Writing Practices of the English Benedictine Nuns of Cambrai and Paris." In Burke and Gibson, *Early Modern Women's Manuscript Writing*, 135–56.

Workman, Samuel Klinger. *Fifteenth Century Translation as an Influence on English Prose.* Princeton: Princeton University Press, 1940.

Woudhuysen, H.R. *Sir Philip Sidney and the Circulation of Manuscripts, 1558–1640.* Oxford: Clarendon Press, 1996.

Wright, Nancy E. "Accounting for a Life: The Household Accounts of Lady Anne Clifford." In *Early Modern Autobiography: Theories, Genres, Practices*, edited by Ronald Bedford, Lloyd Davis and Philippa Kelly, 234–51. Ann Arbor: University of Michigan Press, 2006.

Zaret, David. *The Heavenly Contract: Ideology and Organization in Pre-Revolutionary Puritanism.* Chicago: University of Chicago Press, 1985.

Zim, Rivkah. *English Metrical Psalms: Poetry as Praise and Prayer 1535–1601.* Cambridge: Cambridge University Press, 1987.

Index

Printed in Great Britain
by Amazon

59906282R00154